AF147679

Information Technology and Law Series

Volume 24

For further volumes:
http://www.springer.com/series/8857

Simone van der Hof · Bibi van den Berg
Bart Schermer
Editors

Minding Minors Wandering the Web: Regulating Online Child Safety

Editors
Simone van der Hof
Bibi van den Berg
Bart Schermer
Faculty of Law, Center for Law in
the Information Society (eLaw)
Leiden University
Leiden
The Netherlands

ISSN 1570-2782
ISBN 978-94-6265-004-6 ISBN 978-94-6265-005-3 (eBook)
DOI 10.1007/978-94-6265-005-3

Library of Congress Control Number: 2014931424

Published by T.M.C. ASSER PRESS, The Hague, The Netherlands www.asserpress.nl
Produced and distributed for T.M.C. ASSER PRESS by Springer-Verlag Berlin Heidelberg

Printed on acid-free paper

Springer is part of Springer Science+Business Media (www.springer.com)

Series Information

The *Information Technology & Law Series* was an initiative of IT*e*R, the national programme for Information Technology and Law, which was a research programme set up by the Dutch government and The Netherlands Organisation for Scientific Research (NWO) in The Hague. Since 1995 IT*e*R has published all of its research results in its own book series. In 2002 IT*e*R launched the present internationally orientated and English language *Information Technology & Law Series*. This well-established series deals with the implications of information technology for legal systems and institutions. Manuscripts and related correspondence can be sent to the Series' Editorial Office, which will also gladly provide more information concerning editorial standards and procedures.

Editorial Office

Contents

Part III Privacy, Data Protection and Online Marketing

Part IV Cyberbullying

Part V Online Grooming

Contributors

Rachele Ciavarella has an M.D. in Law (Università degli Studi di Genova, Italy). During her studies, she completed an Erasmus appointment period of 5 months at the University of Louvain where, besides having honed and refined her linguistic capability in French, she has acquired an excellent ability to adapt to multicultural environments. Most significantly, this afforded her a great opportunity to profoundly enhance her knowledge of European law and to observe the key European legislative institutions of Commission, Council and Parliament at close quarters. During the academic year 2010/2011, she has undergone a postgraduate study, namely a Master in Laws of new technologies and the Law of Internet at the University of Namur. This programme has offered her the opportunity to avail of a 1-month internship at The European Consumers' Organisation, BEUC. After 3 months of Internship in the Brussels office of the Italian Law Firm De Berti Jacchia Franchini Forlani, since February 2012 she is a Researcher in the 'Freedoms in the Information Society' Unit of the Research Centre in Information, Law and Society (CRIDS—University of Namur).

Colette M.K.C. Cuijpers is an Assistant Professor at TILT—the Tilburg Institute for Law, Technology and Society at Tilburg University. Colette holds a degree in European Law and in Dutch Law, and received her Ph.D. from Tilburg University in 2004. Her main field of expertise relates to the way in which technology and society influence privacy and data protection regulation and vice versa. She has been involved in several large-scale EU-funded research projects such as FIDIS, Breaking Barriers to eGovernment and VIRTUOSO. In 2010, she worked for the Dutch Scientific Council for Government Policy (WRR), where she participated in a project on the transformation of eGovernment to iGovernment. Lately she was involved in several projects carried out by PIlab, commissioned by the Ministry of Economic Affairs, Ministry of Internal Affairs and The Netherlands Competition Authority.

Jos de Haan is Head of the Care, Emancipation and Time Use research sector at The Netherlands Institute for Social Research (SCP) and Professor at Erasmus University Rotterdam on ICT, Culture and the Knowledge Society. He obtained a Ph.D. in Sociology in 1994 at Utrecht University on the topic of research groups in Dutch sociology. He specialises in research on cultural interests and media use.

His recent research on new media focuses on the digital divide, the digital generation and the rise of e-culture. For publications see www.scp.nl.

Cécile De Terwangne has a M.D. in Law (University of Louvain), a Ph.D. in Law (University of Namur) and a LL.M. in European and International Law (European University Institute of Florence). She is a Professor at the Law Faculty of the University of Namur (Belgium). She teaches courses in Computer and Human Rights, and in Data Protection. She is a Director of the postgraduate Program in IT Law at the University of Namur and a Research Director in the 'Freedoms in the Information Society' Unit of the Research Centre in Information, Law and Society (CRIDS—University of Namur). She has taken part in numerous European and national researches in the fields of data protection, privacy and ICT, freedom of information, eGovernment, etc. She is an expert for the Council of Europe and for the European Commission.

Virginia Dignum is an Associate Professor at the Faculty of Technology, Policy and Management, Delft University of Technology. She got her Ph.D. in 2004 from the Utrecht University. Previously, she worked for more than 12 years in consultancy and system development in the areas of expert systems and knowledge management. Her research focuses on agent-based models of organisations, in particular in the dynamic aspects of organisations and the applicability of agent organisations to support knowledge creation, sharing and representation in distributed environments and the interaction between people and intelligent systems in particular the behaviour of hybrid teams. Her work ranges from the engineering of practical applications and simulations to the development of formal theories that integrate agency and organisation, and includes a strong design methodology component. In 2006, she was awarded the prestigious Veni grant from the Dutch Organization for Scientific Research (NWO) for her work on agent-based organisational frameworks, which includes the Opera framework for analysis, design and simulation of organisational systems. She has organized many international conferences and workshops, and was co-organiser of AAMAS 2005. She is involved in national and EU projects and has more than 120 peer-reviewed publications, including ten edited books.

Sarah Genner studied in Zurich and Berlin specialising in Internet research. She holds a Master's degree in Political Science, Linguistics and Media Studies from Zurich University and is currently a Research Associate in Media Psychology at Zurich University of Applied Sciences (ZHAW) in Switzerland. Her professional experience is in journalism, communications, and teaching. Among other publications, she is the initiator and lead author of 'FAQ Media Literacy'—a Swiss guidebook for parents and teachers to deal with youth and online risks and opportunities based on recent research. A fully revised edition of the guidebook is funded and distributed by the Swiss government for many schools, parents' organisations and professionals in education and therapy in German, French and Italian. In 2013, she has been awarded a Swiss National Science Foundation

Fellowship in order to spend a year at the Berkman Center for Internet and Society at Harvard University.

Marga M. Groothuis is an Assistant Professor at the Faculty of Law of Leiden University in The Netherlands. She obtained her LL.M. at Queen Mary and Westfield College in London. From 2001 until 2005 she worked as a legal specialist at the Constitutional Affairs Department of the Dutch Ministry of the Interior. In 2004, Marga Groothuis obtained her Ph.D. for a thesis on legal aspects of automatic decision making by government agencies. Her research currently focuses on legal aspects of eGovernment in Europe and on fundamental rights and the rule of law in the digital age. Marga Groothuis is a fellow at the Meijers Research Institute of Leiden University and a member of the LDE Research Centre for Safety and Security of Leiden University, Delft University and Erasmus University.

Catholijn M. Jonker (1967) is Full Professor of Man-Machine Interaction at the Faculty of Electrical Engineering, Mathematics and Computer Science of the Delft University of Technology. She studied Computer Science, and did her Ph.D. studies at Utrecht University. After a postdoc position in Bern, Switzerland, she became an Assistant (later Associate) Professor at the Department of Artificial Intelligence of the Vrije Universiteit Amsterdam. From September 2004 until September 2006, she was a full-time Professor of Artificial Intelligence/Cognitive Science at the Nijmegen Institute of Cognition and Information of the Radboud University Nijmegen. She chaired De Jonge Akademie in 2005 and 2006, and she was a member from 2005 through 2010. Her recent publications address cognitive processes and concepts such as trust, negotiation, and the dynamics of individual agents and organisations. In Delft, she works with an interdisciplinary team to engineer human experience through multi-modal interaction between natural and artificial actors in a social dynamic context. At the end of 2007, her NWO-STW VICI project ‘Pocket Negotiator’ has been awarded. In this project she develops intelligent decision support systems for negotiation.

Eva Lievens Ph.D., obtained a law degree at the University of Ghent and a Master’s degree in Transnational Communications and Global Media at Goldsmiths College, London. Eva has been a member of the Interdisciplinary Centre for Law and ICT (K. U. Leuven) since 2003 and obtained her Ph.D. in law in June 2009. Since October 2011 she is a postdoctoral Fellow of the Research Fund Flanders, working on a project entitled ‘Risk-Reducing Regulatory Strategies for Illegal and Harmful Conduct and Content in Online Social Networks’. Her research deals with legal challenges posed by new communication phenomena, such as the regulation of audiovisual media services, user-generated content and social networks, with a particular emphasis on the protection of minors. She also is the Associate Editor of the International Encyclopaedia of Laws—Media Law.

Sonia Livingstone is Professor of Social Psychology, Department of Media and Communications at LSE. She is author or editor of 17 books and many academic articles and chapters. Taking a comparative, critical and contextualised approach, Sonia's research examines the opportunities and risks afforded by digital and online technologies in a range of contexts, including children and young people's experience of digital media at home and school, developments in media and digital literacies and the implications of the changing media environment for audiences, publics and the public sphere. More broadly, she is interested in how citizen values (public sphere, rights-based, equity-focused, diversity-promoting) can be better embedded in information and communication infrastructures in institutions, regulators and the lifeworld. Currently, she directs a 33-country network, EU Kids Online, funded by the EC's Safer Internet Programme. She also directs The Class, as part of the MacArthur Foundation-funded Connected Learning Research Network. She participates in the European COST network, Transforming Audiences, Transforming Societies, leads ECREA's Children, Youth and Media group and blogs for the LSE Media Policy Project. She was President of the International Communication Association in 2007–2008, and serves on the Executive Board of the UK's Council for Child Internet Safety, for which she is the Evidence Champion.

Jamie-Lee Mooney began her Ph.D. following graduating with first class honours from Lancaster University Law School in 2010. Alongside being a Ph.D. candidate for the school, she is also a Postgraduate Teaching Assistant within the areas of Criminal law, Criminal Justice, Family and Child law. Her research explores the legal and societal challenges posed by misconceptions of the phenomenon of child sexual grooming. Her recent publications provide a critical analysis of the growing awareness of group localised grooming and the ways in which offenders operate in groups to facilitate contact and sexual abuse/exploitation of vulnerable children. She has also published in the area of prevention of crime exploring the effectiveness of proactive police investigations. Since 2011, she has been working within the Publication Protection Unit of Lancashire Constabulary to develop the effectiveness of the criminal justice system and frontline response to sexual violence and child exploitation.

Natascha Notten is an Assistant Professor at Radboud University Nijmegen, Department of Sociology. Her research interests include social stratification in media use and cultural consumption, healthy lifestyles and risk behaviours. More specifically, she focuses on family issues, parenting practices and the intergenerational transmission of (un)equal opportunities. Natascha is an expert on parents' socialisation efforts regarding media use and their lasting consequences. She has published her research in several international and Dutch journals, see www.nnotten.nl for more information and publications.

Brian O'Neill is Head of the School of Media at Dublin Institute of Technology. He is a member of the Management Group for EU Kids Online (EC Safer Internet Programme) and leads the work package on policy. In 2012, he held a Government of Ireland senior research fellowship leading a project called Digital Childhoods with a focus on children's use of ICTs and implications for national digital strategy. This includes disseminating findings to a wide range of stakeholders in education, policy, civil society and industry. He was chair of the IAMCR Audience section (2007–2013) and is vice-chair of the ECREA's Temporary Working Group for Children, Youth and Media. He is a member of Ireland's Internet Safety Advisory Committee and is the author of reports on media literacy for the Broadcasting Authority of Ireland and UNICEF. He co-edits a new book to be published this year by Nordicom entitled Towards a Better Internet for Children: Policy Pillars, Players and Paradoxes.

Bart Schermer is an Assistant Professor at the University of Leiden, Faculty of Law (eLaw research group) and a fellow at the E. M. Meijers Institute for Legal Studies. Furthermore, he is co-founder and editor of the Dutch Journal of Internet Law (Tijdschrift voor Internetrecht) and a member of the Cybercrime expert group for the Court of Appeal in The Hague. Apart from his work at the University Bart is a partner at Considerati, a legal consultancy specialising in the legal and policy aspects of IT and new media (www.considerati.com).

Nathalie Sonck obtained a Ph.D. in Social Sciences at the University of Leuven (Centre for Sociological Research) and a Master's degree in Communication Science at the University of Antwerp. Since 2011, she works as media researcher at The Netherlands Institute for Social Research (SCP). She specialises in research on media use in the public, and in particular related to skills and cultural interest. Recent publications include SCP-reports (for general public, policy-makers and social researchers) about children's internet risks, and cultural participation by new media, as well as academic articles (published in the *International Journal of Public Opinion Research*, *Journal of Children and Media*). As representative of The Netherlands in the EU Kids Online network, she investigates the consequences of Internet use by young people, their digital skills and the role of parental mediation strategies and discusses related policy issues with national stakeholders.

Isolde Sprenkels studied philosophy at Tilburg University. In 2007, she started as a junior researcher at the Infonomics and New Media Research Centre at Zuyd University, where she conducted research on digital identities and identity management systems and contributed to publications on social and ethical aspects of identification technologies such as biometrics used in migration and border management. She co-developed and taught a minor on Digital Identity and on Marketing and New Media, and has worked as a teacher in secondary school. Currently, Isolde is a Ph.D. researcher with the ERC funded DigIDeas project: Social and Ethical Aspects of Digital Identities. Towards a Value Sensitive Identity Management: www.digideas.com. Her work concerns socio-technical configurations in which children's identities as consumers in a digitising society are enacted.

Adam Thierer is a senior research fellow at the Mercatus Center at George Mason University where he works in the Technology Policy Program. Thierer covers technology, media, Internet and free speech policy issues with a particular focus in online child safety and digital privacy policy issues. Thierer has spent over two decades in the public policy research community and is the author or editor of seven books on diverse topics such as media regulation and child safety issues, mass media regulation, Internet governance and jurisdiction, intellectual property, regulation of network industries and the role of federalism within high-technology markets. He earned his B.A. in Journalism and Political Science at Indiana University, and received his M.A. in International Business Management and Trade Theory at the University of Maryland. Thierer has served on several distinguished online safety task forces, including Harvard Law School's Internet Safety Technical Task Force, a 'Blue Ribbon Working Group' on child safety organized by Common Sense Media, the iKeepSafe Coalition and the National Cable and Telecommunications Association, and the National Telecommunications and Information Administration's 'Online Safety and Technology Working Group'. In 2008, Thierer received the Family Online Safety Institute's 'Award for Outstanding Achievement'.

Bibi van den Berg (1975) is an Assistant Professor at eLaw, the Center for Law in the Information Society of Leiden University. In 2004, Van den Berg obtained an M.A. (with distinction) in Philosophy, with a specialisation in philosophy of technology and philosophical anthropology, at Erasmus University Rotterdam in The Netherlands. In 2009, she completed her dissertation on Identity and Technologies of the Near Future, at the same university. The title of her dissertation was 'The Situated Self: Identity in a world of Ambient Intelligence'. After her Ph.D., Van den Berg had a postdoc position at the Tilburg Institute for Law, Technology and Society (TILT) at Tilburg University for a few years. In 2012, she transferred to Leiden to take up her current position. Her research focuses on four themes: (1) regulation by technology (techno-regulation), (2) identity and privacy, (3) regulation and governance of/on the Internet and (4) robotics and artificial intelligence. Aside from her role as Assistant Professor, Van den Berg is also a Meijers Fellow at Leiden Law School and research director of eLaw.

Simone van der Hof is Full Professor of Law and Information Society at the Center for Law and the Information Society of Leiden Law School at Leiden University. Simone's research concentrates on the impact of new technologies on individuals and their rights. Her current research topics include online privacy, data protection and privacy statements, digital identities, digital child rights, (legal, social, technological) regulation of online child safety and empowerment of individuals through technology.

Leontien M. van der Knaap is an Associate Professor at the International Victimology Institute Tilburg (INTERVICT) at Tilburg University. She is a developmental psychologist and received her Ph.D. at the Free University of Amsterdam (2003). Her main research interests cover developmental victimology, domestic violence and risk assessment. She is involved in studies on ethnic differences in child abuse and delinquency, child sexual abuse of youth with an ethnic minority background, and the developmental effects of poly-victimisation in childhood and adolescence. Previously, she was a senior researcher at the Research and Documentation Centre of the Dutch Ministry of Justice where she studied, among other things, topics such as risk assessment in forensic populations, domestic violence offenders and violence prevention.

Irma van der Ploeg (1964) holds degrees in Philosophy and Science and Technology studies. In 2006, she was appointed as an Associate Professor of Infonomics and New Media at Zuyd University, Maastricht/Heerlen, The Netherlands, where she is heading the Infonomics and New Media Research Centre (http://infonomie.hszuyd.nl); in addition, she is employed by UNU-MERIT at Maastricht University. She has published extensively on philosophical, normative and gender aspects of medical technologies and information technologies, in particular on biometric identification technologies, digital identities and the relation between technology and the body. She is author of 'The Machine-Readable Body'. Essays on Biometrics and the Informatisation of the Body (Maastricht: Shaker, 2005). In 2008, she was awarded a Starting Grant for Independent Researchers from the European Research Council, for a 5-year research project entitled 'Social and Ethical Aspects of Digital Identities. Towards a Value Sensitive Identity Management'. (www.digideas.nl).

Janneke M. van der Zwaan is a Ph.D. candidate at the Faculty of Technology, Policy and Management of Delft University of Technology, The Netherlands. She has a background in Artificial Intelligence (2006, University of Amsterdam) and Science Communication (2008, VU University). Her research concerns the design and evaluation of a virtual empathic buddy that provides emotional support and practical advice to victims of cyberbullying. In 2010, she was a finalist for the Google Anita Borg Memorial Scholarship.

Heidi Vandebosch is an Associate Professor at the Department of Communication Studies at the University of Antwerp (Belgium). She is a member of the Research Group MIOS (Media and ICT in Organisations and Society). Heidi Vandebosch is the promotor of several studies on cyberbullying amongst youngsters aimed at gaining a deeper knowledge on the causes of this phenomenon. She is also involved in interdisciplinary projects focusing on the development of an evidence-based serious game to prevent (and remedy) cyberbullying (http://www.friendlyattac.be) and of automatic cyberbullying detection tools for Social Network Sites (http://www.clips.ua.ac.be/amica/). Heidi Vandebosch was member of the management committee of the international COST action «Cyberbullying: coping with negative and enhancing positive uses of new technologies, in relationships in educational settings». She has published extensively on cyberbullying in national and international journals and books.

Abbreviations

ANDI	Brazilian News Agency for Children's Rights
ANT	Actor Network Theory
CEO	Chief Executive Officer
CEOP	Child Exploitation and Online Protection Centre
COPA	Child Online Protection Act
COPPA	US Children's Online Privacy Protection Act
ECHR	European Convention on Human Rights
ECtHR	European Court on Human Rights
EDRi	European Digital Civil Rights Movement
FTP	File Transfers
HUDOC	Human Rights Documentation
ICT	Information and Communication Technology
IGF	Internet Governance Forum
ISCED	International Standard Classification of Education
ISP	Internet Service Provider
ISPs	Internet Service Providers
IT	Information Technology
ITU	International Telecommunication Union
IVE	Intelligent Virtual Environment
JAMES	Youth, Activities, Media—Survey Switzerland
LEA	Law Enforcement Agencies
NGO	Non-governmental Organisation
OECD	Organisation for Economic Co-operation and Development
PEGI	The Pan-European Game Information
PFF	The Progress and Freedom Foundation
RQ	Research Question
SES	Socio-Economic Status
SNS	Social Network Sites
SOA	British Sexual Offences Act 2003
SOA	Sexual Offences Act
SNS	Social Networking Service
SSNP	Safer Social Networking Principles for the EU
UN	United Nations
UNCRC	UN Convention on the Rights of the Child

UNESCO	United Nations Educational, Scientific and Cultural Organization
UNICEF	United Nations Children's Fund
US	United States
WSIS	World Summit on the Information Society

Chapter 1
Regulating Online Child Safety: Introduction

Bibi van den Berg

Contents

1.1 Introduction

In Western societies, a vast majority of children and teenagers are online every day. Growing up in a world with always-on, fully connected technologies, the boundaries between the online and the offline world have ceased to exist for these youngsters. They engage with friends and peers in online social networks, through Skype and Twitter as easily as they do during playtime at school. And their skills with modern technologies, including mobile phones and laptops, are often amazing, and at times even bewildering, to their parents and older generations.

Using the Internet provides children and teenagers with tremendous opportunities. Online activities enable them to develop their personality, make and maintain friendships, generate (creative) content and acquire digital skills. However, there are downsides as well. When going online, youngsters may encounter various risks, ranging from cyberbullying and encountering harmful content, to abuse of personal data or becoming victims of fraud, reputation damage or online sexual solicitation. Moreover, aside from encountering risky situations, the Internet also provides children, and especially teenagers, with a wealth of

Bibi van den Berg is Assistant Professor at eLaw, the Center for Law in the Information Society at Leiden University's Law School, Leiden, The Netherlands.

B. van den Berg (✉)
Center for Law in the Information Society, University of Leiden, Leiden, The Netherlands
e-mail: b.van.den.berg@law.leidenuniv.nl

S. van der Hof et al. (eds.), *Minding Minors Wandering the Web: Regulating Online Child Safety*, Information Technology and Law Series 24, DOI: 10.1007/978-94-6265-005-3_1,

opportunities to actively engage in risky behaviour, seeking—and sometimes crossing—boundaries. A good example is texting sexually explicit messages to lovers ('sexting'), which is part of exploring sexuality but can also lead to utterly embarrassing situations, and even fierce bullying, when these messages are forwarded to third parties.

While most online risks and risk-taking issues also apply to adults, they warrant greater concern in relation to children and teenagers for several reasons. First, children are often more easily misled and less proficient in seeing through (potentially) awkward and perilous situations. Second, it is more difficult for children and teenagers to grasp the long-term consequences of their activities. Actions in the present, such as sharing embarrassing images or spreading copyright-protected content, may come to haunt them years down the line, and it is difficult for children and teenagers to keep in mind such an extended horizon. Finally, it is unclear for youngsters (and adults alike) who the audience is that they are sharing information or content with; this audience is potentially global, since content can easily be searched and copied, and sometimes may spread like wildfire, leading to a loss of control over its dissemination. Deleting content that has been posted on the Internet is not an easy feat, therefore, and in some cases becomes entirely impossible. This entails that individuals may be haunted by content (text, images, audio, video) that has been posted online for a lifetime.

In the past decades a lot of empirical research has been conducted to uncover how the Internet affects the lives of youths, both positively, in terms of the opportunities it offers and the skills it teaches them, and negatively, in terms of the risks they may encounter or the risky behaviours they may engage in. The potential risks and harms that children may encounter online have also caught the attention of policymakers and regulators. Ensuring online safety has become a topic on the regulatory agenda in many Western societies. However, regulating for online safety is far from easy, due to the wide variety of national and international, private and public actors and stakeholders that are involved. What is more, as we have seen above there are many different kinds of online risks for children and teenagers, and the exposure of youth to such risks ought to vary with their age and level of experience in using the Internet. Moreover, when regulating online risks for children it is important to strike the right balance between protection against harms on the one hand, and safeguarding their fundamental freedoms and rights on the other. The opportunities that the Internet provides children ought not to be hampered too much in an attempt to combat its negative sides.

Each of the authors in this book attempts to grapple with precisely this theme: striking the right balance between ensuring safety for children on the Internet while at the same time enabling them to experiment, to learn, to enrich their lives, to acquire skills and to have fun using this global network. The authors come from various scientific disciplines, ranging from law to social science and from media studies to philosophy. This means that the book provides the reader with both empirical and theoretical/conceptual chapters, and sheds a multi-disciplinary light on the complex topic of regulating online safety for children. The book is divided into four parts.

1.2 An Overview of This Book

Part I discusses the regulatory horizon against which questions relating to children and their safe Internet use takes place. The authors in this part of the book reflect on current regulatory solutions, be they legal (laws, rules), social (norms) or technological (technical tools), and evaluate these regulatory solutions in terms of their reach, impact and effectiveness.

In Chap. 2, Sonia Livingstone and Brian O'Neill look at the UN Convention on the Rights of the Child (UNCRC), which sets out the basic human rights that apply to all children and specifies the minimum rights and freedoms that all children ought to have. This Convention complements the Universal Declaration of Human Rights and establishes both the rights that children have and the various forms of protection they require. The UNCRC was ratified in 1989 and has since become one "of the most universally recognised international legal instruments". In this chapter, Livingstone and O'Neill ask whether, and how, the key provisions of this Convention apply to children on the Internet. They open the chapter with a discussion of the various so-called 'protection rights' the UNCRC stipulates, for example children's right to be protected against sexual exploitation and abuse, or against trafficking. Protecting children against this type of online risk has received a lot of attention in many Western countries. However, in as Livingstone and O'Neill point out, there are many other online risks that are harder to grapple with and regulate, and that hence have received much less attention. What is more, so far, almost all focus has been on ensuring the protection of children on the Internet. Children's rights in terms of provision and participation, which also figure prominently in the UNCRC, have been left unaddressed. Until now, the focus has predominantly been on combating risk (protection), rather than on the opportunities that the Internet also offers children (provision and participation). But risks and opportunities oftentimes are positively linked—"the more one enables provision and participation, the more the need for protection". This entails, the authors argue, that we need to develop policy approaches that may resolve the potential conflict between protection on the one hand, and provision and participation on the other. Rather than focusing on protection only, Livingstone and O'Neill point out what is needed is an integrated framework that includes all three provisions. And this integrated framework, moreover, ought to build on "real needs, [target] specific and evidence-based risks, and [include] measurable goals on which policy implementation is independently evaluated". Next, Livingstone and O'Neill ask how such a framework would have to be operationalized. They point out that most efforts to improve child safety on the Internet today take a multi-stakeholder approach, viz. a combination of state regulation (through legislation), industry self-regulation, and "the expectation of responsible action on the part of citizens (parents and children, often supported by schools and non-governmental organisation [NGO] actions)." While this seems like a reasonable division of labour on paper, in practice, the authors argue, it turns out that the responsibility for ensuring online safety for children befalls parents and teachers to a significant degree. This is worrying since empirical research shows "that a minority of parents are ill-equipped to manage this". Finally, the authors also point out that more clarity is needed regarding the "responsibility for implementing digital rights, since many governments prefer self-regulation in relation to Internet governance". They conclude that we need a global body to govern the protection, implementation and delivery of children's rights in relation to the Internet.

In Chap. 3, Adam Thierer critically assesses the ways in which society tends to respond to technological risks, ranging from prohibiting the proliferation of technologies, to adapting to the risks they may generate through, for instance, the development of coping mechanisms and new social norms. He develops a four--step framework for analysing such risks, which can be used to find the optimal response strategy for each of them. The first step is "defining the problem to be addressed and determining whether harm exists", which is followed by a cost–benefit analysis of any potential form of regulatory or legal activity to curb the harm. The third step consists of assessing whether or not other, non-legal solutions could be equally or more effective, and after a solution has been chosen, the final step involves evaluating it on a regular basis. With this analysis in place, Thierer turns to a discussion of online risks for children, and asks which regulatory measures, if any, ought to be considered in light of the framework above. He states that while, for example, child pornography is a harm that clearly needs to be combatted, deciding on whether or not many other online risks for children warrant a regulation-based solution is much less clear. Thierer argues that online risks, especially for children, are often the result of so-called 'techno-panics', and prohibition and other regulation-based strategies may threaten free speech and can stifle progress. What is more, Thierer discusses five fundamental medium-specific characteristics of digital technologies that make it exceptionally difficult to regulate them. Examples include digital technologies' decentralised, distributed nature, and the fact that they have facilitated unprecedented (personal) information sharing on a global scale. Because of these five characteristics of digital media it is incredibly difficult to use prohibition or other regulation-based strategies to combat risks, also in the realm of youth online. Therefore, Thierer proposes to look elsewhere for solutions, and focuses especially on resiliency and adaptation as potential areas where successful action against online risks for children and teenagers could take place. To him "[e]ducation and awareness-building strategies can be particularly effective. Empowerment-based strategies are also useful".

In the last chapter of this part, Chap. 4, Bibi van den Berg looks at some of the technical tools that are currently in use to combat risks for children and teenagers on the Internet. She argues that different approaches could be used to regulate online behaviour in these target audiences through technical means. On the one hand, parents, teachers, regulators, businesses and technology developers could opt for technical tools that nudge or persuade children to behave in certain ways, or to avoid other behaviours. This would leave children and teenagers with 'room to manoeuvre', to experiment and make choices themselves. In practice, however, almost all technical tools in use in this domain build on the principle of what has come to be known as 'techno-regulation', the process of hard-coding normative or legal codes into technologies to make certain behaviours impossible and prompt others. While persuasive technologies and nudging still leave room for manoeuvring in users, i.e. still allow users to 'opt out' and choose an alternative path of action than the one suggested by the technology, techno-regulatory measures leave no such room at all. Van den Berg discusses three examples of what she calls 'technological influencing', i.e. the use of technical tools to steer, guide and regulate behaviour of children and teenagers on the Internet: the use of filtering software and parental controls, the use of kids' browsers, and a proposal to zone the Internet through the use of ports. All these examples hard-code an action space for children and teenagers, thereby ensuring that potential online risks, and potential online risky behaviour, are made impossible. When viewed from the perspective of effectiveness each of them can be considered a success. However, what makes these systems successful also makes them problematic: by hard-coding rules into the technology, and by making it impossible to 'colour outside the lines' children have no room for manoeuvring, and do not learn about online risks or the choices and opportunities they themselves have in learning to protect themselves from such risks. These tools clearly do not lead to awareness of, or resilience against, potential risks. This is especially problematic, Van den Berg concludes, for older children and teenagers. She proposes, therefore, that technology developers and regulators ought to focus more on creating and disseminating technical tools that nudge and persuade rather than force through code, so that children can gradually grow into more robust, risk-aware adolescent Internet users.

When studying online risks for children it is important to note that this involves two parts: on the one hand children and teenagers may encounter risks on the Internet, while on the other hand they may actively engage in risky online behaviours themselves. **Part II** contains two chapters that address each of these two parts.

In Chap. 5, Nathalie Sonck and Jos de Haan start from the oft-heard credo that children's online safety could be improved by providing them with the right skills. While this sounds straightforward enough, Sonck and De Haan point out that there are many different types of digital skills, and that some may contribute more to safer Internet use than others. For example, research shows that children have good instrumental skills (i.e. they know how to use the technology to get simple tasks done), but that their structural and strategic skills in using the Internet lag behind. Structural skills relate to knowing how and where to find information, and how to evaluate it, whereas strategic skills revolve around knowing how to use digital skills in daily life. Moreover, research also shows that there is room for improvement in children's social skills, e.g. knowing what the netiquette is, most importantly when using social network sites and other communication channels on the Internet. And the majority of children do not use the full potential of Web 2.0 to create and share content because they lack the necessary creative and production skills. While it is often assumed that a "higher level of digital skills reduces the number of online risks children experience", research reveals that children with more skills encounter more online risks. This is so mainly because they engage in more risky behaviour themselves. Sonck and De Haan point out that age is a partial explanation of this finding. Children with a higher level of skills are often older and hence may be more inclined to actively look for risks on the Internet, while younger children, with lower levels of skills, are more likely to encounter risks accidentally. When looking at skills for children to protect them against Internet risks, Sonck and De Haan remark that the oft-used typology of digital skills (especially the distinction between instrumental, informational and strategic ones) does not suffice. Instrumental skills, i.e. knowing how to use a computer or the Internet in a technical sense, does not help children protect themselves from harm. The same applies to the other skill types discussed. Instead, children need different skills, for example relating to risk-awareness, to proper forecasting and to coping with harm from online activities. Sonck and De Haan end the chapter with a discussion of the ways in which children's digital skills could be improved to enhance safe Internet use, for example through parental mediation, through lessons at school, and through co-regulatory schemes in which government and industry cooperate to enhance online safety for children.

In the last chapter of this part, Chap. 6, Natascha Notten focuses on online risk-taking by adolescents. She points out that research often "does not distinguish between children's intentional engagement in risky online behaviour and their (unintentional) encountering of risks", while these are different issues. This is why she has conducted empirical research into adolescents' risky online behaviour, with a focus on (a) the socioeconomic status of the adolescents' families, (b) their family structure and (c) the level of Internet diffusion in different countries in relation to risk-taking behaviours. Notten begins with a definition of 'risky' behaviour on the Internet, which includes, for examples, sharing personal information with people one has never met offline, or pretending to be someone else. Notten found that teenagers from single parent homes were significantly more inclined to engage in risky online behaviours than teenagers who lived in two-parent households. Similarly, adolescents whose parents had lower levels of education were more likely to engage in online risk-taking than adolescents whose parents had higher levels of education. She also found that active parental mediation in teenagers' Internet use appears to be an effective way to diminish risky online behaviour. "[R]estrictive mediation, as in rules set by parents on children's Internet use, seems most effective in preventing or inhibiting risky behaviour online." The level of Internet diffusion in various countries did not appear to have an effect on the risk-taking behaviour of adolescents.

In **Part III** we turn to three of the most hotly debated topics in the Internet age: privacy, data protection and online marketing. All three are well researched in the academic community. Moreover, various forms of regulation have been developed to protect citizens from harms related to these issues in the EU and the US. Privacy and data protection are also highly relevant topics when it comes to protecting children on the Internet. The same applies to online marketing and profiling. The three chapters in this part explain why this is so and which protections are, or ought to be, in place to ensure children's online safety in these areas.

In Chap. 7, Simone van der Hof assesses the current EU data protection directive and the proposed EU data protection regulation with respect to their applicability on, and attention to, online child safety. In recent years data protection for children has gained much attention. This is due to, on the one hand, an increased interest in child rights in general, and, on the other hand, the realisation that as children's Internet use rises, so does the need for their proper online protection. For one, as children increasingly use the Web, they run a number of specific risks related to data sharing, for example becoming victims of identity theft, online sexual solicitation, cyberbullying or reputational damage. So what can be done to protect children's privacy and safeguard their data on the Internet? Van der Hof looks at different forms of regulation to study the effectiveness of each. She begins by looking at two self-regulatory (i.e. industry-driven) initiatives: the 'Safer Social Networking Principles for the EU' (SSNP) and the 'Coalition to make the Internet a better place for kids'. She concludes that it is difficult to assess the impact of these initiatives, since it is unclear whether the principles these initiatives have developed on paper are actually implemented on a large scale in practice, or whether they are effective. Next, Van der Hof discusses the new data protection regulation, and especially those articles that speak of, or are relevant for, the protection of children's data on the Internet. While there are several articles in the new regulation that mention (means for) the protection of children's personal data on the Internet explicitly, much remains unclear as to the practical implications and applications of the rules that are stipulated. For example, as Van der Hof points out Article 8 of the new regulation stipulates that lawful processing of personal data of children under 13 depends on verifiable parental consent when offering online services. Van der Hof points out that it is unclear what 'verifiable consent' consists of. Similarly, the new regulation appears to prohibit automatic profiling of children. However, profiling is mentioned in several articles, and it is unclear whether in some cases the interests of businesses to profile may or may not trump the protection of individuals, and children in particular. Van der Hof points out that this issue, too, needs clarification. Most importantly, she raises questions regarding one particular omission in the new regulation, that of risks arising in the private sphere, due to the fact that children share one another's data—e.g. disclose embarrassing information—in social network sites and other online communication channels. This type of information sharing falls "outside the scope of the proposed regulation". Van der Hof points out that other regulatory influences, such as education and raising awareness could be used to remedy this gap, and would perhaps be more suitable in practice as well to increase the protection of children on the Internet.

In Chap. 8, Marga Groothuis analyses recent case law of the European Court of Human Rights on the right to respect for private life (Article 8 ECHR) for children on the Internet, to investigate whether or not the medium-specific characteristics of online forms of communication have sufficiently been taken into account by the European Court in its case law on the right to privacy of children. The right to respect for private life is one of the key elements of Article 8 of the Convention. Groothuis discusses two cases to see whether or not the fact that these involved communications via the Internet (and not, for example, in face-to-face interaction) was taken into account sufficiently. She argues that the Court does factor in specific characteristics of the Internet, and of online communication. For example, in several rulings the Court has weighed in the fact that communications via the Internet can have a major impact, due to the Internet's worldwide reach and high accessibility. Since information posted on a website potentially has a much larger audience than, for example, if the same information were published in a newspaper, this calls for extra caution in revealing personally identifiable information of a child. Another factor that has been taken into consideration by the Court is the degree of accessibility of a particular Web page: when potentially harmful content, such as pornographic images, are posted on a freely accessible website, chances are that minors will (also) access this content. Hence, the fact that such information is displayed on a publicly accessible website is a factor of consideration in the Court's ruling. But does the Court do enough in this respect? Here Groothuis is critical. She argues that the Court could strengthen its reasoning by also referring to the articles from the UN Convention of the Rights of the Child. She notes that there is a difference between taking into account the consequences that online experiences may have for children, versus taking into account the degree of dissemination of content online. While the Court clearly factors in the former, it is unclear how this degree of dissemination is established, and hence how the 'impact' is defined in this sense.

Rachele Ciavarella and Cécile de Terwange also write about the new data protection regulation in Chap. 9, but they focus on the 'right to be forgotten' that is to be implemented in this regulation, and the meaning this has for online safety for children. Ciavarella and De Terwange worry about the traces children leave when they go on the Internet, both actively, e.g. by sharing information in social network sites, or passively, as they surf the Web. They point out that children do not properly understand the long-term consequences this may have. The EU has now proposed to incorporate a 'right to be forgotten' into the new data protection regulation, and Ciavarella and De Terwange evaluate this right. They begin by pointing out that no clear definition or description exists of what this right to be forgotten is or ought to be, but that the European Commission refers to this right as "the right of individuals to have their data no longer processed and deleted when they are no longer needed for legitimate purposes. This is the case, for example, when processing is based on the person's consent and when he or she withdraws consent or when the storage period has expired." Ciavarella and De Terwange then raise the following question in this chapter: Could the application of such a 'right to have their data deleted' offer adequate protection to children and young people on social network sites? To answer this question the authors begin by discussing the way in which the right to be forgotten is embedded in the current data protection directive, and is reworked/made more explicit in the proposed data protection legislation. It is not explicitly mentioned or defined in the current data protection directive, but there are provisions in that directive that facilitate the same ends. Think of, for example, the purpose specification principle (data can only be processed until the specified purpose is accomplished and then they must be deleted or anonymised), and the right to object. In the current proposal for the new data protection regulation there is a separate article devoted to the right to be forgotten. Ciavarella and De Terwange argue that the current formulation of the right to be forgotten in the new regulation has some clear limitations. For example, the right to be forgotten "is not an absolute right. In fact, it is in major conflict and permanent tension with other rights and interests including the right to free speech, the right to information and the duty to remember". Moreover, there are considerable technical limits to implementing and executing this right. However, the authors also point out the positive sides of this new right: one of the key elements of the article on the right to be forgotten is that it stipulates that users can withdraw previously given consent for data processing. This is vital, for example in social networks where data subjects have given consent for the processing of data when they were children, but would like to have this data removed as they become older. It could, thus, contribute to safer Internet use for children.

In the last chapter of this part, Chap. 10, Isolde Sprenkels and Irma van der Ploeg focus on online advertising by companies aimed at children, and evaluate this phenomenon. They point out that businesses increasingly use advertising formats and cross-media approaches to target children as potential (future) customers. For example, businesses are present in online virtual worlds, or they provide children with fun games that function as advertising tools at the same time. This latter phenomenon is called 'gamevertising', 'advertisements as game' or 'advergames for short'. Advergames offer businesses a way "to meet corporate goals, such as building brand awareness and stimulating product purchase amongst children and their parents. And [they] also [enable] them to collect valuable information about children". Sprenkels and Van der Ploeg begin the chapter with a description of a Dutch advergame, developed by the OLA Ice cream brand in cooperation with Nickelodeon, the children's television channel. Using this example, the authors explain how OLA goes about invoking a trust relationship with the brand in children, for example by letting children 'become assistants' to the main characters in the game, and enabling them to personalise the game environment. Next, the authors delve into the ethics of advergames, with a special focus on fairness. One could argue that advergames are 'fair' as long as they respect the different levels of experience in children, and hence their differences in degree of awareness relating to the fact that they are the targets of advertising. However, empirical research shows that despite the fact that older children are supposed to be more experienced and media literate, they can still be influenced or persuaded by advertising. This is why, according to Sprenkels and Van der Ploeg, advergames are worrying: "While advergames may be seen as an opportunity to play and have fun for free, children remain unaware of the commercial intent and goals behind the advergame." Using Actor Network Theory, the authors investigate the scripts that are embedded in advergames, and that obliterate "correct recognition as commercial text". They express concern over the fact that children are targeted as consumers, through a hidden machinery of advertising, brand awareness and brand identification, and put on the same level as adults.

In the last two parts of this book, we address two online risks that are especially prevalent among, and dangerous for, children: cyberbullying (**Part IV**) and online grooming (**Part V**).

Part IV opens with a chapter by Eva Lievens. In Chap. 11, she asks to what extent minors may be held liable for certain risky behaviours according to existing criminal or civil law, such as cyberbullying, or posting harmful or illegal content. Lievens also asks whether third parties, such as parents, could be held liable for the behaviour of minors on social network sites. She focuses on provisions from Belgian (civil and criminal) law to find answers to these questions. Lievens points out that while children used to be viewed predominantly as potential victims in online environments, over the years it has become clear that they can also be participants or actors in inflicting harm on others. This is especially the case in social network sites. Major risks that occur in these sites, and that take place between peers, are sexting and cyberbullying. Lievens asks whether existing articles in the Criminal Code in Belgium are relevant for such harmful behaviours. She answers this question affirmatively, and discusses several relevant articles that could apply to sexting. However, while they may be applicable, Lievens still wonders whether it would be right to employ these articles for children. For example, some of the articles she has discussed "aim to address child pornography and to punish adults who intend to sexually abuse children", and while these would, technically, also be relevant to sexting, she argues that it would seem "to be disproportionate to apply [such] legislative provisions [...] to situations where minors send or post sexually suggestive pictures to each other". After this, Lievens looks into the issue of liability. She explains that while Belgian law does not hold minors liable in the same way as adults, they may be put under disciplinary measures when they commit crimes, for example under supervision or guidance. Minors may also be held civilly liable for harmful behaviours, for example sexting. Moreover, sometimes parents or teachers may be held liable for the harmful acts of their children or pupils. Next, Lievens looks at alternative regulatory instruments that may be used to increase online child safety. She pleads for co-regulatory solutions: "A transparent co-regulatory framework, with an unambiguous division of responsibilities, strong incentives to comply and clearly defined evaluation criteria, would lead to more accountability and certainty for all actors involved and would thus, in our view, be in everyone's best interest." Finally, Lievens notes that more and more focus is placed on empowerment and improving the children's digital skills, in order to make them more resilient against potential harms, rather than remedying harms after their occurrence. Improving children's media literacy and skills, and providing children with efficient reporting mechanisms could be very effective means in increasing online child safety.

Chapter 12, focuses on cyberbullying. Janneke van der Zwaan, Virginia Dignum, Catholijn Jonker and Simone van der Hof use a number of empirical studies to show how significant this risk is: victimisation rates in these studies range from 20 to 40 %, and it has a high impact on victims. The authors of this chapter focus on the ways in which technologies can be deployed to protect and empower youngsters against cyberbullying. Van der Zwaan et al. begin the chapter with an explanation of what cyberbullying is, and how it relates to, overlaps with and differs from 'traditional' (offline) bullying. They explain, for example that cyberbullying "has a strong connection with the offline world; between 44 and 82 % of cyberbullying victims know their bullies offline". Next, they turn to the question of what is to be done about cyberbullying. They state that existing research often focuses on the importance of education and awareness to combat cyberbullying. Many researchers argue that cyberbullying ought to become part of existing, conventional anti-bullying programs. Van der Zwaan et al. argue that aside from this, or perhaps in conjunction with it, one could also use technological tools against cyberbullying, or to help children deal with the consequences thereof. The authors discuss a number of existing examples of such tools, for example the use of filtering, monitoring or tools to report content. They compare and contrast these tools to see which ones would be (most) effective with regard to cyberbullying. They conclude that

> the effectiveness of these technologies against cyberbullying is still limited. Technologies such as age/identity verification, filtering and monitoring, reporting, and blocking undesirable contacts have not been designed to protect against cyberbullying, but with other online risks in mind. Some of these technologies primarily target access to undesirable content. Their success in protecting against cyberbullying, which is mostly communication-based, is therefore limited.

Moreover, with a few exceptions, none of the existing technologies that the authors discuss are designed to empower children and teenagers. The only technical solution in the list that they have reviewed that is quite promising in combating cyberbullying is blocking undesirable contacts. There is room for improvement in this area, then.

In Chap. 13, Sarah Genner looks at the effectiveness of legal regulation with regard to violent online video games and cyberbullying, with a focus on Switzerland. She argues that while attempts to regulate these online risks through law may be well intentioned, in practice it often has no effect at all. More importantly, oftentimes cries for a ban on online video games or cyberbullying are politically informed and aimed at quickly 'scoring' with voters. Genner starts her chapter with a discussion of public and political debates on violence as a result of playing online video games. Every time a shocking event occurs, such as the Columbine high school shooting in 1999, or the Zurich-Hoengg shooting in Switzerland in 2007, politicians want quick fixes to prevent such horrors from happening again. "After both tragic events [...], violent computer games were found at the killers' homes. This leads to the widespread conclusion that these games are the cause for the atrocities, or at least made significant contributions." However, scientific evidence does not substantiate that claim. Playing violent video games alone does not lead to violence. When violence occurs, this only happens in combination with other social or personal factors. Despite this scientific evidence, Swiss politicians have passed a law on banning violent video games in 2010, in the name of child safety, as they claimed. However, Genner explains that such bans are ineffective. While they may send a social signal, they cannot prevent the spreading of games, especially not when these are played online, since the Internet is a transnational network. Enforcement of bans is also very difficult. Next, Genner turns to the topic of cyberbullying. In Switzerland, a government-issued report investigating the scope of cyberbullying and the potential legal remedies required to remedy it was published in 2010. It stated that the Swiss Penal Code provided adequate protection against cyberbullying (e.g. by framing it as defamation or name-calling), and that no further regulation was required. The report recommended that the best road to follow would be to invest in improving media literacy and increasing knowledge, both for children and their parents. Since attempts to tackle both cyberbullying and the potential negative consequences of violent video games through legal means are largely symbolic and have proven ineffective, Genner sides with the recommendation of this report, and argues that investing in making children more resilient would be the most fruitful solution to combating cyberbullying.

In the last chapter of this part, Chap. 14, Heidi Vandebosch argues that, in order to combat cyberbullying effectively, we must consider carefully what the characteristics of this form of bullying are. It is important to do so, since due to the nature of cyberbullying, different actors may (need to) be involved compared to offline bulling.

> Because cyberbullying is mostly initiated at home, is only directly observable online, and often done by a perpetrator who takes advantage of the relative anonymity provided by ICT, school staff is probably less aware of this type of bullying and less able to react immediately. Therefore, other types of actors—i.e. parents, Internet Service Providers, and the police—should also be engaged in actions aimed at the prevention, detection and solution of cyberbullying.

Moreover, Vandebosch argues that mass media may also play an important role in preventing and combating cyberbullying. Using findings from a range of different scientific studies, Vandebosch begins her chapter with a description of what cyberbullying is, who its perpetrators and victims are, why perpetrators decide to bully others using the Internet and what the impact of cyberbullying is. She explains, for example, that cyberbullying is quite a common problem, but that it is still less prevalent than traditional bullying. One of the key features of cyberbullying is its anonymity. Interestingly, however, Vandebosch writes that while "[p]erpetrators often cyberbully anonymously [...], most of their actions are targeted towards victims they know in person". Vandebosch concludes that while cyberbullying has considerable overlap with traditional forms of (offline) bullying, there are also significant differences. Most importantly, cyberbullying can take place around the clock, literally 24/7. Moreover, its potential audience is much larger than that of traditional bullying, and may even be worldwide. And finally, as mentioned before, cyberbullying can be conducted anonymously. Because cyberbullying has certain characteristics that set it apart from 'regular' bullying, it also requires different responses. For one, as Van der Zwaan et al. also explained, many researchers argue that cyberbullying should become part of existing anti-bullying programs that are run by schools. However, Vandebosch argues that since cyberbullying is often initiated at home, it falls outside the school's perception and hence is much harder for schools to address or combat. Therefore, other types of actors should be involved in attempting to tackle cyberbullying. Vandebosch organises these actors along three levels. On the first level, we find the children themselves (both as perpetrators and as victims), their parents and schools. On the second level, we find Internet Service Providers, the police and e-safety organisations. Finally, on the third level we find the news media, policy makers and researchers. Vandebosch discusses the ways in which each of these actors play a role in reducing cyberbullying and/or helping youngsters deal with the impact of cyberbullying, and uses examples from Flanders (Belgium) to explain how this works.

The final part of this book, **Part V**, discusses another risk for children when they use the Internet: online grooming or online sexual solicitation. The authors in this section explain what this phenomenon consists of, and how it is, can or ought to be addressed.

In Chap. 15, Leontien van der Knaap and Colette Cuijpers argue that we have little empirical knowledge of the consequences of online sexual solicitation, or about how prevalent (or not) this harm really is. They argue that, therefore, "important regulatory initiatives are developed without substantiating empirical evidence of the risk and protective factors that bear relevance to the actual conduct of victims and offenders. From a regulatory perspective, this raises several questions regarding the European regulatory strategies adopted to curtail online sexual solicitation." In this chapter, they analyse a number of legal documents from the EU relating to online sexual solicitation, to critically assess the underlying assumptions of these documents. They begin by analysing the 2007 Lanzarote Convention, in which online sexual solicitation of children was criminalised for the first time. This criminalisation was based on the assumption "that children and youth are harmed by online sexual solicitation". But there is no empirical evidence that this is necessarily the case. It is unclear how many children actually receive sexual messages from adults, and it is also unclear how children respond to online sexual solicitation. Moreover, it is also unclear which groups of children run the biggest risk of becoming victims of online sexual solicitation. Van der Knaap and Cuijpers discuss a number of empirical studies that reveal that only a small group of all children say that they were upset by receiving online sexual requests. What is more, evidence also shows that the prevalence of online sexual solicitation is "less wide-spread than public anxiety may lead people to believe". Finally, when youth receive sexual requests, these are often sent by peers "and in the majority of cases the sender is also known to youth in the offline context. A large proportion of youth who receive such messages feel free to choose whether or not to respond to online sexual solicitation and if they do, most of them do so because they liked the other person or thought it was fun or exciting to do so." Based on this empirical evidence, Van der Knaap and Cuijpers question whether existing regulation aligns enough with factual evidence of the risk of online sexual solicitation. More specifically, they argue that the current EU legislation in this area could benefit from a stronger empirical basis in three respects: to prevent overregulation, to prevent underregulation and to ensure that the type of regulation employed best matches the issue at hand.

In the final chapter of this book, Chap. 16, Jamie-lee Mooney discusses the role of digital, networked technologies in facilitating grooming. According to Mooney, these technologies make it easier to groom children, and increase the perpetrators' chances of success. For one, this is due to the fact that groomers can operate relatively anonymously when using these technologies to approach children. They can conceal their real identities, and reveal these only at a later stage, when the children have already built up a relationship of trust with them. Moreover, the Internet enables them to easily locate vulnerable children, for example by browsing profile pages on social network sites, and accessing other personal information left behind by children. The wealth of personal information that is available on the Internet about children also enables them to strike up a conversation more easily and provides them with topics for conversation. Finally, because children can now also access the Internet on their mobile phones, it becomes easier for predators to engage in more frequent contact with children, and harder for parents to monitor their children's activities. In the next part of the chapter, Mooney discusses the British Sexual Offences Act 2003 (SOA), which has a special section on grooming. She argues that this section can be considered an example of underregulation, since "the offence only targets the arranging of and/or meeting a child, with the coupled intent, following a period of grooming." This entails that virtual meetings between adults and children are not covered. Mooney also points to other risks of underregulation in relation to the same act. For one, she discusses the issue of 'third-party grooming', whereby a perpetrator grooms child A to get access to child B, for example a younger sibling. This form of grooming is underresearched, she argues, and is not covered by existing legislation. Mooney also argues that grooming is a gradual process, which largely takes place on the Internet, and eventually may result in an offline meeting with the child. Currently, only the offline meeting itself is punishable by law. But Mooney argues that perhaps children would be better protected should the process leading up to the meeting also be considered part of the criminal act. However, she does acknowledge that this is not as straightforward as it seems, given "the ambiguity and fluidity of grooming behaviour presented alongside practical issues surrounding evidence of ulterior intent".

1.3 Challenging Perspectives

As this overview of chapters may already show, this book challenges perspectives in several senses of the phrase. First, this book aims to challenge existing ideas about child safety. It contains analyses of existing (forms of) regulation to reveal both its strengths and weaknesses, and presents ideas on, or areas that have room for improvement. Whether conceptual or empirical, all chapters in one way or another challenge aspects of online child safety and the debates surrounding this topic.

But the book also contains 'challenging perspectives' in another sense. It contains positions that clash and ideas that oppose one another. As editors we have deliberately chosen to include opposing viewpoints on the same (or a similar) topic to show the full range of potential positions within debates on online child safety. Online child safety is not an uncontested topic, and we have opted for the aforementioned approach to provide the reader with a balanced, nuanced overview of this theme.

Two examples may reveal how starkly positions in this book can contrast: in Chap. 3, Adam Thierer discusses the need for a thorough, rigorous framework to analyse whether regulation of a perceived harm is necessary, and which type of regulation would work best. According to him, there are some online risks that obviously need a regulatory intervention, to protect children from harm—child pornography is an example in case. But in many other cases, whether or not an actual harm exists is not all that obvious. He writes:

> Harm is a particular nebulous concept as it pertains to online safety and digital privacy debates where conjectural theories abound. [...] ...many moral panics have come and gone through the years as critics looked to restrict speech or expression they found objectionable. In cases such as these, 'harm' is very much an eye-of-the-beholder issue. It is important to keep in mind that no matter how objectionable some media content or online speech may be, none of it poses a direct threat to adults or children.

Hence, Thierer does not believe that advertising or even forms of targeted marketing harm children. They may make us feel 'creepy', but this is not the same thing as causing harm. And hence we should ask ourselves if regulating these forms of advertising in relation to children would be a wise course of action. In Chap. 10, Sprenkels and Van der Ploeg take quite a contrary stance. Using a case study of an advergame, they show that online marketing strategies targeted at children contain a host of hidden mechanisms that lead to more brand awareness and brand identification. These mechanisms not only entice and seduce children in non-transparent ways, but also effectively treat them as though they are adult consumers. While Sprenkels and Van der Ploeg do not draw explicit conclusions with regard to the regulation of advergames, it is clear that their chapter is a plea against this practice. The hidden assumption in their chapter, therefore, is that advertising aimed at children does cause harm, and must be tackled.

A second example revolves around the topic of online sexual solicitation or grooming. This is the topic of the last section of this book, which consists of two chapters. In Chap. 15, Van der Knaap and Cuijpers argue that current regulation of online sexual solicitation may not always be built on factual evidence, and point out that there is a risk of overregulating online sexual solicitation. They argue that in the vast majority of cases online sexual solicitation takes place between peers, and even if this is not the case, it might not always be perceived as negative, let alone be harmful to the minor(s) in question. This applies especially to older minors, for who engaging in online interactions about sex may be seen as part of their normal development. While Van der Knaap and Cuijpers acknowledge that online sexual solicitation can lead to harm for children in some cases, and argue that regulation and policy should be targeted at these victims, they claim that "research on the prevalence and nature of online sexual solicitation clearly shows that online sexual solicitation of youth may be less wide-spread than public anxiety may lead people to believe." More research is needed, therefore, to establish whether current regulatory initiatives and practices are adequate and suitable, both in their form and in their means. In contrast, in the final chapter of this book Mooney expresses grave concern over the fact that information and communication technologies offer new possibilities for grooming children, i.e. gradually building up a relationship of trust that will, at some point, be used to seduce the child into engaging in sexual acts. Mooney analyses the British Sexual Offences Act 2003 and argues that it underregulates the criminalisation of grooming, since grooming is only qualified as an offence when an actual meeting with the child takes place. While Van der Knaap and Cuijpers also acknowledge this risk, the tenor of their chapter lies with the potential of overregulating.

What these two examples, and the many other contrasting ideas in this book, reveal is that finding answers to the core question of this book—how to strike the right balance between ensuring child safety online and respecting children's freedoms and rights at the same time—is far from straightforward. With this book, we hope to contribute to untangling the complicated conceptual and regulatory knot of child safety in the age of the Internet.

Part I
The Regulatory Horizon

Chapter 2
Children's Rights Online: Challenges, Dilemmas and Emerging Directions

Sonia Livingstone and Brian O'Neill

Contents

Sonia Livingstone is Professor of Social Psychology, Department of Media and Communications at LSE. Brian O'Neill is Head of the School of Media at Dublin Institute of Technology. This chapter draws on the work of the EU Kids Online network funded by the European Commission (Directorate-General Information Society) Safer Internet plus Programme (SIP-KEP-321803); see www.eukidsonline.net. We thank members of the network for their collaboration in developing the research underpinning this chapter. Thanks also to Anne Collier, Nóirín Hayes, Simone van der Hof, Jenny Kuper, Peter Lunt, Robin Mansell and Sharon McLaughlin for their comments on an earlier version of this chapter.

S. Livingstone (✉)
Department of Media and Communications, London School of Economics, London, UK
e-mail: s.livingstone@lse.ac.uk

B. O'Neill
Dublin Institute of Technology, Dublin, Ireland

S. van der Hof et al. (eds.), *Minding Minors Wandering the Web: Regulating Online Child Safety*, Information Technology and Law Series 24, DOI: 10.1007/978-94-6265-005-3_2,

2.1 Positioning Children's Rights Within Debates over Internet Governance

Although it is widely held that a more inclusive and trusted Internet can support a competitive knowledge economy, a digitally skilled labour force, civic participation and a pluralistic media sector, governments and regulators have tended to avoid intervening directly to achieve these aims, believing that industry is best positioned to respond to the fast pace of change in information and communication technologies (ICT).[1] This reflects a wider policy shift away from top-down government measures towards flexible, dispersed and indirect forms of governance, encompassing industry self-regulation as well as elements of cooperation or co-regulation with relevant state agencies.[2]

In these debates, the interests of children figure unevenly and can prove surprisingly contentious. Only partial progress has been made in supporting children's rights online and there have been a number of significant hurdles.[3] In the early days of the Internet, public policy concern for children centred on inappropriate content, since it seemed that pornography of all kinds was pushed via pop-ups and other uninvited means into users' emails and web searches, along with efforts to prevent grooming and related paedophilic contact risks. In the US, early legislative responses were heavy-handed, risking contravention of fundamental rights to freedom of expression (as established by the Universal Declaration of Human Rights 1948 and as afforded legal protection in the US by the First Amendment).[4] But approaches to Internet governance have since shifted from the (largely, but not entirely discredited) view that 'cyberspace' is a distinct sphere in need of distinct regulation to the growing acceptance that what is illegal or inappropriate offline is or should be illegal or inappropriate online. This approach, now concerned with a range of risks far beyond that of pornography, has largely guided European policies, is our main focus in this chapter.[5]

Yet, even the effort to apply offline regulation and governance practices online tends to conflict with liberal and libertarian efforts to keep the Internet open and free (e.g. Open Rights Group).[6] Consequently, advocacy for children's

---

[1] Green 2010; Lembke 2003; Marsden 2011.

[2] Lunt and Livingstone 2012; Schulz and Held 2004; Tambini et al. 2008.

[3] Livingstone and Bulger 2013; Preston 2009.

[4] Early battles included the successful fight against the US Communications Decency Act 1996 (Nesson and Marglin 1996) and, in 2007, the striking down as unconstitutional of the Child Online Protection Act (COPA) 1998 (McNamee 2010). See also www.ftc.gov/privacy/coppafaqs.shtm.

[5] European Commission 1996, 2009a, 2010. For research in other parts of the world, see OECD 2011, ITU 2010 and Livingstone & Bulger 2013 for global reports, Gasser et al. 2010, on developing countries, and Palfrey et al. 2008 on the US.

[6] See also Dutton and Peltu 2007; Thierer 2011.

empowerment and protection online has seemed to swim against the tide of a dominant liberal discourse which posits that the Internet should not be regulated if this undermines freedom of expression, that it cannot easily be regulated through law, and/or that there are higher priorities than those of children's interests. These include, from media reform activists, principles of 'net neutrality' and Internet 'generativity'[7] and, from business interests, policies for market freedom and economic competitiveness. In this context, children's rights and protection measures are readily viewed as a threat to adult rights or as a secondary complication in the larger debate over citizens' rights versus the rights of the state or commerce. At worst, they figure as covert efforts to promote the state's power to survey, censor or even criminalise private citizens' acts.[8]

As Alderson explains, "Rights are collective not individual, 'ours' not 'mine'. Anyone's claim to a right automatically states concern for everyone else's equal claim to it."[9] Can society find a way to advance children's rights online without unduly trampling on business or (adult) citizens' interests? As the Internet and surrounding debates have matured, there is growing acceptance that diverse forms of governance, including but not only national or international intervention, are required to facilitate online opportunities while also reducing or managing the associated risks. This conclusion has been reached not only by child rights advocates but also those concerned with citizen and consumer rights and those concerned to sustain a secure and trusted online infrastructure for commerce, civil society and the state.[10] After all, as Lessig influentially observed,[11] early utopian cheerleading for the so-called freedom of the Internet has had to recognise that the Internet is already governed through its design, code and practises of use—although much of this remains experimental and open to negotiation, given the competing interests at stake.

---

7 Powell and Cooper 2011; Zittrain 2008.

8 Livingstone 2011. Indeed, although there is now widespread acceptance of the need for Internet governance, meaning that the libertarian position (for which expression even of illegal content may be claimed as an unqualified right) receives little support, there is still a need to address the concerns of critics who, often with justification, have learned to be sceptical of the stated good intentions of the state or commerce; too often, it has come about that, using the defence of child protection, or the tools thereby developed, various acts of state or commercial intrusion or censorship occur, whether deliberately (by politically motivated governments or for commercial exploitation) or inadvertently (by incompetent systems of Internet filtering or surveillance).

9 Alderson 2000, p. 442.

10 Mansell 2012.

11 Lessig 2000.

2.2 Applying the UN Convention on the Rights of the Child to the Internet

In the absence of a formal statement of online rights, this chapter argues that the UN Convention on the Rights of the Child (UNCRC), which sets out the basic standards that apply without discrimination to all children and specifies the minimum entitlements and freedoms that governments should implement, offers a sound guide to policy action. This international treaty recognises the human rights of children, defined as persons up to the age of 18 years.[12] It complements the Universal Declaration of Human Rights[13] and clarifies that children 'count' in terms of human rights; indeed, 'the child, by reason of his physical and mental immaturity, needs special safeguards and care, including appropriate legal protection, before as well as after birth' (Preamble). Ratified in 1989, the UNCRC is one of the most universally recognised international legal instruments and incorporates the full range of human rights—civil, cultural, economic, political and social rights—in its 54 articles and two Optional Protocols.

A cornerstone of the UNCRC is the statement that 'in all actions concerning children, whether undertaken by public or private social welfare institutions, courts of law, administrative authorities or legislative bodies, the best interests of the child shall be a primary consideration' (Article 3) although the question of determining what are the child's 'best interests' remains a vexed one.[14] Moreover, although few would claim that the framework offers strong guarantees (see critics of its implementation around the world[15]: its three core principles of the '*provision* of basic needs, *protection* against neglect and abuse and children's *participation* in their families and communities'[16] have widespread support. Thus, they provide a consensual starting point for considering the rights of the child online, as extended by the Oslo Challenge,[17] adopted by UNICEF on the tenth anniversary of the UNCRC to recognise the importance of the media and information environment as a relevant context for the realisation of children's rights.[18] The UNCRC's assertion

---

[12] See www2.ohchr.org/english/law/crc.htm.

[13] See www.un.org/en/documents/udhr/index.shtml. Note that children 'are entitled to special care and assistance' (Article 25) and that 'Parents have a prior right to choose the kind of education that shall be given to their children' (Article 26). Beyond this, there is no implication that children should be treated in any way differently from adults as regards fundamental rights.

[14] Freeman 2007.

[15] Guggenheim 2005; Holzscheiter 2010; O'Neill 1988; Purdy 1992; Veerman 2010. Article 4 requires governments to undertake all relevant legislative, administrative and other measures to implement the rights of the child, to submit evidence and to have progress on their implementation as a subject of public review (Article 44), while making the principles of the Convention widely known to adults and children alike (Article 42).

[16] Alderson 2000, p. 440 (emphasis added).

[17] See www.unicef.org/magic/briefing/oslo.html.

[18] Hamelink 2008; Livingstone 2009b. Consider the world of traditional mass media, where children's rights have long been debated. The Children's Television Charter applies the principles

that children are rights-bearing individuals is particularly pertinent in Internet governance discourses that tend to oppose adult rights and child protection. And its particular articles specifying children's rights dovetail with the emerging challenges that the Internet poses to children and families.[19]

At present, children's rights are commonly referred to but little examined in relation to the Internet.[20] Nor, must it be said, are they necessarily supported by the advent of the digital media and information environment. Indeed, while the rapid development of the Internet as a mass phenomenon has presented children with unprecedented opportunities to achieve their rights to learn, express themselves and participate in their communities in meaningful ways, it has also created new and sometimes threatening conditions in which children are abused or exploited, with varying incidence and severity. Early in the history of the Internet, governments recognised the seriousness of the child protection issues involved and, through the second Optional Protocol on the sale of children, child prostitution and child pornography,[21] gave effect to international legislation outlawing online child abuse images.[22] There are, however, many aspects of children's use of online, digital and mobile technologies that give rise to concern or which require attention by policy makers to assess their impact on children and to ensure children's interests are incorporated.

So, how might the key provisions of the UNCRC apply to the Internet? In what follows, we consider the application of the so-called three Ps—protection, provision and participation rights—to the online environment. As will be seen, two broad strategies have emerged—a regulatory approach that transposes individual rights and preventative measures into appropriate legal or other (self- or co-) regulatory instruments, and a broader policy approach that focuses on child well-being, emphasising appropriate provision for children and support for their participation.

(Footnote 18 continued)
of the UNCRC to television and may, surely, also be applied to the Internet (Livingstone 2009b). Relatedly, the concept of 'child-friendly journalism' has been promoted by the Brazilian News Agency for Children's Rights (ANDI), founded on legislative recognition of children's rights (including communicative rights), proactive production of positive content and an accountability system in which all stakeholders play an active role (see www.andi.org.br/).

[19] McLaughlin 2013.

[20] In Europe, the Directorate-General for Justice is charged with coordinating efforts regarding children's rights; see http://ec.europa.eu/justice/fundamental-rights/rights-child/index_en.htm. There are, however, many other European Commission efforts relevant here, including the European Commission Communication, 'Towards an EU Strategy on the Rights of the Child' (2006), 'An EU Strategy for Youth' (2009) and 'An EU Agenda for the Rights of the Child' (2011). Advancing these concerns is not always straightforward, however—witness the struggle in formulating the 2011 Directive on combating sexual abuse and sexual exploitation of children and child pornography about whether the blocking of illegal child abuse images should be discretionary or mandatory in member states. See the overview in European Parliament 2012. Little is said regarding the digital environment in any of these documents.

[21] See www2.ohchr.org/english/law/crc-sale.htm.

[22] Flint 2000; Jones 1998.

2.3 Protection Rights

To date, most national and international effort has gone into children's protection rights, including protection against all forms of abuse and neglect (Article 19), and sexual exploitation and sexual abuse (Article 34). Present measures offer a robust legal framework for classifying illegal content and activity on the Internet involving the sexual abuse of children that member states have, or are in the process of, transposing into national law.[23] Additionally, children have the right to be protected from trafficking (Article 35) and from 'all other forms of exploitation prejudicial to any aspects of the child's welfare' (Article 36). These rights point to some serious risks of harm, many of which are now mediated, even exacerbated by mass use of the Internet. The production and circulation of illegal child abuse images, the incidence of sexual grooming for abuse and the conduct of child trafficking and other forms of exploitation—all have their online dimension and, many would argue, all have been amplified, worsened, by the Internet's astonishing convenience, anonymity and means to evade law enforcement.[24] Protecting children against online sexual abuse has justifiably been one of the most important policy goals of online child protection since the earliest days of the Internet, and the subject of extensive international efforts in law enforcement, detection through various technological means, self-regulatory initiatives on the part of industry through an international network of hotlines, and wide international cooperation on 'notice and take down' procedures to make the Internet a safer place.

Less clear-cut is the imperative for initiatives designed to protect children from material injuries to the child's well-being (Article 17(e)). Alongside Article 18, enjoining governments to support parents in their caregiving role, this is a wide domain in which the protection of children has been addressed through self-regulatory initiatives to promote the use of parental controls and filters on devices and platforms, the development of advisory classification and labelling schemes. To varying degrees in different countries and cultures, children's widespread exposure to online pornography, 'race' hate, self-harm and violent content attest to the only partial success thus far in protecting children.[25] On the other hand, theory and evidence also make it clear that risk is distinct from harm: not all those who

[23] Relevant to the digital dimension of Article 34, which requires governments to protect children from all forms of sexual abuse and sexual exploitation, is the 2007 Council of Europe's *Convention on the Protection of Children against Sexual Exploitation and Sexual Abuse* (the 'Lanzarote Convention'), which criminalises the use of new technologies to sexually harm or abuse children. Other European legal instruments include the 1996 *Communication on Illegal and Harmful Content on the Internet,* the 2006 *Recommendation on the Protection of Minors* and the 2011 *Directive on Combating the Sexual Abuse and Sexual Exploitation of Children and Child Pornography*. Child protection online setting is also implied by Article 19's call for 'appropriate legislative, administrative, social and educational measures to protect the child' and which promote governmental action in Internet safety provision.

[24] Ainsaar and Loof 2012; Muir 2005; Quale and Taylor 2011; Webster et al. 2012.

[25] Livingstone et al. 2011b.

encounter risk are harmed by it, for risk refers only to the probability of harm. Moreover, the factors that account for risk encounters are not the same as those that explain harm.[26] Thus, the wholesale elimination of risk is neither feasible nor desirable; society does not wish to keep children forever in a 'walled garden', recognising that they must explore, make mistakes and learn to cope in order to develop into resilient adults and responsible digital citizens. This leaves policy makers with the difficult balancing act of supporting and empowering children online, given that increased use and higher levels of digital skills also mean increased exposure to risk and, for some, actual harm.[27]

Also difficult in an online environment is addressing children's right to be protected from 'arbitrary or unlawful interference with his or her privacy, family, or correspondence, nor to unlawful attacks on his or her honour and reputation' (Article 16). Relatedly, Article 8's obligation to respect the right of the child to preserve his or her identity raises new challenges for legislators to keep pace with new technologies that may threaten the security and privacy of children's personal information online. It is noteworthy, for instance, that children's primary concerns regarding the Internet centre on privacy, (cyber-)bullying and online reputation.[28] Yet efforts to address these problems are sporadic and of uncertain efficacy.[29] Many children lack the competence to manage the settings provided to protect their privacy or reputation, and only a minority use the available tools to report bullying or racist insults online,[30] although they are learning to keep their social networking profiles private and to take care in disclosing personal information.[31] Whether responsibility to protect children from such online harms lies with industry, parents, child welfare or law enforcement agencies remains hotly contested. The concept of a 'right to be forgotten',[32] as proposed in the new *Regulation for a European Data Protection Framework*,[33] promises to tackle some of the risks to young people's reputation from online preservation of information and give them the right to have their personal data removed. Ensuring the availability of user-friendly and age-appropriate privacy controls to enable young people to exercise their rights to privacy is also addressed by self-regulatory codes of practise (e.g. *Safer Social Networking Principles for the EU*; see also Vice President Kroes' CEO coalition[34]), although the continued updating and independent evaluation of such codes and guidelines remains uncertain.

---

[26] Schoon 2006.

[27] O'Neill et al. 2011.

[28] Lusoli and Miltgen 2009.

[29] Anthonysamy et al. 2012; Eurobarometer 2011; Lusoli et al. 2011.

[30] Livingstone et al. 2012b.

[31] Livingstone et al. 2011a.

[32] Mayer-Schönberger 2009; Rosen 2012.

[33] European Commission 2012b.

[34] Announcing a coalition of chief executive officers (CEOs) of major Internet companies on 1 Dec 2011, European Commission Vice President Neelie Kroes established five work streams to

2.4 Provision Rights

Article 17 is not only concerned with protection from harm, but it also recognises 'the important function performed by the mass media' and encourages the production by industry of information and material of social and cultural benefit to the child from a diversity of sources so as to promote the social and moral well-being of the child. Meeting such a right is, however, expensive for governments, especially in small language communities (and if supported by advertising this extends market logic to public services). At present, it seems that sufficient provision is lacking—a simple example: only 34 % of European 9- to 10-year-olds say there are lots of good things for children of their age to do online.[35] In response, the European Commission launched a European Award for Best Children's Online Content[36] and initiated efforts to stimulate industry investment in positive content for children.[37]

Also little developed as yet is the extent to which other aspects of the UNCRC can and should apply online. Article 31 requires governments to provide for children's rights to recreation and leisure as appropriate to their age—here it is relevant that the majority of children in the digital age seek recreation and leisure online. Even more importantly, Article 28 underpins the child's right to an education that will support the development of their full potential. Again, in relation to the Internet, such a right clearly entails online resources and support for information and learning valuable to children, along with the acquisition of the necessary digital skills that develop the 'child's personality, talents and mental and physical abilities' and prepare young people 'for responsible life in a free society' (Article 29). Increasingly, educators argue that digital competence as an essential skill for life-long learning represents a vital contemporary extension of the right to education, requiring governments and other agencies to make appropriate provision for the development of children's full potential in the digital age.[38]

Yet in much of the world, within and beyond the Global North, even basic provision of hardware and connectivity has proved challenging. Consider efforts to overcome the digital divide, now reframed in a more nuanced fashion in terms of digital inclusion and digital literacy.[39] Over and again, interventions intended to support greater provision tend to exacerbate rather than ameliorate social

(Footnote 34 continued)
make the Internet better for children; see http://europa.eu/rapid/pressReleasesAction.do?reference=IP/11/1485&format=HTML&aged=0&language=EN&guiLanguage=en.

[35] Livingstone et al. 2011b.

[36] Awarded at the Digital Agenda Assembly, Brussels, by Commissioner Neelie Kroes (17 June 2011); see http://ec.europa.eu/information_society/activities/sip/events/competition/winners/index_en.htm. The prize was awarded again on 11 February 2014.

[37] European Commission 2012a.

[38] Ala-Mutka et al. 2008; Council of Europe 2006; OECD 2012a.

[39] Helsper 2012.

inequality as they are taken up disproportionately by the already advantaged—the so-called 'knowledge gap' problem.[40] Meanwhile, market developments are likely to continue targeting the relatively better-off, again exacerbating inequalities in provision. Delivering skills to ensure children truly gain the benefits of full participation in the network society is proving beyond the capacity of many governments. And the result is that, even within Europe, Internet use for many children remains narrow, unimaginative, centred on the reception of mass communication, with only a minority (typically the already-advantaged) attaining the interactive, creative, participatory and civic vision that has been held out for the Internet.[41]

2.5 Participation Rights

While protecting children's rights is frequently interpreted as 'protecting' children from harm, the UNCRC—uniquely within international treaties—also places equal emphasis on provision, as discussed above, and on children's rights to social, cultural and political participation. Children's participation rights include the right to be consulted in all matters affecting them, with due weight being given to children's views in accordance with the age and maturity of the child (Article 12). They also have the right to freedom of expression (Article 13), 'the right of the child to freedom of thought, conscience and religion' (Article 14) and 'the rights to freedom of association and to freedom of peaceful assembly' (Article 15). Each of these finds expression in the digital world, although each receives far less attention than children's rights to protection online.

Article 13 is particularly relevant to the Internet in its reference to fundamental freedom of expression, holding that children should have the freedom 'to seek, receive and impart information and ideas of all kinds, regardless of frontiers, either orally, in writing or in print, in the form of art, or through any other media of the child's choice.' Note that, relevant to problems of cyberbullying, sexting and more, this is a contingent freedom, for the child must also respect 'the rights or reputations of others' (which the evidence shows a significant minority do not do), while parents too bear responsibility for the child's upbringing (Article 18). Article 15's reference to freedom of association is also particularly relevant to the Internet, given that children may now meet anyone and go anywhere online. Here it is obvious that efforts to protect children can come into conflict with their rights to freedom of thought, expression, assembly and association. The best interests of the child may be served by restricting their access to content that is potentially harmful for their development, but this also depends on the age and maturity of the child, with judgements varying according to cultural context. Does it extend to banning

[40] Warschauer and Matuchniak 2010.

[41] Pruulmann-Vengerfeldt and Runnel 2012.

or restricting social networking services in school settings (as is common practise in many countries)? Tricky issues include determining when rights must be limited by responsibilities, and who is best placed to determine what is in the child's best interests. Youth themselves may be expected to have a view on this question, and although they are occasionally consulted,[42] it is not obvious that they are carefully listened to in this as in other policy domains.

2.6 Unanswered Questions Regarding Children's Rights Online

The creation of a body of rights specifically for children remains controversial.[43] Some contend that human rights codes already address the needs of children and adults alike; indeed, this is even implied within the vision offered by the UNCRC where children are represented as competent and resilient agents. Yet, as the argument in favour of a dedicated convention maintains, it is because they are children—to varying degrees immature, vulnerable, in need of care and protection—that their rights are frequently ignored, denied or abused, and this is the case online as offline. Hence the UNCRC sets out the rights of the child as a distinct subset of human rights, outlining fundamental obligations of society to meet the needs of children, on the assumption that greater awareness of rights better enables their realisation.[44]

But the UNCRC provides little guidance when these rights are contradictory, as is often the case, especially in the online environment where norms are fragile and expectations are immense. For example, an online encounter that for many is harmless, part of their right to participate, may at the same time be harmful for a minority, part of their right to protection. Evidence shows that opportunities and risks are positively correlated—the more one enables provision and participation, the more the need for protection; similarly, the more one seeks to protect, the more one risks undermining participation.[45] This clash, potential and actual, between children's need for protection and for freedom is most evident in the heavily contested policy debate over the use of filtering software, whether applied by parents as end users or, to protect children even from insufficient or negligent parenting, applied centrally (e.g. by governments or at server level).[46]

42 E.g., Nordic Youth Forum 2012.

43 Griffin 2009; Guggenheim 2005.

44 Archard 2004; Foley et al. 2012.

45 Livingstone et al. 2012a.

46 See CEO coalition discussion earlier. At present, parental tools (filters, monitoring software, age ratings, etc.) are still flawed in design and operation (e.g. they over-block legitimate content, and work poorly for user-generated content, Deloitte and European Commission 2008.

Nor is the UNCRC clear on when rights are met or on how they must be met. A strong claim would be that any evidence of a child being harmed shows their protection rights are not met, but given the conflict between protection and participation, a weaker case may fairly be advanced. Defining a basic level of provision when norms regarding digital infrastructure are rising rapidly is also problematic; in many contexts, mere connectivity would be a huge benefit, but in the privileged West, lacking super-fast broadband may be disadvantageous. Last, asserting a child's right to participation in matters that concern him or her as an individual may be relatively straightforward, but how should society enable such rights for children in general? Should all children participate in civic deliberation regarding their school or community, for instance, or is the participation of some sufficient to meet the needs of all? Evidence shows that the often-valiant efforts to mediate such participation via the Internet can struggle to engage more than the few already privileged and already engaged, rendering children's actual levels of online deliberation or e-participation less than hoped.

2.7 Persistent Policy Challenges

Although children's need for protection is recognised in the Audiovisual Media Services Directive,[47] the situation is less clear in relation to the converging digital and online media landscape (regarding the regulation of media content, converged platforms, privacy, data protection, Internet security, e-commerce and so forth). Three practical problems significantly impede effective Internet governance, contributing to the tendency to side-line consideration of children's online rights. First, it is difficult to draw the line in relation to judgements of 'inappropriate' content or contact. While the challenge of defining risk is hardly new (for which representations harm children has long proved contentious[48]), public norms of offence or acceptability typically rest on 'community standards', which are unclear and contested in the cross-national context that characterises the borderless Internet.[49] Second, there are considerable difficulties of jurisdiction, given the global and networked nature of the Internet. Especially challenging here are the lack of trusted and authoritative international regulatory institutions, numerous differences in legal systems and significant practical difficulties of compliance and enforcement. Third, there is the problem of addressing the rights of children in particular (rather than those of citizens and consumers in general) in the absence of reliable means of age verification (i.e. knowing whether a user is a child or not). This problem arises both from the lack of reliable databases and a widespread

[47] European Union 2010.

[48] Millwood Hargrave and Livingstone 2009.

[49] As Holzscheiter observes, the UNCRC also 'poses serious problems in translation into different cultural contexts'; Holzscheiter 2010, p. 17.

distrust of the companies or governments that maintain them. Whether or not addressing children separately from adults is the desirable way forward is also contested.[50]

How, then, should the public policy objective of supporting children's rights online be achieved? Nationally and internationally, most efforts to secure children's interests online adopt a multi-stakeholder approach, combining legislation (albeit, for the most part, the application of general laws to the Internet), industry self-regulation (achieved through codes of practise and consumer-facing service provision) and the expectation of responsible action on the part of citizens (parents and children, often supported by schools and non-governmental organisation [NGO] actions). Policy frameworks such as Europe's *Safer Internet Programme*,[51] and the continuing policy discussions of child online protection at fora such that the Internet Governance Forum (IGF) and the International Telecommunication Union (ITU) have made substantial contributions to a better and safer online world,[52] putting Internet safety on the political agenda of many governments. Internet safety policy in the European Union has evolved within an environment that has moved away from top-down, state-led models of regulation in favour of collaborative and cooperative arrangements between the state and industry. Particularly, other than in relation to illegal harms, most emphasis is on a combination of education/awareness-raising and industry self-regulation.[53]

---

[50] Palfrey et al. 2008.

[51] Founded in 1999, the Directorate-General Information Society's *Safer Internet Programme* (renamed: Better Internet for Children) has provided an overarching framework for European initiatives for combating illegal content, promoting safer use of Internet and communication technologies and for awareness-raising activities, following a prescient 1996 *Communication on Illegal and Harmful Content on the Internet.* This established an international network of hotlines for reporting illegal child abuse images and a parallel network of awareness-raising centres, together with a programme to build the knowledge base regarding emerging trends in children's use and consequences of online technologies. See http://ec.europa.eu/information_society/activities/sip/policy/program5me/current_prog/index_en.htm.

[52] Child online protection features prominently in the work of international bodies such as the Internet Governance Forum (IGF), the Organisation for Economic Cooperation and Development (OECD) and the Council of Europe, as well as many national governments around the world. The International Telecommunication Union (ITU), as the lead United Nations (UN) agency with responsibility for the Internet, has actively raised the profile of cyber-security, and the role of child Internet safety within that, both in developed countries and across the developing world where burgeoning Internet adoption in Asia, Latin America and Africa greatly expands the reach of the Internet and the potential risks for children. Linking Internet safety with confidence and trust in the infrastructure of the Internet was a theme that emerged from the World Summit on the Information Society (WSIS) in 2005 when the ITU assumed leadership of Action C5: 'building confidence and security in the use of ICTs'. Its Global Cyber-security Agenda acts as the framework for international cooperation aimed at enhancing confidence and security in the information society, a central pillar of which is its Child Online Protection initiative (ITU 2009), designed to tackle the legal, technical and institutional challenges posed by cyber-security. See *Global Security Agenda*, accessed on 5 Sept 2010 at www.itu.int/osg/csd/cybersecurity/gca/index.html.

[53] European Commission 2009b; GSMA 2007; ICT Coalition 2012.

But policy remains largely a reactive response to a phenomenon that is not entirely understood, demanding a tight balancing act between supporting the innovation and diffusion of new online technologies while attempting to manage their diverse and unpredictable social consequences. Protectionist approaches tend to overshadow efforts to promote the role of ICTs in enhancing children's development and participation (as also important to the 2005 Tunis Commitment, for example).[54] Moreover, there is little independent monitoring or evaluation of policy effectiveness. For example, rather than the hoped-for concerted action by the industry according to transparent codes of practise, we are witnessing the semi-coordinated activity of consumer and complaint services, sporadically informed by child welfare organisations and with uncertain benefit. As a result, considerable responsibility falls on consumers (here, parents, teachers and children) to be aware of risks and to educate themselves to manage online risks appropriately,[55] and this can mean that a burden falls disproportionately hard on those least able to bear it,[56] as explored below.

2.8 Can Children's Rights Online Be Left to Parents?

A popular solution to the governance of an inappropriate or harmful (as opposed to illegal) content, contact and conduct is to say that parents bear the primary responsibility for their children's online experience. Parents are generally best placed to judge what their child should see or do (online as offline), and parental mediation is surely the most adaptable and flexible form of governance; it might even be claimed that if only parents would to take on this responsibility, managing their children's Internet access effectively, no other measures would be needed. This responsibility may be construed in terms of parental empowerment, and a fair amount of resources are devoted to raising awareness among parents and educating them in the ways of the Internet, along with the development (and marketing) of software solutions to support their role.[57] But, many parents experience this task as something of an imposition—burdening them with a technically and socially difficult task for which they are ill-equipped and under-resourced[58] and which often falls disproportionately on mothers.[59] The evidence confirms that while many parents do their best, not all are entirely competent or reliable, leaving some children's rights and safety at risk.[60] Nor do all act as expected by child welfare

---

54 See WSIS 2005.

55 Helberger 2008; O'Neill 2010.

56 Livingstone 2009a.

57 Criddle 2006; Thierer 2009.

58 Livingstone 2009a; Oswell 2008.

59 Olsen 1992.

60 Clark 2013; Dueraeger and Livingstone 2012.

experts, for the application of top-down domestic restrictions clash with the values of the modern 'democratic family' in which parents and children ground their relationship in trust rather than control.[61]

The question of parental versus state responsibility for children's rights has long cultural roots, with the US keener to leave matters to parents than Europe. In connection with the US's decision not (yet) to ratify the UNCRC, Bartholet observes that the Convention 'makes children's best interests "primary" in all matters concerning children' (Article 3), [while] in the US 'the emphasis is on parents' rights to make decisions related to their children and on states' rights to protect children's best interests, with states limited in their ability to do so by parents' rights'.[62] This has consequences in relation to the Internet for questions of parental surveillance versus state (or industry) management of children's online experiences. For example, it seems that US parents find it more acceptable than European parents to check their children's social networking or mobile phone contacts and conversations, with or without permission.[63]

Particularly problematic for policy makers hoping to rely on parental mediation is the fact that those parents whose children are most at risk are precisely those least likely to mediate their child's Internet use effectively. For the majority of children, it seems that parental mediation is fairly constructive, although both parents and children prefer active mediation to top-down restrictive strategies. Further, there is little evidence that children's exposure to risks is effectively reduced by parental efforts (except insofar as restricting Internet use prevents both risks and opportunities).[64] For a few, whether by acts of omission or commission, parents may actively threaten or undermine children's well-being (and such arguments lead to calls for children's right to privacy from their parents, since 'there is a privacy problem when parents monitor their children'.[65] Indeed, for the 'at risk' minority, a generic policy of reliance on parenting may precisely exacerbate their vulnerability, since the main source of online vulnerability appears to be vulnerability offline.[66]

2.9 Conclusion: Children's Rights and Responsibilities in a Digital Age

The rapid and enthusiastic way in which children are going online offers a strong endorsement of the policies, infrastructural investment and initiatives undertaken

61 Giddens 1991.

62 Bartholet 2011, p. 85.

63 Mathiesen 2012.

64 Duerager and Livingstone 2012.

65 Shmueli and Blecher-Prigat 2011, p. 793.

66 Livingstone et al. 2012a; OECD 2011; Palfrey et al. 2008.

to make the Internet so widely accessible and available.[67] Yet, the evidence shows that children and young people, frequently the pioneers of Internet adoption, not only gain (potentially, at least) extraordinary new opportunities but also routinely encounter content or contact that is problematic and engage in behaviour that is risky and potentially harmful.[68] In developing Internet governance policies to underpin children's rights to protection, provision and participation in the digital era, it seems that the differences between once-rival perspectives are reducing: freedom of expression advocates are often as committed to protecting children from harm online as child protection advocates are keen not to undermine adult (or children's) rights to free expression.[69] However, it is still the case that each side fears the over-extended or ineffective implementation of the policies advocated by the other, to the point where adult or child rights are undermined by poor or unaccountable regulation. We suggest that common ground alone is insufficient to overcome the challenges facing Internet governance in the interests of children. Moreover, even if common ground were attained, positively providing for children's rights and ensuring their full participation would remain expensive and demanding, requiring a concerted determination to act by governments that is only unevenly in evidence.

What is needed is a new framework for child protection, provision and participation online that results in a clear and effective policy that is born of real needs, targets specific and evidence-based risks, and includes measurable goals on which policy implementation is independently evaluated. In this chapter, we hope to have established that the UNCRC provides a valuable framework for formulating Internet governance policy in the interests of children. The work of applying its provisions to the digital realm is receiving increasing attention by researchers (Van der Hof, Groothuis, this volume) and policy makers—most notably in the *Communication on the European Strategy for a Better Internet for Children*, which brings within the Digital Agenda the priorities of the EU Agenda on the Rights of the Child,[70] although much remains to be done. As researchers, our evidence-based priorities are as follows[71]:

---

[67] As affirmed in the 2009 Prague Declaration, ministers of the European Union have committed to direct coordinated, intergovernmental action to combat illegal content and to minimise risks to Internet users. As a result, the European Commission has made proposals for the adoption of a new directive on combating sexual abuse, sexual exploitation of children and child pornography (European Commission 2010). Also, it is committed through the *Digital Agenda*, Europe's digital policy successor to i2010 (European Commission 2010), to creating a flourishing digital economy by 2020. This includes a set of measures to promote the building of digital confidence (p. 6); guaranteeing universal broadband coverage with fast and ultrafast Internet access (pp. 18–19); enhancing digital literacy, skills and inclusion (p. 28); and promoting cultural diversity and creative content (p. 30). See *Digital Agenda for Europe*, accessed on 5 Sept 2010 at http://ec.europa.eu/information_society/digital-agenda/index_en.htm.

[68] Livingstone et al. 2011b.

[69] Powell et al. 2010, p. 5.

[70] European Commission 2012a.

[71] Livingstone et al. 2011b; O'Neill et al. 2011.

- The protection of children in the digital world from diverse forms of sexual, violent and other abuses continues to be an urgent priority for governments, parents and caregivers, industry and civil society, requiring inclusive, effective and accountable forms of governance to be ensured by all stakeholders.
- Provision of appropriate support and resources is vital to enable all children to reach their full potential within a complex and fast-changing digital environment, including those who are vulnerable or disadvantaged or with special needs.
- Educators are particularly important in supporting provision and digital literacy (or 'digital citizenship') for young people, being uniquely placed to reach all children and so counteracting the risks of a digital divide.
- Children's participation rights, their right to be heard and their involvement in the life of their communities can and should be greatly enhanced through fostering opportunities for safer and better online participation.
- Children's rights are necessarily counterbalanced and limited by responsibilities—obligations requiring action by the state, including the allocation of resources, investment in education and careful negotiation when one set of rights are or appear to be in conflict with others.

But how shall this be achieved? In February 2012, the OECD recommended a framework for the empowerment and protection of children online that encompasses the rights discussed in this chapter.[72] Citing the evidence for online risk produced by EU Kids Online,[73] the European Parliament's Committee on Culture and Education proposed similarly, in April 2012, to call on the European Commission for 'a single framework directive on the rights of minors in the digital world, in order to integrate all the provisions regarding minors envisaged in the previous provisions of the EU'.[74] We support these initiatives. To advance this cause, we also support the call not only for policy but also for a governance body charged with its implementation that is inclusive in engaging multiple stakeholders and that is widely trusted not to overstep its remit in governing the Internet in ways that inappropriately limit the rights of others—adults or children. Such a body should probably be international in scope and should have the responsibility and authority to encourage (and enforce) action at a national level.[75] It is hard to see otherwise how children's needs and rights in the globalised, commercialised and technologically complex Internet can be ensured in a coherent, consistent and effective manner.

---

[72] OECD 2012b.

[73] Livingstone et al. 2011b.

[74] Until this is taken forward, the current policy of the European Commission is widening its focus: the Digital Agenda includes a 'new strategy for safer Internet and better Internet content for children and teenagers' (Kroes 2012). It is to be hoped that, in times of austerity, a 'better' Internet does not seem less pressing than a 'safer' one.

[75] eNACSO 2012a, b.

References

Ainsaar M, Loof L (eds) (2012) Online behaviour related to child sexual abuse: literature report. Council of the Baltic Sea States. ROBERT, European Grooming Project

Ala-Mutka K, Punie Y, Redecker C (2008) Digital competence for lifelong learning. JRC technical reports. European Commission, Luxembourg

Alderson P (2000) UN Convention on the Rights of the Child: some common criticisms and suggested responses. Child Abuse Rev 9:439–443

Anthonysamy P, Greenwood P, Rashid A (2012) Can privacy policies be traced to privacy controls on social networking sites? A qualitative study. Computer 99:1

Archard D (2004) Children: rights and childhood, 2nd edn. Routledge, London

Bartholet E (2011) Ratification by the United States of the Convention on the Rights of the Child: pros and cons from a child's rights perspective. Ann Am Acad Polit Soc Sci 633(1):80–101

Clark LS (2013) The parent app: understanding families in the digital age. Oxford University Press, Oxford

Council of Europe (2006) Recommendation Rec (2006)12 of the committee of ministers to member states on empowering children in the new information and communications environment

Criddle L (2006) Look both ways: help protect your family on the internet. Microsoft Press, Redmond, Washington

Deloitte and European Commission (2008) Safer internet: protecting our children on the net using content filtering and parental control techniques. European Commission Safer Internet Programme, Luxembourg

Duerager A, Livingstone S (2012) How can parents support children's internet safety? EU Kids Online, London School of Economics and Political Science, London. http://eprints.lse.ac.uk/42872/

Dutton WH, Peltu M (2007) The emerging internet governance mosaic: connecting the pieces. Inf Polity 12(1):63–81

eNACSO (2012a) CEO coalition to make the internet a better place for kids. eNACSO's response to the working groups' interim reports

eNACSO (2012b) The next click. European NGO Alliance for Child Safety Online, Brussels

Eurobarometer (2011) Special eurobarometer 359. Attitudes on data protection and electronic identity in the European Union. Directorate-general justice, Information Society & Media and Joint Research Centre, Brussels

European Commission (1996) Illegal and harmful content on the internet. COM(96) 487. Brussels

European Commission (2009a) Commission recommendation on media literacy in the digital environment for a more competitive audiovisual and content industry and an inclusive knowledge society. Brussels

European Commission (2009b) Safer social networking principles for the EU. European Commission safer internet programme. Luxembourg

European Commission (2010) A digital agenda for Europe. http://eur-lex.europa.eu/LexUriServ/LexUriServ.do?uri=COM:2010:0245:FIN:EN:PDF

European Commission (2012a) Communication on the European strategy for a better internet for children. Brussels

European Commission (2012b) Safeguarding privacy in a connected world. A European data protection framework for the 21st century. http://eur-lex.europa.eu/LexUriServ/LexUriServ.do?uri=COM:2012:0009:FIN:EN:PDF

European Parliament (2012) EU framework of law for children's rights. DG for internal policies, citizens' rights and constitutional affairs. Brussels

European Union (2010) Audiovisual media services directive 2010/13/EU. Brussels

Flint D (2000) The internet and children's rights: suffer the little children. Comput Law Secur Rev 16(2):88–94

Foley M, Hayes N, O'Neill B (2012) Journalism education and children's rights: new approaches to media development in CEE/CIS countries. Ir Stud Int Aff 23:1–12

Freeman M (2007) Article 3: the best interests of the child. In: Alen A, Lanotte JV, Verhellen E, Ang F, Berghmans E, Verheyde M (eds) A commentary on the United Nations Convention on the Rights of the Child. Martinus Nijhoff Publishers, Leiden

Gasser U, Maclay C, Palfrey J (2010) Working towards a deeper understanding of digital safety for children and young people in developing nations. Berkman Center for Internet and Society, Cambridge

Giddens A (1991) Modernity and self-identity: self and society in the late modern age. Polity Press, Cambridge

Green L (2010) The internet: an introduction to new media. Berg, Oxford

Griffin J (2009) On human rights. Oxford University Press, Oxford

GSMA (2007) European framework for safer mobile use by younger teenagers and children. GSMA Europe, Brussels

Guggenheim M (2005) What's wrong with children's rights?. Harvard University Press, Cambridge

Hamelink CJ (2008) Children's communication rights: beyond intentions. In: Drotner K, Livingstone S (eds) The international handbook of children, media and culture. Sage Publications, London, pp 508–519

Helberger N (2008) The media-literate viewer. In: van Eijk N, Hugenholtz PB (eds) Dommering-bundel: opstellen over informatierecht aangeboden aan Prof Mr E. J. Dommering. Otto Cramwinckel Uitgever, Amsterdam, pp 135–148

Helsper E (2012) Which children are fully online? In: Livingstone S, Haddon L, Görzig A (eds) Children, risk and safety online: research and policy challenges in comparative perspective. The Policy Press, Bristol, pp 45–58

Holzscheiter H (2010) Children's rights in international politics: the transformative power of discourse. Hampshire, Palgrave Macmillan, Houndmills

ICT Coalition (2012) Principles for the safer use of connected devices and online services by children and young people in the EU. www.gsma-documents.com/safer_mobile/ICT_Principles.pdf

ITU (2009) Child online protection. ITU, Geneva

ITU (2010) Child online protection statistical framework and indicators. www.itu.int/pub/D-IND-COP.01-11-2010

Jones LM (1998) Regulating child pornography on the internet: the implications of Article 34 of the United Nations convention on the rights of the child. Int J Child Rights 6(1):55–79

Kroes N (2012) Digital agenda: new strategy for safer internet and better internet content for children and teenagers. http://europa.eu/rapid/press-release_IP-12-445_en.htm?locale=en

Lembke J (2003) Competition for technological leadership: EU policy for high technology. Edward Elgar Publishing, Cheltenham

Lessig L (2000) Code: and other laws of cyberspace. Basic Books, New York

Livingstone S (2009a) Children and the internet: great expectations, challenging realities. Polity Press, Cambridge

Livingstone S (2009b) A rationale for positive online content for children. Commun Res Trends 28(3):12–17. http://eprints.lse.ac.uk/48922/

Livingstone S (2011) Regulating the internet in the interests of children: emerging British, European and international approaches. In: Mansell R, Raboy M (eds) The handbook on global media and communication policy. Blackwell, Oxford, pp 505–524

Livingstone S, Bulger M (2013) A global agenda for children's rights in the digital age: recommendations for developing UNICEF's research strategy. UNICEF Office of Research, Florence. http://www.unicef-irc.org/publications/702

Livingstone S, Ólafsson K, Staksrud E (2011a) Social networking, age and privacy. EU Kids Online, London School of Economics and Political Science, London. http://eprints.lse.ac.uk/35849/

Livingstone S, Haddon L, Görzig A, Ólafsson K (2011b) Risks and safety on the internet: the perspective of European children, full findings. EU Kids Online, London School of Economics and Political Science, London. http://eprints.lse.ac.uk/33731/

Livingstone S, Haddon L, Görzig A, Ólafsson K (2012a) EU Kids Online final report. EU Kids Online, London School of Economics and Political Science, London. http://eprints.lse.ac.uk/39351/

Livingstone S, Ólafsson K, O'Neill B, Donoso V (2012b) Towards a better internet for children. EU Kids Online, London School of Economics and Political Science, London. http://eprints.lse.ac.uk/44213/

Lunt P, Livingstone S (2012) Media regulation: governance and the interests of citizens and consumers. Sage Publications, London

Lusoli W, Miltgen C (2009) Young people and emerging digital services. An exploratory survey on motivations, perceptions and acceptance of risks, JRC technical reports. European Commission, Institute for Prospective Technological Studies, Luxembourg

Lusoli W, Bacigalupo M, Lupiañez F, Andrade N, Monteleone S, Maghiros I (2011) Pan-European survey of practices, attitudes and policy preferences as regards personal identity data management JRC technical reports. European Commission, Luxembourg

Mansell R (2012) Imagining the internet: communication, innovation, and governance. Oxford University Press, Oxford

Marsden CT (2011) Internet co-regulation: European law, regulatory governance and legitimacy in cyberspace. Cambridge University Press, Cambridge

Mathiesen K (2012) The internet, children, and privacy: the case against parental monitoring. Springer

Mayer-Schönberger V (2009) Delete: the virtue of forgetting in the digital age. Princeton University Press, Princeton, NJ

McLaughlin S (2013) Rights v. Restrictions. Recognising children's participation in the digital age. In: O'Neill B, Staksrud E, McLaughlin S (eds) Towards a better internet for children policy pillars, players and paradoxes. Nordicom, Goteborg, pp 301–319

McNamee J (2010) Internet blocking: crimes should be punished and not hidden. European Digital Rights, Brussels

Millwood Hargrave A, Livingstone S (2009) Harm and offence in media content: a review of the empirical literature. Intellect Press, Bristol. http://eprints.lse.ac.uk/49000/

Muir D (2005) Violence against children in cyberspace: a contribution to the United Nations study on violence against children. ECPAT International, Bangkok

Nesson C, Marglin D (1996) The day the internet met the first amendment: time and the communications decency act. Harv J Law Technol 10(1):113

Nordic Youth Forum (2012) Youth have their say on internet governance. Nordicom, Gothenburg

O'Neill B (2010) Media literacy and communication rights: ethical individualism in the new media environment. Int Commun Gaz 72(4–5):323–338

O'Neill B, Livingstone S, McLaughlin S (2011) Final recommendations for policy, methodology and research. EU Kids Online, London School of Economics and Political Science, London. http://eprints.lse.ac.uk/39410

O'Neill O (1988) Children's rights and children's lives. Ethics 98(3):445–463

OECD (2011) The protection of children online. Risks faced by children online and policies to protect them. OECD Working Party on Information Security and Privacy, Paris

OECD (2012a) Connected minds: technology and today's learners. www.oecd-ilibrary.org/education/connected-minds_9789264111011-en

OECD (2012b) Recommendation of the council on the protection of children online. http://webnet.oecd.org/oecdacts/Instruments/ShowInstrumentView.aspx?InstrumentID=272&InstrumentPID=277&Lang=en&Book=False

Olsen F (1992) Children's rights: some feminist approaches to the United Nations Convention on the Rights of the Child. Int J Law Fam 6:192–220

Oswell D (2008) Media and communications regulation and child protection: an overview of the field. In: Livingstone S, Drotner K (eds) International handbook of children, media and culture. Sage Publications, London, pp 469–486

Palfrey J, boyd d, Sacco D (2008) Enhancing child safety and online technologies: final report of the internet safety technical task force to the multi-state working group on social networking of state attorneys general of the United States. Berkman Center for Internet and Society, Cambridge, MA

Powell A, Cooper A (2011) Discourses of net neutrality: comparing advocacy and regulatory arguments in the US and the UK. The inf soc 27:311–325

Powell A, Hills M, Nash V (2010) Child protection and freedom of expression online. Oxford Internet Institute forum discussion paper no 17, Oxford

Preston CB (2009) All knowledge is not equal: facilitating children's access to knowledge by making the internet safer. Int J Commun Law Policy 13:115–132

Pruulmann-Vengerfeldt P, Runnel P (2012) Online opportunities. In: Livingstone S, Haddon L, Görzig A (eds) Children, risk and safety online: research and policy challenges in comparative perspective. The Policy Press, Bristol, pp 45–58

Purdy LM (1992) In their best interest? The case against equal rights for children. Cornell University Press, Ithaca, NY

Quale E, Taylor M (2011) Social networking as a nexus for engagement and exploitation of young people. Inf Secur Tech Rep 16:44–50

Rosen J (2012) The right to be forgotten. Stanford Law Rev Online 64:88

Schoon I (2006) Risk and resilience: adaptations in changing times. Cambridge University Press, New York

Schulz W, Held T (2004) Regulated self-regulation as a form of modern government: an analysis of case studies from media and telecommunications law. John Libbey Publishers for University of Luton Press, Luton

Shmueli B, Blecher-Prigat A (2011) Privacy for children. Columbia Hum Rights Law Rev 42:758–795

Tambini D, Leonardi D, Marsden CT (2008) Codifying cyberspace: communications self-regulation in the age of internet convergence. Routledge, London

Thierer A (2009) Parental controls and online child protection: a survey of tools and methods. The Progress and Freedom Foundation, Washington, DC

Thierer A (2011) Kids, privacy, free speech and the internet: finding the right balance. Mercatus Centre working paper 11. Mercatus Center, Arlington, VA

Veerman PE (2010) The ageing of the UN Convention on the Rights of the Child. Int J Child Rights 18(4):585–618

Warschauer M, Matuchniak T (2010) New technology and digital worlds: analyzing evidence of equity in access, use, and outcomes. Rev Res Educ 34(1):179–225

Webster W, Davidson J, Bifulco A, Gottschalk P, Caretti V, Pham T et al (2012) European online grooming project. Final report. European Commission safer internet plus programme, Brussels

WSIS (2005) Tunis commitment. www.itu.int/wsis/documents/doc_multi.asp?lang=en&id=2266%7C2267

Zittrain J (2008) The future of the internet and how to stop it. Penguin, London

Chapter 3
A Framework for Responding to Online Safety Risks

Adam Thierer

Contents

Adam Thierer is Senior Research Fellow at the Mercatus Center at George Mason University, Arlington, Virginia, USA. Portions of this chapter are based on: Adam Thierer, 'Technopanics, Threat Inflation, and the Danger of an Information Technology Precautionary Principle', 14(1) Minnesota Journal of Law, Science & Technology, Winter 2013, http://purl.umn.edu.

A. Thierer (✉)
Mercatus Center at George Mason University, Arlington, VA, USA
e-mail: athierer@mercatus.gmu.edu

S. van der Hof et al. (eds.), *Minding Minors Wandering the Web: Regulating Online Child Safety*, Information Technology and Law Series 24, DOI: 10.1007/978-94-6265-005-3_3,

3.1 Introduction

This chapter develops a framework for evaluating how individuals and society respond to technological risks and then discusses why some "risk response strategies" will work better than others as it pertains to online safety risks. Four generic risk response strategies are identified—prohibition, anticipatory regulation, resiliency, and adaptation—and the trade-offs associated with each option are discussed.

It will be argued that resiliency-based strategies present the optimal risk response strategy to address most online safety risks. Specifically, education and empowerment-based initiatives offer society the greatest return on investment by ensuring that (a) parents and guardians are equipped with the tools and methods needed to guide the mentoring process, and (b) children are better prepared for the inevitable surprises the future will always throw at them.

3.2 Possible Responses to Technological Risk

This section considers different strategies that individuals and society use to respond to technological risk and considers the relative strengths and weaknesses of each.

3.2.1 Risk Response Continuum

Many different strategies exist for how individuals and society responds to technological risk. For purposes of this discussion, the locus of decision making is assumed to be public policymakers instead of individual citizens, although individuals often adopt similar strategies at the household level.

These strategies can be described as follows:

1. Prohibition

Prohibitionary strategies attempt to eliminate potential risk through suppression of technology, product or service bans, information controls, or outright censorship. As applied to technology, such prohibitionary strategies are sometimes referred to as "the precautionary principle." The precautionary principle holds that, since a given technology or technological advance could pose some theoretical danger or risk, public policies should prevent people from using those innovations until their developers can prove that they won't cause any harms. In other words, the precautionary principle suggests that—either at the individual or society wide level—"play it safe" should be the default disposition toward technological progress.

Like the next strategy (anticipatory regulation), prohibition represents a *risk mitigation* strategy that focuses on *top-down* solutions. Prohibitionary solutions tend to be far more sweeping than anticipatory regulation, however, in that they propose the complete control of the content or activity in question. For this reason, prohibitionary strategies tend to be less popular today that in the past. Outright bans or censorial measures are increasingly shunned by governments either because they are impractical, costly, unpopular, or illegal. Some governments still seek to regulate certain types of speech and content deemed hateful or even blasphemous, but such restrictions are increasingly less likely to be effective over time.

Less controversially, any form of child abuse imagery is prohibited in most nations since the harm is abundantly clear.

2. Anticipatory Regulation

Anticipatory regulation includes any public policy action short of prohibition that attempts to deal with technological risk by controlling or curbing the uses of that technology. There exists a diverse array of possible legal strategies and regulatory safeguards that can be very context-specific. Those strategies include: administrative regulation and sanctions, government ownership or licensing controls, or restrictive defaults. For example, fines for airing "indecent" media content during certain hours of the day have long been a popular form of anticipatory regulation for television and radio programming.[1] Such regulation is facilitated by the licenses that many of those operators must obtain from government officials before they are allowed to operate.

Another example: Restrictive defaults are often proposed as a form of anticipatory regulation in the video game and online search contexts. In both cases, restrictive defaults could be imposed pre-emptively to limit access to content that is considered sensitive or rated above the age of certain audiences.[2]

Anticipatory regulation can sometimes lead to prohibition, although it is equally likely that prohibition will give way to regulation when efforts to completely ban a specific type of technological risk prove futile. Like prohibition, anticipatory regulation is a *risk mitigation* strategy that is more top-down in nature, but not nearly as sweeping or restrictive in character.

3. Resiliency

Resiliency-based strategies addresses technological risk through education, awareness-building, transparency, and labeling, and empowerment steps and tools. Resilience represents "the capacity of a system, enterprise, or a person to maintain its core purpose and integrity in the face of dramatically changed circumstances."[3]

---

[1] Thierer 2007c.

[2] Thierer 2008, http://papers.ssrn.com/sol3/papers.cfm?abstract_id=1120324.

[3] Zolli and Healy 2012, p. 7.

Resiliency-based strategies can be highly informal or very formal and can be undertaken by governments, companies, communities, institutions, and individuals. For example, governments, trade associations, and advocacy organizations have utilized public service announcements and other mechanisms to promote awareness about the dangers of distracted driving. Using communication technology (i.e., talking or texting) while driving can pose a serious threat to those in the vehicle and others around them. While some governments have passed laws to address this danger, education and awareness-based initiatives are helping to change public attitudes about this activity and encouraging drivers to adapt their behavior while operating vehicles.

Compared to the first two strategies, which focused on *top-down risk mitigation*, resiliency represents a form of *risk adaptation* that focuses on *bottom-up* strategies. But, unlike a strategy of pure adaptation, resilient strategies encourage more active steps by various institutions and individuals to prepare for, or adjust to, technological risk. This may include some public policies to facilitate the educational and empowerment-based strategies mentioned, although they cannot be unnaturally forced upon individuals or institutions from above.[4]

4. Adaptation

Adaptation involves learning to live with technological risks through trial-and-error experimentation, experience, coping mechanisms, and social norms. Adaptation strategies often begin with, or evolve out of, resiliency-based efforts. It might be overly simplistic to refer to adaptation as a "just-get-over-it" strategy, although it is sometimes conceptualized that way. The essence of adaptation lies in the *bottom-up, organic, and evolutionary* coping mechanisms that individuals and societies develop to deal with technological risks (Fig. 3.1).

3.2.2 Generic Framework for Determining Optimal Strategy

Different technological risks require different responses along this continuum, and those responses will vary depending on whether the unit of analysis is the individual or society as a whole. When individuals and society confront new technological risks, they must conduct a cost-benefit test to weigh which option makes the most sense. Those responses will often evolve over time.

To understand how this calculus works, consider two illustrative examples: Power tools and weapons of mass destruction.

All tools represent technologies that can pose risks to individuals and society—from fire and hammers to power saws and power drills. When used improperly, the

[4] Zolli and Healy 2012, p. 211. ("This capacity cannot simply be imposed from above – instead it must be nurtured in the social structures and relationships that govern people's everyday lives.")

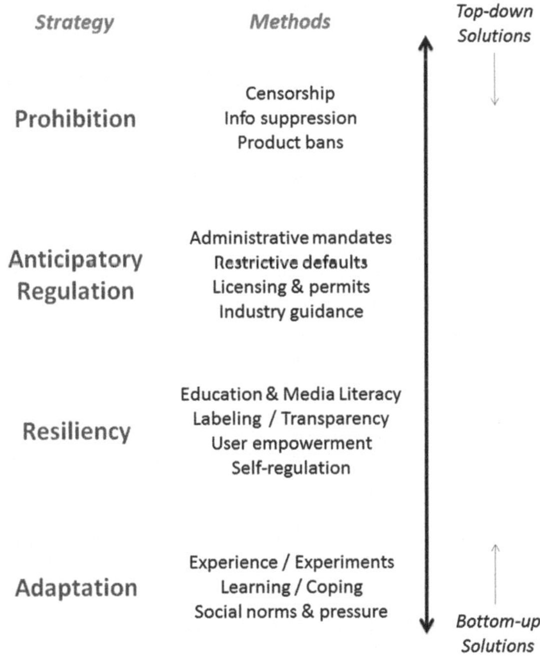

Fig. 3.1 The risk response Continuum. A range of responses to technological risk

results can be damaging—even deadly. Despite that risk, most individuals and cultures have generally chosen to rely on adaptation strategies for this sort of technological risk. Put simply, people are expected to be responsible with those tools and, if it comes to it, to learn from their mistakes. Prohibition is generally viewed as unnecessary or too costly by most societies, even if some individuals may prohibit or curtail the use of specific tools in their own homes. But most countries and cultures also place no special restrictions on the sale or use of such tools, no special permits or licenses are needed for their use, and governments don't even bother requiring courses about how to use them safely. In other words, most countries and cultures choose *not* to "play it safe" when it comes to the use of power tools as the precautionary principle would counsel.

At the opposite end of this spectrum, there are some tools or technologies for which prohibition is potentially the right answer. Heavy ordnance and "weapons of mass destruction"—tanks, bazookas, uranium, biological weapons, chemical explosives, etc.—are deemed illegal in most countries. The potential costs associated with private ownership or use are considered unbearable due to the potential for catastrophic destruction or loss of life. Thus, most governments throughout the world impose the ultimate "play it safe" strategy and ban private ownership outright. For somewhat less destructive weapons, however—crossbows and knives, for example—anticipatory regulation or even resiliency strategies are the preferred alternative.

A generic four-part framework can be used to analyze the risks associated with new technological developments and determine the optimal response strategy for any given risk.[5]

1. Defining the problem/harm

The first step involves defining the problem to be addressed and determining whether harm exists. Defining the problem is sometimes easier said than done, and it is vital that "harm" not be too casually defined. Harm is a particular nebulous concept as it pertains to online safety and digital privacy debates where conjectural theories abound. Some cultural critics insist that provocative media content "harms" us or our kids. As Sect. 3.3 notes, many moral panics have come and gone through the years as critics looked to restrict speech or expression they found objectionable. In cases such as these, "harm" is very much an eye-of-the-beholder issue. It is important to keep in mind that no matter how objectionable some media content or online speech may be, none of it poses a *direct* threat to adults or children.

Likewise, some privacy advocates claim that advertising is inherently "manipulative" or that more targeted forms of marketing and advertising are "creepy" and should be prohibited. "But creating new privacy rights cannot be justified simply because people feel vague unease", notes Solveig Singleton, formerly of the Cato Institute.[6] If harm in this context is reduced to "creepiness" or even "annoyance," it raises the question whether the Internet as we know it can continue to exist since it represents an open-ended standard by which to regulate online speech and interactions over digital networks.[7] Such an amorphous standard simply leaves much to the imagination, thus making credible cost-benefit analysis virtually impossible since the debate becomes purely about emotion instead of anything empirical.[8]

As it pertains to online safety, the most serious harms are those that involve a direct physical threat to life or limb. Online child predation, abduction, and abuse would be the primary examples. While those harms can be real, their frequency can also sometimes be greatly overstated, as Sect. 3.3 notes. Nonetheless, given their potential severity, such harms demand a different risk response than supposed

---

[5] This framework is based on Williams and Ellig 2011, http://mercatus.org/publication/regulatory-oversight.

[6] Singleton 1998, www.cato.org/pubs/pas/pa-295.html.

[7] Szoka and Thierer 2009b, www.scribd.com/doc/12597638/Targeted-Online-Advertising-Whats-the-Harm-Where-Are-We-Heading.

[8] Thierer 2011, pp. 24–28, http://mercatus.org/publication/public-interest-comment-protecting-consumer-privacy-era-rapid-change.

psychic or social harms, which tend to be far more ambiguous and, in some cases, largely conjectural.

Some psychic or social harms—cyberbullying and hate speech, for example—can have very real impact on psychological well-being.[9] That does not mean prohibition or anticipatory regulation is automatically the best response to those harms, however, since regulation can impose major economic and speech-related trade-offs on many other users. More importantly, as Sect. 3.4 will elaborate, other remedies are available to deal with such concerns, including counter-speech opportunities and education and awareness-building initiatives that highlight the ways harassing or hateful speech can hurt others.

Other asserted psychic or social harms are often highly subjective and are best dealt with using more flexible risk response strategies. For example, debates over the impact of pornography on society have raged for decades. In light of the diversity of views about its impact, as well as the formidable enforcement challenges noted in Sect. 3.4, it seems wise to shift the locus of decision making about its regulation to the household level. As Sect. 3.4 will argue, this is where empowerment tools and solutions can help a diverse citizenry to craft individualized risk response strategies so that the decision need not be made for everyone from the top-down. This is also a useful way of addressing many perceived privacy risks, where consensus does not exist about the actual harm of data collection or online advertising on children or others.

2. Considering legal and economic constraints

The second step in determining the optimal risk response strategy is to identify legal and constitutional constraints on government action and then conduct cost-benefit analysis of any proposed legal or regulatory activity.[10]

If harm can be demonstrated, the costs associated with government action must be considered.[11] Even where there is some potential risk of harm, it does not necessarily follow that regulation can effectively solve the problem. Proposed rules should always be subjected to rigorous cost-benefit analysis.[12] Regulation is not a costless exercise, and sometimes its benefits are artificially inflated.[13] Daniel Gardner notes that "the public often demands action on a risk without giving the

[9] Levy et al. 2012, http://papers.ssrn.com/sol3/papers.cfm?abstract_id=2146877.

[10] Williams 2012, http://mercatus.org/publication/comment-ombs-draft-2012-report-congress-benefits-and-costs-federal-regulations.

[11] Gardner 2009, p. 83. ("[R]egulations can also impose costs on economic activity and since wealthier is healthier, economic costs can, if they are very large, put more lives at risk than they keep safe.")

[12] Gardner 2009, p. 286. ("To ensure money is doing the greatest good possible, cost-benefit analysis is essential.")

[13] Abdukadirov and Yazigi 2012, http://mercatus.org/publication/inflated-benefits-agencies-economic-analysis.

slightest consideration to the costs of that action".[14] Yet, all government action entails trade-offs, both economic and social.

Of course, not all legal solutions entail the same cost or complexity as direct regulatory approaches. For example, some online safety problems might be better dealt with through the enforcement of private contracts or terms of service. Likewise, antifraud statutes and antiharassment laws, which are generally applicable to all industries and technologies, might work better than sector-specific or technology-specific regulations.

Importantly, information technology is, by definition, tied up with the production and dissemination of speech. Consequently, as will be noted further below, free speech values may be implicated and limit government action in many cases.

3. Considering alternative, less restrictive approaches

The third step in determining the optimal risk response strategy involves an assessment of the effectiveness of alternative, nonlegal approaches to addressing the perceived risk or harm.

As noted above, and as Sect. 3.4 will make clear, because preemptive, prophylactic regulation of information technology can be costly, complicated, and overly constraining, it is often wise to consider such alternative, less restrictive approaches. Section 3.4 will argue that education and awareness-building strategies can be particularly effective, as well as being entirely constitutional. Empowerment-based strategies are also useful. These strategies can help build resiliency and ensure proper assimilation of new technologies into society.

Transparency and disclosure are particularly useful options for many online safety and privacy concerns. Voluntary media content ratings and labels for movies, music, video games, and smartphone apps have given parents and others more information to make determinations about the appropriateness of content they may want to consume.[15] Regarding privacy, consumers are better served when they are informed about online privacy and data collection policies of the sites they visit and the devices they utilize. Such steps can help alleviate the need for more sweeping regulation of digital technologies.

4. Evaluating actual outcomes

Finally, if and when regulatory solutions are pursued, it is important that actual outcomes be regularly evaluated and, to the extent feasible, that results be measured against well-established baselines.[16] To the extent that regulatory policies are deemed necessary, it is usually wise to revisit and even sunset them on a

[14] Gardner 2009, p. 83.

[15] Thierer 2009b, www.pff.org/parentalcontrols.

[16] Lutter 2012, http://mercatus.org/publication/how-well-do-federal-regulations-?tjl=20mm?>actually-work-role-retrospective-review.

regular basis, unless policymakers can justify their continued existence.[17] Importantly, even if regulation is necessary in the short-term, resiliency, and adaptation strategies may emerge or become more evident over time that alleviate the need for continued regulation.

3.3 The Problem with Prohibition and Anticipatory Regulation

We can now apply the framework developed in Sect. 3.2 to online child safety issues and begin by asking when, if ever, prohibition might be a desirable strategy for responding to online risks. The answer is, very rarely.

3.3.1 Prohibition and Regulation Often Based on Irrational Technopanics

Would prohibition *ever* represent a sensible response to online safety risks? It certainly would when child pornography is the risk in question. Almost all societies agree that child pornography—not only the practice but the resulting imagery that can be widely distributed via digital networks—is a scourge that must be addressed with prohibitionary measures. The harm to minors is obvious, but there also exists a societal harm from allowing such images to be circulated and viewed. Thus, efforts to control the production and dissemination of such content clearly pass any cost-benefit analysis.

But other prohibitionary responses are often driven by "technopanics" or knee-jerk reactions to new technologies that are not actually harmful to either youth or society. A "technopanic" refers to an intense public, political, and academic response to the emergence or use of media or technologies, especially by the young.[18] It is a variant of "moral panic" theory. Christopher Ferguson, professor at Texas AM's Department of Behavioral, Applied Sciences, and Criminal Justice, offers the following definition: "A moral panic occurs when a segment of society believes that the behavior or moral choices of others within that society poses a significant risk to the society as a whole."[19] Authoritative research on moral panic theory was conducted by British sociologist Stanley Cohen in the 1970 s. He defined a moral panic as a moment when:

---

[17] Thierer 2012, www.forbes.com/sites/adamthierer/2012/03/25/sunsetting-technology-regulation-applying-moores-law-to-washington.

[18] Thierer 2009a, http://techliberation.com/2009/07/15/against-technopanics.

[19] Ferguson 2008, pp. 25–37, http://onlinelibrary.wiley.com/doi/10.1002/jip.76/abstract.

> a condition, episode, person, or group of persons emerges to become defined as a threat to societal values and interests; its nature is presented in a stylized and stereotypical fashion by the mass media; the moral barricades are manned by editors, bishops, politicians, and other right-thinking people; socially accredited experts pronounce their diagnoses and solutions; ways of coping are evolved or resorted to [...] Sometimes the panic passes over and is forgotten, except in folklore and collective memory; at other times it has more serious and long-lasting repercussions and might produce such changes as those in legal and social policy or even the way the society conceives itself.[20]

By extension, a "technopanic" is simply a moral panic centered on societal fears about a particular contemporary technology (or technological method or activity) instead of merely the content flowing over that technology or medium. In a 2008 essay on "The MySpace Moral Panic," Alice Marwick noted that technopanics have the following characteristics:

First, they focus on new media forms, which currently take the form of computer-mediated technologies. Second, technopanics generally pathologize young people's use of this media, like hacking, file-sharing, or playing violent video games. Third, this cultural anxiety manifests itself in an attempt to modify or regulate young people's behavior, either by controlling young people or the creators or producers of media products.[21]

This pattern has played out for dime novels, comic books, movies, rock-and-roll music, video games, and other types of media or media platforms.[22] While protection of youth is typically a motivating factor, some moral panics and technopanics transcend traditional "it's-for-the-children" rationales for information control. The perceived threat may be to other segments of society or involve other values that are supposedly under threat, such as privacy or security.

During all panics, the public, media pundits, intellectuals, and policy makers articulate their desire to "do something" to rid society of the apparent menace, or at least tightly limit it. Thus, the effort (a) *to demonize* and then (b) *to control* a particular type of content or technology is what really defines a true panic. Sociologists Erich Goode and Nachman Ben-Yehuda, authors of *Moral Panics: The Social Construction of Deviance*, observe that

> whenever the question, "What is to be done?" is asked concerning behavior deemed threatening, someone puts forth the suggestion, "There ought to be a law." If laws already exist addressing the threatening behavior, either stiffer penalties or a law enforcement crackdown will be called for. Legislation and law enforcement are two of the most obvious and widely resorted to efforts to crush a putative threat during a moral panic.[23]

Unsurprisingly, a rush to judgment is a common feature of many panics. Such hasty judgments are often accompanied by, or the direct result of, "threat inflation" tactics. The concept of threat inflation has received the most attention in the

---

20 Cohen 1972, p. 9.

21 Marwick 2008, www.uic.edu/htbin/cgiwrap/bin/ojs/index.php/fm/article/view/2152/1966.

22 Corn-Revere 2011.

23 Goode and Ben-Yehuda 1994, p. 82.

field of foreign policy studies.[24] In that context, political scientists Jane K. Cramer and A. Trevor Thrall define threat inflation as "the attempt by elites to create concern for a threat that goes beyond the scope and urgency that a disinterested analysis would justify."[25]

Threat inflation involves the use of fear-inducing rhetoric to inflate artificially the potential harm a new development or technology poses to certain classes of the population, especially children, or to society or the economy at large. These rhetorical flourishes are empirically false or at least greatly blown out of proportion relative to the risk in question.

The initial response of US policymakers to the rise of social networking sites offers a particularly vivid example of the technopanic mentality and threat inflation in action. As social networking sites began growing in popularity in the mid-2000 s, some policymakers began claiming that sites like MySpace.com and Facebook represented a "predators' playground," implying that youth could be groomed for abuse or abduction by visiting those sites.[26] To address this supposed threat, legislation was introduced in the US Congress proposing a federal ban on access to social networking sites in schools and libraries.

Unsurprisingly, this measure was given a provocative title: "The Deleting Online Predators Act."[27] Beyond restricting access to popular social networking sites, the measure would have impacted a wide swath of online sites and services that had interactive functionality.[28] In 2006, the measure received 410 votes in the US House of Representatives before finally dying in the US Senate. It was introduced in the subsequent session of Congress, but did not see another vote and was never passed into law.

During this same period, many US states, including Georgia,[29] Illinois,[30], and North Carolina, introduced legislative measures that sought to restrict underage access to social networking sites.[31] Several state attorneys general also proposed mandatory online age verification for all online social networking users.[32] This

[24] Kaufmann 2004, pp. 5–48, http://belfercenter.ksg.harvard.edu/files/kaufmann.pdf.

[25] Cramer and Trevor Thrall 2009, p. 1.

[26] Steel and Angwin 2006, http://online.wsj.com/public/article/SB115102268445288250-YRxkt0rTsyyf1QiQf2EPBYSf7iU_20070624.html?mod=tff_main_tff_top.

[27] H.R. 5319, "The Deleting Online Predators Act", 109th Cong., (2006). See also Thierer 2006, http://articles.philly.com/2006-05-31/news/25400396_1_web-sites-social-networking-block-access.

[28] Thierer 2007d, http://techliberation.com/2007/03/10/would-your-favorite-website-be-banned-by-dopa.

[29] S.B. 59, 149th Gen. Assem., Reg. Sess. (GA, 2007).

[30] S.B. 1682, 95th Gen. Assem. (Ill. 2007).

[31] S.B. 132, 2007 Gen. Assem., Reg. Sess. (N.C. 2007).

[32] Steel and Angwin 2006, http://online.wsj.com/public/article/SB115102268445288250-YRxkt0rTsyyf1QiQf2EPBYSf7iU_20070624.html?mod=tff_main_tff_top.

represented a form of anticipatory regulation that, in theory, would have limited youth access to some social networking services or restricted their interactions with adults on those sites. Doubts were raised about the effectiveness and constitutionality of age verification mandates, however, and those efforts were largely abandoned within a few years.[33]

Although none of these efforts were implemented, they all represented forms of prohibition or anticipatory regulation. The case for these regulatory responses was premised on the fear that predators were lurking everywhere online. Despite the heightened sense of fear aroused by policymakers over this issue, it turned out that there was almost nothing to the predator panic. It was based almost entirely on threat inflation. "As with other moral panics, the one concerning MySpace had more to do with perception than reality", concluded social media researcher danah boyd.[34] "As researchers began investigating the risks that teens faced in social network sites, it became clear that the myths and realities of risk were completely disconnected."[35]

Generally speaking, the fear about strangers abducting children online was always greatly overstated since it was obviously impossible for them to "snatch" them at a distance. Abduction after Internet contact requires long term, and usually long distance, grooming, and then meticulous planning about how to commit the crime. This is not to say there were no cases of abduction that involved Internet grooming, but such cases were exceedingly rare and did not represent the epidemic that some suggested.

A 2002 study conducted for the US Department of Justice's Office of Juvenile Justice and Delinquency Prevention found that abductions by strangers "represent an extremely small portion of all missing children [cases]".[36] Although the survey is a decade old and suffers from some data and methodological deficiencies, it remains the most comprehensive survey of missing and abducted children in the United States. The study reported that the vast majority of kidnapping victims were abducted by family, friends of the family, or people who had a close relationships with (or the trust of) the minors. Only 115 of the estimated 260,000 abductions—or less than a tenth of a percent—fit the stereotypical abduction scenario that parents most fear: complete strangers snatching children and transporting them miles away.[37] Lenore Skenazy, author of *Free-Range Kids*, puts

[33] Internet Safety Technical Task Force to the Multi-State Working Group on Social Networking of State Attorneys General of the United States 2008, p. 10, http://cyber.law.harvard.edu/pubrelease/isttf; and Thierer 2007b, www.pff.org/issues-pubs/pops/pop14.5ageverification.pdf, http://papers.ssrn.com/sol3/papers.cfm?abstract_id=976936.

[34] boyd 2008, p. 266, www.danah.org/papers/TakenOutOfContext.pdf.

[35] boyd 2008.

[36] Sedlak et al. 2002, p. 7, www.missingkids.com/en_US/documents/nismart2_overview.pdf.

[37] A 2005 study of cases about missing children in Ohio revealed a similar trend. Of the 11,074 documented missing child cases in 2005, only five involved abduction by strangers compared with 146 abductions by family members. Ohio Missing Children Clearinghouse 2005, p. 4, www.ag.state.oh.us/victim/pubs/2005ann_rept_mcc.pdf.

things in perspective: "the chances of any one American child being kidnapped and killed by a stranger are almost infinitesimally small: 0.00007 percent."[38] A May 2010 report by the Department of Justice confirmed that "family abduction [remains] the most prevalent form of child abduction in the United States."[39]

As with all other technopanics, the "predator panic" eventually ran its course, although some of these fears remain in the public consciousness.

3.3.2 Prohibition and Regulation-Based Strategies Can Threaten Free Speech and Expression

When the technological risk in question is the Internet and digital technology, it is vital to remember that we are talking about platforms and technologies that facilitate speech and expression. That fact makes the trade-offs associated with prohibition and anticipatory regulation even more profound. More restrictive forms of risk control would limit many socially beneficial types of speech and forms of social interaction.

For example, most daily interactions on social networking sites are entirely innocuous and would likely be considered beneficial by the parties involved. Hence, a move to limit access to social networking sites would be drastic and overly restrictive compared to the (mostly hypothetical) dangers of online interactions for youth.

3.3.3 Prohibition and Regulation Can Constrain Progress

Another problem with prohibition and regulatory-based risk response strategies is that they are often premised on the precautionary principle mindset. The problem with the precautionary principle, notes Kevin Kelly, editor of *Wired* magazine, is that because "every good produces harm somewhere […] by the strict logic of an absolute precautionary principle no technologies would be permitted".[40] Under an information policy regime guided at every turn by a precautionary principle, digital innovation and technological progress would become impossible because social trade-offs and economic uncertainly would be considered unacceptable.

"If the burden of proof is on the proponent of the activity or processes in question," he argues, "the Precautionary Principle would seem to impose a burden of proof that cannot be met," observes University of Chicago legal scholar Cass

---

[38] Skenazy 2009, p. 16.

[39] US Department of Justice, Office of Justice Programs 2010, https://www.ncjrs.gov/pdffiles1/ojjdp/229933.pdf.

[40] Kelly 2011, pp. 247–248.

Sunstein.[41] The problem is that one cannot prove a negative. An innovator cannot prove the absence of risk or harm, but a critic or regulator can always prove that *some* theoretical harm exists. Consequently, putting the burden of proof on the innovator when that burden cannot be met essentially means no innovation is permissible. This means many innovations that could enhance speech or improve consumer welfare would be sacrificed.

In addition, forestalling innovation because of theoretical risk could mean that other risks develop or go unaddressed. For example, if online social networking was encumbered by a precautionary principle mentality, it could mean youth substitute other types of real-world networking that carry other risks.

3.3.4 Enforcement Challenges Constrain Prohibition and Regulatory-Based Strategies

It is also worth considering the formidable challenges that await any effort to clamp down on the flow of information on digital networks—even if that regime is pursued in the name of protecting online child safety or digital privacy. The administrative or enforcement burdens associated with modern information control efforts are as important as the normative considerations at play here. Some of those practical considerations are itemized below, and they should be factored into discussions about which risk response strategies make the most sense.

Information control can be complex and costly. This was equally true in the era of media and information scarcity, with its physical and analog distribution methods of information dissemination. All things considered, however, the challenge of controlling information in the analog era paled in comparison to the far more formidable challenges governments face in the digital era when they seek to limit information flows.

The movement of binary bits across electronic networks and digital distribution systems creates unique problems for information control efforts, even when that control might be socially desirable. In particular, efforts to control spam, objectionable media content, hate speech, copyrighted content, and even personal information are greatly complicated by five phenomena unique to the Information Age: (1) media and technological convergence; (2) decentralized, distributed networking; (3) unprecedented scale of networked communications; (4) an

---

[41] Sunstein 2002–2003, p. 34, www.cato.org/pubs/regulation/regv25n4/v25n4-9.pdf. "The most serious problem with the Precautionary Principle is that it offers no guidance – not that it is wrong, but that it forbids all courses of action, including inaction", Sunstein says. "The problem is that the Precautionary Principle, as applied, is a crude and sometimes perverse method of promoting various goals, not least because it might be, and has been, urged in situations in which the principle threatens to injure future generations and harm rather than help those who are most disadvantaged. A rational system of risk regulation certainly takes precautions. But it does not adopt the Precautionary Principle." Sunstein 2002–2003, pp. 33, 37.

explosion of the overall volume of information; and (5) unprecedented individual information sharing through user-generation of content and self-revelation of data.

Each of these phenomena is facilitated by the underlying drivers of the information revolution: digitization; dramatic expansions in computing/processing power ("Moore's Law"); a steady drop of digital storage costs; and the rise of widespread Internet access and ubiquitous mobile devices and access.

1. Media and technological convergence

First, content platforms and information distribution outlets are blurring together today thanks to the rise of myriad new technologies and innovations. New digital communication tools and entities generally ignore or reject the distribution-based distinctions and limitations of the past. In other words, convergence means that information is increasingly being "unbundled" from its traditional distribution platform and can find many paths to consumers.[42]

For example, a piece of personal information voluntarily uploaded to a blog can be reproduced instantaneously on other blogs or on a social network site (such as Facebook, LinkedIn, or MySpace), sent to Twitter (where it could be re-Tweeted countless times), or sent directly via e-mail or text messages. Again, this can, and often does, happen within minutes, even seconds. If the information in question contains a picture or video, it can also be reproduced across countless sites virtually instantaneously.

As a result of media and technological convergence, it is now possible to disseminate, retrieve, or consume the same content and information via multiple devices or distribution networks. When copying costs are essentially zero and platforms are abundant, information can flow across communications and media platforms seamlessly and instantly.

In this way, technological convergence complicates efforts to create effective information control regimes. This is will be just as true for privacy regimes as it is for other regulatory efforts.

2. Decentralized, distributed networking

Second, information creation, curation, storage, and dissemination are all increasingly highly decentralized and distributed in nature. Milton Mueller, author of *Networks and States: The Global Politics of Internet Governance*, notes that "Internet protocols decentralized and distributed participation in and authority over networking and ensured that the decision-making units over network operations are no longer closely aligned with political units."[43]

---

[42] Henry Jenkins, founder and director of the MIT Comparative Media Studies Program and author of *Convergence Culture: Where Old and New Media Collide*, defines convergence as "the flow of content across multiple media platforms, the cooperation between multiple media industries, and the migratory behavior of media audiences who will go almost anywhere in search of the kinds of entertainment experiences they want". Jenkins 2006, p. 2.

[43] Mueller 2010, p. 4.

Thus, shutting down a website, blog, social network site, etc., to control information flows is often ineffective since the information in question could be hosted in multiple places and might have been copied and reproduced by countless individuals who perpetuate the process by uploading it elsewhere.[44] By contrast, controlling information in the past could have been accomplished by smashing a printing press, cutting power to a broadcast tower, or confiscating communications devices. While imperfect, such measures—or even less extreme regulatory measures—were often reasonably effective at controlling information flows. But this was facilitated by the highly centralized nature of those older systems or networks. Because modern digital technologies are far more decentralized and distributed, it complicates efforts to centralize information control. Hierarchical or top-down regulatory schemes must contend with the atomization of information and its mercurial nature within these modern digital systems.

3. Unprecedented scale of networked communications

Third, in the past, the reach of speech and information was limited by geographic, technological, and cultural/language considerations. Today, by contrast, media can now flow across the globe at the click of a button because of the dramatic expansion of Internet access and broadband connectivity. Content and commentary that appears in one obscure corner of the globe can be instantaneously viewed across the world. Offshore hosting of content also makes it harder to know where content originates or is being stored.[45]

While restrictions by government are certainly still possible, the scale of modern speech and content dissemination greatly complicates government efforts to control information flows.[46]

4. Explosion of the overall volume of information

Fourth, the volume of media and communications activity taking place today also complicates regulatory efforts. In simple terms, there is just too much stuff for regulators to police today relative to the past. "Since 1995 the sheer volume of information – personally identifiable and otherwise – that has become digitized and can be cheaply transported around the world has grown by orders of

---

44 "[S]hort of unplugging the Internet, it is difficult to control its networking capabilities because they can always be redirected to a backbone somewhere else on the planet. True, it is possible to block access to some designated sites, but not the trillions of e-mail messages and the millions of web sites in constant process of renewal.... [T]he best governments can do to enforce their legislation is to prosecute a few unfortunate culprits who are caught in the act, while millions of others enjoy their merry ride over the web.... [W]hile a few of the messengers are punished, the messages go on, most of them surfing the ocean of global, seamless, communication." Castells 2009, p. 113.

45 "The bits are everywhere; there is simply no locking them down, and no one really wants to do that anymore." Abelson et al. 2008, p. 68.

46 Pager and Candeub 2012, p. 3, ["the Internet has revolutionized scale."].

47 Downes 2009, p. 69.

magnitude," notes Larry Downes, author of *The Laws of Disruption*.[47] Mueller concurs, noting: "The sheer volume of transactions and content on the Internet often overwhelms the capacity of traditional government processes to respond" to developments in this space.[48] Almost a decade ago, a blue ribbon panel assembled by the National Research Council to examine the regulation of objectionable content had already concluded that, "The volume of information on the Internet is so large – and changes so rapidly – that it is simply impractical for human beings to evaluate every discrete piece of information for inappropriateness."[49]

The problem has only grown larger since then. IDC's 2009 report, *The Digital Universe Ahead—Are You Ready?*[50] offers the following snapshot of the digital "data deluge" that is upon us: "[In 2009], despite the global recession, the Digital Universe set a record. It grew by 62 % to nearly 800,000 petabytes. A petabyte is a million gigabytes. Picture a stack of DVDs reaching from the earth to the moon and back."

This year, the Digital Universe will grow almost as fast to 1.2 million petabytes, or 1.2 zettabytes.

This explosive growth means that by 2020, our Digital Universe will be 44 times as big as it was in 2009. Our stack of DVDs would now reach halfway to Mars.

Also, a February 2011 study by Martin Hilbert and Priscila Lopez of the University of Southern California, calculated "The World's Technological Capacity to Store, Communicate, and Compute Information," and found that "in 2007, humankind sent 1.9 zettabytes of information through broadcast technology such as televisions and GPS. That is equivalent to every person in the world receiving 174 newspapers every day."[51] This "volume problem" for information control efforts will only grow more acute in coming years, especially when the next consideration is taken into account.

5. Unprecedented individual information sharing through user-generation of content and self-revelation of data

Finally, in this new world in which every man, woman and child can be a one-person publishing house or self-broadcaster, restrictions on information uploading, downloading, or subsequent aggregation/use will become increasingly difficult to devise and enforce.[52] This is particularly relevant to any discussion of online safety and privacy regulation since millions of individuals, including children, are

---

47 Downes 2009, p. 69.

48 Mueller 2010, p. 4.

49 Computer Science and Telecommunications Board, National Research Council 2002, p 187.

50 Gantz and Reinsel 2010, http://idcdocserv.com/925.

51 Hilbert and Lopez 2011, http://annenberg.usc.edu/News%20and%20Events/News/110210Hilbert.aspx.

52 "The material requirements for effective information production and communication are now owned by numbers of individuals several orders of magnitude larger than the number of owners of the basic means of information production and exchange a mere two decades ago," notes Yochai Benkler. "Individuals can reach and inform or edify millions around the world. Such a

currently placing massive volumes of personal information online—both about themselves and others.

For example, in 2011, Facebook reported that users submit around 650,000 comments on the 100 million pieces of content served up *every minute* on its site.[53] And Hilbert and Lopez found that "Humankind shared 65 exabytes of information in 2007, the equivalent of every person in the world sending out the contents of six newspapers every day."[54] Not all of that shared information was personal information, of course, but much of it probably was.

This problem will be exacerbated by the increasing ubiquity of mobile devices that capture and reproduce information instantaneously. For example, practically every teenager today carries a powerful digital "sensor" or surveillance technology in their pocket: their mobile phones.[55] They use them to record audio and video of themselves and the world around them and instantaneously share it with the planet. They also use geolocation technologies to pinpoint the movement of themselves and others in real time. This will create new online safety and privacy challenges, but it is unclear how prohibitionary or anticipatory regulation-based strategies could address those concerns without limiting the accessibility or functionality of devices and services that the public increasingly demands.

Taken together, the end result of these five phenomena, as David Friedman of Santa Clara Law School has noted, is that "Once information is out there, it is very hard to keep track of who has it and what he has done with it."[56] This has important ramifications for which risk response strategy is optimal. Prohibition and regulation-based strategies will increasingly backfire or be less effective because of these new realities. This makes resiliency-based strategies even more desirable. Section 3.4 outlines additional benefits of adopting resiliency strategies.

3.4 Why Resiliency and Adaptation Make More Sense for Online Safety Risks

Because efforts to prohibit or regulate information technology can be costly, complicated, and overly constraining, it is often wise to consider alternative, less restrictive approaches. Education and awareness-building strategies can be particularly effective. Empowerment-based strategies are also useful. These strategies

(Footnote 52 continued)
reach was simply unavailable to diversely motivated individuals before", he says. Benkler 2006, p. 4.

[53] Deeter 2011, www.facebook.com/note.php?note_id=496077348919.

[54] Hilbert and Lopez 2011.

[55] "Young people are turning to mobile devices in droves. They use them to post more information about themselves and their friends into the ether." Palfrey and Gasser 2008, p. 62.

[56] Friedman 2008, p. 62.

can help build resiliency and ensure proper assimilation of new technologies into society.

3.4.1 Education, Media Literacy, and Digital Citizenship

Collecting information and learning from online sites clearly has great value to children. More generally, children also benefit from being able to participate in online interactions because they learn essential social skills. As a recent MacArthur Foundation study of online youth Internet use concluded:

> Contrary to adult perceptions, while hanging out online, youth are picking up basic social and technological skills they need to fully participate in contemporary society. Erecting barriers to participation deprives teens of access to these forms of learning. Participation in the digital age means more than being able to access "serious" online information and culture.[57]

Nonetheless, fears persist about youth and online environments and drive the panics and regulatory responses discussed above. The greatly overblown "predator panic" discussed earlier is the most obvious example. But when concerns about online cyberbullying arose, regulatory solutions were the knee-jerk response in the US as well.[58] Some US lawmakers suggested that cyberbullying by youth should be addressed by creating a new a new federal felony that would have incarcerated those found guilty.[59]

For the reason outlined in the previous sections, such "legislate and regulate" responses are most often not sensible approaches to most online safety concerns. The better approach might be labeled "educate and empower," which is a resiliency-based response.

The "educate and empower" approach focuses on encouraging better social norms and coping strategies through parental and social mentoring. We need to assimilate children gradually into online environments and use resiliency strategies to make sure they understand how to cope with the challenges they will face in the digital age.[60]

In recent years, many child safety scholars and child development experts have worked to expand traditional online education and media literacy strategies to

---

[57] The MacArthur Foundation 2008, p. 2, http://digitalyouth.ischool.berkeley.edu/files/report/digitalyouth-WhitePaper.pdf.

[58] Szoka and Thierer 2009a, www.pff.org/issues-pubs/pops/2009/pop16.12-cyberbullying-education-better-than-regulation.pdf.

[59] In May 2008, Rep. Linda Sánchez (DCA) introduced the "Megan Meier Cyberbullying Prevention Act", a bill that would create a new federal felony that stated "Whoever transmits in interstate or foreign commerce any communication, with the intent to coerce, intimidate, harass, or cause substantial emotional distress to a person, using electronic means to support severe, repeated, and hostile behavior", could be prosecuted under federal law. The measure did not pass into law, however.

[60] Newton and Monks 2011, www.gamersdailynews.com/articlenav-2984-page-1.html.

place the notion of digital citizenship at the core of their lessons.[61] Online safety expert Anne Collier defines digital citizenship as "critical thinking and ethical choices about the content and impact on oneself, others, and one's community of what one sees, says, and produces with media, devices, and technologies."[62] Common Sense Media, a prominent US-based online safety organization, notes that "digital literacy programs are an essential element of media education and involve basic learning tools and a curriculum in critical thinking and creativity." "Digital Citizenship," it notes, "means that kids appreciate their responsibility for their content as well as their actions when using the Internet, cell phones, and other digital media. This is part of an effort to develop and practice safe, legal, and ethical behaviors in the digital media age. Digital Citizenship programs involve educational tools and a basic curriculum for kids, parents, and teachers."[63]

As online safety educator Nancy Willard notes, responsible digital citizens: (1) understand the risks: they know how to avoid getting into risk, detect if they are at risk, and respond effectively, including asking for help; (2) are responsible and ethical: they do not harm others, and they respect the privacy and property of others; (3) pay attention to the well-being of others: they make sure their friends and others are safe, and they report concerns to an appropriate adult or site; and, (4) promote online civility and respect.[64] Only by teaching our children to be good cyber-citizens can we ensure they are prepared for life in an age of information abundance. This can also alleviate anxieties among parents and policymakers about these new technologies.[65]

Many of these same principles and strategies can help us address privacy concerns for both kids and adults. "Again, the solution is critical thinking and digital citizenship," argues online safety expert Larry Magid. "We need educational campaigns that teach kids how to use whatever controls are built into the browsers, how to distinguish between advertising and editorial content and how to evaluate whatever information they come across to be able to make informed choices."[66] Teaching our kids smarter online hygiene and "Netiquette" is vital. "Think before you click" should be lesson #1. Children must be taught the dangers

---

[61] Willard 2008, www.cyberbully.org/PDFs/yrocomprehensiveapproach.pdf; Collier 2009b, www.netfamilynews.org/2009/11/from-users-to-citizen-how-to-make.html; Magid 2010, www.huffingtonpost.com/larry-magid/we-need-to-rethink-online_b_433421.html; Collier and Magid 2009, www.connectsafely.org/Commentaries-Staff/online-safety-30-empowering-and-protecting-youth.html; and Hancock et al. 2009.

[62] Collier 2009a, www.netfamilynews.org/2009/09/definition-of-digital-literacy.html. *Also see* Collier 2012, www.netfamilynews.org/?p=31427.

[63] Common Sense Media 2009, p. 1, www.commonsensemedia.org/sites/default/files/CSM_digital_policy.pdf.

[64] Willard 2008, pp. 1–2.

[65] Balkam and Gifford 2012, www.fosi.org/images/stories/resources/calming-parental-anxiety-while-empowering-our-digital-youth.pdf.

[66] Magid 2011, www.safekids.com/2011/08/29/digital-literacy-critical-thinking-accomplish-more-than-monitoring-tracking-laws.

of over-sharing personal information about themselves and others. They should also be encouraged to delete unnecessary online information occasionally.[67]

While much of this mentoring will be conducted within schools, digital citizenship ultimately begins at home with parental guidance and mentoring. Some of those mentoring strategies will be discussed in Sect. 3.4.2 on user empowerment strategies.

3.4.2 *User Empowerment, Self-regulation, and Best Practices*

This section discusses how user empowerment plays a role in helping to advance resiliency-based strategies. Three types of user empowerment strategies are identified and discussed.

1. Informal parental controls/household media rules

Some of the most important parental control efforts take the form of household level rules that parents and guardians establish to govern how media content and online technologies are used in the home or other places where children are present. In a previous report, I noted that these household media consumption rules can be grouped into four general categories[68]:

- *"Where" rules*: These are rules regarding where in the home or elsewhere that children are allowed to consume media or use digital/online technologies. For example, many parents impose household restrictions of televisions, computers, or other media devices in kids' bedrooms.
- *"When and how much" rules*: These are household rules limiting the overall number of hours that children can consume various types of media/digital content, or dictating when they can do so.
- *"Under what conditions" rules*: These rules represent a carrot-and-stick approach to media consumption. Parents can incentivize their children by requiring that other tasks or responsibilities be accomplished before media consumption or use of digital technologies is permitted.
- *"What" rules*: These are household rules that dictate the substance of the media that the child can consume. While different families have different values, most parents have pre-established rules for what types of content are off-limits for children, usually determined by age/maturity.

In many ways, these household efforts represent the most important steps that most parents can take in dealing with potentially objectionable content or teaching their children how to be sensible, savvy digital citizens. To the extent that many

[67] Collier 2011, www.netfamilynews.org/?p=30376.

[68] Thierer 2009b, pp. 25–43, www.pff.org/parentalcontrols.

households never take advantage of the technical parental control tools discussed below, it is likely because they rely instead on the informal household media rules instead. Importantly, however, many technical parental control tools can be used in combination with these informal household media rules to guide or control kids' media exposure or online interactions.

2. Technical parental controls

A stunning array of parental control tools and methods exist today that parents and guardians can tap to better protect children from various online risks.[69] These tools, which all offer some form of content filtering or tailoring, include:

- *Stand-alone filtering and monitoring products*: Many parents and most schools already use Internet filtering software and monitoring tools control their children's online surfing activities.[70]
- *Operating system controls/web browser controls*: Firms like Microsoft and Apple have integrated parental control tools directly into PC operating systems and web browsers. In addition, major web browsers from Microsoft, Google, Firefox, and Apple all have some parental control and privacy controls. For example, they can allow "whitelisting" or "blacklisting" of websites and there are many plugins available for most browsers that allowed expanded parental control and privacy options.
- *"Safe search" engine filters*: Major search providers (Google, Microsoft, and Yahoo) offer "safe search" features that allows users to filter unwanted content. Search results are set to a default "moderate" position but can be adjusted by parents to provide added protection.
- *Web portals for kids*: A broad array kid-oriented web portals now exist. Kidzui.com is a good example. These search portals are massive white lists of acceptable sites and content that have been prescreened to ensure that they are appropriate for very young web surfers. The only downside of using such services is that a lot of wonderful material available on the Internet might be missed, but many parents will be willing to make that trade-off since they desire greater protection of their children from potentially objectionable content.

Many of these parental control technologies are available on major smartphone and video gaming platforms.[71] Also, many excellent privacy-enhancing tools exist for people seeking to safeguard their child's online experiences or their own online privacy.[72] A host of tools are available to block or limit various types of data collection, and every major web browser has cookie-control tools to help users

---

69 Thierer 2009a, b, c, pp. 45–143.

70 Lazansk 2012, www.adamsmith.org/sites/default/files/research/files/parentledprotection.pdf.

71 Klosowski 2011, http://lifehacker.com/5868750/how-do-i-set-up-non+annoying-parental-controls-on-all-my-devices.

72 Thierer 2011, pp. 24–28, http://mercatus.org/publication/public-interest-comment-protecting-consumer-privacy-era-rapid-change.

manage data collection.[73] Many nonprofits—including many privacy advocates—offer instructional websites and videos explaining how privacy-sensitive consumers can take steps to protect their personal information online.

These technical controls should not be considered substitutes for talking to children about what they might see or hear while online. Even though empowerment tools and strategies can help parents control the vast majority of objectionable content that their kids might stumble upon while online, no system is perfect. In the end, education, oversight, and ongoing communication and mentoring are vital.[74] That being said, these tools and strategies can supplement the mentoring role.

3. Industry self-regulation: Best practices

Companies also have an important role to play in creating "well-lit neighborhoods" online where kids will be safe and others can feel their privacy is relatively secure. Many companies and trade associations are also taking steps to raise awareness among their users about how they can better protect their privacy and security. Online operators should also be careful about what (or how much) information they collect—especially if they primarily serve young audiences. Most widely trafficked social networking sites and search engines already offer a variety of privacy controls and allow users to delete their accounts.

Sites that cater mostly to children must be particularly cautious. These sites should develop best practices or codes of conduct that establish smart ground rules for acceptable behavior and limitations on certain types of functionality and data collection. Everloop, a leading social media site for kids and tweens, offers a good example. Everloop's "3 Cs of Conduct" for social interaction and sharing on its site are as follows:

- "BE COOL: Everloop is a safe, fun place for everyone…so no swearing, cheating, bullying or general bad behavior allowed. If you do any of that, we might have to boot you from the loop."
- "BE CLEAN: Everloop is not about drugs, alcohol, sex, race or any inappropriate stuff like that. We will block offensive posts."
- "BE CONFIDENTIAL: Play safe on Everloop – don't share your real name, address, phone number, e-mail or passwords with anybody."

---

[73] Importantly, just as most families leave the vast majority of parental control technologies untapped, many households will never take advantage of these privacy-enhancing empowerment tools. That fact does not serve as proof of "market failure" or the need for government regulation, however. What matters is that the tools exist for those who wish to use them, not the actual usage rates of those tools. Thierer 2009c, www.pff.org/issues-pubs/pops/2009/pop16.5parental-controlsmarket.pdf.

[74] Julia Angwin of the *Wall Street Journal* argues: "For most parents, it seems that our best bet is to treat the Internet like an unsupervised playground in a sketchy neighborhood: You shouldn't drop your kids off there and walk away. You are obligated to stick around and make sure some kid doesn't beat up your kid – even if you're just watching from a bench on the sidelines." Angwin 2009, http://online.wsj.com/article/SB123238632055894993.html.

Everloop closely monitors behavior on the site to ensure compliance with these ground rules.

A more extreme example is Disney's popular Club Penguin, a hugely popular virtual world for kids. To ensure the site is safe for children, Disney intentionally limits functionality within a well-protected walled garden. For example, once kids are there, they cannot find any "back doors" that lead them off the site and onto the Internet. All content and communication is self-contained within the walls of the site and highly moderated. Functionality is also limited by nature of the fact that certain types of information (e-mail addresses, phone numbers, etc.) cannot be uploaded or shared within the virtual community. In essence, Disney has intentionally "crippled" the social networking functionality and social sharing features on the site to guarantee safety and privacy on the site. Of course, such limitations will not work for all websites, especially sites geared toward tweens and older audiences who expect greater social sharing capabilities. Nonetheless, Club Penguin offers a model for how other sites for very young audiences can ensure the ultimate safe and secure experience.

3.4.3 Hybrid Approaches

Hybrid risk response strategies are certainly possible, especially between anticipatory regulation and resilience-based strategies. For example, transparency, disclosure, and labeling policies can be either top-down (government-driven) or bottom-up (norms-based) in nature.

As part of the best practices they establish for their online sites and services, private entities should be encouraged to be as transparent as possible about site practices and clearly disclose what information is being collected and retained. In the case of sites that generate or host content, when possible, that content should be clearly labeled to highlight what users might expect to see or hear. To go a step further, they should allow media content to be tagged with metadata that is searchable and can be filtered in some fashion.

Of course, all these policies could be mandated or encouraged by public policymakers. Many governments across the globe already enforce labeling and transparency requirements for various media practices, especially as it pertains to marketing to children. However, some media labeling efforts may be limited by free speech considerations or constitutional constraints, as is the case in the United States.

But voluntary steps can be encouraged by governments and have already resulted in much progress. Voluntary media content ratings and labels for movies, music, video games, and smartphone apps have given parents and others more information to make determinations about the appropriateness of content they may want to consume.[75] Many of those rating and labeling efforts were encouraged by government.

[75] Thierer 2009b, www.pff.org/parentalcontrols, pp. 57–113.

Hybrid strategies can be particularly appropriate when it comes to complex problems like cyberbullying and sexting among youth. While criminalization would be unwise in these contexts, governments can work with public health experts, child safety organizations, and companies, to craft educational strategies and mentoring responses that help youth understand the dangers of such behavior. Government funding for public awareness campaigns and targeted educational initiatives in this area can help protect children from either objectionable content or various other cyber-dangers.[76]

3.5 Conclusion

This chapter has presented a conceptual framework for how to evaluate safety risks that youth may confront online. This framework can help policymakers determine the most sensible risk responses as digital technologies and online networks proliferate and evolve.

It has been argued that resiliency-based strategies offer many advantages when compared with prohibitionary and regulatory-based responses. Resiliency-based strategies do not impose a burden on free speech or technological innovation. Moreover, resiliency-based strategies offer greater flexibility in terms of how individuals and institutions respond to evolving technological challenges.

Instilling principles and lessons to last a lifetime will ultimately do more to make children smart, savvy cyber-citizens and prepare them for the worst of what the world might throw their way. In this sense, the resiliency approach builds on the logic of the Chinese proverb: "Give a man a fish and you feed him for a day. Teach a man to fish and you feed him for a lifetime." Except in this case it is: "Teach a child to think and you prepare them for a lifetime."

In many ways, this is precisely what has been happening over the past decade. Both parents and kids have been "learning on the job," so to speak. They have been adapting to new digital technologies and online worlds and gradually assimilating them into their lives. In the process, they have learned important lessons and become more resilient.

Of course, some risks are serious enough that they demand anticipatory regulation, perhaps even prohibition. Child porn and online child abuse of any sort are the primary examples. For most other risks, however, resiliency and social adaptation responses generally trump prohibition.

[76] Thierer 2007a, www.pff.org/issues-pubs/pops/pop14.3beanbillinternetsafety.pdf.

References

Abdukadirov S, Yazigi D (2012) Inflated benefits in agencies' economic analysis. Mercatus Center at George Mason University, Arlington, VA. http://mercatus.org/publication/inflated-benefits-agencies-economic-analysis

Abelson H, Ledeen K, Lewis HR (2008) Blown to bits: your life, liberty, and happiness after the digital explosion. Addison-Wesley Professional, New York

Angwin J (2009) How to keep kids safe online. Wall Street J. http://online.wsj.com/article/SB123238632055894993.html

Balkam S, Gifford N (2012) Calming parental anxiety while empowering our digital youth. Family Online Safety Institute, Washington, DC. www.fosi.org/images/stories/resources/calming-parental-anxiety-while-empowering-our-digital-youth.pdf

Benkler Y (2006) The wealth of networks: how social production transforms markets and freedom. Yale University Press, New Haven, CT

boyd d (2008) Taken out of context, American teen sociality in networked publics. Doctoral dissertation, University of California, Berkeley. www.danah.org/papers/TakenOutOfContext.pdf

Castells M (2009) Communication power. Oxford University Press, Oxford

Cohen S (1972) Folk devils and moral panics: the creation of the mods and rockers. MacGibbon and Kee, London

Collier A (2009a) A definition of digital literacy citizenship. Net family news. www.netfamilynews.org/2009/09/definition-of-digital-literacy.html

Collier A (2009b) From users to citizens: How to make digital citizenship relevant. Net family news. www.netfamilynews.org/2009/11/from-users-to-citizen-how-to-make.html

Collier A (2011) 'Delete day': Students putting messages that matter online. NetFamilyNews.org. www.netfamilynews.org/?p=30376

Collier A (2012) Literacy for a digital age: transliteracy or what? Net family news. www.netfamilynews.org/?p=31427

Collier A, Magid L (2009) ConnectSafety.org. Online safety 3.0: empowering and protecting youth. www.connectsafely.org/Commentaries-Staff/online-safety-30-empowering-and-protecting-youth.html

Common Sense Media (2009) Digital literacy and citizenship in the 21st century: Educating, empowering, and protecting America's kids. San Francisco, CA. www.commonsensemedia.org/sites/default/files/CSM_digital_policy.pdf

Computer Science and Telecommunications Board, National Research Council (2002) Youth, pornography, and the internet. National Academy Press, Washington, DC

Corn-Revere R (2011) Moral panics, the first amendment, and the limits of social science. Commun Lawyer 28(3)

Cramer JK, Trevor Thrall A (2009) Framing Iraq: threat inflation in the marketplace of values. In: Trevor Thrall A, Cramer JK (eds) American foreign policy and the politics of fear. Routledge, London

Deeter K (2011) Live commenting: behind the scenes. Facebook.com. www.facebook.com/note.php?note_id=496077348919

Downes L (2009) The laws of disruption. Basic Books, New York

Ferguson CJ (2008) The school shooting/violent video game link: Causal relationship or moral panic? J Invest Psychol Offender Prof 5(1–2):25–37. http://onlinelibrary.wiley.com/doi/10.1002/jip.76/abstract

Friedman D (2008) Future imperfect: technology and freedom in an uncertain world. Cambridge University Press, Cambridge

Gantz J, Reinsel D (2010) The digital universe ahead—are you ready? IDC. http://idcdocserv.com/925

Gardner D (2009) The science of fear: how the culture of fear manipulates your brain. Plume, New York

Goode E, Ben-Yehuda N (1994) Moral panics: the social construction of deviance. Blackwell, Malden, MA

Hancock M, Randall R, Simpson A (2009) From safety to literacy: digital citizenship in the 21st century. Threshold

Hilbert M, Lopez P (2011) The world's technological capacity to store, communicate, and compute information. Science. http://annenberg.usc.edu/News%20and%20Events/News/110210Hilbert.aspx

Internet Safety Technical Task Force (2008) Enhancing child safety online. Final report http://cyber.law.harvard.edu/pubrelease/isttf

Jenkins H (2006) Convergence culture: where old and new media collide. New York University Press, New York

Kaufmann C (2004) Threat inflation and the failure of the marketplace of ideas: the selling of the Iraq war. Int Secur 29:5–48. http://belfercenter.ksg.harvard.edu/files/kaufmann.pdf

Kelly K (2011) What technology wants. Viking, New York

Klosowski T (2011) How do I set up non-annoying parental controls on all my devices? Lifehacker. http://lifehacker.com/5868750/how-do-i-set-up-non+annoying-parental-controls-on-all-my-devices

Lazansk D (2012) Parent-led protection: Market-based solutions to child safety. Adam Smith Institute. www.adamsmith.org/sites/default/files/research/files/parentledprotection.pdf

Levy N, Cortesi S, Gasser U, Crowley E, Beaton M, Casey J, Nolan c (2012) Bullying in a networked era: a literature review. Research publication no. 2012-17. Berkman Center for Internet Society, Cambridge, MA. http://papers.ssrn.com/sol3/papers.cfm?abstract_id=2146877

Lutter R (2012) How well do federal regulations actually work? The role of retrospective review. Mercatus Center at George Mason University, Arlington, VA. http://mercatus.org/publication/how-well-do-federal-regulations-actually-work-role-retrospective-review

Magid L (2010) We need to rethink online safety. The Huffington post. www.huffingtonpost.com/larry-magid/we-need-to-rethink-online_b_433421.html

Magid L (2011) Digital citizenship and media literacy beat tracking laws and monitoring. SafeKids.com. www.safekids.com/2011/08/29/digital-literacy-critical-thinking-accomplish-more-than-monitoring-tracking-laws

Marwick A (2008) The myspace moral panic. First Monday 13(6–2). www.uic.edu/htbin/cgiwrap/bin/ojs/index.php/fm/article/view/2152/1966

Mueller M (2010) Networks and states: the global politics of internet governance. The MIT Press, Cambridge, MA

Newton R, Monks E (2011) Who's minding the e-children: why kids can sensibly participate on the net. Gamer Daily News. www.gamersdailynews.com/articlenav-2984-page-1.html

Ohio Missing Children Clearinghouse (2005) 2005 annual report. www.ag.state.oh.us/victim/pubs/2005ann_rept_mcc.pdf

Pager SA, Candeub A (eds) (2012) Transnational culture in the internet age. Edward Elgar, Northampton

Palfrey J, Gasser U (2008) Born digital: understanding the first generation of digital natives. Basic Books, New York

Sedlak A J, Finkelhor D, Hammer H, Schultz D J (2002) National estimate of missing children: an overview, national incidence studies of missing, abducted, runaway, and thrownaway children. National Center for Missing Exploited Children, Alexandria, VA. www.missingkids.com/en_US/documents/nismart2_overview.pdf

Singleton S (1988) Privacy as Censorship: a skeptical view of proposals to regulate privacy in the private sector. Policy Analysis 295:8. www.cato.org/pubs/pas/pa-295.html

Skenazy L (2009) Free-range kids: giving our children the freedom we had without going nuts with worry. Jossey-Bass, San Francisco, CA

Steel E, Angwin J (2006) MySpace receives more pressure to limit children's access to site. Wall Street J, June 23, 2006. http://online.wsj.com/public/article/SB115102268445288250-YRxkt0rTsyyf1QiQf2EPBYSf7iU_20070624.html?mod=tff_main_tff_top

Sunstein C (2002–2003) The paralyzing principle. Regulation 34. Cato Institute, Washington, DC. www.cato.org/pubs/regulation/regv25n4/v25n4-9.pdf

Szoka B, Thierer A (2009a) Cyberbullying legislation: why education is preferable to regulation. Progress on point 16.2. The Progress Freedom Foundation, Washington, DC. www.pff.org/issues-pubs/pops/2009/pop16.12-cyberbullying-education-better-than-regulation.pdf

Szoka B, Thierer A (2009b) Targeted online advertising: what's the harm where are we heading. Progress on point no. 16.2. Progress Freedom Foundation. Washington, DC. www.scribd.com/doc/12597638/Targeted-Online-Advertising-Whats-the-Harm-Where-Are-We-Heading

The MacArthur Foundation (2008) Living and learning with new media: Summary of findings from the digital youth project. Chicago, IL. http://digitalyouth.ischool.berkeley.edu/files/report/digitalyouth-WhitePaper.pdf

Thierer A (2006) The middleman isn't the problem. Philly.com. http://articles.philly.com/2006-05-31/news/25400396_1_web-sites-social-networking-block-access

Thierer A (2007a) Rep. Bean's 'SAFER net act': an education-based approach to online child safety. Progress on point 14.3. Progress Freedom Foundation, Washington, DC. www.pff.org/issues-pubs/pops/pop14.3beanbillinternetsafety.pdf

Thierer A (2007b) Social networking and age verification: many hard questions; No easy solutions. Progress on point no. 14.5. Progress Freedom Foundation, Washington, DC. www.pff.org/issues-pubs/pops/pop14.5ageverification.pdf, http://papers.ssrn.com/sol3/papers.cfm?abstract_id=976936

Thierer A (2007c) Why regulate broadcasting: toward a consistent first amendment standard for the information age. CommLaw Conspectus 15:431

Thierer A (2007d) Would your favorite website be banned by DOPA? Technology liberation front. http://techliberation.com/2007/03/10/would-your-favorite-website-be-banned-by-dopa

Thierer A (2008) The perils of mandatory parental controls and restrictive defaults. Progress Freedom Foundation progress on point no. 15.4. http://papers.ssrn.com/sol3/papers.cfm?abstract_id=1120324

Thierer A (2009a) Against technopanics. Technology liberation front. http://techliberation.com/2009/07/15/against-technopanics

Thierer A (2009b) Parental controls online child protection: a survey of tools, version 4.0. Progress Freedom Foundation, Washington, DC. www.pff.org/parentalcontrols

Thierer A (2009c) Who needs parental controls? Assessing the relevant market for parental control technologies. Progress on point 16.5. Progress Freedom Foundation, Washington, DC. www.pff.org/issues-pubs/pops/2009/pop16.5parentalcontrolsmarket.pdf

Thierer A (2011) Public interest comment on protecting consumer privacy in an era of rapid change. Mercatus Center at George Mason University, Arlington, VA. http://mercatus.org/publication/public-interest-comment-protecting-consumer-privacy-era-rapid-change

Thierer A (2012) Sunsetting technology regulation: applying Moore's law to Washington. www.forbes.com/sites/adamthierer/2012/03/25/sunsetting-technology-regulation-applying-moores-law-to-washington

US Department of Justice, Office of Justice Programs (2010) The crime of family abduction: a child's and parent's perspective. Washington, DC. https://www.ncjrs.gov/pdffiles1/ojjdp/229933.pdf

Willard N (2008) Comprehensive layered approach to address digital citizenship and youth risk online. Center for Safe and Responsible Internet Use, Eugene, OR. www.cyberbully.org/PDFs/yrocomprehensiveapproach.pdf

Williams R (2012) Comment on OMB's draft 2012 report to congress on the benefits and costs of federal regulations. Public comment. Mercatus Center at George Mason University, Arlington, VA. http://mercatus.org/publication/comment-ombs-draft-2012-report-congress-benefits-and-costs-federal-regulations

Williams R, Ellig J (2011) Regulatory oversight: the basics of regulatory impact analysis. Mercatus Center at George Mason University, Arlington, VA. http://mercatus.org/publication/regulatory-oversight

Zolli A, Healy AM (2012) Resilience: why things bounce back. Free Press, New York

Chapter 4
Colouring Inside the Lines: Using Technology to Regulate Children's Behaviour Online

Bibi van den Berg

Contents

4.1 Introduction

In recent years, both in research and in popular media, debates have emerged on a wide variety of risks to which children and teenagers may be exposed when using the Internet. Such risks range from attracting spam or malware, to encountering offensive or harmful content, to engaging in contact with unknown others (especially adults), to sharing too much or the wrong kind of information with (unintended) audiences, to bullying and harassment. Extensive empirical research has

Bibi van den Berg is Assistant Professor at eLaw, the Center for Law in the Information Society at Leiden University's Law School, Leiden, The Netherlands.

B. van den Berg (✉)
Center for Law in the Information Society, University of Leiden, Leiden, The Netherlands
e-mail: b.van.den.berg@law.leidenuniv.nl

S. van der Hof et al. (eds.), *Minding Minors Wandering the Web: Regulating Online Child Safety*, Information Technology and Law Series 24, DOI: 10.1007/978-94-6265-005-3_4,

revealed that it is not easy to quantify the 'dangers' of Internet use among children and teenagers, nor straightforward to establish their impact. Large empirical studies leave us with a nuanced picture with regard to the frequency and the effects of online risks. In practice, such risks materialise less often than their discussion in popular media would sometimes lead us to believe.[1] Moreover, the impact that potentially negative experiences may have on children is also less clear-cut than one might believe based on the ways in which online risks are discussed in popular media and by policy makers and regulators.[2]

At the same time, there is substantial pressure on technology designers, policy makers and regulators to come up with measures—either technical, educational, normative or legal—to counter the risks to which children and youngsters may be exposed on the Internet.[3] Of course, there are valid reasons for creating such measures, most importantly the fact that children and teenagers are worthy of proper protection in any sphere of life, and hence should also receive any safeguards necessary to ensure safe Internet use. Moreover, almost everyone will agree that it is wise to empower children in their online skills so that they may make the most of the Internet's vast array of opportunities, while at the same time maximising their abilities to steer clear of its downsides.

However, as a rule, any attempt to combat risk, in whatever form, through regulation, legislation, norm-setting or through technical means, ought to be applied only and insofar as it provides an effective, realistic, balanced and adequate remedy for the problem to be tackled. This means that if the empirical data do not show convincingly that online risks are, in fact, as clear-cut of a problem as they are sometimes made out to be, both in their magnitude and their effects, then we would be justified in raising questions with respect to the widespread and extensive application of technologies, regulations and norms to counter such risks. This article aims to critically address the debate on remedying, preventing or countering online risks for children and teenagers, and to assess whether existing measures are, in fact, reasonable and effective. It will do so by critically evaluating one specific solution that is commonly used in preventing children from encountering online risks, viz. the use of technical means to affect, limit, shape and guide youngsters' behaviours in the online world. This phenomenon can be labelled 'technological influencing' and it comes in several different forms, some less stringent than others. I will begin this article with a discussion of the theoretical underpinnings of (these different forms of) technological influencing. Next, I will showcase a number of examples of practical technical measures that are in use today to afford and constrain the behaviour of children and teenagers on the Internet. I will end this article with an analysis of the effectiveness, the benefits and the limitations of using technological influencing to protect children and teenagers from online risks.

---

[1] Hasebrink et al. 2011; Livingstone and Haddon 2009a; OECD 2011.

[2] Livingstone et al. 2011.

[3] ITU 2009.

4.2 Understanding Technological Influencing

One of the ways in which technology developers, regulators and policy makers aim to contribute to increased security and safety for children and teenagers[4] in online environments is through technological influencing, i.e. through the use of *technical tools.*[5] Such tools are implemented into the architecture of websites, social media, chat boxes or even the network architecture of the Internet itself, and shape what children and teenagers can and cannot do when they go online. They limit children's access to certain websites or content that is deemed harmful or inappropriate and they make certain actions, for example downloading specific (types of) content impossible. Some of these tools are also used to create a protected, circumscribed environment, a fenced-in garden so to speak, in which children are free to (inter)act. In all of these cases, the explicit goal is to ensure that children and teenagers will 'colour inside the lines', that their behaviour will stay within boundaries set by parents, educators, regulators, policy makers and/or technology developers. This can be brought about in more or less stringent ways. Some technical tools merely attempt to encourage users to avoid certain behaviours or embrace others, and hence leave them with the freedom to choose to comply or not. Other tools make it impossible for users to 'be bad'. With such tools users cannot but follow the proscribed course of action. Let's look at the ideas underlying these various forms of technological influencing in more detail.

4.2.1 *Persuasive Technologies and Nudging*

In the past few decades, many studies in various scientific disciplines have revealed that the design of technologies and their interfaces has profound effects on the ways in which users interact with them, or are affected by them.[6] For the purpose of this chapter, the work of B.J. Fogg on *captology* and that of Thaler and Sunstein on *nudging* is particularly relevant. Both of these concepts build on the idea that technologies can gently stimulate users to adopt certain courses of action, which are deemed, e.g. safer, healthier, or contribute to their wellbeing in some way or other.

---

[4] And, of course, also for adults.

[5] Cf. ITU 2009. The ITU report focuses almost exclusively the policy measures that should be taken, both on national and international levels, to combat the rise and spread of child abuse material (or CAM for short) via the internet. However, many of the policy recommendations in this report also apply to other areas that have been defined as online risks for children and teenagers.

[6] Duffy 2003; Fogg 2003; Friedman et al. 2003; Friedman and Millett 1995; Nass and Moon 2000; Nass et al. 1994a, b; 1993; Reeves and Nass 1996; Thaler and Sunstein 2008; Turkle 1984, 2007; Van den Berg 2010a, b; Verbeek 2005.

B.J. Fogg's work focuses on the ways in which information and communication technologies can be used to *persuade* individuals to do certain things or abstain from others, or to adopt certain beliefs and reject others.[7] According to Fogg, examples of the persuasive capacities of these technologies are everywhere around us. Sometimes technologies are designed explicitly to convince a target audience that certain (types of) actions may have undesirable consequences. A drunk-driving simulator or a robotic doll that mimics the behaviours of a baby is an example in case. These technologies are used to let specific groups of individuals experience what the consequences can be of certain behaviours in a very direct fashion—*in casu* to let teenagers experience the effects of drunk driving, and to let teenage girls experience what it's like to live with a baby, thus aiming to teach them to avoid teenage pregnancies. The goal of these persuasive technologies, thus, is to expose teenagers to the effects of certain types of 'risky' behaviour, and to do so in such an immersive, technologically facilitated fashion that the teenagers will become convinced that it's better to avoid such risky behaviour in the future.

Aside from these technologies, which are designed specifically to persuade users to avoid risky behaviours, computers and other information technologies in general offer unique opportunities to persuade users to change their behaviour, their attitudes or beliefs. For example, there is the effect of 'tunnelling': (computer) technologies tend to take users through a predetermined path of steps, and persuade them to follow this path. Installing software is a good example of this kind of process, as is the checking out and paying for products in an online store. Tunnelling narrows users' scope of behavioural choices, and in the process their sense of having choices as well. Therefore, chances are that users will be persuaded to act precisely in the intended fashion: once a given sequence is set in motion, the user is tempted to 'colour inside the lines' and do what is requested of him or her.

But tunnelling is not the only form of persuasion that may be at work in computer technologies. There are many others as well. For one, users can also be persuaded through technology by what Fogg calls 'conditioning'.[8] This happens, for example, in computer games. When users play a game correctly they are rewarded with points and all kinds of bonuses, such as gaining extra lives, getting extra capabilities, tools or weapons. And then there is the mechanism of 'self-monitoring': technologies allow users to monitor some aspect of themselves (for example their heart rates or their calorie intake), and by providing them with regular feedback on the monitored parameter, they may persuade users to adjust their behaviour in such a way as to work toward a predetermined goal.

The idea of persuading users through technological means is quite similar to the concept of 'nudging', which has spread far and wide in recent years through a book called *Nudge: Improving decisions about health, wealth and happiness* by Richard Thaler and Cas Sunstein.[9] Like Fogg, these authors, too, argue that human

[7] Fogg 2003.

[8] Fogg 2003, p. 49.

[9] Thaler and Sunstein 2008.

behaviours and human choices may be intentionally affected by, for example, the design of technologies, but they take this idea one step further and claim that the same applies to the design of spaces, institutions and systems. Building on findings from behavioural economics, Thaler and Sunstein introduce the concept of a 'choice architecture', the idea that designers have a "*responsibility for organizing the context in which people make decisions*".[10] Some contexts invoke choices that are qualitatively better than others, according to Thaler and Sunstein, i.e. choices that promote individuals' health, happiness or wellbeing. Other contexts inhibit such choices, undermine them, or obliterate them. According to the authors, politicians, regulators, designers and developers have an obligation to create options to meet the choice criteria of the first and avoid those in the second category, thus adopting an attitude that is designated 'libertarian paternalism'.[11]

One way in which technologies can be used to nudge people towards 'better' choices is through the use of default settings. Banking on the fact that most users do not change the default settings offered to them with a product or service by the designers thereof, a 'benign' default setting may be an easy, effective and efficient means to improve the quality of (aspects of) individuals' lives. For example, a social network site that reminds users of the size and makeup of the audience that will view a message once it is posted gently nudges these users in the direction of greater safety, of improved privacy protection and more privacy awareness.[12] Similarly, an alarm clock[13] that jumps off the nightstand and wheels around the room until its sleepy/lazy owner gets out of bed to switch it off, nudges him or her to get up in an entertaining, playful manner.

Both persuasive technologies and nudging through benign defaults build on the idea that many users, much of the time, will not deviate from the paths that designers and regulators create for them, and hence will automatically adhere to the option that is deemed best for them by these parties. When using these techniques, so-called 'regulative rules'[14] are embedded into the technology, i.e. rules that influence behaviour, yet not in a deterministic manner—people may still choose to act otherwise. Both persuasive technologies and nudging *do* leave room for alternative choices. If a user does not want to go in the direction in which (s)he is being nudged by the choice architect, or does not want to follow through on the conditioning path that (s)he is guided along, then (s)he has the possibility to choose otherwise. For example, users can (almost) always choose to change the default settings, or to ignore messages intended to evoke actions for the protection of their safety or privacy. The behavioural pull generated by persuasive and nudging techniques in ICTs is quite strong, so in practice most users will not step

[10] Thaler and Sunstein 2008, p. 3.

[11] Thaler and Sunstein 2008; for a critical reading of this concept, cf. Yeung 2012; Amir and Lobel 2009; Burgess 2012.

[12] Van den Berg and Leenes 2010, 2011.

[13] See 'clocky' and 'Tocky' at www.nandahome.com.

[14] Hildebrandt 2008, 2009, 2011.

off the intended path, yet the ways in which these techniques are designed and implemented does enable individuals to break free from the envisioned pattern and choose to act differently. The regulatory (as in steering) power of these technologies is limited in a sense, therefore. This is different for the next category of technological influencing I will discuss: techno-regulation.

4.2.2 Techno-Regulation

Techno-regulation can be defined as the process of hard-coding normative or legal codes into technologies to make certain behaviours impossible and prompt others. While persuasive technologies and nudging still leave room for manoeuvring in users, i.e. still allow users to 'opt out' and choose an alternative path of action than the one suggested by the technology, techno-regulatory measures leave no such room at all. They prescribe actions in such a way that there is no freedom to choose an alternative course of action.[15]

There are numerous examples of this type of regulation.[16] A ticket gate at an underground station (see Fig. 4.1), which only opens when travellers have a valid ticket is one example in case,[17] especially those gates that extend from floor to ceiling so that jumping over them is no longer an option. In this example, the enforcement of the rule—in this case 'one can only travel by public transport with a valid ticket'—has been delegated to a technological artefact (the gate), and through its design compliance is complete. This form of regulation is fool-proof (no one can evade it), it's cheap (no need for a human checking tickets), efficient and effective.

A second example of techno-regulation is the use of road blockers, viz. movable road elements that can be raised or lowered to prevent traffic from passing without permission (see Fig. 4.2). When encountering a road blocker, the driver has no other option but to stop and wait until the blocker is lowered before being able to continue. The rule 'no access without permission' has been hard-coded into a technological artefact, which enforces this rule in an efficient, effective and fool-proof fashion.

Examples of techno-regulation also abound on the Internet.[18] We will discuss several examples in the next section, when addressing the ways in which the behaviour of children and teenagers is influenced, shaped and steered on the Internet through technical means.

---

[15] Hildebrandt 2011.

[16] Cf. Brownsword 2008; Latour 1992; Leenes 2010; Leenes 2011;Van den Berg 2011; Van den Berg and Leenes 2013.

[17] Morgan and Yeung 2007; Yeung 2008.

[18] Cf. Lessig 2006.

Fig. 4.1 Entry gates to the Paris subway

Fig. 4.2 A road blocker

What distinguishes techno-regulation from persuasion and nudging is that 'opting out' is not an option. Techno-regulatory measures shape the action space of the regulatees in such a way that freedom of choice is minimised and alternative patterns of action are made impossible. Regulatees *must* adhere to the rule. Moreover, since the rule is implemented into a technological device, most users, most of the time, will not be aware of the fact that they are being regulated. They will simply execute the required action(s), and will do so automatically, unthinkingly, since there is no option for acting otherwise or pondering over different choices. The embedded rule's consequences are (almost) inevitable when triggered.

4.3 Implementations of Techno-Regulation in Online Safety for Children

As we have seen at the beginning of this article, there is substantial pressure on regulators, politicians, parents, teachers and technology designers to ensure that children and teenagers can use the Internet safely, and to minimise the chance that youth will encounter risky situations of various kinds on the Internet, or engage in risky behaviour. The technical mechanisms described in this article—persuasive technologies, nudging and techno-regulation—have all been adopted in numerous forms to meet this requirement. In this section, I will discuss a number of implementations of these forms of technical influencing used especially to increase children's safety on the Internet.

4.3.1 Parental Control and Filtering Content

One of the easiest ways in which parents and teachers can attempt to shield children from unwanted materials or block unwanted contacts is through the use of filtering software.[19] Livingstone and Haddon found that "among parents whose children use the Internet at home, 49 % across Europe claim that they have installed filtering software; another 37 % say they have monitoring software, and 27 % use both tools".[20] In some cases, filtering software comes as part of the operating system of the computer, but it can also be offered as a service by the Internet Service Provider (ISP) with which the parents have a subscription.

Filtering software often offers a set of different options, not just with respect to blocking or filtering content, but also, for example, to limit the time children and

[19] Cf. ITU 2009; Hasebrink et al. 2011.

[20] Livingstone and Haddon 2009b, p. 19. Note that having the software installed does not mean that parents are actually *using* it.

teenagers spend online. Figure 4.3 provides an overview of the options. Parents can create different accounts, assigning access rights and filtering/blocking levels to each account, so that adults using the same computer will be allowed access to sources that are disabled for their children. Moreover, parents can check a log file to see which sites children have visited and they can set a timer on children's Internet use, shutting down the Internet connection after a specific interval. They can also define traffic limits, to ensure that children do not download or upload large files (e.g. music or movie files). Finally, parents can define filtering and blocking settings, i.e. they can define search terms that will become blocked by the technology, for instance 'sex' or 'porn'.

Note, first of all, that all these options are forms of techno-regulation, and not nudging or persuading. By using filtering/blocking technologies children will be unable to access certain content or connect with certain individuals. Of course, tech-savvy children and teenagers will be able to find workarounds if they really want to, since none of the existing filtering and blocking concepts is completely fool-proof,[21] but most users will lack the skills, knowledge or awareness to do so. Shutting down the network connection after a specified amount of time spent browsing the web is also a form of limiting children's behaviour that leaves no room for manoeuvring, as is defining the maximum file size that they can upload or download. In all cases, a rule is hard-coded into the Internet filtering system that defines the action space of children and teenagers and forces them to 'colour inside the lines'.

As Adam Thierer points out, never before in history have parents had such an extensive repertoire of tools at their disposal to regulate what media their children are exposed to.[22] He points out, moreover, that parents can do more than merely limit their children's access to specific types of content using these technologies. They can also tailor youth's access to some materials or sources, to ensure that they will "see, hear, or consume content [the parents] would regard as 'better' (i.e., more educational, enriching, or ethical) for them".[23] Here we see a second level of the deployment of filtering software: it is not only used in a prohibitive, techno-regulatory fashion to block access to persons or content, but can also be utilised in a more constructive way, to steer children and teenagers towards content or persons that are deemed useful or beneficial in some way or other. By using filtering or blocking software parents may thus strike two birds with one stone: they can enhance their children's safety and reduce the risk of encountering unwanted content or persons through the software's techno-regulatory workings, and move them towards desirable/desired content.

However, there are clear downsides to the use of filtering and blocking software by parents as well. Most importantly, using filtering software—not just for the protection of children but in general—may lead to 'overblocking' and

[21] Cf. ITU 2009; Deibert et al. 2008.

[22] Thierer 2009.

[23] Thierer 2009, p. 15.

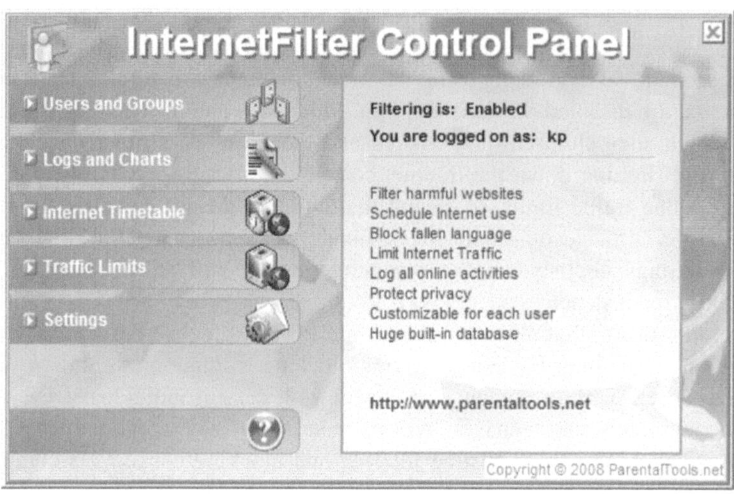

Fig. 4.3 Example of the control panel of an Internet filtering tool for parents

'underblocking'. Filtering software is quite a crude tool, in the sense that it makes content unavailable based on lists of keywords, such as 'sex' or 'breast' or any other search term deemed politically, religiously, ethically or socially sensitive.[24] These keywords are filtered indiscriminately, without looking at the context in which they are used. This entails that when filtering the word 'breast' content from, e.g. pornographic websites is made inaccessible (as was intended), but so is a host of content from innocent websites, for example those discussing breast cancer, or providing users with recipes for chicken breast, or information on breast feeding.[25] In other words, because filtering is such a crude mechanism, in the process a lot of harmless material accidentally gets 'overblocked'. The inverse sadly happens as well. Since content creators are aware of the workings of filtering software, some go out of their way to avoid its detection, and hence creatively 'misspell' commonly filtered terms, or use technical tools to avoid blocking.[26] This entails that despite the use of filtering software unwanted content may still be accessible to children and teenagers as a result of 'underblocking'.

More in general, one could argue that using filtering software also deprives children and teenagers of the possibility to freely explore the Internet to find information about things they may not wish or dare to ask their parents or teachers,

[24] The list of keywords that must be filtered can, in many cases, be composed or adjusted by parents themselves. Many internet filtering packages also come with a preinstalled list. In the broader context of using filtering and blocking software governments and other regulatory forces may also define lists of keywords to be filtered within the boundaries over which they hold sovereign power.

[25] Preston 2007, p. 1451; also see Deibert et al. 2008, p. 34.

[26] Preston 2007; also see Deibert et al. 2008, p. 34.

but about which they are curious. This is especially true for teenagers, who gradually start developing an interest in, e.g. matters related to sexuality. As Karen Yeung points out, referring to the work of Justice Michael Kirby, "internet filters designed to prohibit access to materials considered 'harmful to minors' may inadvertently prevent access to a range of legitimate materials, such as lawful erotic material…".[27] Using filtering or blocking software always entails a trade-off between enhanced safety and risk-reduction on the one hand, and limiting children's and teenagers' Internet freedom on the other.[28] Therefore, it taps directly into the much larger debate on Internet freedom and freedom of expression on the Internet,[29] and this entails that its deployment must always be "evaluated for its effectiveness – not only in terms of usability but also in risk reduction outcomes and, equally important, in terms of any trade-off in restricting freedoms".[30]

4.3.2 Browsers for Kids

A second way of ensuring that children can access the Internet in a safer and more risk-free manner is by using a browser specifically designed for them. The most well-known example of such a browser is KidZui,[31, 32] a "browser […] stuffed with millions of websites, games, and videos which are all pre-screened and approved by our editorial staff, teachers, and parents like you", as the KidZui website tells parents. Figure 4.4 shows KidZui's home screen.

By providing children with their own designated browser, in which all channels and content are verified and approved for them, and even categorised for different age groups, parents and teachers can rest assured that their children will not accidentally stumble upon undesirable content when they go online. Children no longer access the Wild West of the Internet whenever they start up the computer's browser, but play inside a 'walled garden' instead,[33] in which no risky behaviour is possible, or harmful content is available. Browsers for children such as KidZui offer much the same functionality as the filtering software discussed above: they allow parents to check which sites their child has visited, offer time restrictions on Internet use, and enable parents to create lists of sites or keywords to be blocked.

---

27 Cf. Yeung 2011, p. 7.

28 Cf. Livingstone and Haddon 2009b.

29 Zittrain and Palfrey 2008, p. 44.

30 Livingstone and Haddon 2009b, p. 26.

31 See www.kidzui.com (last accessed on 12 June 2013).

32 The Netherlands has its own browser especially designed for children, called MyBee (see www.mybee.nl (last accessed on 12 June 2013)). This browser was created and is owned by KPN, the Netherlands' largest cable and telephone company.

33 Burt 2010.

Fig. 4.4 The home screen of the KidZui children's browser

What's more, some browsers for children, such as the Buddy Browser,[34] contain locking scripts, which, if switched on by the parent, make it impossible for children to launch any other browser on the computer, such as Firefox or Internet Explorer. What sets apart these browsers from filtering software, of course, is that they provide a fenced-in Internet environment for children, rather than a browser add-on for parents.

Browsers for children are a clear-cut example of techno-regulation. By allowing children to access the Internet only through software that is designed especially for them, they cannot but stay within the boundaries set by the technology. They have no alternative but to 'colour inside the lines'. Browsers for children do not use mechanisms of persuasion or nudging. Children are not invited to behave in certain ways or discouraged to behave in others, nor are they guided and influenced by 'benign' default settings. The 'fence' that these walled gardens provide is hard-coded, and hence leaves no room for manoeuvring, no choice on how to behave, and no space for risk—not for encountering risks, nor for acting in a risky manner. The action space that children have is literally and figuratively defined in and through the code.

There are clear advantages to using kids' browsers. It is a safe and secure way for children to 'experiment' with the Internet—but the reason why 'experiment' is between inverted commas is, of course, that their experimenting is significantly limited and explicitly regulated. For older children and especially for teenagers the boundaries set by browsers for children are clearly too stringent, since for them the balance between security and protection on the one hand and freedom to explore and experiment on the other tips towards the latter rather than the former. For

[34] See www.buddybrowser.com/Free-Parental-Controls.cfm (last accessed on 12 June 2013).

younger children, however, many parents feel that experimentation is less important than safety, and for them using a specially designed browser for children is a workable, effective tool.

4.3.3 Using Ports and Zoning

As we have seen above, filtering and blocking software has clear limitations in its level of protectiveness; overblocking and underblocking are the main issues. Because of this, Cheryl B. Preston came up with another idea.[35] She proposes that it is better to prevent undesirable information from getting into the computer in the first place, because that way kids cannot circumvent it, it is not necessary for parents to know about filters or other technical measures, and there is no risk of overblocking or underblocking. One way to accomplish this, says Preston, is to cut up the Internet into different 'zones', based on different types of content. This could work, according to Preston, through the use of one of the key architectural features of the Internet: ports. A port is a "virtual entranceway between [one's] computer and the Internet".[36] Currently, ports are mainly used to distinguish between different types of *information*. For example port 80 is used for html traffic, while ports 25 and 110 are used for email traffic, and port 21 is used for file transfers (FTP). Secure information, such as credit card information, travels over its own specified ports, and some institutions, such as government agencies and the military also use designated ports to keep their information from prying eyes.[37] For purposes of the idea of zoning the Internet, it is important to note that in the current architecture of the Internet, "all standard Web content [i.e. content in html] uses the same port for transmission – port 80. Whether it is sport scores, financial information, news, children's programming, or pornography on the Web, the information packets are transmitted over port 80".[38] However, this is not an architectural necessity. There are over 65,000 ports that can be used for the transmission of information, but only a fraction of that number is currently in use.[39] Preston argues that we could use ports not only to distinguish between different types of information, as we do today, but also between different types of *content*. This way certain types of content, i.e. especially types of content that could be labelled offensive or harmful to some audiences (e.g. children, teenagers), could be channelled into the computer only via certain ports, and this would provide greater control over the management and blockage of this content. By routing different types of content via different ports the Internet would effectively

---

35 Preston 2007.

36 Gralla 2007, p. 312.

37 Preston 2007.

38 Preston 2007, p. 1431.

39 Cf. Gralla 2007; Nunziato 2008.

be divided into different zones. Users could open or close ports to their computer, and thus have control over the type of content that will enter their machines. If a user would decide to close off specific ports, (s)he would no longer be exposed to content (s)he deemed unwelcome, risky or harmful, for example to online pornographic materials. As Preston points out, this is a fool-proof solution: "Access is impossible, rather than subject to imperfect computer-installed filters, which users can hack past, circumvent, or disable, and which must be regularly updated and monitored."[40]

Using ports to create different content zones is a yet another clear example of techno-regulation. One cannot but 'obey' this form of regulation, because information simply does not enter the household anymore, and unwanted information is screened so effectively at the gateway into the computer that workarounds or accidental transgressions are made impossible. As Nunziato remarks "Unlike user-based filtering software, which users (especially teenage users) frequently disable with ease, port-filtering software [...] is much more difficult to circumvent."[41] It could therefore be an efficient, effective and fool-proof way of preventing children from encountering content that is deemed inappropriate for them.[42]

However, Preston's proposal received critique from several directions. First, there are technical questions surrounding the labelling of different types of content. Such labelling is required to make distinctions between different types or content and routing them via different ports. Distinguishing between content that is 'harmful to minors' and content that is 'not harmful to minors' entails that providers must be able to draw clear lines between these two categories. In many cases, this will not be too difficult, but in some cases it may very well be. For example, it is virtually impossible to provide a clear-cut definition of what counts as pornography and what does not. Second, there is a legal implication in being unable to delineate clearly what counts as harmful content, in terms of penalties for the content provider or site owner. Since the penalties of inadvertently passing on information that is 'harmful to children' would be high, Nunziato points out that, if zoning the Internet according to Preston's proposal would materialise, then almost all website owners would remove their content from the old port 80. Instead, they would start passing on their content via designated other ports, merely to avoid the risk of accidentally making their information available to a child that considers it 'harmful' in some way or other, and hence get sued.[43] While this is obviously not the intended goal of Preston's proposal, it is a realistic side-effect and one of the reasons why it will be difficult to create a workable system of Internet zones. Third, and most importantly for this chapter, zoning the Internet would remove a large degree of control over the management of content from parents and educators, and place it in the hands of the government, and the Internet service

[40] Preston 2007, p. 1432.

[41] Nunziato 2008, p. 1573.

[42] Also see Weekes 2003.

[43] Nunziato 2008.

providers complying to the government's rules instead. But is this really a good idea? Should we not let parents themselves decide, and take responsibility for the media consumption of their children? Using ports is, potentially, and even cruder mechanism than using filtering or blocking software. Literally all content that is deemed potentially harmful to children will become unavailable to children and teenagers. No 'experimenting' of any kind is available to kids and youngsters in such an (online) environment. No nudging, no persuasive mechanisms are available to them. Zoning would obliterate any possibility to experiment and discover, which, as we have also seen when discussing the use of kids' browsers, is especially problematic for teenagers. Most parents tend to gradually allow an increased level and potential of (online) risks as their children grow older, to help them grow into resilient adolescents and to allow them to discover novel topics as befitting their age. Using ports does not allow for such gradual exposure to more (potential) risk. 'Risky' content is either entirely unavailable or entirely available, with no options in between. This makes it a very effective and efficient form of ensuring children's safety online, yet one with no room to spare for any freedom to choose or experiment whatsoever.

4.4 Evaluating the Use of Technological Tools for Online Child Safety

In this chapter, I have discussed several examples of technical tools that are used on, or in relation to, the Internet, to ensure (greater) safety for children. As we have seen all of these rely heavily on techno-regulatory solutions, that is, they hard-code what can and cannot be done with the technology to ensure that children 'colour inside the lines' defined by parents, educators, regulators and/or technology-designers. In the last part of this chapter, I will discuss the merits and shortcomings of these solutions and provide some thoughts on potential alternative approaches to keeping children and teenagers safe on the Internet.

4.4.1 Effective Does Not Mean Absolutely Safe

As I have argued at the beginning of this chapter tools for 'technological influencing' are often adopted by technology designers, regulators and policy makers because they offer a very efficient, effective, cheap and fool-proof means to ensure that individuals will act in a desired fashion or refrain from acting in an undesired fashion. By implementing rules and regulations into technological artefacts the enforcement thereof is delegated to these artefacts, and the more strict the enforcement is made, the greater the chance of compliance. Especially in light of the latter it is unsurprising that in the case of increasing demands for child safety on the Internet a choice is generally made to use techno-regulation as the preferred technical means to bring this about. Techno-regulation does not leave room for manoeuvring, as we have seen, and hence provides a fool-proof and very effective way to make sure that children do not encounter risky situations or engage in risky behaviours on the Internet.

Of course, any technical system can be hacked or circumvented and thus even techno-regulatory solutions for the protection of children and teenagers on the Internet are not entirely fail-safe. Of the examples discussed in this chapter, as we have seen, filtering and blocking software is the 'weakest' solution. It can be circumvented by tech-savvy children, and hence has more limited techno-regulatory force than kids' browsers or using ports to zone different types of content. But for most children, most of the time, any of these technical safety measures provide a set of boundaries they cannot and will not (be able to) cross. Moreover, note that for a technical solution to be effective it need not be perfect. As Adam Thierer remarks:

> instead of thinking of [...] technological controls as absolute barriers, it makes more sense to think of them in terms of training wheels and speed bumps. In other words, if we want to make our kids slow down and be more cautious, we can affix training wheels to their bikes when they are young and add more speed bumps along the roads they travel once they start to drive. But even with training wheels, kids will still fall off their bikes sometimes. And long after they learn how to ride without training wheels and have given up their bikes for cars, speed bumps can only slow them down so much; they won't stop them from speeding entirely.[44]

The fact that techno-regulatory solutions to protect children may not always be 100 % effective is important to note, though, since such measures may evoke a illusory sense of security in parents and educators that is unjustified. What's more, by relying heavily on techno-regulatory solutions only, parents and educators may forget that they also have responsibilities in increasing children's media literacy and digital skills. After all, when the technology ensures that children cannot but colour inside the lines, parents and educators need not concern themselves with raising children's awareness of potential risks and risky behaviours on the Internet, thus precluding their development into tech-savvy, risk-aware and resilient adolescents. An overly strong focus on technical means to increase the safety of children and teenagers online, therefore, leads to risks for both parents and educators, and for the children themselves. This is why policy makers and regulators must combine the use of technical solutions with educational programs for both children themselves and their parents and educators. Thierer calls such a more integrated approach the '3E Solution': education, empowerment and enforcement.[45]

---

[44] Thierer 2009, p. 56.

[45] Thierer 2009, p. 195, also see Thierer 2013.

4.4.2 A Need to Run Risks?

But this is not the only issue with the current technical means implemented to improve child safety online. As we have seen in the examples discussed in this chapter, all technical tools for child safety on the Internet use techno-regulatory solutions, i.e. they hard-code an action space for children and teenagers, leaving them no room to behave other than within the boundaries defined by that (risk-free) space. The rest of the spectrum of technological influencing, and most importantly nudging or using persuasion to evoke children to behave in certain ways is currently not used. This is a serious shortcoming indeed. Experts in online child safety consistently emphasise that it is vital to balance children's ability to freely explore and experiment with the potential of the Internet, lest they become competent Internet users on the one hand, and to protect them from harm on the other. However, in the current practice techno-regulatory solutions for child safety are the standard, and hence all emphasis is on the latter, at the expense of the former.

Using technical tools to increase child safety on the Internet is efficient and effective, yet the choice of tools to be used should be broadened, maybe not for small children, but certainly for older ones and teenagers. Using nudging or persuasion, instead of techno-regulation only, would provide several benefits. First and foremost, (older) children and teenagers would have more freedom to experiment and discover and in the process to become more competent, risk-aware and resilient while protective measures for their security would still be in place. They could be persuaded or nudged towards 'safe(r)' behaviours, yet experience more room for manoeuvring than is the case with techno-regulatory solutions. This could lead to a second benefit, viz. the fact that teenagers could learn about risks and risky behaviour in the process. When risky behaviours or situations are 'coded away', children and teenagers have no possibility of encountering them, nor even reflecting on them, because they are simply not part of their online reality. When using nudging or persuasion, teenagers could be actively invited to reflect on Internet risks and hence make more informed decisions on how to behave on the Internet and how to avoid risks in the future. In the end, the goal of using technological tools to increase child safety on the Internet ought not just to be to protect our children from harm, but also to help them grow into adults that are risk-aware and can protect themselves. Technical tools can play a fruitful role in accomplishing this goal, especially when they don't force but rather invite, nudge and convince children and teenagers to behave in ways that will strengthen their digital skills. A move away from techno-regulatory solutions, and towards persuasive technologies and nudging solutions, therefore, could be a worthwhile contribution to improving child safety on the Internet.

References

Amir O, Lobel O (2009) Stumble, predict, nudge: how behavioral economics informs law and policy. Columbia Law Rev 108:2098–2139

Brownsword R (2008) So what does the world need now? Reflections on regulating technologies. In: Brownsword R, Yeung K (eds) Regulating technologies: legal futures, regulatory frames and technological fixes. Hart, Oxford, pp 23–46

Burgess A (2012) 'Nudging' healthy lifestyles: the UK experiments with the behavioural alternative to regulation and the market. Eur J Risk Regul 3(1):3–30

Burt D (2010) Kid safe browsers: product comparison 2010. http://filteringfacts.files.wordpress.com/2010/02/pckidsafebrowsers2010.pdf

Deibert R, Palfrey J, Rohozinski R, Zittrain J (2008) Access denied: the practice and policy of global Internet filtering. The information revolution and global politics. MIT Press, Cambridge, MA

Duffy BR (2003) Anthropomorphism and the social robot. Robot Auton Syst 42:177–190

Fogg BJ (2003) Persuasive technology: using computers to change what we think and do. The Morgan Kaufmann series in interactive technologies. Morgan Kaufmann, Amsterdam, Boston

Friedman B, Millett L (1995) 'It's the computer's fault'—reasoning about computers as moral agents. Paper read at Conference companion of the conference on human factors in computing systems: CHI'95, May 1995, New York

Friedman B, Kahn Jr PH, Hagman J (2003) Hardware companions? What online AIBO discussion forums reveal about the human-robotic relationship. Paper read at computer-human interaction (CHI) conference 2003, 5–10 April, Ft. Lauderdale, FA

Gralla P (2007) How the Internet works, 8th edn. Que Pub, Indianapolis

Hasebrink U, Görzig A, Haddon L, Kalmus V, Livingstone S (2011) Patterns of risk and safety online: in-depth analyses from the EU kids online survey of 9- to 16-year olds and their parents in 25 European countries. EU kids online. LSE, London

Hildebrandt M (2008) A vision of ambient law. In: Brownsword R, Yeung K (eds) Regulating technologies. Legal futures, regulatory frames and technological fixes. Hart, Oxford, pp 175–192

Hildebrandt M (2009) Technology and the end of law. In: Claes E, Devroe W, Keirsbilck B (eds) Facing the limits of the law. Springer, Berlin, Heidelberg

Hildebrandt M (2011) Legal protection by design: objections and refutations. Legisprudence 5(2):223–249

ITU (2009) Guidelines for policy makers on child online protection. www.itu.int/osg/csd/cybersecurity/gca/cop/guidelines/policy_makers.pdf

Latour B (1992) Where are the missing masses? The sociology of a few mundane artifacts. In: Bijker WE, Law J (eds) Shaping technology/building society: studies in sociotechnical change. MIT Press, Cambridge, MA

Leenes R (2010) Harde lessen: apologie van technologie als reguleringsinstrument. Universiteit van Tilburg, Tilburg

Leenes R (2011) Framing techno-regulation: an exploration of state and non-state regulation by technology. Legisprudence 5(2):143–169

Lessig L (2006) Code: version 2.0, 2nd edn. Basic Books, New York

Livingstone S, Haddon L (2009a) Conclusions. In: Livingstone S, Haddon L (eds) In kids online: opportunities and risks for children. The Policy Press, Bristol

Livingstone S, Haddon L (2009b) EU kids online: Final report. In EU kids online. EC safer internet plus programme deliverable D6.5. LSE, London

Livingstone S, Haddon L, Görzig A, Ólafsson K (2011) Risks and safety on the internet: the perspective of European children. Full findings. In EU kids online. LSE, London

Morgan B, Yeung K (2007) Regulatory instruments and techniques. In: Morgan B, Yeung K (eds) An introduction to law and regulation: text and materials. Cambridge University Press, Cambridge, pp 79–150

Nass CI, Moon Y (2000) Machines and mindlessness: social responses to computers. J Soc Issues 56(1):81–103

Nass CI, Steuer J, Tauber ER, Reeder H (1993) Anthropomorphism, agency, and ethopoeia: computers as social actors. Paper read at computer-human interaction (CHI) conference 1993. Amsterdam, The Netherlands

Nass CI, Steuer J, Henriksen L, Dryer DC (1994a) Machines, social attributions, and ethopoeia: performance assessments of computers subsequent to 'self-' or 'other-' evaluations. Int J Hum Comput Stud 40(3):543–559

Nass CI, Steuer J, Tauber ER (1994b) Computers are social actors. Paper read at computer-human interaction (CHI) conference: Celebrating interdependence. Boston, MA

Nunziato DC (2008) Technology and pornography. Brigham Young University Law Review 1535–1585

OECD (2011) The protection of children online: risks faced by children online and policies to protect them. www.oecd.org/sti/ieconomy/protectingchildrenonline.htm

Preston CB (2007) Zoning the internet: a new approach to protecting children online. Brigham Young University Law Review 1417–1467

Reeves B, Nass CI (1996) The media equation: how people treat computers, television, and new media like real people and places. CSLI Publications/Cambridge University Press, Stanford/ New York

Thaler RH, Sunstein CR (2008) Nudge: improving decisions about health, wealth, and happiness. Yale University Press, New Haven, CT

Thierer A (2009) Parental controls and online child protection. In PFF special report. The Progress & Freedom Foundation, Washington, DC

Thierer A (2013) The pursuit of privacy in a world where information control is failing. Harvard J Law Public Policy 36(2):409–456

Turkle S (1984) The second self: computers and the human spirit. Simon and Schuster, New York

Turkle S (2007) Evocative objects: things we think with. MIT Press, Cambridge, MA

Van den Berg B (2010a) I-object: intimate technologies as 'reference groups' in the construction of identities. Technè 14(3):176–193

Van den Berg B (2010b) The situated self: identity in a world of ambient intelligence. Wolf Legal Publishers, Nijmegen

Van den Berg B (2011) Robots as tools for techno-regulation. Law Innov Technol 3(2):317–332

Van den Berg B, Leenes R (2010) Audience segregation in social network sites. In: Proceedings for SocialCom2010/PASSAT2010, Second IEEE international conference on social computing/second IEEE international conference on privacy, security, risk and trust. IEEE, Minneapolis, MI

Van den Berg B, Leenes R (2011) Masking in social network sites: translating a real-world social practice to the online domain. IT Inf Technol (1):26–34

Van den Berg B, Leenes R (2013) Abort, retry, fail: scoping techno-regulation and other techno-effects. In: Hildebrandt M, Gaakeer J (eds) Human law and computer law: comparative perspectives. Springer, Berlin, pp 67–88

Verbeek P-P (2005) What things do: philosophical reflections on technology, agency, and design. Pennsylvania State University Press, University Park, PA

Weekes RB (2003) Cyber-zoning a mature domain: the solution to preventing inadvertant access to sexually explicit content on the internet? Virginia J Law Technol 8(1)

Yeung K (2008) Towards an understanding of regulation by design. In: Brownsword R, Yeung K (eds) Regulating technologies: legal futures, regulatory frames and technological fixes. Hart, Oxford, pp 79–108

Yeung K (2011) Can we employ design-based regulation while avoiding brave new world? Law Innov Technol 3(1):1–29

Yeung K (2012) Nudge as fudge. Mod Law Rev 75(1):122–148

Zittrain J, Palfrey J (2008) Internet filtering: the Politics and mechanisms of control. In: Deibert R, Palfrey J, Rohozinski R, Zittrain J (eds) Access denied: the practice and policy of global Internet filtering. MIT Press, Cambridge, MA, pp 29–56

Part II
Encountering Risk Versus Engaging in Risky Behaviour

Chapter 5
Safety by Literacy? Rethinking the Role of Digital Skills in Improving Online Safety

Nathalie Sonck and Jos de Haan

Contents

Dr. Nathalie Sonck is a senior media researcher in the Care, Emancipation and Time Use research group at the Netherlands Institute for Social Research/SCP. Professor Dr. Jos de Haan is Head of the Care, Emancipation and Time Use research group at the Netherlands Institute for Social Re search/SCP and a Professor at Erasmus University Rotterdam.

N. Sonck (✉) · J. de Haan
Netherlands Institute for Social Research/SCP, The Hague, The Netherlands
e-mail: n.sonck@scp.nl

S. van der Hof et al. (eds.), *Minding Minors Wandering the Web: Regulating Online Child Safety*, Information Technology and Law Series 24, DOI: 10.1007/978-94-6265-005-3_5,

5.1 Digital Skills and Online Safety: An Indistinct Relationship

It is generally assumed that children can avoid negative consequences from using the Internet by acquiring and improving their digital skills. These skills are part of the broader concept of digital literacy.[1] They encompass several types of skills or dimensions, ranging from basic skills to strategic skills, related to the technology of computers and the Internet, as well as to the use and evaluation of information online.[2] Due to the current characteristics of interactive—Web 2.0—Internet use, digital skills also increasingly comprise social skills and the creative skills needed to produce and upload content to the Web.[3] Some publications do not support the assumption that more skills mean fewer Internet risks. In fact they suggest precisely the opposite, namely that more skills are associated with more risks.[4]

The main questions addressed in this chapter are: To what extent do children acquire the skills needed to use the Internet safely? How do the different types of skills relate to online risk experience? How can children learn to master the skills needed to use the Internet safely?

In this chapter, we focus particularly on the situation in the Netherlands, as this country ranks among the highest scorers for Internet penetration and use, both among the general public and among young people. Dutch Internet penetration increased from 69 % of all individuals aged between 12 and 75 years in 2002 to 95 % in 2011,[5] with virtually all Dutch teenagers accessing the Internet at home.[6] Among Dutch, 9–16 year olds who use the Internet, 80 % do so (almost) every day and 56 % use the Internet in their own bedroom. More than a third of Dutch young people go online using a mobile phone or another hand-held device.[7] These high Internet access figures might implicitly suggest that children are also automatically highly skilled in using the Internet safely. In this chapter, we present some empirical findings about children's mastery of the different dimensions of digital skills. We will then explore the relationship between skills and online safety, as well as the implications for children's acquiring of digital literacy via peers, parents, schools, government and industry.

---

[1] Sonck et al. 2012a.

[2] Steyaert 2000; Van Deursen 2010.

[3] De Haan et al. 2011.

[4] Livingstone and Helsper 2010; Sonck and De Haan 2012a.

[5] CBS 2012, p. 104.

[6] Livingstone and Haddon 2009.

[7] Livingstone et al. 2011.

5.2 Mastering Skills

In order to address the question of which digital skills children master, we need to distinguish between different types or dimensions of skills. Broadly, skills can be divided into three dimensions[8]: instrumental, structural/informational and strategic skills.

5.2.1 *Instrumental Skills*

First, there are instrumental skills, which refer to the ability to use the technology of computers and the Internet. These skills are also called operational skills.[9] They relate primarily to the ability to install programmes and click the correct buttons.

Duimel and De Haan[10] observed that almost all teenagers (13–18 years old) in the Netherlands have a mastery of the basic instrumental skills needed to add pictures to a document (97 %), move sentences within a document (94 %) and compile an e-mailing list (89 %). However, a much smaller proportion of Dutch teenagers have mastered the rather more complex instrumental skills needed to install an anti-virus programme (56 %) or a new version of Windows (54 %) or to install a hard drive in a computer (28 %). Compared with the reports from parents on their own skills, more teenagers indicate they are able to perform these basic and complex instrumental activities. The only exception is that more fathers than teenagers indicate that they are able to install software and hardware on a computer.[11]

International research corroborates the findings concerning the mastery of basic skills. The large-scale European EU Kids Online survey[12] provides an indication of mainly safety-related instrumental skills. For this study, children aged between 11 and 16 years were asked to assess their ability to perform specific tasks on the Internet. Most Dutch teenagers reported that they were able to block messages from people they do not wish to hear from (87 %), bookmark websites (85 %),

[8] Steyaert 2000; Van Deursen 2010.

[9] Van Deursen and Van Dijk 2010.

[10] In 2001, 2005 and 2008, students from all levels of secondary education (13–18 year olds) were interviewed at an average of 50 schools throughout the Netherlands. About 1,500 children were surveyed in each wave, and in 2005 one of their parents was also surveyed ($n = 1100$). The survey was part of a broader academic research project (Young People and Culture—Jongeren en Cultuur) conducted by researchers from VU University Amsterdam. Duimel and De Haan 2009.

[11] Duimel and De Haan 2009.

[12] In the EU Kids Online survey, a random stratified sample of 25,142 children aged 9–16 years who use the Internet were interviewed during the spring and summer of 2010 in 25 European countries. In the Netherlands, 1,004 children were interviewed, partly face-to-face and partly by means of a self-administered written questionnaire. For more information about this European project, see www.eukidsonline.net. Livingstone et al. 2011.

find information about using the Internet safely (79 %) and change the privacy settings for a social networking profile (78 %). A minority of teenagers reported that they had mastered the skills to change filter settings (30 %), which illustrates once again that they are not very Internet savvy when it comes to the rather more complex instrumental skills.[13]

5.2.2 *Structural/Informational Skills*

The second skill dimension comprises structural skills, which relate to the unique structure of the Internet, with hyperlinks and dynamic information that need to be accessed and used differently from offline information. On one hand, this set of competences comprises formal Internet skills, or the competency to navigate the Web. On the other hand, it also refers to informational or evaluation skills, i.e. the ability to evaluate the reliability of information found on websites and to cross-reference information correctly (e.g. mentioning the source of information).

Although both teenagers and parents in the Netherlands say they check several search results to verify online information (63 and 69 %, respectively), only a minority of teenagers check more than just the first page of search engine results (32 %) or check who placed the information online when they find useful information (26 %). By contrast a majority of parents (59 and 51 %, respectively) report that they do this.[14] Walraven et al. observed similar findings in Belgium in an actual skill measurement test focusing on informational skills among secondary school students.[15] Although young people report that they are aware of the criteria necessary for evaluating information, they do not apply those criteria very often when searching for online information. The results indicated that the students did not evaluate search results or the source and the content of websites on the Internet very frequently, for example.[16] In another test involving secondary school students, it was found that websites were only evaluated in light of the relevance for the specific task to be performed, not their reliability in general. The researchers found that during the assignments, many students literally overlooked the right answer or missed the link where the answer could be found. Furthermore, students merely scanned the websites rather than reading them in detail.[17] These results suggest that young persons perform particularly poorly on informational (structural) skills. Somewhat rhetorically, the Joint Information Systems Committee concludes that young people have a poor understanding of their information needs, find it difficult to develop effective search strategies and spend little time on

13 Sonck and De Haan 2011.

14 Duimel and De Haan 2009.

15 Walraven et al. 2009.

16 Walraven et al. 2009.

17 Kuiper et al. 2008.

evaluating information, either for its relevance, accuracy or authority.[18] Having a mastery of basic instrumental skills does not guarantee adequate handling of content.

5.2.3 Strategic Skills

Finally, strategic skills relate to the capacity to apply digital skills in everyday life. Examples are benefiting financially from comparing products online, or saving time after checking timetables online (e.g. for trains). In such cases, people need to search for information proactively and take decisions based on this information that have consequences in real life.[19]

A specific example of strategic skills is using the Internet to compare the quality and price of products. Dutch parents, and especially fathers, compare different handsets online when they are looking to buy a mobile phone (73 % of parents; 86 % of fathers), and search online to see whether they can find an item cheaper than in a traditional shop (71 % of parents; 79 % of fathers). Their children (13–18 year olds) say they perform these comparisons on the Internet less frequently (64 % for buying a mobile phone and 52 % for online searches).[20] The differences between generations might be due to adults having more purchasing opportunities, but might also point to a more careless attitude among young people. They certainly do not support the image of young people as 'digital natives' who have an easy mastery of all aspects of digital life, while their parents, as 'digital immigrants', are merely ignorant outsiders.[21] In Dutch research among adults, performance tests revealed that young persons (aged 18–29 years) successfully completed more tasks requiring instrumental skills than older age groups. However, the younger groups performed less well than the older groups in tasks requiring informational and strategic skills.[22] The kind of skills mastered thus clearly differs with age. Children master instrumental skills, but lack capability when it comes to handling information and using online opportunities effectively.

5.2.4 Social Skills

In addition to the three dimensions of digital skills mentioned above, children also need online social skills in order to use the Internet effectively, especially given the

---

[18] Joint Information Systems Committee 2008, p. 12.

[19] Steyaert 2000; Van Deursen 2010.

[20] Duimel and De Haan 2009.

[21] Prensky 2001.

[22] Van Deursen 2010.

increasingly social character of children's Internet use due to the popularity of social network sites (such as Facebook, Twitter, etc.). These online skills mainly relate to communication, self-disclosure and privacy. For example, children need to be aware of current 'netiquette' rules, such as which personal information they should and should not post online and who they should allow to see it (i.e. posting on a public website or a private profile).[23]

Although there is a lack of research on the level of children's online social skills, it has been shown (in the EU Kids Online project) that children use the Internet very frequently to communicate with others. For example, 9–16 year olds in the Netherlands go online to send and receive e-mails (77 %), visit social network sites (74 %) and use messaging services (65 %).[24] Frequent social use of the Internet does not imply that all social contacts will go smoothly. On the contrary, many studies have been conducted into the risks children face online and the harm they might encounter from using social media.[25] There is therefore also scope for improving their online social skills.

5.2.5 *Creative and Production Skills*

Crucial innovations in Web 2.0 include increased interactivity and the possibility of producing user-generated content, which can be disseminated online to a wide public. Consequently, the skills and knowledge to create, produce and upload content have become more important.[26]

Although there are currently a lot of online interactive and creative opportunities, it seems that the general public do not automatically use these possibilities. For example, less than a third of the Dutch adult population (aged 18+) use the Internet actively or creatively to create and upload their self-made pictures, films, music and/or written content.[27] Similarly, among children a relatively small group seem to perform activities online which involve creating new content. For example, only 13 % of Dutch 9–16-year old Internet users write a blog or an online diary, and just 15 % create a virtual character or avatar. Fewer than half (45 %) upload pictures, films or music to share with others, but it is unclear whether or not this content is self-made. In fact, most children use the Internet in a fairly 'receptive' way, in which they do not produce content themselves, for example to watch video clips (89 %) or play games (84 %).

As far as we are aware, creative skills have so far not been taken into account in research on children's online safety, yet a link has been established between basic

---

[23] De Haan et al. 2011.

[24] Sonck and De Haan 2012a; Livingstone et al. 2011.

[25] Walrave 2012.

[26] Sonck and De Haan 2011; Livingstone et al. 2011.

[27] Sonck and De Haan 2012b.

digital skills and the level of online creativity. Teenagers who possess good digital skills are more active in creating new content than teenagers with poor skills. These skills are an important factor in determining which teenagers take part in online creation and which do not. This creative activity is influenced more by the level of digital skills than by the social context, the education level of teenagers or that of their parents.[28] Digital skills can thus be quite a powerful predictor of uploading user-generated content, but do they also prevent young people from getting into trouble on the Internet?

5.3 More Skills, Higher Risks

Young people are exposed to Internet risks to a lesser extent than is often generally assumed (based on media reports about ad hoc incidents). Fewer than a quarter of Dutch Internet users aged between 9 and 16 years say they have seen pornographic images online, while 15 % say they have received sexually explicit messages via the Internet (sexting). A third of Dutch youngsters engage in online contacts with strangers, of whom 6 % actually meet those online contacts in person. Finally, less than 5 % of the young people surveyed reported that they had experienced repeated bullying via the Internet.[29]

Only a minority of children who are exposed to risks actually experience harm as a result of those risks. Most young people are not upset by these experiences, but a small minority are. They report being upset most often by seeing sexually explicit images on the Internet, followed by receiving sexually explicit messages and meeting an online contact in person. Being bullied is seen as a negative experience in itself.[30]

There are some striking differences in risk behaviour between groups of young people. Young people are exposed to or elicit risks on the Internet to differing degrees. The extent to which they undergo negative experiences also varies from one group to another. Boys and older teenagers are particularly exposed to online risks, but girls and younger teenagers more often report that they find these experiences negative.

It is generally assumed that a higher level of digital skills reduces the number of online risks children experience, such as cyberbullying, grooming or violation of privacy.[31] Only a handful of studies have investigated the relationship between skills and risks. Livingstone and Helsper,[32] for example, examined the influence of skills on online opportunities and risks among 12–17 year olds in the UK. They

[28] Schols et al. 2011.

[29] Sonck and De Haan 2011.

[30] Sonck and De Haan 2011.

[31] Hasebrink et al. 2009.

[32] Livingstone and Helsper 2010.

observed that children who have better access, wider usage and more skills seem not only to benefit more from the Internet, but also to exhibit more risky behaviour online. The researchers observed a positive relationship between online opportunities, digital skills and online risks: thus, the more positive experiences children have online and the more skilled they are, the more they also encounter risks online.[33]

Sonck and De Haan reach a similar conclusion based on data collected in 25 European countries.[34] They also investigated to what extent children's self-reported Internet skills influence the degree to which they encounter online risks. It was observed that more experienced and skilled 11–16-year old Internet users also encountered more online risks. For example, young people with a wider online repertoire and a higher level of self-reported Internet skills were found to see more sexual images online or to meet online contacts in person more frequently.[35]

Thus, contrary to the general assumption, both these studies indicate that children with more online experience and a higher claimed level of Internet skills not only benefit more from online opportunities, but also encounter more online risks. This finding should first be placed in a life-course perspective. The diversity of Internet use, the available skills and risk-taking behaviour all increase as children grow older. Young children may encounter more risks by chance, while teenagers may be looking for them consciously. During adolescence, in particular, young people challenge the boundaries of acceptable behaviour and seek the excitement of risk as part of their identity experimentation. As an example, 15-year olds might consider seeing pornography or receiving sexually explicit messages as an opportunity rather than as a risk.

Young people's evaluation of what constitutes risky behaviour is likely to be different from the judgement of adults—first and foremost their parents, but also teachers and researchers who share their evaluation that certain online activities are risky. These differences in risk perception make it difficult to interpret the relationship between risks and skills in an unambiguous way. Digital skills may well be instrumental in prompting teenagers to engage in activities that are positively evaluated by them but disapproved of by parents and others. The positive relationship between the level of digital skills and the risks that young people encounter thus warrants closer inspection.

Not being harmed by what is believed to be risky behaviour is a more clear-cut criterion for assessing negative influences of Internet use, and also for discussing the influence of digital skills. As older children report being less bothered by their experience of risks compared to younger children, the role of online maturity cannot be denied. Older children may be more aware of what they are doing, better able to foresee the potential consequences or more capable of coping with negative outcomes. Awareness, forecasting and coping are relevant capabilities for the

---

[33] Livingstone and Helsper 2010.

[34] Sonck and De Haan 2012a.

[35] Sonck and De Haan 2012a.

prevention of harm from online activities. They differ from the usual indicators for digital skills. Instrumental skills, especially, are unlikely candidates for improving online safety; it would be verging on the absurd to suggest that skills such as 'moving sentences within a document' or 'compiling an e-mailing list' contribute to greater safety. Informational skills are also hedged in with ambivalence. These skills might equally well be used to search for educational material, for entertaining music or for pornographic material. At best, what are described here as online social skills would come closest to a skill base that is effective enough to prevent harm. However, these skills have not yet been adequately measured in research. In general, the issue of digital skills in relation to online safety is too ambivalent. Hence, quantitative research shows no clear influence of skills in preventing harm, and the models show very low explained variance. The conceptual issues (What are relevant skills? Can some abilities be regarded as safety skills?) have to be solved first before the effectiveness of these skills can be properly investigated.

5.4 Policy Implications for Children's Digital Safety

Empirical research has thus far produced inconclusive results with regard to the effectiveness of digital skills in keeping young people safe on the Internet. It has been found that more skills coincide with more risks and have no significant effect in preventing unwanted experiences. Based on the empirical findings presented in this chapter, we suggest a rethink of the relationship between digital skills and online risks. Young people prove to have a different perspective on risks compared to parents, teachers and regulators; improving their digital skills might therefore equally well serve as an encouragement to explore online risks further. Educators need to accept that risks exist and that these risks are part of the increasingly digital lifestyles of young people. Risk-taking behaviour is tied up with their identity experiments. Growing up in a digital age entails encountering online risks and also calls for the development of coping strategies when actual harm is experienced. Avoidance of risks might still be an important task of educators for young children, but for older children prevention from harm through coping strategies should be given more prominence. Our recommendation is to broaden the notion of skills to include the empowerment of children on the Internet when they face harm. We will reflect on the different responsibilities in this regard.

5.4.1 Young People's Own Responsibility

Young people mostly manage by themselves when using computers and the Internet. Furthermore, peers have a substantial influence on how they discover new things to do with the Internet. Mutual learning and teaching practices between peers are common.[36] Such peer-to-peer teaching might improve children's skills in coping with negative experiences online; on the other hand, peers might also encourage each other in undertaking risky online behaviour (e.g. viewing sexual images online).

Exposure of young people to online risks cannot and should not be entirely avoided. However, it is important that if children and teenagers actually feel threatened on the Internet they know where to find help and advice—and, perhaps more importantly, that they should not feel embarrassed about discussing negative experiences openly with others. Offline, they can contact peers, parents or teachers. But online, too, a number of initiatives have been launched to support young people in using the Internet safely. In the Netherlands, for example, there is the website Helpwanted where young people can report online sexual abuse.[37] Additionally, several organisations, including the police, have developed an online reporting button for all kinds of Internet problems. These initiatives can help raise awareness among young people of the opportunity to talk openly about their online experiences.

5.4.2 Mediation by Parents

Children are learning to use computers at an ever younger age, and increasingly also mobile devices, such as tablets and smartphones, by playing with them at home.[38] Consequently, we can attribute a major part of responsibility for children's online safety to parents. Most parental attention is given to 10–11 year old; it is lower before this age and decreases thereafter.[39] Younger children are more susceptible to negative online experiences and more dependent upon their parents for online safety. Exposure to online risks increases during adolescence, but this exposure does not necessarily result in harm. Parents should therefore focus less on avoiding such exposure altogether among older age groups. There are limits to what parents can achieve with these groups, as older teenagers turn away from parents in order to build their own identities and establish their own peer culture. However, this is no reason not to be interested and involved in their digital lives. This involvement and mutual trust can provide a basis for ongoing discussions and thus for improving the online safety of children and teenagers.

Parents can mediate their children's Internet use in several ways. Previous research has found that parents mostly use one or more of the following strategies: active mediation, applying technical restrictions, setting rules about content restrictions and/or monitoring Internet use.[40] By actively mediating children's

[36] De Haan and Huysmans 2002; Kalmus 2012.

[37] www.helpwanted.nl

[38] De Haan and Pijpers 2010.

[39] Hasebrink et al. 2009.

[40] Livingstone and Helsper 2008; Sonck et al. 2012b.

Internet use, parents can give advice and suggestions on using the Internet safely. They discuss potential risks and the harm that can be experienced online. Applying technical restrictions involves using filter software or other systems that block Internet access. Setting rules about content means that parents restrict which websites their children can access or decide whether their children can have a social network profile. Finally, monitoring entails checking the history of websites visited, what messages children have posted or what personal information they have published online.[41] Most of these mediation strategies contribute to the development of skills. Children learn which situations to avoid, what information to ignore and which persons not to 'like' on social network sites. Successful mediation contributes to more awareness of potential problems, better anticipation of risky situations and improved ability to cope with unpleasant events. In short, it contributes to the empowerment of young people.

A possible impediment for parents in seeking to mediate their children's Internet use adequately might be their own digital skills. A lack of these skills is more apparent in countries that occur late on the Internet diffusion curve, such as Estonia,[42] compared to countries that appear early on the curve, such as the Netherlands, where parents are a better source of advice in learning to use the computer.[43] On the other hand, parents everywhere are becoming more familiar with using the Internet. This increasing knowledge may be sufficient to enable them to guide the Internet use of young children, but probably falls short in guiding teenagers' use. Teenagers are often more familiar with social network sites, games and other platforms than their parents. For these media, parents may need to be more aware of which problems their children might face and need more knowledge about how to help them deal with them.[44]

Another obstacle that applies to restrictive mediation and monitoring strategies, in particular, relates to the rapid spread of new technologies and devices for accessing the Internet. As more and more children use their own computers in their bedrooms, and are able to be online any time and anywhere using tablets and smartphones, it becomes increasingly difficult for parents to check and restrict their children's online activities. Consequently, active mediation may become more important in order to empower children to use the Internet safely. In the same way that children need to learn to cope with negative experiences offline, they also need to learn to do so online.

Supporting parents in protecting minors acquired a stronger legal basis with the United Nations Convention on the Rights of the Child, which came into effect in 1990 and was subsequently ratified by almost every country in the world. The Convention sets out the civil, political, economic, social, health and cultural rights of children. It gave governments a responsibility to engage with child-rearing

---

41 Livingstone and Helsper 2008; Sonck et al. 2012b.

42 Kalmus 2012.

43 De Haan and Huysmans 2002.

44 De Haan and Livingstone 2009.

practices and a formal obligation to support parents. In 2011, the European Parliament and the Council issued and approved a new legislative resolution on combating the sexual abuse and exploitation of children, as well as child pornography.[45] In addition to prescribing higher sanctions for perpetrators, the European Parliament realises that making the Internet safer for children also means raising awareness among children and parents about the dangers of the Internet, and that it is necessary to talk about these issues within families.

5.4.3 Support from Schools

Schools can play a role by teaching skills to children and raising awareness among parents about children's online safety.

Children learn all kinds of skills at school, related to reading, writing and mathematics, but also to safe behaviour in different situations (e.g. traffic, sexuality, etc.). One option would be to integrate all aspects of digital skills in one course, but it would also be possible to cover the various skill dimensions in different courses. Dealing with online privacy issues might require different skills from those needed to deal with cyberbullying or with sexually oriented risks online. It is crucial that schools not only target older (e.g. secondary school) students, but also younger (primary school) children, as the age at which children first use the Internet continues to reduce. In most European countries, online safety is part of the obligatory school curriculum. However, there are exceptions, such as the Netherlands.[46] As a consequence, schools might differ greatly in the extent to which they adopt online safety in their school programmes.

In addition, since it has been found that two-thirds of Dutch parents were not aware of their children's negative experiences online,[47] schools could play a greater role in raising awareness, for example by organising information meetings for parents. It is important to reach not only those parents who are already very aware of their children's experiences, but also those who are not, or to a lesser degree. Schools could also report bullying behaviour among children, as it seems that those who are bullied offline are also often bullied online.[48] Also, the value of peer-to-peer teaching could be more effectively resourced and integrated as part of media education in schools.

One potential impediment to school support for safer Internet use by children is the lack of sufficient knowledge and skills among teachers. Although they seem to

---

[45] For more information, see Directive 2011/92/EU of the European Parliament and of the Council of 13 December 2011 on combating the sexual abuse and sexual exploitation of children and child pornography, and replacing Council Framework Decision 2004/68/JHA (OJ L 335/1, 17.12.2011).

[46] Eurydice 2010.

[47] Sonck and De Haan 2011.

[48] Livingstone et al. 2011.

be catching up in terms of their instrumental skills, their more advanced skills may still be deficient. However, there is a lack of research on the mediating role of teachers. New research should focus both on teachers' digital skills and literacy (including their training needs) and on their mediating practices in the classroom.[49]

5.4.4 Co-regulation by Government and Industry

Although governments mostly consider the Internet to be a domain which they cannot or should not regulate closely, the government in the Netherlands explicitly seeks to protect minors from potentially harmful effects of media, including the Internet.[50] For example, under Dutch law, the possession and viewing of child pornography is illegal. Moreover, since 2010, the contacting of minors by adults for sexual purposes (i.e. grooming) has been a criminal offence.

As there are already a lot of ad hoc initiatives to improve digital literacy and online safety of children, the primary task of a government may be to continue, improve and coordinate these initiatives. In the Netherlands, the Ministry of Education, Culture and Science launched a project in 2008 (*Mediawijzer*) aimed at bringing together all the available expertise about media literacy. This turned out to be particularly difficult, since the issue of children's online safety is a responsibility of several ministries, each with a different focus. For example, the Ministry of Security and Justice deals with safer Internet use and illegal behaviour; the Ministry of Education, Culture and Science focuses on media literacy projects and social safety in schools (e.g. protocols for combating cyberbullying); the Ministry of Security and Justice deals with privacy issues; the Ministry of Economic Affairs addresses misleading mobile services and other consumer issues and the Ministry of Health, Welfare and Sport is concerned with youth programmes and problems within families. Such governmental fragmentation does nothing to contribute to an integrated approach to children's online safety.

Given the global character of the Internet, it is crucial that governments and industry cooperate at an international level. Through co-regulation they could and should work proactively on issues concerning online safety. An important development in this regard is the recent establishment by EC Vice-President Neelie Kroes of an industry coalition of 28 leading Internet companies in Europe to take action in five specific areas in a commitment to make the Internet a better and safer place for kids: (1) Simple and robust reporting tools; (2) Age-appropriate privacy settings; (3) Wider use of content classification; (4) Wider availability and use of parental controls and (5) Effective takedown of child abuse material.

---

[49] De Haan and Livingstone 2009.

[50] TK 2010.

5.4.5 Conclusion and Discussion

This chapter has shown that although children may have the reputation of being Internet-savvy users, there is substantial doubt about their actual skill levels. On somewhat closer inspection, they seem to rely on their fathers for more complex instrumental skills, and lack sufficient capability to handle information and effectively use a wide variety of online opportunities. Furthermore, their online social skills are in need of improvement and their creative skills need to be strengthened if they are to become content producers themselves. As children grow older their digital skills increase, but so does their online risk behaviour. Living in a mobile youth culture has brought their identity play and associated risk-seeking behaviour to a wide variety of online platforms.[51] Children with more online experience and a higher claimed level of Internet skills not only benefit more from online opportunities, but also encounter more online risks. Empirical research has also found no significant effect of digital skills in preventing unwanted experiences.

These unexpected findings give rise to reflections both on the research methodology and the policy implications. In this chapter we have suggested that a careful examination of conceptual and measurement problems in relation to digital skills is needed. The wide variety of these skills related to participating in different online settings is in need of better definitions. Which safety skills are needed to keep children safe on the Internet, and are these the same for every platform or application? As quantitative research stumbles along with rather crude measurements, a closer examination through qualitative research might shed more light on the protective potential of digital skills. An exploration by way of open interviews seems appropriate and might yield better measurement instruments for quantitative research.

Notwithstanding the outcomes of empirical research, improving digital skills is still seen as a form of empowerment and a possible contribution to online safety. It is still important to strengthen young people's sense of responsibility for their online behaviour. For young children, protection by parents seems more appropriate, although they could also improve the online agency of their children. Most parents mediate their children's Internet use, but many of them might be uncertain about the most appropriate approach. A minority of parents are unable or unwilling to act, and their children might be the most vulnerable online. Luckily, parents are not on their own. A web of advice has been built around parents, raising their awareness and knowledge and skill levels is seen as relevant by both policymakers and industry. Teachers are in a vitally important position, both for improving children's skills and raising awareness among parents and stimulating strategies to keep their children safe. With combined efforts, it seems clear that online safety will benefit from digital literacy.

---

[51] Castells et al. 2007.

References

Castells M, Fernandez-Ardevol M, Linchuan Qiu J, Sey A (2007) Mobile communication and society: a global perspective. The MIT Press, Cambridge

CBS (2012) ICT, knowledge and the economy 2012. Statistics Netherlands, The Hague

De Haan J, Huysmans F (2002) Van huis uit digitaal: Verwerving van digitale vaardigheden tussen thuismilieu en school [Home-based skills: Acquiring digital skills at home or at school]. Netherlands Institute for Social Research, The Hague

De Haan J, Livingstone S (2009) Policy and research recommendations. LSE/EU Kids Online, London

De Haan J, Pijpers R (2010) Contact!: children and new media. Bohn Stafleu van Loghum, Houten

De Haan J, Kuiper E, Pijpers R (2011) Young children and their digital skills in the Netherlands. Int J Media Cult Polit 3(3):327–333

Duimel M, De Haan J (2009) Instrumental, information and strategic ICT skills of teenagers and their parents. Paper presented at the EU kids online conference in London

Eurydice (2010) Education on online safety in schools in Europe. Summary report. Education, Audiovisual and Cultural Executive Agency (EACEA), Brussels

Hasebrink U, Livingstone S, Haddon L, Ólafsson K (2009) Comparing children's online opportunities and risks across Europe. Cross-national comparisons for EU kids online, deliverable D3.2, 2nd edn. EU kids online, London

Joint Information Systems Committee (2008). Information behaviour of the researcher of the future. UK: Joint Information Systems Committee. http://www.jisc.ac.uk/media/documents/programmes/reppres/gg_final_keynote_11012008.pdf

Kalmus V (2012) 'Estonian adolescents' expertise in the internet in comparative perspective. Cyberpsychology: J Psychosoc Res Cyberspace 1(1). www.cyberpsychology.eu/view.php?cisloclanku=2007070702&article=3. Accessed 14 Aug 2012

Kuiper E, Volman M, Terwel J (2008) Students' use of web literacy skills and strategies: searching, reading and evaluating web information. Information research, paper 351, 13(3)

Livingstone S, Haddon L (2009) EU kids online: final report. LSE/EU kids online, London

Livingstone S, Helsper E (2008) Parental mediation and children's internet use. J Broadcast Electron Media 52(4):581–599

Livingstone S, Helsper E (2010) Balancing opportunities and risks in teenagers' use of the Internet: the role of online skills and family context. New Media Soc 12(2):309–329

Livingstone S, Haddon L, Görzig A, Ólafsson K (2011) Risks and safety on the internet. The perspective of European children. Full findings and policy implications from the EU kids online survey of 9-16 year-olds and their parents in 25 countries. LSE/EU kids online, London

Prensky M (2001) Digital natives, digital immigrants. On the Horizon 9(5):1–6

Schols M, Duimel M, De Haan J (2011) Hoe cultureel is de digitale generatie? [How cultural is the digital generation?]. Netherlands Institute for Social Research, The Hague

Sonck N, De Haan J (2011) Kinderen en internetrisico's [Children and Internet risks]. Netherlands Institute for Social Research, The Hague

Sonck N, De Haan J (2012a) How digital skills mediate between online risk and harm. J Child Media (special issue). doi:10.1080/17482798.2012.739783

Sonck N, De Haan J (2012b) De virtuele kunstkar: Cultuurdeelname via oude en nieuwe media [The virtual culture consumer: Cultural participation through old and new media]. The Netherlands Institute for Social Research, The Hague

Sonck N, Kuiper E, De Haan J (2012a) Digital skills in the context of media literacy. In: Livingstone S, Haddon L, Görzig A (eds) Children, risk and safety online: research and policy challenges in comparative perspective. Polity Press, Bristol, pp 87–98

Sonck N, Nikken P, De Haan J (2012b) Determinants of internet mediation: a comparison of the reports by parents and children. J Child Media (special issue). doi:10.1080/17482798.2012.739806

Steyaert J (2000) Digitale vaardigheden: geletterdheid in de informatiesamenleving [Digital skills: Literacy in the information society]. Rathenau Institute, The Hague

TK [Lower House of Dutch Parliament] (2010) Mediabeleid. Brief van de staatssecretaris van onderwijs, cultuur en wetenschap, 32 033, nr. 4 [Media policy. Letter from the state secretary for education, culture and science]. The Hague

Van Deursen A (2010) Internet skills: vital assets in an information society. Ph.D. thesis. University of Twente, Enschede

Van Deursen A, Van Dijk J (2010) Measuring internet skills. Int J Hum Comput Interact 26(10):891–916

Walrave M (2012) eYouth: between trust, concern and science. In: Walrave M, Heirman W, Mels S, Timmermann C, Vandebosch H (eds) eYouth: balancing between opportunities and risks. P.I.E Peter Lang, Brussels

Walraven A, Brand-Gruwel S, Boshuizen E (2009) How students evaluate sources and information when searching the world wide web for information. Comput Educ 52(1):234–246

Chapter 6
Taking Risks on the World Wide Web: The Impact of Families and Societies on Adolescents' Risky Online Behavior

Natascha Notten

Contents

Natascha Notten is Assistant Professor at Radboud University Nijmegen, Department of Sociology. A different and Dutch version of this study was published as: N. Notten, *Risicogedrag en het wereldwijde web. De invloed van gezin en samenleving op het online risicogedrag van adolescenten vanuit een Europees perspectief.* Mens & Maatschappij, 88(4):350–374.

N. Notten (✉)
Radboud University Nijmegen, Nijmegen, The Netherlands
e-mail: n.notten@maw.ru.nl

S. van der Hof et al. (eds.), *Minding Minors Wandering the Web: Regulating Online Child Safety*, Information Technology and Law Series 24, DOI: 10.1007/978-94-6265-005-3_6,

6.1 Introduction

Internet offers children a wealth of opportunities. But unfortunately, it poses risks as well.[1] Children's engagement in risky online behavior—such as providing personal information or agreeing to meet with a stranger—is an important predictor of whether they will encounter harmful content on the World Wide Web or be confronted with situations such as sexual harassment and privacy violations.[2] Of course, risky online behavior does not always result in harm or exposure to undesirable content. Furthermore, and in line with research on risk taking in general, most children are not heavily engaged in risky online activities.[3] Nevertheless, the potential consequences of adolescents' risky online behavior are a major concern among parents and policymakers.

Not all children engage in risky online behavior. Among those who do, the intensity and frequency of the risks taken varies. Family characteristics are a relevant indicator of children's media and Internet use. In some family homes, children participate in online activities more than in others, including both more and less risky activities.[4] This may be due to different household characteristics, such as family structure (e.g., one vs. two-parent households) and parents' socioeconomic background. Parents' efforts to guide their children's online activities are also socially differentiated. Parents differ in their own experience with the Internet, their strategies for coping with their children's Internet use, and the supply of Internet access in the family home.[5]

Alongside the family, wider society seems to influence children's online behavior as well. That is, the general level of computer skills and usage differs not only between individuals, but between nations as well.[6] In general, a higher prevalence of Internet usage in a country seems to correlate with more online risks.[7] It is therefore of interest to explore how national characteristics, and in particular the prevalence of Internet use, affects adolescents' engagement in risky online behavior, as well as parents' efforts to mediate the risks that their adolescents take online.

The current study explores the effect of contextual factors on adolescents' engagement in risky online behavior from a cross-national and comparative perspective. To do so, it uses EU Kids Online survey data and employs a hierarchical multilevel design. The general research question (RQ) underlying the study is twofold: (1) Do differences in adolescents' risky online behavior stem from differences in family characteristics, parental Internet mediation, and the prevalence of Internet use in a country? (2) Is the relation between parental mediation and

[1] See e.g., Livingstone et al. 2011b.

[2] Hasebrink et al. 2008; Lobe et al. 2011.

[3] Livingstone et al. 2011b.

[4] Livingstone and Helsper 2010; Notten et al. 2009.

[5] Livingstone and Helsper 2008; Lee 2012; Notten and Kraaykamp 2009b.

[6] DiMaggio et al. 2004; Hargittai 2010; Notten et al. 2009.

[7] Hasebrink et al. 2008; Lobe et al. 2011.

children's risky online behavior dependent on how widespread Internet use is in a country? In today's globalized societies, Internet usage plays an increasingly important role within the home and in society as a whole. Answers to these questions will therefore be of great interest to parents, educators, and policymakers.

6.2 Children and Risky Online Behavior

Prior research shows that, when it comes to screen media, high levels of consumption and harmful content may hurt a child's development and well-being in a number of ways, even in the long run. For instance, television seems to hinder a child's cognitive development, arouse aggression, and increase children's risk of becoming overweight.[8] Aside from positive outcomes of specific types of Internet consumption, studies repeatedly show negative effects of Internet use as well. For instance, time spent on social media and playing (violent) computer games, online and offline, may adversely affect a child's healthy development.[9]

Nowadays, most adolescents are online. Social networking has become an immersive phenomenon,[10] and adolescents are highly experienced online communicators.[11] However, young people are often reckless producers of information, which is a major concern.[12] Research shows a correlation between children and adolescents' risky online behavior and consequences like online sexual intimidation and harassment.[13] However, comparative research on particular adolescents' deliberate risk-taking online is rather scarce.[14] Most research does not distinguish between children's intentional engagement in risky online behavior and their (unintentional) encountering of risks. Though they are related, these are two different concepts. The current study focuses explicitly on individual and contextual factors that explain adolescents' deliberate engagement in risky online behavior.

6.3 Family Background and Risky Online Behavior

Children grow up within a social context, and generally their immediate family is most influential in guiding their development.[15] Families differ in many ways. Some parents offer their offspring beneficial opportunities; others are less generous

8 Notten et al. 2013; Valkenburg 2004.

9 Livingstone et al. 2011b; Valkenburg and Peter 2011.

10 Lenhart et al. 2010.

11 Valkenburg and Peter 2011.

12 Rockman 2002; Deursen et al. 2011.

13 Görzig and Ólafsson 2013; Lobe et al. 2011; Peter and Valkenburg 2006.

14 See e.g., Fogel and Nehmad 2009 for an exception.

15 Bandura 1977; Bronfenbrenner 1979.

or even expose their children to a rather disadvantageous (media) socialization environment.[16] Since parents are not homogeneously equipped with resources and skills to beneficially guide their children's online activities, in some family homes children are more exposed to negative aspects of Internet use and are more prone to use the Internet in a risky way.[17] With this in mind, the current study examines family socioeconomic status (represented by educational level) and family structure and the impact of these factors on adolescents' risky online behavior.

In general, higher educated parents have more advantageous cognitive and cultural skills to transmit to their children compared to lower educated parents.[18] Moreover, higher educated parents are themselves more experienced and sophisticated users of digital technologies. They tend to have a more positive attitude toward the educational benefits of computers and the Internet, and they are more apt to mediate their children's online activities.[19] Adolescents whose parents are more highly educated are therefore probably more skilled and better informed Internet users, and they are also likely to be more aware of the Internet's potential risks.[20] Accordingly, adolescents from higher socioeconomic parental homes probably engage less in risky online behavior than their peers from lower socioeconomic households.

Family structure is another aspect of social background and is highly important for a child's development and behavior. Children with married or cohabiting parents may benefit from having two adults at home who can bundle their resources and family time.[21] Generally, children from broken homes and single-parent households are 'worse off'. They tend to show more deviant and risky behavior than children from two-parent families.[22] This may be due to stress factors or to financial strains and a more restricted availability of time for parenting. Media research shows that children from single-parent families use digital technologies more often than their peers from two-parent homes.[23] In addition, in single-parent households less time is spent guiding children's media use.[24] Consequently, adolescents from single-parent households are likely riskier online compared to children with two parents at home.

---

[16] Hoeve et al. 2009; Patterson et al. 1990; Notten and Kraaykamp 2009b.

[17] D'Haenens 2001; Livingstone and Helsper 2010; Notten et al. 2009.

[18] Bourdieu 1984.

[19] Clark et al. 2005; Pasquier 2001; Paus-Hasebrink et al. 2013.

[20] Livingstone and Helsper 2010; Notten et al. 2009.

[21] Brown et al. 1990; Sayer et al. 2004.

[22] McLanahan and Sandefur 1994; Dornbusch et al. 1985.

[23] Notten et al. 2009.

[24] Notten and Kraaykamp 2009a; Warren 2005.

6.4 Parental Internet Mediation and Risky Online Behavior

Even when adjusting for family background considerations, parents may still have different manners and styles for dealing with their children's Internet use. Hence, when studying adolescents' risky online behavior, it is important to include parenting practices and, in particular, parents' mediation of their children's Internet use. Parents vary in the warmth and support they offer their children, but also in the extent and strictness of family rules and supervision. Generally, parental warmth and support, in combination with a certain amount of supervision and family rules, benefits children's development, and reduces their odds of (future) antisocial behavior. The converse is also true: ineffective parenting, as in neglect or inconsistency, is associated with a higher risk of antisocial behavior.[25] Related to these general aspects of parenting, research has defined different types of parental mediation of children's media use.[26] Accordingly, the current study distinguishes two overarching categories of parental Internet mediation: 'instructive' or supportive mediation (i.e., active and co-use forms of mediation of Internet use and safety) and 'restrictive' mediation (i.e., Internet rules and restrictions on use, monitoring, and technical restrictions such as filter software). Note that prior studies show that the intensity of parents' mediation may change as children mature.[27] Therefore, this study focuses on adolescents and controls for age within this group.

Instructive mediation by parents, characterized by parent–child interaction on media use, is generally aimed at enhancing a child's beneficial media use, skills and understanding of media content.[28] Children who were taught by their parents to use media in a responsible way have been found to have higher levels of well-being.[29] Children taught to value privacy offline are cautious with privacy online as well; these children are less likely to disclose personal information on the Internet.[30] Instructive mediation by parents is therefore expected to limit adolescent children's risky online behavior.

The second type under study here, restrictive mediation, is usually aimed at reducing or preventing children from engaging in unwanted behavior. Prior research has shown that parental supervision and restrictions are associated with less involvement of children in delinquent and norm-breaking behavior, offline and online.[31] An important predictor of risky online behavior is the time children spend

[25] Baumrind 1991; Steinberg et al. 1994; Patterson et al. 1990; Hoeve et al. 2009.

[26] Valkenburg et al. 1999; Livingstone and Helsper 2008; Nikken and Jansz 2006; Sonck et al. 2013.

[27] See e.g., Clark 2011.

[28] Lobe et al. 2011.

[29] Notten et al. 2013.

[30] See e.g., De Souza and Dick 2009.

[31] E.g., Steinberg et al. 1994; Leung and Lee 2011.

using online media.[32] Parental restrictions on both the time children spend online and the content of their activities is highly effective in reducing a range of online risks.[33] Overall, restrictive mediation by parents, as in setting rules for Internet use, monitoring Internet use, and implementing technical constraints (such as filters), is expected to prevent or at least inhibit risky behavior of adolescents online.

6.5 Country Characteristics, Risky Online Behavior, and Parental Mediation

Children's Internet access and use vary not only between families but also between countries.[34] Not only do households differ in their media socialization, the effects of the media climate at home differ between countries as well.[35] Prior research shows that children's odds of encountering online risks correlates with contextual factors, such as a country's rate of broadband penetration and level of schooling.[36] However, these studies do not examine both individual-level and country-level indicators simultaneously, nor do they focus on children's deliberate risk-taking online. The current study concurrently analyzes the impact of family indicators and the level of Internet diffusion in a country on adolescents' engagement in risky online behavior. Moreover, since parents deal with their children's Internet use in different manners, due to individual level and national-level characteristics, this study also relates the impact of parents' Internet mediation to the prevalence of Internet use within the country.

In countries where Internet access is more widespread, that is, where more people use the Internet, children seem to spend more time online than in countries with an overall lower rate of Internet diffusion.[37] A social context with more Internet users suggests more opportunities for digital media use.[38] Since time spent online correlates with risky online behavior,[39] a social context in which Internet use is more common might stimulate experimentation online and greater participation in risky online activities. Hence, it might be expected that in countries with a higher level of Internet diffusion, adolescents will engage more in risky online behavior.

Furthermore, the diffusion of Internet within a country might affect the mediation efforts of parents.[40] In countries where Internet use is widespread, some types

[32] Lobe et al. 2011; Livingstone and Helsper 2010.

[33] Livingstone and Helsper 2008, Lee 2012; Mitchell et al. 2003.

[34] Lobe et al. 2011; Notten et al. 2009.

[35] Kirwil 2009; Notten and Kraaykamp 2009b.

[36] See e.g., Hasebrink et al. 2008; Lobe et al. 2011.

[37] Livingstone et al. 2011a, b.

[38] Lobe et al. 2011.

[39] Livingstone and Helsper 2010.

[40] Paus-Hasebrink et al. 2013; Lobe et al. 2011.

of parental mediation might be less effective in preventing children from taking risks online. For instance, when more people are online (including teachers and peers), digital knowledge and skills become more widespread, and Internet guidance within the family home might become less essential in determining adolescents' online behavior. However, from a contrasting viewpoint, parents in digitally developed countries will likely be more aware of online risks.[41] These parents might be particularly conscientious in applying preventions and limitations. The current study aims to provide more insight into this intriguing issue.

6.6 Data, Measurements, and Method

To answer the research question, the study makes use of 'EU Kids Online' survey data gathered in 2010. This offers information on households, parental Internet mediation, and children's online activities in 25 European countries.[42] The aim of the EU Kids Online project is to enhance knowledge about children and parents' experiences and practices regarding risky and safe use of online technologies. See www.eukidsonline.net for more information about the project.[43] The EU Kids Online survey data is combined with country-level data from Eurostat 2012 and UNESCO 2012. Although children between 9 and 16 years of age were included in the original dataset, for reasons of consistency, this study analyzes adolescents between ages 11 and 16 (N = 18,709 respondents). Deliberate risk-taking online is hardly an issue for the younger children (those aged 9 and 10), as also indicated by their high proportion of missing scores (26 %) on the dependent variable risky online behavior. Note that since this study uses cross-sectional data, results and conclusions about causality should be interpreted with care.

6.6.1 Measurements

1. Risky online behavior

In the EU Kids Online survey, children answered questions on five risky activities, modeled on the UK Children Go Online survey[44]: 'Have you done any

---

[41] Lobe et al. 2011.

[42] Countries included in the EU Kids Online survey: Austria, Belgium, Bulgaria, Cyprus, the Czech Republic, Denmark, Estonia, Finland, France, Germany, Greece, Hungary, Ireland, Italy, Lithuania, The Netherlands, Norway, Poland, Portugal, Romania, Slovenia, Spain, Sweden, Turkey and the UK.

[43] This article draws on the work of the EU Kids Online network, funded by the European Commission (DG Information Society) Safer Internet Programme (project code SIP-KEP-321803). See www.eukidsonline.net.

[44] See Livingstone et al. 2011a.

of the following things in the past 12 months; if yes, how often have you done each of these things?': (i) looked for new friends on the Internet; (ii) sent personal information (e.g., my full name, address, or phone number) to someone that I have never met face to face; (iii) added people to my friends list or address book that I have never met face to face; (iv) pretended to be a different kind of person than I really am; (v) sent a photo or video of myself to someone that I have never met face to face. Answer categories were (0) 'never/not in the past year', (1) 'less than once a month', (2) 'one or twice a month', (3) 'once or twice a week', (4) 'every day or almost every day'. A scale was created measuring adolescents' risky online behavior using the mean score on all five items, ranging from 0 to 4 ($\alpha = 0.76$) (6.6 % missing scores).

2. Family background

The variable *parental educational level* represents the highest educational level of either parents, ranging from (0) 'none or primary only' to (6) 'tertiary (second stage)', in line with the International Standard Classification of Education (ISCED). Respondents' family structure is measured as living in a (0) 'two-parent' or (1) 'single-parent' household.

3. Parental Internet mediation

The EU Kids Online data includes five different types of parental Internet mediation (see, e.g., Livingstone et al. 2011b), which were confirmed by performing a factor analysis.[45] All questions on Internet mediation were answered by the parents. *Active parental mediation of Internet use* (including co-use), is measured by the following questions about things parents sometimes do with their child: (i) sit with him/her while he/she uses the Internet; (ii) stay nearby when he/she uses the Internet; (iii) encourage the child to explore and learn things on the Internet on their own; (iv) do activities together with the child on the Internet. Answer categories were (0) 'no' and (1) 'yes'. A scale was constructed by taking the mean of all four items ($\alpha = 0.63$) (0.3 % missing).

Active parental mediation of Internet safety includes six questions asking parents whether they (i) explained why some websites are good or bad, (ii) helped the child when something is difficult to do or find on the Internet, (iii) suggested ways to use the Internet safely, (iv) suggested ways to behave toward others, (v) helped the child when something disturbing happened on the Internet, (vi) talked with the child about what to do when something disturbing happened on the Internet ($\alpha = 0.82$) (0.4 % missing scores).

The variable *parental restrictive mediation on Internet use,* as in parental Internet rules, is measured by asking parents whether their child is allowed to do the following six online activities (0) 'all of the time' or (1) 'only with permission/

[45] A factor analysis (oblimin rotation) confirmed the five parental Internet mediation indicators (together explaining 52 % of the variance) and showed that two items loaded on more than one dimension: "Talk to the child about what he/she does on the internet" and "Do you make use of software to prevent spam or junk mail or viruses?" These items were therefore excluded.

supervision or never allowed': (i) use instant messaging; (ii) download music or films; (iii) watch video clips; (iv) have his/her own social networking profile; (v) give out personal information to others; (vi) upload photos, videos or music to share with others. A scale was constructed by taking the mean of all four items ($\alpha = 0.83$) (1.6 % missing scores).

Parental monitoring of Internet use is measured by four questions on whether parents (0) 'never' or (1) 'sometimes' checked up on what the child was doing on the Internet: (i) which websites the child had visited; (ii) the child's profile on a social network or online community; (iii) which friends or contacts the child had added to social networking profiles; (iv) the messages in the child's email or instant messaging account ($\alpha = 0.82$) (9.3 % missing).

The variable *parental technological restrictions* is constructed using the mean of the following items: Do you make use of any of the following? (i) parental controls or other means of blocking or filtering some types of website, (ii) parental controls or other means of keeping track of the websites your child visits, (iii) a service or contract that limits the time your child spends on the Internet. Answer categories were coded (0) 'no' and (1) 'yes'. A scale was constructed using the mean of the three items ($\alpha = 0.65$) (9.4 % missing).

4. Individual-level control variables

Children's frequency of Internet use and online skills are related to encountering online risks.[46] Therefore, this study includes a measure of *adolescents' Internet use,* indicating whether the adolescent uses the Internet (0) 'once a month or less', (1) 'once or twice a month', (2) 'once or twice a week', (3) '(almost) every day'. Furthermore, parents' own media consumption influences their children's use of media, but also the intensity and type of parental mediation.[47] Thus, the current study controls for parents' frequency of Internet usage. The variable *parental Internet use* indicates whether parents use the Internet (0) 'never' to (4) '(almost) daily'.

This study also takes into account the *age* and *gender* of the respondents (i.e., adolescents), since these factors are highly relevant in risk taking in general and also in Internet use and risk taking online,[48] even within the narrow age group of adolescence. Moreover, effects and type of parental media socialization are found to differ with the age and gender of their children.[49]

5. Country-level characteristics

This study includes a measure of how widespread Internet use is within a country. A *country's Internet diffusion* indicates the proportion of the total

---

[46] Livingstone and Helsper 2010.

[47] Notten and Kraaykamp 2009a; Lee 2012.

[48] Notten et al. 2009; Peter and Valkenburg 2006.

[49] Paus-Hasebrink et al. 2013; Notten and Kraaykamp 2009a; Sonck et al. 2013.

Table 6.1 Descriptive statistics of all variables

	Mean	Std. Dev.	Min	Max
Adolescents' risky online behavior	0.49		0.00	4.00
Individual level (level 1)				
Parental educational level	3.52	1.40	0.00	6.00
Single-parent family (1 = yes)	0.21		0.00	1.00
Age adolescent	13.57	1.68	11.00	16.00
Gender adolescent (1 = female)	0.50		0.00	1.00
Daily Internet use adolescent	2.78	0.47	0.00	3.00
Daily Internet use parent	3.11	1.40	0.00	4.00
Parental active mediation use	0.52	0.33	0.00	1.00
Parental active mediation safety use	0.64	0.33	0.00	1.00
Parental restrictive mediation use	0.43	0.32	0.00	1.00
Parental monitoring	0.39	0.39	0.00	1.00
Parental technological restrictions	0.19	0.30	0.00	1.00
Country level (level 2)				
Internet diffusion (%users) (62 = 0)	0.00	16.64	−31.60	26.40
Educational level (years) (16 = 0)	0.00	1.10	−4.05	2.05

Source EU Kids online, *N* level 1 = 15431, *N* level 2 = 25

population of that country that used the Internet on a weekly basis in the year preceding measurement (2009).[50] For reasons of interpretation this variable is centered to its mean ($M = 62$). Since different measures of a nation's Internet usage and penetration (e.g., broadband penetration, percentage of households with Internet access) highly correlate,[51] the percentage of frequent Internet users in a country may also be perceived as a general indicator of a country's ICT readiness and development. The current study controls for a *country's educational level*, which is represented by the years of expected education.[52] This indicator relates to the informational aspect of Internet use ('information society') and a country's general level of development.[53] See Appendix A for more detailed information on the country-level characteristics.

Finally, respondents with missing scores on one of the included variables were omitted, resulting in a final sample of 15,431 respondents. Table 6.1 presents the descriptive statistics for all variables included in the analyses.

[50] Eurostat 2012.

[51] Lobe et al. 2011; Notten et al. 2009.

[52] UNESCO 2012.

[53] See e.g., Lobe et al. 2011; Notten et al. 2009.

6.6.2 *Methods and Models*

In this study several multivariate multilevel models are estimated to provide insight into the relation between family characteristics, Internet diffusion within a country, and risk-taking online by adolescents.[54] Multilevel modeling takes into account the hierarchical structure of the EU Kids Online dataset, that is, the fact that the adolescents under study (individual level) are nested in 25 different European countries (country level). This method enables simultaneous estimation of the effects of individual *and* country-level factors on adolescents' engagement in risky behavior online, resulting in more correct estimates than models that do not take the nesting structure into account.[55]

Several multilevel models are estimated and presented in Table 6.2. In model 1, all control variables and family social background features are included. Model 2 adds parental Internet mediation, and model 3 includes the country-level characteristics (all fixed effects). Table 6.3 presents the results of the estimated cross-level interactions; that is, interactions are estimated between a specific type of parental Internet mediation (individual level) and the Internet diffusion within a country (country level). These cross-level interactions test whether the effects of parental mediation on adolescents' risk-taking online might differ between countries (random effects) with different levels of Internet diffusion.

6.7 Results

Table 6.2 shows the results for the multilevel regression models. Model 1 shows that, as expected, adolescents with higher educated parents are less likely to engage in risky online behavior compared to peers with lower educated parents ($b = -0.025$). Also, adolescents growing up in a single-parent household engaged significantly more in risky behavior online than their peers in two-parent households ($b = 0.045$). This finding is in line with previous research on the effects of single-parent families on various types of deviant behavior. Model 1 also includes several control variables. The findings reveal that older adolescents engage more in risky online behavior ($b = 0.057$). The results also show that adolescents who spend more time online participate more in risky online activities ($b = 0.150$), and girls seem to participate in such activities less often than boys ($b = -0.041$). Finally, controlled for all other variables, parents' frequency of Internet use does not have a significant effect on their adolescent children's engagement in risky online behavior. Model 1 also shows that most of the variance in adolescents' risky

---

[54] Although the variable 'risky online behavior' is skewed, a robustness check showed that logistic modeling resulted in the same substantive findings.

[55] Snijders and Bosker 1999.

Table 6.2 Multilevel regression models on adolescents' risky online behavior

	Model 1		Model 2		Model 3	
	b	s.e.	*b*	s.e.	*b*	s.e.
Intercept	−0.583***	0.055	0.102	0.056	−0.112	0.061
Individual level (level 1)						
Family background						
Parental educational level	−0.025***	0.004	−0.023***	0.004	−0.023***	0.004
Single-parent family (1 = yes)	0.045***	0.013	0.039**	0.012	0.040***	0.012
Parental Internet mediation						
Parental active mediation use			−0.041*	0.018	−0.042*	0.018
Parental active mediation safety			0.024	0.018	0.024	0.018
Parental restrictive mediation use			−0.309***	0.018	−0.310***	0.018
Parental monitoring			0.035*	0.015	0.035*	0.015
Parental technological restrictions			0.022	0.018	0.021	0.018
Control variables						
Age adolescent	0.057***	0.003	0.038***	0.003	0.038***	0.003
Gender adolescent (1 = female)	−0.041***	0.010	−0.038***	0.010	−0.039***	0.010
Daily Internet use adolescent	0.150***	0.011	0.136***	0.013	0.112***	0.011
Daily Internet use parent	−0.007	0.004	−0.008	0.004	−0.007	0.004
Country level (level 2)						
Internet diffusion/10 (% users/10)					−0.014	0.014
Educational level (years) (16 = 0)					−0.016	0.019
Individual-level variance	0.374***	0.004	0.367***	0.004	0.367***	0.004
Country-intercept variance	0.012***	0.004	0.010***	0.003	0.009***	0.003
Log likelihood	28686.622		28382.388		28378.730	

Significance *** $p \leq 0.001$, ** $p \leq 0.01$, * $p \leq 0.05$ two-tailed test
Source EU Kids Online, *N* level 1 = 15431, *N* level 2 = 25

behavior is due to variations at the individual level (here including characteristics of the family and the child); only a small proportion of the variance in risk-taking online is due to differentiation between countries (3.3 %).

Model 2 includes the five different types of parental Internet mediation, representing instructive, and restrictive parenting, next to family background indicators and controls. The results suggest that active parental mediation of Internet use does reduce adolescents' engagement in risky online behavior. Hence, adolescents engage less in risky behavior online if their parents are involved with their Internet use ($b = -0.041$). Overall, restrictive mediation, as in rules set by parents on children's Internet use, seems most effective in preventing or inhibiting risky behavior online ($b = -0.309$). When parents set rules for Internet use, their

Table 6.3 Multilevel regression models on adolescents' risky online behavior

	Model 3(a)		Model 3(b)		Model 3(c)		Model 3(d)		Model 3(e)	
	b	s.e.	*b*	s.e.	*b*	s.e.	*b*	s.e.	*b*	s.e.
Cross-level interactions[a]										
Parental active mediation use × Internet spread	0.026*	0.011								
Parental active mediation safety use × Internet spread			0.014	0.011						
Parental restrictive mediation use × Internet spread					0.014	0.015				
Parental monitoring × Internet spread							0.023*	0.011		
Parental technological restriction × Internet spread									0.016	0.012
Log likelihood	28367.931		28375.762		28347.167		28360.216		28374.947	

Significance $^{***}p \leq 0.001$, $^{**}p \leq 0.01$, $^{*}p \leq 0.05$ two-tailed test

Source EU Kids Online, N level 1 = 15431, N level 2 = 25

[a] All variables are included (similar to model 3 Table 6.2). For reasons of presentation, only the estimates for the cross-level interactions are shown

(adolescent) children are significantly less likely to engage in risky online behavior compared to adolescents whose parents do not set rules for Internet use. In contrast to the expectation, the findings show a significant positive relation between parental monitoring and adolescents' risky online behavior ($b = 0.035$). It is unlikely that parental monitoring, such as checking up on what their children are doing on the Internet, stimulates adolescents' risky behavior. This positive relation therefore most likely represents a reversed causality. That is, when adolescents are reckless online, their parents probably increase their level of supervision. This coincides with conclusions of other studies on parenting and deviant media behavior, some of which use the same dataset.[56] When controlling for all other factors, active parental mediation of Internet safety and technological restrictions, such as Internet filters in the family home, appear to have no influence on adolescents' risky behavior.

Model 2 shows that the significant effect of parental social background is hardly affected by including the mediation strategies. For parental educational level, only 8 % of the effect is explained by parental Internet mediation. The effect of single-parent families on adolescent children's risky behavior online also runs partly via parent's Internet mediation (14 %), though the direct effect of growing up in a single-parent household is still highly relevant. These findings suggest that parental Internet mediation might function as a useful tool for guiding adolescents' online activities, regardless of family background.

Model 3 includes the country-level characteristics. The results suggest that Internet diffusion within a country and its level of schooling do not significantly affect adolescents' risk-taking online. Thus, contrary to the expectation, the proportion of people using the Internet in a country does not affect 11–16-year old adolescents' risky online behavior.

Table 6.3 presents the estimates of the cross-level interactions.[57] Model 3a seems to suggest that the impact of parents' active mediation of Internet use becomes somewhat less pronounced (i.e., more positive) with increased Internet diffusion in a country ($b = 0.026$). This means that active mediation by parents is less successful in reducing adolescents' risky online behavior in countries where Internet use is more common. The positive impact of parental monitoring, on the other hand, seems to increase in countries where more people use the Internet, as presented under model 3d ($b = 0.023$). This suggests that parents are more likely to monitor adolescents' online activities in countries with greater Internet penetration. All other cross-level interactions are non-significant, meaning that the prevalence of Internet use in a country does not affect the impact of parental safety-related mediation, Internet rules, and technological restrictions on adolescents' engagement in risky online behavior. This also implies that, regardless of the level of diffusion of Internet in a country, parental restrictions on Internet use

[56] See e.g., Kalmus et al. 2013.

[57] Due to collinearity and non-convergence of the model, it was not possible to include all cross-level interactions simultaneously.

are highly relevant in preventing and inhibiting adolescents from engaging in risky online behavior.

6.8 Conclusions

Internet use is inescapable in European societies today, for parents, but also for children and adolescents. Internet is a source of valuable information and means of communication. But it also poses risks, especially for young people. This study focused on adolescents' engagement in risky online behavior. The first aim of the study was to explore the extent to which adolescents' risky online behavior is related to parental social background, the intensity of parents' mediation of Internet use, and the diffusion of Internet use within a country. The second aim was to find out whether the impact of parental mediation differs depending on how widespread Internet use is in a country. To accomplish these aims, this study used the EU Kids Online dataset, including 15,431 adolescents in 25 countries.

The findings of this study point to four general conclusions. First, adolescent children from lower educated and single-parent households engage more in risky online behavior than children from more 'advantageous' households. Adolescents in lower educated and single-parent homes are more attracted to risky online behavior, which is possibly due to factors like a lower stock of beneficial parental resources and various stress factors within the home. Educators and media-education programs might therefore give increased consideration to this consistently more vulnerable group of adolescents and their parent(s).

Second, Internet mediation seems to be an effective tool for parents to influence their adolescents' risky online behavior. Parents' active involvement in their children's Internet use prevents or at least reduces adolescents' risky online behavior. Rules restricting Internet use are especially effective in reducing children's risky online behavior. By teaching children to use the Internet in a beneficial way and by limiting the amount of time that children spend online, parents reduce their children's odds of participating in risky online activities. Parental monitoring is positively correlated with risky online behavior. This probably indicates that parents are more likely to check up on what their adolescent child does online if they have a history of risky online behavior.

Third, in countries where Internet use is widespread, adolescents are not more likely to participate in risky online behavior than in countries where Internet use is less prevalent. Hence, engaging in risky online behavior does not seem to depend on the number of Internet users in the wider social context or the level of digital development of a country. Therefore, in limiting adolescents' risky online behavior, this study suggests that policy programs should predominantly focus on the immediate environment of children.

Fourth, the findings of this study suggest that the spread of Internet use somewhat alters the impact of some parental mediation styles on adolescents' risky online behavior. For instance, in countries where Internet use is more prevalent, also among peers and within school environments, parent–child interaction on adolescents' use of the Internet seems less influential in limiting risky online behavior. The correlation between parental monitoring and risky behavior increases as Internet use becomes more common. This might reflect parents' growing concerns about their children's risky online behavior in more digitalized countries. Above all, applying rules for Internet use in the family home proves to be a key way to reduce adolescents' risky online behavior, regardless of the level of Internet diffusion within a country. This suggests that in modern countries, where parenting styles are often more permissive, parents should nonetheless be encouraged to restrict their children's Internet use.

In exploring the impact of several contextual factors on adolescents' risky online behavior, this study used cross-sectional data. Since parental and adolescents' behavior are measured at one point in time, especially regarding parental mediation and children's risky online behavior, conclusions about causality should be interpreted with care. Another relevant point of discussion is the relation between parental Internet mediation and children's age. As children mature, parents tend to adjust their mediation strategies, and children respond differently to parental mediation as they mature. Although this study takes into account the variation in age among adolescents, future research concerning risky online behavior might differentiate more explicitly between ages. Also, this study suggests that parents are more likely to check up on their adolescent children's Internet use when their children show more risky online behavior. However, what these parents do with the information they gather remains unclear. Since the relevance of monitoring seems to increase in more digitalized countries, research unraveling the causality and implications of parental monitoring and online risks seems highly relevant.

Overall, since Internet use and digital applications are ever more ubiquitous, the findings of this study urge policymakers and educators to further stimulate parents to be involved in and, especially, to set rules for their children's Internet use. Many parents might find it difficult to restrict adolescents' online activities. They might therefore benefit from policies supporting them in keeping their rules and in guiding their children into critical online users. It is also worthwhile to recognize that adolescents from problematic and less supportive family backgrounds are more vulnerable to risky behavior, including online. With Internet use becoming increasingly common in schools and more mobile, a more active role will be called for, for instance, of teachers, and youth workers.

Appendix A

Table A.1 Country-level characteristics

	N	Risky online behavior (mean)	Internet diffusion (% users)	Schooling (expected years)
Austria	586	0.51	67	15.0
Belgium	635	0.44	70	15.9
Bulgaria	646	0.52	40	13.7
Cyprus	585	0.56	45	13.8
Czech Republic	673	0.58	54	15.2
Germany	696	0.47	71	15.6
Denmark	658	0.38	82	16.9
Estonia	667	0.71	67	15.8
Greece	473	0.49	38	16.5
Spain	605	0.22	54	16.4
Finland	724	0.41	79	17.1
France	588	0.45	65	16.1
Hungary	585	0.32	57	15.3
Ireland	616	0.38	60	17.9
Italy	645	0.56	42	16.3
Lithuania	581	0.73	55	16.0
Netherlands	724	0.39	86	16.7
Norway	734	0.40	88	17.3
Poland	629	0.40	52	15.2
Portugal	564	0.48	42	15.5
Romania	587	0.70	31	14.8
Sweden	704	0.57	86	15.6
Slovenia	705	0.58	58	16.7
Turkey	227	0.58	30	11.8
UK	594	0.41	76	15.9

Source EU Kids Online, *N* level 1 = 15431; *N* level 2 = 25

References

Bandura A (1977) Social learning theory. General Learning Press, New York

Baumrind D (1991) The influence of parenting style on adolescent competence and substance use. J Early Adolesc 11:56–95

Bourdieu P (1984) Distinction: a social critique of the judgement in taste. Routledge, London

Bronfenbrenner U (1979) The ecology of human development. Experiments by nature and design. Harvard University Press, Cambridge, MA

Brown JD, Childers KW, Bauman KE, Koch GG (1990) The influence of new media and family structure on young adolescents' television and radio use. Commun Res 17:65–82

Clark LS (2011) Parental mediation theory for the digital age. Commun Theory 21:323–343

Clark LS, Demont-Heinrich C, Webber S (2005) Parents, ICTs, and children's prospects for success: interviews along the digital 'access rainbow'. Crit Stud Media Commun 22:409–426

D'Haenens L (2001) Old and new media: access and ownership in the home. In: Livingstone S, Bovill M (eds) Children and their changing media environment: a European comparative study. Lawrence Erlbaum Associates, Mahwah, pp 53–84

De Souza Z, Dick GN (2009) Disclosure of information by children in social networking—not a case of 'you show me yours and I'll show you mine'. Int J Inf Manage 29:255–261

DiMaggio P, Hargittai E, Celeste C, Shafer S (2004) Digital inequality: from unequal access to differentiated use. In: Neckerman K (ed) Social inequality. Rusell Sage Foundation, New York, pp 355–400

Dornbusch SM, Carlsmith JM, Bushwall SJ, Ritter PL, Leiderman H, Hastorf AH, Gross RT (1985) Single parents, extended households, and the control of adolescents. Child Dev 56:326–341

Eurostat (2012) Information retrieved in July 2012. http://appsso.eurostat.ec.europa.eu/nui/show.do?dataset=isoc_ci_ifp_iuandlang=en

Fogel J, Nehmad E (2009) Internet social network communities: risk taking, trust, and privacy concerns. Comput Hum Behav 25:153–160

Görzig A, Ólafsson K (2013) What makes a bully a cyberbully? Unraveling the characteristics of cyberbullies across 25 European countries. J Child Media 7:9–27

Hargittai E (2010) Digital na(t)ives? Variation in internet skills and uses among members of the 'net generation'. Sociol Inq 80:92–113

Hasebrink U, Livingstone S, Haddon L, Ólafsson K (eds) (2008) Comparing children's online opportunities and risks across Europe: cross-national comparisons for EU kids online, 2nd edn. LSE, EU kids online, London. http://eprints.lse.ac.uk/24368/

Hoeve M, Semon Dubas J, Eichelsheim VI, Van der Laan PH, Smeenk W, Gerris JRM (2009) The Relationship between parenting and delinquency: a meta-analysis. J Abnorm Child Psychol 37:749–775

Kalmus V, Blinka L, Ólafsson K (2013) Does it matter what mama says: evaluating the role of parental mediation in European adolescents' excessive internet use. Child Soc. doi:10.1111/chso.12020

Kirwil L (2009) Parental mediation of children's internet use in different European countries. J Child Media 3:394–409

Lee SJ (2012) Parental restrictive mediation of children's internet use: effective for what and for whom? New media & society. http://nms.sagepub.com/content/early/2012/07/12/1461444812452412

Lenhart A, Purcell K, Smith A, Zickuhr K (2010) Social media & mobile internet use among teens and young adults. Pew Interet & American Life Project

Leung L, Lee PSN (2011) The influence of information literacy, internet addiction and parenting styles on internet risks. New Media Soc 14:117–136

Livingstone S, Helsper E (2008) Parental mediation of children's internet use. J Broadcast Electron Media 52:581–599

Livingstone S, Helsper E (2010) Balancing opportunities and risks in teenagers' use of the internet: the role of online skills and self-efficacy. New Media Soc 12:309–329

Livingstone S, Haddon L, Görzig A, Ólafsson K (2011a) Technical report and user guide: the 2010 EU kids online survey. LSE, EU kids online, London

Livingstone S, Haddon L, Görzig A, Ólafsson K (2011b) Risks and safety on the internet: the perspective of European children. Full findings. LSE, EU kids online. London

Lobe B, Livingstone S, Ólafsson K, Vodeb H (2011) Cross-national comparison of risks and safety on the internet: initial analysis from the EU kids online survey of European children, EU kids online, Deliverable D6. EU Kids Online Network, London

McLanahan S, Sandefur G (1994) Growing up with a single parent. What hurts, what helps. Harvard University Press, Cambridge, MA

Mitchell K, Finkelhor D, Wolak J (2003) The exposure of youth to unwanted sexual material on the internet. A national survey of risk, impact and prevention. Youth Soc 34:330–358

Nikken P, Jansz J (2006) Parental mediation of children's videogame playing: a comparison of the reports by parents and children. Learn Media Technol 31:181–202

Notten N, Kraaykamp G (2009a) Parents and the media. A study of social differentiation in parental media socialization. Poetics 37:185–200

Notten N, Kraaykamp G (2009b) Home media and science performance: a cross-national study. Educ Res Eval 15:367–384

Notten N, Peter J, Kraaykamp G, Valkenburg PM (2009) Research note: digital divide across borders—a cross-national study of adolescents' use of digital technologies. Eur Sociol Rev 25:551–560

Notten N, Kraaykamp G, Tolsma J (2013) Parents, television and children's weight status. J Child Media 7(2):235–252

Pasquier D (2001) Media at home: domestic interactions and regulation. In: Livingstone S, Bovill M (eds) Children and their changing media environment: a European comparative study. Lawrence Erlbaum Associates, Mahwah, pp 161–177

Patterson GR, Debaryshe B, Ramsey E (1990) A developmental perspective on antisocial behavior. Am Psychol 44:329–335

Paus-Hasebrink I, Bauwens J, Dürager AE, Ponte C (2013) Exploring types of parent-child relationship and internet use across Europe. J Child Media 7:114–132

Peter J, Valkenburg P (2006) Adolescents' exposure to sexually explicit material on the internet. Commun Res 33:178–204

Rockman IF (2002) Strengthening connections between information literacy, general education, and assessment efforts. Library Trends 51:185–198

Sayer LC, Bianchi SM, Robinson JP (2004) Are parents investing less in children? Trends in mothers' and fathers' time with children. Am J Sociol 110:1–43

Snijders TAB, Bosker RJ (1999) Multilevel analysis. An introduction to basic and advanced multilevel modeling. Sage Publications, London

Sonck N, Nikken P, De Haan J (2013) Determinants of internet mediation: a comparison of the reports by Dutch parents and children. J Child Media 7:96–113

Steinberg L, Lamborn SD, Darling N, Mounts NS, Dornbusch SM (1994) Over-time changes in the adjustment and competence among adolescents from authoritative, authoritarian, indulgent, and neglectful families. Child Dev 65:754–770

UNESCO Institute for Statistics (2012) Information retrieved July 2012 via http://stats.uis.unesco.org. See also http://hdr.undp.org/en/media/HDR_2010_EN_Tables_reprint.pdf

Valkenburg PM (2004) Children's responses to the screen. Lawrence Erlbaum Associates, Mahwah, NJ

Valkenburg PM, Peter J (2011) Online communication among adolescents: an integrated model of its attraction, opportunities, and risks. J Adolesc Health 48:121–127

Valkenburg PM, Krcmar M, Peeters AL, Marseille NM (1999) Developing a scale to assess three styles of television mediation: 'Instructive mediation', 'restrictive mediation', and 'social coviewing'. J Broadcast Electron Media 43:53–66

Van Deursen A, Van Dijk JA, Peeters O (2011) Rethinking internet skills. The contribution of gender, age, education, internet experience, and hours online to medium- and content-related internet skills. Poetics 39:125–144

Warren R (2005) Parental mediation of children's television viewing in low-income families. J Commun 55:847–863

Part III
Privacy, Data Protection and Online Marketing

Chapter 7
No Child's Play: Online Data Protection for Children

Simone van der Hof

Contents

7.1 Introduction

The vastly increased Internet usage by children has boosted attention for their online privacy, more particularly, the protection of their personal data. It is, therefore, not surprising that the European Commission has added provisions specifically focused on protecting children in the proposal for a general data

---

Simone van der Hof is Full Professor of Law and Information Society and chair of eLaw, the Center for Law in the Information Society, Leiden University. This chapter is a translation and adaptation of the following article: S. van der Hof, Online privacybescherming is bepaald geen kinderspel, Over de nieuwe Europese regels voor de persoonsgegevensbescherming van minderjarigen, *Tijdschrift voor Internetrecht*, November 2012, pp. 134–141.

S. van der Hof (✉)
Center for Law in the Information Society, Leiden University, Leiden, The Netherlands
e-mail: s.van.der.hof@law.leidenuniv.nl

S. van der Hof et al. (eds.), *Minding Minors Wandering the Web: Regulating Online Child Safety*, Information Technology and Law Series 24, DOI: 10.1007/978-94-6265-005-3_7,

protection regulation. This chapter aims to analyse these provisions and assess them in the broader scope of technological developments and the interest of the child. To this end, the chapter first describes the current legal framework for the protection of children's online privacy and the concerns that are raised in this respect. Then it goes on to explore the changes intended to be brought on by the proposed regulation. The chapter wraps up with an assessment of these changes in light of technological complexities, privacy concerns and the interests of children.

7.2 Protection of Online Privacy and Data Protection of Children in Europe

Current European data protection law[1] lacks child-specific rules, which means that the provisions apply to children as well as adults. However, parents exercise their children's data protection rights when they are still under the age of 16. Over the last years, attention for special personal data protection for children has vastly increased, the two most important reasons for which are: (1) the growing relevance of child rights and (2) concerns about online child safety. Each of these reasons will be briefly elaborated first. Then we turn to the emerging self-regulation for online child safety and, particularly, also the protection of children's online privacy therein, since the European Commission has put self-regulation forward as an important regulatory instrument for online child safety.

7.2.1 Growing Relevance of Child Rights and Protecting Children's Data

The importance of the 1989 UN Convention on Child Rights is increasingly more expressly recognised in law, policy and practice. Under the convention, children are persons under the age of 18 years, unless national law provides for an earlier age of adulthood.[2] Children are provided with a special legal position, given their psychological and physical immaturity and, hence, their need for care and pro-

---

[1] Directive 95/46/EC of the European Parliament and of the Council of 24 October 1995 on the protection of individuals with regard to the processing of personal data and on the free movement of such data, OJ L 281, 23/11/1995, p. 31; Directive 2002/58/EC of the European Parliament and of the Council of 12 July 2002 concerning the processing of personal data and the protection of privacy in the electronic communications sector (Directive on privacy and electronic communications), OJ L 201, 31/07/2002, p. 37.

[2] Article 1, 1989 UN Child Rights Convention.

tection by others.[3] Article 16(1) of the Convention[4] provides that children have a right to privacy,[5] which also encompasses a right to the protection of their personal data.[6] The twentieth birthday of the 1989 UN Child Rights Convention has been reason for the European Commission to endorse child rights as a priority in EU policy-making in its Communication 'Towards an EU Strategy on the Rights of the Child'.[7] The special status of children in personal data protection was further elaborated at the European level by the Article 29 Working Party[8] in one of their opinions by providing guidelines in the educational context that are, however, relevant more generally as well.[9] The working group stresses that, in light of privacy principles, the processors of personal data need to be particularly meticulous when processing children's data.[10] They should provide children with information on personal data practices in words of one syllable in order for it to be understandable to children.[11] Personal data of children (e.g. pupils) should be published on private websites and the use of privacy-infringing technologies, such CCTV surveillance and biometrics, should be proportional. In line with the theories underlying the UN Convention,[12] children should be given more responsibility in independently exercising their personal data rights, and, e.g. consenting to

---

[3] See the Preambule of the 'Declaration of the Rights of the Child': [T]he child, by reason of his physical and mental immaturity, needs special safeguards and care, including appropriate legal protection, before as well as after birth. See also: Article 24(1), EU Charter of fundamental rights.

[4] This provision states: No child shall be subjected to arbitrary or unlawful interference with his or her privacy, family or correspondence, nor to unlawful attacks on his or her honour and reputation.

[5] See also Article 8 ECHR and Article 7 EU Charter of fundamental rights, which apply regardless a person's age.

[6] Pursuant to Article 8, EU Charter of fundamental rights, citizens have the right to data protection, and Article 24, EU Charter, requires that the interest of children be taken into account. See also Article 3, 1989 UN Child Rights Convention.

[7] COM(2006) 367 final. See further Decision No. 1351/2008/EC of the European Parliament and of the Council of 16 December 2008 establishing a multi-annual Community programme on protecting children using the Internet and other communication technologies, OJ L 348, 24/12/2008, p. 118; Commission Communication on a comprehensive approach on personal data protection in the European Union, COM(2010)609 final, at http://ec.europa.eu/justice/news/consulting_public/0006/com_2010_609_en.pdf; EU agenda for the rights of the child, 2011, at http://ec.europa.eu/justice/fundamental-rights/rights-child/eu-agenda/index_en.htm.

[8] The Article 29 Working Party is an independent body of the European data protection authority that advises the European Commission on issues related to personal data protection.

[9] Working Document 1/2008 on the protection of children's personal data, WP 147, February 2008. Previous opinions pay attention also to particular issues regarding the position of children under data protection law; see Opinion 2/2010 on online behavioural advertising and Opinion 5/2009 on online social networking.

[10] Working Document 1/2008 on the protection of children's personal data, WP 147, February 2008, p. 7.

[11] Working Document 1/2008 on the protection of children's personal data, WP 147, February 2008, p. 10.

[12] See also Article 5, 1989 UN Child Rights Convention.

the use of their personal data (even contrary to their parents' wishes), while growing up and becoming more and more mature.[13]

7.2.2 Complexity of the Technology Mediated Environment

New technologies have instigated a rising interest in the online protection and empowerment of children. Children increasingly use the Internet and mobile devices that bring along risks related to personal data misuse or abuse. Publishing personal data online can result in identity theft, sexual abuse, cyberbullying or reputational damage, et cetera. Online safety may, hence, be improved by safeguarding adequate personal data protection. Even more fundamentally, online activities and communications of children are constantly and meticulously tracked and mapped by companies and governments, and ultimately they are sorted into economically and socially relevant categories.[14] This process is called profiling, which entails that sets of correlated data are translated into personal or group profiles that can represent individual persons and be used for decision-making concerning individuals, including, e.g. decisions to (not) offer particular services, to differentiate between prices or to label a person as (potentially) fraudulent. To the extent that children or parents are aware of profiling practices at all, it will probably not be easy to find out by whom and how they are being profiled, how online profiles are used and how online surveillance and profiling practices can be stopped.[15] The Article 29 Working Party has expressly stated that parents must provide informed consent in case of tracking and tracing children's online behaviour for commercial purposes.[16] Ensuring that data processing practices are actually transparent is not an easy task though, given the legal-technological complexities and the commercial interests to collect personal data. Moreover, adequate instruments for age verification do not yet exist and it is, therefore, difficult to determine if and when children are involved.[17] So far, existing laws have not stood the test of time as a result of these developments and offer insufficient protection to individuals who live in an increasingly smarter

[13] Working Document 1/2008 on the protection of children's personal data, WP 147, February 2008, pp. 5–6 and 9.

[14] David Lyon calls these developments 'social sorting'; see Lyon 2003.

[15] In this respect, the Article 29 Working Party's opinion that marketing is not an issue of data protection, but consumer protection, is outdated, Working Document 1/2008 on the protection of children's personal data, WP 147, February 2008, p. 12.

[16] Opion 2/2010 on behavioural advertising, WP 171, 22 June 2010.

[17] Previously the Article 29 Working Party had already insisted that the implementation of proof of consent and age verification should be studied further, Opinion 5/2009 on online social networking, WP 163, p. 13.

environment that continuously monitors their actions.[18] Whether the proposed general data protection directive will improve this situation will be discussed later on in this chapter. First, however, let's turn to the ways in which the industry is involved in regulating online child safety.

7.2.3 Self-Regulation in the EU

Interestingly, self-regulation is one of the cornerstones of EU online child safety policy, including online privacy protection of children.[19] Self-regulation has certain obvious advantages, given that it can be more flexible and efficient than government regulation and directly builds on the socio-technological expertise of the industry. Moreover, the industry may feel more committed to comply with rules that they have been involved in developing and, as a result, regulation may be more effective. On the downside, companies may perceive being part of self-regulation as a way to boost or maintain their reputation, which does not necessarily coincide with legal compliance.[20] Here I will look a bit further into two self-regulatory initiatives that are relevant for online privacy and data protection: the 'Safer Social Networking Principles for the EU' (SSNP) and the 'Coalition to make the Internet a better place for kids'.[21,22]

The SSNP were adopted by the most important social networking providers at the beginning of 2009.[23] The SSNP's goal is: 'to provide good practice recommendations for the providers of social networking and other user interactive sites, to enhance the safety of children and young people using their services'. Principle

---

[18] See, amongst others, Roßnagel and Müller 2004, pp. 625–632; Hildebrandt 2008, pp. 175–191.

[19] For that matter, the Council of Europe has explicitly spoken in favour of self-regulation of online child safety and guaranteeing child rights, see Recommendation Rec(2001)8 of the Committee of Ministers to member states on self-regulation concerning cyber content (self-regulation and user protection against illegal or harmful content on new communications and information services), Draft Recommendation on measures to protect and promote respect for human rights with regard to social networking services. Committee of Experts on New Media, March 2010. See also Opinion 5/2009 on online social networking, WP 163, p. 13.

[20] De Haan et al. 2013.

[21] This coalition works alongside the ICT Coalition, see https://www2.lse.ac.uk/media@lse/research/EUKidsOnline/EU%20Kids%20III/Project%20resources/Coalitionmeetingnote.pdf. The ICT Coalition has adopted the Principles for the Safer Use of Connected Devices and Online Services by Children and Young People in the EU, see www.rcysostenibilidad.telefonica.com/blogs/wp-content/uploads/2012/01/ICT_Principles.pdf.

[22] Another self-regulatory initiative is, e.g. European Framework for Safer Mobile Use by Young Teenagers and Children, http://ec.europa.eu/information_society/activities/sip/self_reg/phones/index_en.htm, see also De Haan et al. 2013.

[23] See for more information on the SSNP: De Haan et al. 2013.

6 of the SSNP, which addresses privacy and data protection, states: 'enable and encourage users to employ a safe approach to personal information and privacy'.

Other principles can, however, also be relevant to assure safe Internet use and protection of personal data.[24] Pursuant to the SSNP, companies need to implement online safety strategies for children,[25] including default privacy settings that provide maximum protection for children, age verification, supervision instruments for parents, understandable and unambiguous terms of use and clear information on online child safety. So far, we do not know, whether the SSNP actually work. In 2011, self-reporting by the companies showed that while they have put in place safety measures the principles have not always been fully or satisfactorily implemented.[26] What's more, implementation of the principles does not necessarily mean that the measures adopted are effective. To find out how effective they are, more research needs to be done.[27]

Another initiative is the *Coalition to make the Internet a better place for kids* (the Coalition),[28] which consists of telecommunications and ICT companies, and—again—social networking providers. In close cooperation with the European Commission and other stakeholders, the Coalition aims to ensure a safe online environment for children by sharing expertise and developing safety tools. Obviously, there is a definite overlap in participants and working areas with the SSNP, but it is not clear how these initiatives are coordinated. One of the Coalition's objectives is to develop age-appropriate privacy settings, i.e. settings that are accessible and understandable for children and allow them to determine who can or cannot view their online profiles and access messages, pictures or other personal information. Default settings (i.e. settings as defined when opening an account at a social networking site or other interactive site) should be as safe as reasonably possible. The former Dutch social networking site Hyves, for instance, has default private profiles for children under 16. If children change their privacy settings they should be informed clearly and unambiguously of the consequences and, more particularly, the potential risks of these changes.

In 2012, a midterm review of the implementation of the principles by the Coalition reveals that achievements with respect to age-appropriate privacy settings are still preliminary, given that they basically involve an inventory of practices and a commitment of mobile operators to implement privacy guidelines, but important issues to actually achieve the commitment still need to be taken up by the companies. These issues include:

---

[24] See, amongst others, Principle 3 which is called: '*Empower users through tools and technology*'.

[25] See on safety strategies on online social networks: Article 29 Working group, Opinion 5/2009 on online social networking, p. 13.

[26] De Haan et al. 2013.

[27] De Haan et al. 2013.

[28] Coaltition to make the Internet a better place for kids, Statement of purpose, Brussels, December 2011, http://ec.europa.eu/information_society/activities/sip/self_reg/index_en.htm.

- Providing transparency of default privacy settings and the consequences of changing these settings,
- Ensuring effectiveness and user-friendliness of privacy settings,
- Working on privacy-by-design solutions and specifications for, e.g. mobile services and apps,[29] and, last but certainly not least,
- Acquiring knowledge on fundamental questions, such as: when are privacy settings age-appropriate, and at what age will children understand the consequences of sharing personal data online?[30]

The process is also closely watched by the European digital civil rights movement EDRi. One of their critiques concerns the fact that the industry solely addresses personal information that SNS users exchange themselves and not the use of behavioural data for targeted advertising.[31] Obviously, the Coalition has a commercial interest in the latter, which will make them reluctant at least to address issues of online marketing to kids. Second, some businesses intend to protect children more than others by, for instance, introducing parental consent before allowing children on their websites. Recently, Facebook was said to also develop instruments to allow children under 13 on their site under parental surveillance, for example, by linking the child's profile to that of their parents.[32] The downside of such protective initiatives may be, however, that children's Internet use is restricted or conditional to parental surveillance, which can negatively impact their freedom of information and personal development. Moreover, it can be very instructive to teach children how to tweak privacy settings and—in line with the 1989 Child Rights Convention—to provide them with increasingly more privacy in relation to their parents. The midterm review rather cryptically mentions that 'for the Coalition the rule of the age of 13 was going to be considered', which could mean that parental consent will be required for children under 13 and would be in line with the data protection regulation discussed in the Sect. 7.3. Finally, besides children others, such as the mentally handicapped, may also be vulnerable in terms of online safety and it's important that these groups are addressed as well.[33]

We will now turn to the amendments of the proposed general data protection regulation to assess how these will impact the protection on children's personal data.

---

29 See also a recent opinion by the Article 29 Working Party in light of the growing use of apps by (very young) children: Opinion 02/2013 on apps on smart devices, February 2013, www.cbpweb.nl/downloads_int/wp202_en_Opinion_on_Mobile_Apps.pdf. See also Federal Trade Commission 2012, www.ftc.gov/os/2012/02/120216mobile_apps_kids.pdf.

30 See CEO Coalition 2012, http://ec.europa.eu/information_society/newsroom/cf/document.cfm?action=display&doc_id=1656.

31 The Article 26 Working Party has stated that children should not be confronted with online behavioural advertising, See Opinion 2/2010 on online behavioural advertising, 22 June 2010, p. 17.

32 Wall Street Journal 2012, http://online.wsj.com/article/SB10001424052702303506404577444711741019238.html?mod=WSJ_hpp_LEFTTopStories. However, there hasn't been a follow-up with, e.g. concrete initiatives by Facebook since then.

33 European Digital Rights 2012, European Digital Rights 2013.

7.3 General Data Protection Regulation

In January 2012, the proposal that will replace data protection Directive 95/46/EC was published and an amended version was adopted in October 2013 by the LIBE Committee of the European Parlement.[34] It intends not only to harmonise, but also modernise data protection law, given that new technologies have had a disruptive effect on the current legal protections for the use of personal data.[35] Since the introduction of the Lisbon Treaty, Article 16 of the Treaty on the functioning of the EU forms the legal basis for regulating personal data protection and free movement of data, and, hence, for the proposed regulation. It expressly puts forward a duty to provide effective protection of citizens, including children, which also entails providing citizens with the instruments to control their data.[36] Earlier, the European Commission had already noted that children need special protection, because research[37] found that 'children are less aware of risks, consequences, safeguards and rights in relation to the processing of personal data'.[38] Moreover, the EU Charter on fundamental rights not only contains a right to data protection, but also states that the protection and interests of children warrant particular attention.[39]

The proposed regulation has adopted the same definition of a child, i.e. a person under 18, as provided in the 1989 UN Child Rights Convention, and provides special protection for children in a number of ways. First, Article 8 specifically addresses the processing of children's personal data. Additionally, other provisions also contain elements focussed on child protection.[40] Relevant topics will be elaborated in the next sections.

---

[34] See also Inofficial consolidated version after the LIBE Committee vote, http://www.janalbrecht.eu/fileadmin/material/Dokumente/DPR-Regulation-inofficial-consolidated-LIBE.pdf. Here we will refer to the official proposal inasmuch as the provisions are still relevant or mention changes as a result of the amendments by the LIBE Committee. Proposal for a Regulation of the European Parliament and of the Council on the protection of individuals with regard to the processing of personal data and on the free movement of such data (General Data Protection Regulation), 25 January 2012, COM(2012) 11 final.

[35] Dutch Parliament has already criticised the proposed regulation for providing a lower level of protection than current data protection law, see www.nl-prov.eu/nl-prov/hnpewcm.nsf/_/68413B7B936DF39BC12579D4002FD99A?OpenDocument.

[36] Hijmans 2012.

[37] See Eurobarometer 2007, Safer Internet for Children—a children's perspectives, at http://ec.europa.eu/information_society/activities/sip/surveys/qualitative/index_en.htm.

[38] See A comprehensive approach to personal data protection in the European Union, COM(2010) 609 def, Brussel 4 November 2010, p. 7.

[39] See Articles 8 and 24 EU Charter.

[40] Article 32A also provides special protection for children but will not be further addressed here.

7.3.1 Consent and Age Verification

The proposed Article 8 provides that lawful processing of personal data of children under 13 is dependent on verifiable parental consent when offering online services. The choice to protect children under 13, rather than 18, is a welcome one in light of the right to freedom of information as laid down in the 1989 UN Child Rights Convention.[41] It endorses the importance of allowing children more and more rights and freedoms while growing up, which can be enjoyed and exercised free from parental supervision, while providing protection to younger children. However, Article 8 is not without problems. With respect to 'consent', the proposed regulation seems to distinguish between children and adults in order to account for the fact that children are less likely to be aware of online risks of personal data disclosure.[42] The distinction is, more specifically, linked to the right to be forgotten as a form of ex post protection, which has been criticised as not being a very effective for protection, though.[43] Preferably, the regulation should provide guidance on how consent of adults and of children over 13 is different to ensure legal certainty and adequate protection. Furthermore, it is important to clarify what verifiable consent entails and how this can be achieved in practice. Verifiability concerns the age of the person providing consent and, more particularly, the extent to which online service providers can—to a certain extent—reliably determine whether a person is over 13, as well as whether—in case of a child under 13—consent was given by one of the parents or caregivers. Will providing date of birth be sufficiently reliable? Will ticking the box that as a parent you are giving consent be sufficiently reliable when the child is under 13? Obviously, these processes can easily be manipulated. Or do service providers need to implement more advanced age verification and parental consent systems? And which of the service providers will be required to implement such systems: those that provide online services particularly focussed on children, or also those that provide services that could potentially be used by children?[44] The European legislator needs to provide more guidance on these issues for the rules to work and be clear, particularly, given that

---

[41] Article 17 UN Child Rights Convention 1989.

[42] See recital 53.

[43] See Sect. 7.3.2.

[44] See also Center for Democracy and Technology 2012, https://www.cdt.org/files/pdfs/CDT-DPR-analysis.pdf, arguing to restrict the requirement to websites for children as is the case under the US Children's Online Privacy Protection Act (COPPA), unless an online service provider has 'actual knowledge' of being in contact with a child. The actual knowledge required does not entail a general duty of online service providers to verify the age of their customers. Moreover, COPPA uses a sliding scale approach, which means that internal use of personal data demands lesser safeguards to verify parental consent than online publication of personal data or sharing personal data with third parties, see further Notice of Proposed Rulemaking seeking comment on proposed changes to the Commission's COPPA Rule, September 2011, p. 59817.

advanced cross-border age verification systems would have to be developed and will likely be quite costly for businesses.[45,46] Another issue is that age verification systems can potentially lead to more personal data being processed, which would not be in line with the proposed regulation.[47] Finally, parental consent should not be confused with parental control and technical solutions must not unnecessarily restrict the rights and freedoms of children.

7.3.2 Deleting Personal Data

Article 17 of the proposed regulation contains a right to erasure, which would allow Internet users to start again with a clean slate. The right to erasure is particularly relevant for children, since they are more often involved in risk-taking online behaviour of which they may not want be remembered as adults, and they may not be well aware of the long-term consequences of such behaviour.[48] The Internet has an iron memory and it can be difficult, if not impossible, to have online information removed once it is out there and spreading freely. Hence, Article 17 of the amended version of the proposed regulation requires the person or organisation responsible for processing personal data to: 'erase personal data relating to a person and abstain from further dissemination of such data if that person no longer consents to the use of his or her personal data. In that case, also third parties have to erase of any links to, or copies or replications of that data'.

In this way the right to erasure has an effect also on third parties that are involved in processing personal information of a particular individual. For instance, personal information can be shared automatically between different social networking services, such as Twitter, LinkedIn and Facebook. Perhaps such information can also be removed automatically if the SNS provider with which the information was posted originally makes a request to other SNS providers following a request by the data subject. Although the right to erasure comes from sympathetic reasoning, it has nevertheless been criticised as being potentially ineffective, given that architecture of Internet makes removing information a tedious, if not hopeless, job.

---

[45] Failure to comply with the conditions for consent (Article 8) can result in a fine of up to € 1.000.000 (Article 79(6)(a), proposed regulation).

[46] A proposed regulation on electronic identification and trusted services for electronic transactions in the internal market intends to accomplish interoperability between national e-identification systems, at http://ec.europa.eu/information_society/policy/esignature/eu_legislation/regulation/index_en.htm.

[47] See Article 10, proposed regulation.

[48] Preventing data abuse remains important beside ex post measures, which entails an important task for data protection authorities to educate children about risks, rules and rights in relation to personal data processing practices. See also Article 52, proposed regulation.

Since the proposed regulation does not apply to the private use of personal data, such as communications between family and friends on social networking sites, the scope of the right to erasure is limited, because it is confined to commercial parties and others outside the personal sphere. We are faced with the question, though, whether on social networking sites it is still appropriate to speak of a private sphere, when online profiles are public or when friends lists include people that are outside the close circle of family and friends.[49]

7.3.3 Profiling

According to article 20 of the amended version of the proposed regulation, natural persons have the right to object to profiling and must be informed about profiling 'in a highly visible manner'. Profiling is allowed when, for instance, a person has consented and adequate safeguards are in place, or when profiling is necessary for the performance of a contract. However, the proposed regulation seems to completely prohibit automated online profiling of children in recital 58, which states:

> Every natural person should have the right not to be subject to a measure which is based on profiling by means of automated processing. However, such measure should be allowed when expressly authorised by law, carried out in the course of entering or performance of a contract or when the data subject has given his consent. In any case, such processing should be subject to suitable safeguards, including specific information of the data subject and the right to obtain human intervention and *that such measure should not concern a child* (emphasis by the author).

An exception for children would be in line with opinions by the Article 29 Working Party, which has on several occasions argued against online behavioural targeting of children, a commercial activity that includes online profiling.[50] Remarkably, this reasoning has not been implemented in the provisions of the proposed regulation itself. Article 20 is silent on the issue. If the European legislator indeed wishes to except children from profiling, it would be wise to expressly say so in the provisions of the regulation. This would then, however, lead to the previously mentioned problem of how businesses will be able to determine the age of their customers. It will be difficult for them to verify with a reasonable amount of certainty that someone is a child or not, as long as there are no adequate and reliable age verification systems.[51]

---

[49] Hijmans 2012.

[50] Opinion 02/2013 on apps on smart devices, February 2013, www.cbpweb.nl/downloads_int/wp202_en_Opinion_on_Mobile_Apps.pdf, p. 26, and Opinion 2/2010 on online behavioural advertising, 22 June 2010, p. 17, http://ec.europa.eu/justice/policies/privacy/docs/wpdocs/2010/wp171_en.pdf.

[51] This is all the more worrying since severe fines are recommended for violating Article 20 of the proposed regulation (see Article 79(6)(d), proposed regulation).

7.3.4 Transparency

Initially, information on data processing practices in privacy statements must be provided in clear and simple ways that are understandable for children as well (Article 11); but this part of the provision has been deleted in the amended version of the proposed regulation. Transparency of data processing is an issue that needs our attention more generally, given that many people—young or old—may not have enough of an overview over the complex ways in which their data are harvested and used by multiple—third—parties.[52] Although Facebook's privacy statement describes, for example, in clear and understandable terms with examples how they process the personal data of their users, the technology is designed in such a way that it is quite difficult to actually understand their data processing practices. As a result even privacy-savvy Facebook users may unintentionally leak personal data and be confronted with potentially embarrassing situations. Moreover, websites other than Facebook do not always deploy transparent data processing practices. This is not surprising, given that the system is meant to nudge or trick users into sharing a lot of personal data to allow for better targeted advertising. Making money may in itself not be a bad thing, but the non-transparent and incontrollable ways in which this happens certainly raises questions. Merely providing understandable and accessible privacy statements is thus insufficient to adequately inform and protect children and two new principles in the proposed regulation aim to address this problem to a certain extent: 'privacy-by-default' en 'privacy-by-design'.

7.3.5 'The Principles of Privacy-by-Default' and 'Privacy-by-Design'

The proposed regulation puts greater responsibility on governments and businesses to comply with data protection rules,[53] amongst others, by introducing duties to implement what are called 'privacy-by-design' and 'privacy-by-default' schemes.[54] The second principle entails that personal information should in principle not be published by default to an unlimited group of people. This would be at odds with business models of most social networking sites, such as Facebook and Twitter, which require users to tweak their privacy settings in order to socialise privately. The first principle intends to obligate processors of personal data to implement privacy rules into the technical design of their online services. How these principles play out conceptually and practically still needs to be

[52] See also Van den Berg and Van der Hof 2012, www.uic.edu/htbin/cgiwrap/bin/ojs/index.php/fm/article/viewArticle/4010/3274.

[53] See Article 22, proposed regulation.

[54] See Article 23, proposed regulation.

determined. Moreover, it is to be expected that more detailed specifications will be set by the European Commission. What seems quite certain though is that they will have a great impact on business processes. However, some businesses have already started defining and perhaps even implementing privacy settings that are adequate for children as part of the SSNP and the Safer Internet Coalition. Nonetheless, enshrining these principles into the general data protection regulation is an important step towards integral, and hopefully effective, technical and organisational compliance with fundamental data protection principles.

7.4 Evaluation of the Proposed Changes in EU Regulation

Special data protection rules for children are extremely welcome in a world where children are avid users of online services and run risks to have their personal data used and abused. Nevertheless, the effect of these rules is expected to be limited in certain respects. Personal data risks may be also implicated in the private sphere, for instance, when peers compromise confidentiality or disclose embarrassing information, which falls, however, outside the scope of the proposed regulation. However, we should not forget that data protection law does not necessarily address all kinds Internet risks, such as slander or harassment. Besides, there are other ways, such as education or training, which may be more effective than laws in addressing or preventing such problems.[55] The proposed regulation should, however, explain much more clearly what 'personal and household activities'[56] entail to clearly define when data processing is in or outside the private sphere. The principles of privacy-by-design and privacy-by-default and requirements on transparency are important improvements in the proposed regulation, although how they will play out in practice remains to be seen.

The proposed regulation is very much in line with the UN Child Rights Convention 1989 by allowing for children to become more autonomous and independent when growing up and not requiring parental consent for data processing when they are over 13. However, the difference in consent by an adult and a child over 13 still needs clarification. Giving young people more responsibility does not necessarily mean they are aware of the consequences of their actions in the same way as adults may be. The proposed regulation leaves us completely in the dark how such factors may play a role in assessing whether consent was given adequately. To be sure, the right to erasure may be brought in when things turn awry for an older child, but this right may be difficult to enforce in practice. Moreover, the proposed regulation does not explain the concept of 'verifiable consent', which amounts to at least two problems. First, legal uncertainty exists for businesses when it is unclear when and how parental consent must be provided. Depending on

[55] Compare Van der Hof and Koops 2011, Article 4.

[56] See Article 2 sub d, proposed regulation.

the more precise conditions for age verification, such systems can become quite costly and have a considerable impact on business processes. Second, 'parental consent' systems should not develop into 'parental control' systems that unnecessarily restrict the online freedom of children. So far, cross-border and fool-proof age verification systems do not exist though.

The proposed regulation shows important progress by regulating profiling and protecting individuals against unfathomable profiling practices. For example, self-regulatory initiatives focussed on creating a safer Internet for children focus particularly on personal information exchanged amongst individual users rather than profiling practices by businesses and governments. The latter, however, entail the harvesting and processing of enormous amounts of personal data—also termed 'big data'—of individuals, including children. Given that current laws focus on personal data as such, not profiles, legal protection is presently inadequate. Unfortunately though, the current version of the proposed regulation is completely ambiguous about if, when and how children are protected against profiling. The recitals state quite clearly that children should not be profiled, however, the text of the proposal itself is silent on the issue. The European legislator needs to clarify this point, given that it would have huge implications for businesses.

7.5 Final Remarks

Two final remarks will wrap up this chapter. First, this chapter focuses on children, but there may very well be other groups of vulnerable individuals, such as people with mental disabilities, that may require similar levels of protection. I think we need to discuss how to include these people in safety schemes, given that the world is getting increasingly more complex.

Second, despite my earlier note of caution on self-regulation, I believe that it is important to engage businesses in ensuring online safety and increasing resilience of children.[57] The proposed regulation lays the groundwork for important issues—such as profiling, consent, right to be forgotten and privacy-by-design—that can become part of self-regulation in a much more meaningful way than is the case today.

References

Center for Democracy and Technology (2012) Analysis of the proposed data protection regulation. https://www.cdt.org/files/pdfs/CDT-DPR-analysis.pdf

De Haan J, Van der Hof S, Bekkers W, Pijpers R (2013) Self-regulating online child safety in Europe. In: O'Neil B, Staksrud E, McLaughlin S (eds) Towards a better internet for children—policy pillars, players and paradoxes. Nordicom, Goteborg

[57] See also Article 38, proposed regulation.

Eurobarometer (2007) Safer internet for children—a children's perspectives. http://ec.europa.eu/information_society/activities/sip/surveys/qualitative/index_en.htm

European Digital Rights (2012) CEO Coalition to make the internet a better place for kids. http://mogis-undfreunde.de/blog/guest-article-for-edri-gram-ceo-coalition-to-make-the-internet-a-better-place-forkids/

European Digital Rights (2013) CEO Coalition. The blind leading the bland. http://edri.org/ceo_coalition/

FTC (2012) Staff report mobile apps for kids: current privacy disclosures are disappointing. http://www.ftc.gov/os/2012/02/120216mobile_apps_kids.pdf

Hijmans H (2012) Nieuwe Europese regels voor privacy: commissie stelt pakket voor om gegevens ook in het informatietijdperk te beschermen. NtEr 4

Hildebrandt M (2008) A vision of ambient law. In: Brownsword R, Yeung K (eds) Regulating technologies: legal futures, regulatory frames and technological fixes. Hart, Oxford

Lyon D (2003) Surveillance as social sorting, privacy risk and digital discrimination. Routledge, London

Roßnagel A, Müller J (2004) Ubiquitous computing—neue Herausforderungen für den Datenschutz, ein Paradigmenwechsel und die von ihm betroffenen normativen Ansätze. Computer und recht 20(98):625–632

Van den Berg B, Van der Hof S (2012) What happens to my data? A novel approach to informing users of data processing practices. First Monday 17(7). www.uic.edu/htbin/cgiwrap/bin/ojs/index.php/fm/article/viewArticle/4010/3274

Van der Hof S (2012) Online privacybescherming is bepaald geen kinderspel, Over de nieuwe Europese regels voor de persoonsgegevensbescherming van minderjarigen. Tijdschrift voor internetrecht, pp 134–141

Van der Hof S, Koops EJ (2011) Adolescents and vybercrime: navigating between freedom and control. Policy & Internet 3(2):Article 4

Chapter 8
The Right to Privacy for Children on the Internet: New Developments in the Case Law of the European Court of Human Rights

Marga M. Groothuis

Contents

8.1 Introduction

In recent years, the European Court of Human Rights has published an increasing number of decisions on the right to privacy for children online. In its case law, the Court addresses the vulnerable position of minors in a digital environment. An example is the decision of the Court in the case of *K.U. v. Finland*.[1] The case concerned the applicant's complaint that an advertisement of a sexual nature had been posted about him on an Internet dating site. The applicant was 12 years old at

Dr. M. M. Groothuis is Assistant Professor at the Faculty of Law of Leiden University in the Netherlands.

[1] *K.U. v. Finland*, no. 2872/02, 2 December 2008.

M. M. Groothuis (✉)
Faculty of Law, Leiden University, Leiden, The Netherlands
e-mail: m.m.groothuis@law.leidenuniv.nl

S. van der Hof et al. (eds.), *Minding Minors Wandering the Web: Regulating Online Child Safety*, Information Technology and Law Series 24, DOI: 10.1007/978-94-6265-005-3_8,

the time. He complained under Article 8 of the European Convention of Human Rights (ECHR) that, under Finnish legislation in place at the time, the police and the courts could not require the Internet provider to identify the person who had posted the advertisement. The Court considered that the posting of the Internet advertisement about the applicant had been a criminal act, which had resulted in a minor having been a target for paedophiles. It stated that such conduct called for a criminal-law response and that effective deterrence had to be reinforced through adequate investigation and prosecution. The Court found that there had been a violation of Article 8.

The aim of this chapter is two-fold. First, it seeks to analyse recent case law of the European Court of Human Rights on the right to respect for private life (Article 8 ECHR) for children on the Internet. Second, it aims to investigate and critically discuss whether the characteristics of online modes of communications have sufficiently been taken into account by the European Court in its case law on the right to privacy of children.

The outline of this paper is as follows. Section 8.2 offers a brief overview of the case law of the European Court of Human Rights on the scope of the right to privacy for minors. Section 8.3 investigates to what extent and in which ways the Court has taken into account the characteristics of online communication in its case law. Section 8.4 focuses on the position of the minor in a digital environment: in which ways does the Court take into account factors such as age and possible vulnerability of minors on the Internet? Finally, Sect. 8.5 draws conclusions on the question whether the characteristics of online modes of communications have sufficiently been taken into account by the European Court in its case law on the right to privacy of children on the Internet.

8.2 The Right to Privacy for Minors: The Legal Framework

8.2.1 Scope of Article 8 of the European Convention

Article 8 of the European Convention on Human Rights (ECHR) imposes upon states the obligation to respect a wide range of interests.[2] Those interests—private and family life, home and correspondence—encompass a variety of matters, some of which are connected with one another and some overlap. In its application of Article 8, the European Court of Human Rights (the Court) has taken a flexible approach to the definition of the individual interests protected, with the result that the provision continues to broaden in scope.

This chapter, which examines the right to privacy of children on Internet, the focus is on one core element of Article 8 of the Convention: the right to respect for

[2] Harris et al. 2009, pp. 361–362.

private life. Although the Court has established that 'private life' is a broad concept, incapable of exhaustive definition,[3] it has in its case law provided some guidance as to the meaning and scope of this concept. In *Niemietz v. Germany* it observed:

> The Court does not consider it possible or necessary to attempt an exhaustive definition of the notion of 'private life'. However, it would be too restrictive to limit the notion to an 'inner circle' in which the individual may live his own personal life as he chooses and to exclude therefrom entirely the outside world not encompassed within that circle. Respect for private life must also comprise to a certain degree the right to establish and develop relationships with other human beings.[4]

It is possible to identify at least six categories of interests and activities which the Court has held to be within the ambit of 'private life'[5]: (i) personal identity,[6] (ii) moral or physical integrity,[7] (iii) private space,[8] (iv) collection and use of information,[9] (v) sexual activities[10] and (vi) social life.[11] Gerards[12] has pointed out that the special character of fundamental rights can be compared to that of a prism. If light is shed on the prism of the right to privacy, it shows a many-coloured spectrum of rights and interests. All these colours can be seen and named individually, yet they also run into one another. The fundamental rights prism continuously discloses new hues of colour: new individual interests are constantly recognised as elements of fundamental rights.

The application of Article 8 of the Convention requires a two-step test.[13] The first step involves consideration of whether the complaint falls under the scope of Article 8(1) as described above. Stage 2 concerns investigating whether the inference with the right to privacy is consistent with the requirements of Article 8(2). In that context, the following issues arise: (1) is the interference 'in accordance with the law'; (2) does it pursue a legitimate aim, and (3) is the interference 'necessary in a democratic society'?[14]

---

[3] White and Ovey 2010, p. 364.

[4] *Niemietz v. Germany*, no. 13710/88, 16 December 1992.

[5] Harris et al. 2009, pp. 366–371; cf. White and Ovey 2010, pp. 358–359.

[6] *Gaskin v. United Kingdom*, no. 10454/83, 7 July 1989.

[7] *X and Y v. The Netherlands*, no. 8978/80, 26 March 1985.

[8] *Von Hannover v. Germany* No. 1, no. 59320/00, 24 June 2004.

[9] *White v. Sweden*, no. 42435/02, 19 September 2006.

[10] *Dudgeon t. United Kingdom*, no. 7525/76, 22 October 1981.

[11] *Slivenko et al v. Latvia*, no. 48321/99, 9 October 2003.

[12] Gerards 2012, pp. 178–179.

[13] Harris et al. 2009, p. 363.

[14] An extensive analysis of the interpretation of these criteria in the case law of the European Court of Human Rights (ECtHR) can be found in White and Ovey 2010, pp. 312–333.

8.2.2 The Right to Private Life of Minors

In its case law on Article 8 ECHR, the Court has found a positive duty on the part of the Contracting states to protect their inhabitants, and in particular minors, in a range of cases.[15] In such cases, the state is not the primary violator of the right to privacy, but rather the state has inadequate structures in place to prevent the violation of this right. This can mean that the state does not provide adequate criminal sanctions for actions that violate the right to privacy of individuals.[16] States may also be compelled to provide regulations and policies that effectively deter and prevent violation of this right. Two cases are illustrative in this context.

In a landmark case in 1985, *X and Y v. The Netherlands*, the Grand Chamber of the Court formulated a positive obligation for a state to protect a child for the first time. The case concerned the rape of an 11-year-old mentally ill girl who had been raped in the home for mentally ill children where she lived. The next day, the father of the child had filed a complaint at the local police station and asked for criminal proceedings to be instituted. The police argued that since the father of the child considered his daughter unable to sign the complaint because of her mental condition and he was not allowed to sign himself, the complaint could not be filed. Because of this procedural obstacle, no criminal proceedings were started. Unable to file a complaint under the Dutch Criminal Code, the parents filed a complaint under Article 8 of the ECHR against the Dutch State and argued that the right to respect for family life meant that parents must be able to have recourse to remedies in the event of their children being the victims of sexual abuse. The European Court held that the Dutch Criminal Code had not provided the child with practical and effective protection. The Court concluded that, taking account of the nature of the wrongdoing in question, the child was the victim of a violation of Article 8 of the Convention.

More than two decades later, in the case *K.U. v. Finland* (2008), the Court formulated a positive obligation for states to protect children online.[17] The case concerned the posting, in 1999, of an advertisement of a sexual nature about a 12-year-old child, K.U., on an Internet dating site. The advertisement mentioned his age and year of birth and gave a detailed description of his physical characteristics. There was also a link to the applicant's web page where his picture and telephone number could be found. The ad announced that he was looking for an intimate relationship with a boy of his age or older "to show him the way". The boy became aware of the announcement when he received an e-mail from a man, offering to meet him and "to then see what he wanted". K.U.'s father asked the

---

15 ECtHR 2011, p. 4, available at www.echr.coe.int/NR/rdonlyres/A055F9CF-47DA-408A-9D90-BBEF8014BB8A/0/RAPPORT_RECHERCHE_Child_sexual_abuse_EN.pdf.

16 *M.C. v. Bulgaria*, no. 39272/98, 4 December 2003. An overview and analysis of the case law of the ECtHR on the positive obligation for states to provide sanctions under criminal law can be found in Tulkens 2011, pp. 582–595.

17 See also on this case: Hughes 2012, pp. 29–30.

police to identify the person who had posted the ad in order to bring charges. The service provider, however, refused as it considered itself bound by the confidentiality of telecommunications as defined under Finnish law. In a decision issued in 2001, the Helsinki District Court also refused the police's request under the Criminal Investigations Act to oblige the service provider to divulge the identity of the person who had posted the ad. It found that there was no explicit legal provision in such a case that could oblige the service provider to disregard professional secrecy and disclose such information. The decision of the District Court was upheld at the Court of Appeal. The Finnish Supreme Court refused leave to appeal. In 2002, the applicant lodged an appeal with the European Court.

In its judgment, the Court considered that the posting of the Internet advertisement about the applicant had been a criminal act, which had resulted in a minor having been a target for paedophiles. The Court remarked that the incident had taken place in 1999, that is, at a time when it had been well known that the Internet, precisely because of its anonymous character, could be used for criminal purposes. The widespread problem of child sexual abuse had also become well known over the preceding decade. It could, therefore, not be argued that the Finnish government had not had the opportunity to put in place a system to protect children from being targeted by paedophiles via the Internet.

The Court added that the national legislature should have provided a framework for reconciling the confidentiality of Internet services with the prevention of disorder or crime and the protection of the rights and freedoms of others. Although such a framework had been introduced in 2004 under the Exercise of Freedom of Expression in Mass Media Act, it had not been in place at the relevant time, with the result that Finland had failed to protect the right to respect for K.U.'s private life. The Court therefore found that there had been a violation of Article 8 ECHR.

A core element in this case is the question from which moment in time the national authorities could be expected to adopt legislation to protect children against paedophiles online. The Finnish government had taken the view that 'any legislative shortcoming' on her side to protect minors such as the applicant should be seen in its social context at the time (the late nineties), when a rapid increase in the use—and abuse—of the Internet was just beginning. For that reason, the Finnish government argued, the legislature could not be expected to already have adopted legislation to protect children online. The European Court rejected this argument. It referred to the negotiations for the Convention on Cybercrime, which had already been in an advanced stage in 1999.[18] It also considered that in the 1990s the Council of Europe and the United Nations had adopted several political

[18] In 1996 the European Committee on Crime Problems set up a committee of experts to deal with cybercrime. The Convention on Cybercrime was opened for signature on 23 November 2001 and entered into force on 1 July 2004. An analysis of this European treaty, which binds the Contracting Parties to provide criminal sanctions for various forms of online child abuse, can be found in Clough 2012, pp. 367–387.

declarations and resolutions on cybercrime.[19] National authorities had, therefore, had ample opportunity to put in place a system to protect children from exposure to paedophiles via the Internet.

This element in the reasoning of the Court has a wider meaning than for the K.U. case by itself: it indicates that the Member States to the ECHR are under an obligation to permanently amend and update their national legislation in order to protect children and other vulnerable individuals against forms of abuse enabled by the newest technological and social developments on the Internet.

8.3 The Role of New Technologies in the Case Law of the European Court

To what extent does the Court in its case law take the particular characteristics of online communication into account? When investigating this question, it is important to be aware that the Court's decisions give direction on individual complaints, but taken together they do not allow for a full characterisation of the Court's stance towards online communication.[20] With this qualification in place, I have attempted to investigate to what extent and how the Court refers to characteristics of the Internet in its judgments in individual cases. In this context I refer, first, to an extensive survey performed by Murphy and Ó Cuinn[21] in which they investigated the Court's position on new technologies, inter alia in its case law on the Articles 8 and 10 ECHR.[22] Using the findings of Murphy and Ó Cuinn as a starting point, I have investigated to what extent the Court explicitly refers to characteristics of the Internet or related applications of information and communication technologies by analysing a selection of the Court's decisions published in the HUDOC database in the period 2005–2012.[23] The outcome of this explorative analysis is as follows.

---

[19] These include Recommendation No. R (95) 13 of the Committee of Ministers of the Council of Europe concerning problems of criminal procedural law connected with information technology and Resolutions 55/63 of 4 December 2000 and 56/121 of 19 December 2001 of the General Assembly of the United Nations on Combating the criminal misuse of information technologies.

[20] This was also emphasised by Murphy and Ó Cuinn, who investigated the Court's stand towards 'new technologies': Murphy and Ó Cuinn 2010, p. 636.

[21] Murphy and Ó Cuinn 2010.

[22] Murphy and Ó Cuinn 2010, pp. 601–638.

[23] The selection was made by applying twenty key words, referring to (elements of) the Internet (such as 'web page', 'online) or to related applications of information and communication technologies (such as 'computer', 'server'), on the collection of the Court's decisions on complaints under Articles 8 and 10 ECHR, published on the English language section of the HUDOC website (www.echr.coe.int/ECHR/Homepage_EN) in the years 2005–2012.

A first factor which the Court has in some cases taken into account is the Internet's ability to create a major impact, due to its worldwide reach and high accessibility. The impact-factor was taken into account in particular in judgments concerning Internet publications in which a child is the subject of the publication. Illustrative is the case *Krone Verlag GmbH & Co KG and Krone Multimedia GmbH & Co KG v. Austria* (2012).[24] Krone Verlag and Krone Multimedia were publishers of two national newspapers that had published news articles about a 10-year-old girl who had been sexually abused by her father and stepmother. In their articles, the newspapers had revealed the identity of the girl. One of the newspapers had published its articles not only in its paper newspaper but also online, and had also published photographs of her. The Austrian courts decided to award the girl compensation, as they had found that her right as a victim of a criminal offence not to have her identity disclosed to the public had been breached. The two publishers filed a complaint with the European Court, relying on Article 10 (freedom of expression) of the ECHR.

In its judgment, the Court considered that the interference with the applicant companies' right to impart information was proportionate. The court indicated that it took into account "the particularly wide circulation of the applicant companies' media". The Court considered further that the news articles at issue dealt with a matter of public concern, a crime involving violence against a child and sexual abuse committed within the family, and could well give rise to a public debate on how the commission of similar crimes could be prevented. However, given that neither the offenders nor the victim were public figures or had previously entered the public sphere, it could not be said that the knowledge of the identity of these persons was material for understanding the particulars of the case. Hence, the Court noted that the newspapers were not prevented from reporting on all the details concerning the case of the child, only from revealing her identity and publishing a picture of her from which she could be recognised.

A second factor that the Court has taken into account—in at least one case, *Perrin v. United Kingdom*[25]—is the degree of accessibility of a particular web page. The Perrin case concerned the complaint under Article 10 ECHR of an individual convicted under the British Obscenity Act for the publication of pornographic photographs on the Internet. In its judgment the Court noted that the web page in respect of which the applicant was convicted was freely available to anyone surfing the Internet and that the material was the very type of material which might be sought out by young persons whom the national authorities were trying to protect. The Court further argued that it would have been possible for the applicant to have avoided the harm and, consequently, the conviction, by ensuring

---

[24] *Krone Verlag GmbH & Co KG and Krone Multimedia GmbH & Co KG v. Austria*, no. 33497/07, 17 January 2012. See also: *Kurier Zeitungsverlag und Druckerei GmbH v. Austria*, no. 3401/07, 17 January 2012.

[25] *Perrin v. United Kingdom*, no. 5446/03, 18 October 2005. Cf. *Mouvement Raëlien Suisse v. Switzerland*, no. 16354/06, 13 July 2012, in which the Court also refers to the extent to which the website of the application organisation is accessible to minors.

that none of the photographs were available on the free preview page (where there were no age checks). The Court pointed out that the applicant chose not to do so, no doubt because he hoped to attract more customers by leaving the photographs on the free preview page. The Court concluded that *in casu* the applicant's criminal conviction could be regarded as necessary in a democratic society in the interests of the protection of morals and the rights of others.

A third factor which is relevant in this context concerns the fact that the publication of information containing personal data on the Internet implies 'automatic processing of personal data'.[26] In a series of judgments[27] published in 2008–2009, the Court emphasised that the protection of personal data is of fundamental importance to a person's enjoyment of his or her right to respect for private and family life, as guaranteed by Article 8 of the Convention. Therefore, the Court argued, the domestic law must afford appropriate safeguards to prevent any such use of personal data as may be inconsistent with the guarantees of this article. The Court stressed that the need for such safeguards is all the greater where the protection of personal data undergoing automatic processing is concerned.

The overview above indicates that the Court is aware of various characteristics of the Internet. It takes these characteristics into account when balancing interests in the application of Article 8(2) ECHR in individual cases. It is important to note, however, that the Court weighs these medium- and ICT-related factors in relation to other factors that are also relevant for the balancing of interests in the particular case.

The recent judgments of *Axel Springer v. Germany*[28] and *Von Hannover v. Germany* (no. 2)[29] illustrate how the Court balances five factors, including the scope of the used media, in relation to each other. Both cases concerned the publication of articles in the media and, in the second case, of photos depicting the private life of well-known people. In these judgments, published on the same date (7 February 2012), the Grand Chamber of the Court formulated five criteria relevant for the exercise of balancing the right to freedom of expression against the right to respect for private life. These criteria are:

1. Do the published photos or articles contribute to a debate of general interest?
2. How well known is the person concerned and what is the subject of the report?

---

[26] Cf. Court of Justice EU, 6 November 2003, C-101/01 (*Lindqvist*).

[27] *S. and Marper v. United Kingdom*, nos. 30562/04 and 30566/04, 4 December 2008; *Bouchacourt v. France*, no. 5335/06, 17 December 2009; *Gardel v. France*, no. 16428/05, 17 December 2009; *M.B. v. France*, no. 22115/06, 17 December 2009; *Liberty v. United Kingdom*, no. 58243/00, 1 July 2008. In these judgments, the Court refers to its earlier case law in which it had formulated principles and safeguards to be respected in case of secretly monitoring communication: *inter alia Malone* v. *United Kingdom*, no. 8691/79, 2 August 1984 and *Rotaru v. Romania*, 28341/95, 4 May 2000. See for an analysis of this case law: Heringa and Zwaak 2006, pp. 666–674 and 734–738.

[28] *Axel Springer AG v. Germany*, no. 39954/08, 7 February 2012.

[29] *Von Hannover v. Germany No.* 2, nos. 40660/08 and 60641/08, 7 February 2012.

3. The conduct of the person concerned prior to publication of the report or the fact that the photo and the related information have already appeared in an earlier publication;
4. The way in which the information was obtained and its veracity;
5. Content, form and consequences of the publication, also taking into account the extent to which the article or photo has been disseminated.

It follows from the above that the Court weighs the factor 'form and scope of the used medium' (factor 5) in conjunction with four other factors.

Section 8.4 will critically discuss whether the characteristics of online modes of communications have sufficiently been taken into account by the European Court in its case law on the right to privacy of children.

8.4 The Position of the Minor on the Internet: Assessment of the Case Law

When assessing the case law of the European Court on the right to respect for private life for children on the Internet, several remarks can be made.

First, it is remarkable that the Court, in its recent case law on Article 8 ECHR, rarely refers to the United Nations Convention on the Rights to the Child,[30] while it has frequently referred to this UN Convention in its case law on the Articles 2 (right to life) and 3 (prohibition of torture and inhuman treatment) ECHR. Already in 1998, in the case of *A. v. United Kingdom*, the Court considered:

> [t]he obligation on the High Contracting Parties under Article 1 of the Convention to secure to everyone within their jurisdiction the rights and freedoms defined in the Convention, taken together with Article 3, requires States to take measures designed to ensure that individuals within their jurisdiction are not subjected to torture or inhuman or degrading treatment or punishment, including such ill-treatment administered by private individuals [..]. Children and other vulnerable individuals, in particular, are entitled to State protection, in the form of effective deterrence, against such serious breaches of personal integrity (see, mutatis mutandis, the *X and Y v. the Netherlands* judgment of 26 March 1985, Series A no. 91, pp. 11–13, §§ 21–27; the *Stubbings and Others v. the United Kingdom* judgment of 22 October 1996, Reports 1996-IV, p. 1505, §§ 62–64; and also the United Nations Convention on the Rights of the Child, Articles 19 and 37).[31]

In my view, in its case law on the right to privacy of children online, the Court could strengthen its reasoning by referring to the Articles 16(2) and 3 of the UN Convention of the Rights of the Child. Article 16(2) of the UN Convention prescribes that no child shall be subjected to arbitrary or unlawful interference with his

[30] An exception is *Mavlov v. Bulgaria*, no. 1638/03, 23 June 2008, in which the Court did, in a case concerning the right to family life of a child who was expulsed from Austria to Bulgaria, refer to Article 3 of the UN Convention on the Rights of the Child.

[31] *A. v. United Kingdom*, no. 100/1997/884/1096, 23 September 1998.

or her privacy, family, home or correspondence, nor to unlawful attacks on his or her honor and reputation. Article 3(2) prescribes that States Parties undertake to ensure the child such protection as is necessary for his or her well-being and, to this end, shall take all appropriate legislative and administrative measures. These two provisions, read in conjunction with Article 8 ECHR, emphasise the need to protect children against breaches of personal integrity, both online and offline. This implies that children have a right to respect for their personal identity and moral or physical integrity and that they are entitled to State protection, in the form of legislation or policy measures, to protect them against serious breaches of personal integrity in case of—inter alia—online publication and dissemination of real or simulated child pornography,[32] 'grooming'[33] and serious forms of cyberbullying.[34]

Second, when taking into account the factor 'impact', it is important to distinguish between impact in the sense of 'consequences for the child' on the one hand, and impact in the sense of 'degree of dissemination of the text, photo or video among an audience' on the other.

When considering the factor 'consequences for the child', the argumentation of the Court is in most cases precise and clear. In *K.U. v. Finland*, for example, the Court emphasised that the act of publishing the advertisement on the dating site made the child a target for approaches by paedophiles. In this context, the Court referred to the potential threat to the child's physical and mental welfare brought about by the impugned situation and to his vulnerability in view of his young age. In *Krone Verlag GmbH & Co KG and Krone Multimedia GmbH & Co KG v. Austria* the Court specified the impact the publication of the articles and photos had on this young girl: following the detailed reports in the press and on Internet the girl—already traumatised as a victim of rape—had a relapse and had to be readmitted to hospital on account of her serious psychological problems.

When considering the 'degree of dissemination of the text, photo or video among an audience', however, the Court is less precise, at times even vague, in its argumentation. In most cases, the Court only indicates to take into consideration "the degree of circulation of the applicant companies' media"[35] or "the extent to which the report and photo have been disseminated".[36] In my view the Court could strengthen its argumentation by specifying in a more concrete way how this degree of dissemination is assessed and which circumstances are taken into consideration. The following aspects could in my view be taken into account when measuring 'degree of dissemination':

[32] See on the legality of regulating simulated child pornography: Nair 2010, pp. 223–232, McIntyre 2010, pp. 209–221.

[33] Clough 2012, pp. 381–382. 'Grooming' can be defined as "the process by which a child is befriended by a would-be abuser in an attempt to gain the child's confidence and trust, enabling them to get the child to acquiesce to abusive activity": Gillespie 2002, pp. 411–412.

[34] Langos 2012, pp. 285–289; Gillespie 2006, pp. 123–136.

[35] *Krone Verlag GmbH & Co KG and Krone Multimedia GmbH & Co KG v. Austria*, para 60.

[36] *Von Hannover v. Germany* No. 2, para 112.

1. Was the text, photo or video distributed via the Internet or via a non-digital (paper) medium (taking into account that digital data can be redistributed much more easily and at much smaller cost than non-digital data)?
2. In the case of publication on the internet: how many page views have there been, millions of only dozens?
3. Is the video, photo or text that constituted an interference in the child's private life still online, or was it removed as soon as a request to do so was received?
4. Has the video, photo or text been published by other websites than the one which first published it, and if so, to what degree? More concretely: has the video, photo or text spread around the World Wide Web (with the result that it can never be removed from the internet anymore), or was there only a limited dissemination from one website during a short period of time?

By explicitly referring to factors such as these, the Court could give more insight in the way it measures 'degree of dissemination' in cases of interference with the privacy of a child online.

Third, the factor 'degree of accessibility of a particular web page' is relevant not only in cases where a distinction can be made between 'preview pages' and 'pages for which payment is required' (such as in the case *Perrin v. United Kingdom*) but also in cases which involve the use of social media. One of the characteristics of social media is the variation in the extent of their accessibility. In social media such as Facebook and Google+, users can determine for each publication (of a text, photo or video) to whom they give access: for example to a limited number of 'friends', to a wider group of 'friends of friends' or to 'everyone'. There has not yet been case law of the Strasbourg Court on publications on social media. These cases can be expected to reach the Court soon, given the fact that they have been brought for national courts throughout Europe in recent years.[37] When a complaint in a case involving the use of a social medium is submitted to the Court, e.g. a case concerning the publication and dissemination on Facebook of a video showing cyberbullying and abuse of a child, it will be necessary to determine the degree of openness (or closeness) of the used medium. An example is a case in Italy, where a video, posted on Google Video in 2006, showed a teenager with autism being bullied by four students in front of more than a dozen others. The posting of the video gave rise to three distinct lawsuits.[38] The first concerned the four students having an active role in the video (three abusers and the movie maker). They were identified and condemned by the Tribunal of Turin with a 1-year sentence (work in social services) for assault and slander. The second lawsuit concerned the teacher and the school (for failing to prevent the offence). The third lawsuit concerned Google: four leading Google executives were accused of violating Italian law by allowing the video to be posted online. On 24 February

---

[37] See for an overview and analysis of case law on social media and the right to privacy in The Netherlands and in Europe: Lodder 2012.

[38] Sartor and Viola de Azevedo Cunha 2010, p. 357.

2010, the Court of First Instance in Milan convicted three of the four Google executives for violation of the Italian Data Protection Act.[39] On 21 December 2012, the Milan Court of Appeal overturned these convictions. This Court rejected the public prosecutor's position that hosting services must pre-emptively screen all material uploaded to the internet, explaining that such a duty could chill freedom of expression.[40]

When balancing the interest of protecting the personal integrity and privacy of a child against the interest of protecting the freedom of expression, a factor to be taken into account is the degree of dissemination of the video in the particular case. Concrete indicators can be the number of web pages on which the video was published, the number of 'views' of the video on these web pages, the degree of openness or closeness of the web pages (accessible to 'all' or to a limited number of users of a social medium) and the length of time during which the video was accessible. Investigating indicators such as these requires substantive knowledge of the internet and specific Internet applications. In order to acquire knowledge of the new developments on the Internet and in particular social media, it is important that judges themselves, both at the national and the European level, participate in social media.[41]

8.5 Conclusion

The goal of this chapter was twofold: (1) to analyse recent case law of the European Court of Human Rights on the right to respect for private life (Article 8 ECHR) for children on the Internet and (2) to investigate and critically discuss whether the characteristics of online modes of communications have sufficiently been taken into account by the European Court in its case law on the right to privacy of children.

I conclude, first, that the European Court has offered strong protection to privacy of children online in its case law in the period 2005–2012. While emphasising the vulnerability of children, especially young children, in a digital environment, the Court has imposed a positive obligation, inherent to Article 8 ECHR, upon States to adopt a legislative framework to protect children from grave

---

[39] Sentenza n. 1972/2010. Tribunale Ordinario di Milano in composizione monocratica. Sezione 4 Penale, available at http://speciali.espresso.repubblica.it/%2Fpdf/Motivazioni_sentenza_Google.pdf. An analysis of this case and critical comments on the decision of the Court can be found in Sartor and Viola de Azevedo Cunha 2010, pp. 356–378.

[40] Corte d'Appello di Milano, case 4889/2010, available at www.penalecontemporaneo.it/upload/1362065204Sentenza%20appello%20google.pdf. An English summary of the decision of the Court of Appeal is available at http://www.lexology.com/library/detail.aspx?g=8a202daf-549a-4abc-b242-1baf983ee355.

[41] Cf. Hull 2012, for an analysis of the debate on judges using online social networks in the United States.

types of interference with their private lives, such as sexual abuse online in several cases. Furthermore, it follows from the case law of the Court that the Member States to the ECHR are under an obligation to permanently update and amend their national legislation in order to protect children and other vulnerable individuals against forms of abuse enabled by the newest technological and social developments on the internet.

Second, I conclude that in its judgments the Court has shown awareness of the basic characteristics of the Internet, such as the internet's ability to create a major impact, due to its worldwide reach. It takes these characteristics into account when balancing interests in the application of Article 8(2) ECHR in individual cases. The Court weighs these medium- and ICT related factors in relation to other factors that are also relevant for the balancing of interests in the particular case.

However, I have found that when assessing the interference into the private life of a child online the Court is not always precise, and at times even vague, in its argumentation. In my view the Court could strengthen its argumentation by specifying in a concrete way how the degree of dissemination of a video, photo or text portraying a child is assessed and which circumstances are taken into consideration. Thus, it could give more guidance to domestic courts in the Member States of the Council of Europe on how to apply Article 8 of the Convention in a digital environment.

Finally, I have argued that handling cases involving children online requires judges to have substantive knowledge of the newest developments on the internet, as well as knowledge of the workings of specific Internet applications, such as social media. A judge is expected to have general knowledge of the aspects of the world he assesses. A judge in the digital age should be expected to know about Web 2.0.

References

Clough J (2012) The Council of Europe convention on cybercrime: defining 'crime' in a digital world. Crim Law Forum 23:363–391

European Court of Human Rights (2011) Child sexual abuse and child pornography in the Court's case law—research report, Council of Europe 2011. www.echr.coe.int/NR/rdonlyres/A055F9CF-47DA-408A-9D90-BBEF8014BB8A/0/RAPPORT_RECHERCHE_Child_sexual_abuse_EN.pdf

Gerards J (2012) The prism of fundamental rights. Eur Const Law Rev 8(2):173–202

Gillespie AA (2002) Child protection on the internet-challenges for criminal law. Child Fam Law Q 14:411–425

Gillespie AA (2006) Cyber-bullying and harassment of teenagers: the legal response. J Soc Welf Fam Law 28(2):123–136

Harris D, O'Boyle M, Bates E, Buckley C (eds) (2009) Harris, O'Boyle & Warbrick: Law of the European Convention on Human Rights, 2nd edn. Oxford University Press, Oxford

Heringa AW, Zwaak L (2006) Right to respect for privacy (article 8). In: Van Dijk P, Van Hoof F, Van Rijn A, Zwaak L (eds) Theory and practice of the European Convention on Human Rights. Intersentia, Antwerp

Hughes K (2012) The child's right of privacy and article 8 of the European convention on human rights. Law Childhood Stud Curr Legal issues 14:1–51

Hull B (2012) Why can't we be 'friends'? A call for a less stringent policy for judges using online social networking. Hastings Law J 63:595–631

Langos C (2012) Cyberbullying: the challenge to define. Cyberpsychology. Behav Soc Netw 15(6):285–289

Lodder AR (2012) Recht rond cyberwar, het internet van dingen en andere internet(on)gemakken [Law on cyber war, the internet of things and other aspects of the internet]. Free University, Amsterdam

McIntyre TJ (2010) Blocking child pornography on the internet: European Union developments. Int Rev Law Comput Technol 24(3):209–221

Murphy T, Ó Cuinn G (2010) Works in progress: new technologies and the European Court of Human Rights. Hum Rights Law Rev 10(4):601–638

Nair A (2010) Real porn and pseudo porn: the regulatory road. Int Rev Law Comput Technol 24(3):223–232

Sartor G, Viola de Azevedo Cunha M (2010) The Italian Google-case: privacy, freedom of speech and responsibility of providers for user-generated contents. Int J Law Inf Technol 18(4):356–378

Tulkens F (2011) The paradoxical relationship between criminal law and human rights. J Int Crim Justice 9:577–595

White RCA, Ovey C (2010) Jacobs, White and Ovey: the European convention on human rights. Oxford University Press, Oxford

Chapter 9
Online Social Networks and Young People's Privacy Protection: The Role of the Right to Be Forgotten

Rachele Ciavarella and Cécile De Terwangne

Contents

Rachele Ciavarella is a lawyer with ICT Legal Consulting Law Firm and a Blue Book Trainee at EU Commission DG CNECT Unit H4 Trust and Security. Cécile De Terwangne is a professor at the Law Faculty of the University of Namur (Belgium) and Research Director in the 'Freedoms in the Information Society' Unit of the Research Centre in Information, Law and Society (CRIDS—University of Namur).

R. Ciavarella (✉)
CRIDS—University of Namur, Namur, Belgium
e-mail: rachele.ciavarella@unamur.be

C. De Terwangne
Faculty of Law, CRIDS, University of Namur, Namur, Belgium

S. van der Hof et al. (eds.), *Minding Minors Wandering the Web: Regulating Online Child Safety*, Information Technology and Law Series 24, DOI: 10.1007/978-94-6265-005-3_9,

9.1 Introduction

A number of social studies have shown that children and young people[1] are increasingly interested in new technologies, and especially in new forms of communication and socialisation.[2] According to a recent study[3] conducted by the EU Kids Online network,[4] 38 % of 9–12 year olds and 77 % of 13–16 year olds have a social networking service (SNS) profile. The way they "feed" these profiles and use the SNS is inevitably influenced by their young age. Moreover, the above-mentioned study has demonstrated that younger children are more likely to have a "public" profile.

Young individuals often do not envisage the long-term consequences of the content that they spontaneously make public. They do not fully comprehend the power of search engines to allow access to any piece of information removed out of its initial context. The majority of youths do not consider the possibility that the content they communicate (be it text, photographs or video) may be copied and stored on third-party computers, fundamentally outside their control. Above all, they are largely unaware of the "eternity effect"[5] of electronic memory. Additionally, when surfing the Internet, children are commonly unconscious that they leave traces of their activity, similar to tattoos, which are rather difficult to remove.

Combined with the actual practical difficulty of content removal once published online,[6] this means that as adults such individuals may suffer life-long consequences of an image influenced by their online activities as teenagers.[7] The consequences are thus multiple. In today's society, digital reputation is at least as important as one's "real life" profile.[8] A negative *e-reputation* has the potential to create significant problems for children and young people who do not exercise

---

[1] For the purposes of this document, the term "young people" will refer to legal minors. The meaning of legal minor depends on the jurisdiction in which the service is offered; normally this refers to users under 18 or 16 years of age. However, in the General Data Protection Regulation (see *infra*), while Article 4(18) states that 'child' means any person below the age of 18 years, Article 8.1 (Processing of personal data of a child) outlines that *the processing of personal data of a child below the age of 13 years shall only be lawful if and to the extent that consent is given or authorised by the child's parent or custodian.*

[2] Casarosa 2010, available at http://ssrn.com/abstract=1561570.

[3] Livingstone et al. 2011, available at http://www2.lse.ac.uk/media@lse/research/EUKidsOnline/ShortSNS.pdf.

[4] EU Kids Online is a multi-national thematic network, founded by the EC Safer Internet Programme, that aims to stimulate and coordinate investigation into the use of new media by children, www2.lse.ac.uk/media@lse/research/EUKidsOnline/Home.aspx.

[5] Walz 1997, p. 3.

[6] For an example of reported cases about people seeking to have their data deleted from a social network and facing practical difficulties, see http://online.wsj.com/article/SB10001424052748703396604576087573944344348.html.

[7] See for example Mayer-Schönberger 2009.

[8] Legrand and Bellamy 2012, www.lesnumeriques.com/divers/touche-pas-a-e-reputation-enquete-a1548.html.

correct control in the use of social networks. Moreover and not insignificantly, the digital traces that they leave behind are easily used for behavioural and contextual advertising.

Due to the expanding possibilities to collect, store and use personal data,[9] we have dismantled the world in which our past is "forgettable" and we have begun to live in a society of permanent memory. The development and diffusion of Information and Communication Technologies has increased simultaneously with the need for an adequate level of privacy on the Internet. Taking such notions into account, in 2009 the Vice President of the European Commission, Viviane Reding, announced her intention to review the 1995 Data Protection Directive[10] and to include a separate "right to be forgotten". She stated, "As somebody once said: 'God forgives and forgets but the Web never does!' This is why the 'right to be forgotten' is so important for me. With more and more private data floating around the Web—especially on social networking sites—people should have the right to have their data completely removed."[11]

Section 9.2 of this chapter will analyse the role of the right to be forgotten, also called the "right to oblivion", in the field of online social networking sites. Section 9.3 outlines the role given to the right to oblivion in the Data Protection Directive of 1995, while Sect. 9.4 focuses on the potential and the limitations of the recent Proposed General Data Protection Regulation that is intended to replace this Directive.[12]

As will be demonstrated, the issue of the right to be forgotten primarily revolves around the conflict between this right and the right to freedom of speech, the duty to remember and marketing purposes.

9.2 The Role of the Right to Be Forgotten

What is the right to be forgotten? Neither the 95/46/EC Directive nor the Proposed General Data Protection Regulation provide any clear definition or description of what the right to be forgotten clearly consists of. However, in its important communication preceding, the revision process of the general legal text on personal data protection, the European Commission refers to the right to be forgotten as "the right of individuals to have their data no longer processed and deleted

---

[9] 'Personal data' means 'any information relating to an identified or identifiable natural person ("data subject")' (Article 2, a) of the directive 95/46).

[10] Directive 95/46/CE of the European Parliament and of the Council of 24 October 1995 on the protection of individuals with regard to the processing of personal data and on the free movement of such data, OJ, 23 November 1995, L281/31.

[11] Reding 2010.

[12] Proposal for a Regulation of the European Parliament and of the Council on the protection of individuals with regard to the processing of personal data and on the free movement of such data (General Data Protection Regulation), 2012/0011 (COD).

when they are no longer needed for legitimate purposes. This is the case, for example, when processing is based on the person's consent and when he or she withdraws consent or when the storage period has expired."[13]

Could the application of such a 'right to have their data deleted' offer adequate protection to children and young people in the field of SNS?

In this day and age forgetting is difficult, if not impossible. The basic idea of informational self-determination[14] has limits.[15] On the Net it appears that we are indeed prisoners of our past. Control of the fate of the data that has been shared in certain circles and control of what is circulated tends to be an illusion. This is notably due to the frightening efficiency of search engines to examine the Web in its entirety and to bring the slightest piece of information to the surface, often out of its initial context.[16] The content that one agrees to disclose to certain recipients, because they belong to a determined circle (friends, family, members of an interest group, etc.), is expected to be inaccessible to others. However, in order to erase what has been said or shared about us on the Internet, or even what we once shared ourselves, represents a pure challenge. This notably derives from the architecture of information systems that have become increasingly complex, with numerous links rendering any deletion of data both tricky and expensive, similar to a Sisyphean activity.[17] It has been demonstrated that on an SNS a user's loss of control is observed at three levels: the creation of personal data, their accessibility and their deletion.[18]

The situation is even worse when the data subject is a child, wholly ignorant of the mechanisms through which the information he "posts" on the Internet can be spread or further transmitted. It is also often the case that the said child simply does not care about the risks of divulging such information. The risks are, however, very real as is demonstrated by the misadventure of an American student who was denied the possibility to graduate from college due to the discovery, on a social networking site, of a post criticising her supervisor and a photo of herself wearing a pirate hat, holding a cup inscribed with the words "drunken pirate".[19] Additionally, innumerable job candidates are refused positions after simple and rapid Internet searches, all too often revealing compromising pictures posted by the individuals when they were mere teenagers.

---

[13] European Commission Communication, 'A comprehensive approach on personal data protection in the European Union', 4 November 2010, COM (2010) 609 final, p. 8.

[14] Informational self-determination means control over one's personal information, that is to say the individuals' right to decide which information about themselves will be disclosed, to whom and for which purpose. See De Terwangne 2012, p. 112, also available at www.idp.uoc.edu.

[15] See Rouvroy 2008, available at http://works.bepress.com/antoinette_rouvroy/5/.

[16] On the risk of de-contextualisation in SNS, see Dumortier 2009, available at http://works.bepress.com/franck_dumortier/1.

[17] De Terwangne 2012, p. 112 and 117, also available at www.idp.uoc.edu.

[18] Moiny 2012.

[19] Copeland 2012, p. 1.

The 'perfection' of the memory of the Internet is contrasted with the imperfections of the human memory. The eternity effect of the Internet preserves past errors, memories, photos and videos that have been 'posted' on the Web and that we would often, at a later stage, like to cancel.[20] The right to be forgotten may appear to be a solution that 'cleans' our past, our errors, and consequently preserves our digital reputation. It is a legal way to reintroduce oblivion in social life. It raises serious concerns, however, regarding the possibility of individuals to re-write their own history. It should not be considered nor built, then, as a way of having elements of one's past completely disappear on a whim of desire. We observe, under Sect. 9.4.2, that this right must indeed face serious limits.

As outlined before, Sect. 9.3 will focus on the elements of what the right to be forgotten could be, as found in the Directive 95/46/EC, Sect. 9.4 will deal with the right to be forgotten under the Proposed General Data Protection Regulation.

9.3 The Right to Be Forgotten Under the Directive 95/46/EC on Data Protection

The right to be forgotten is not evoked as such under the Directive 95/46/EC on data protection. As previously stated, no definition of the right to oblivion appears in the text. Can this logically bring one to conclude that such a right has little or nothing to do with the Directive and is a sort of non-legally-binding principle? Shall we then consider the concept of the right to be forgotten as a new principle, or instead as an old principle only phrased differently?

While the concept is not present as such in Directive 95/46/EC, we find elements of what could be considered a right to oblivion in the current European Union data protection framework. The first element ensues from the so-called principle of purpose.[21] The purpose principle states that personal data must be processed for a determined, legitimate and transparent purpose. Moreover—the most interesting point here—this that the principle specifies that personal data must not be kept longer than necessary for the purposes for which it was collected or further processed. A sort of right to oblivion is therefore directly attained by the means of this principle.[22] According to the EU Data Protection Directive, personal data should be anonymised or deleted once the purposes for which it was processed have been achieved. This rule clearly establishes a right to oblivion in the sense that data is not supposed to remain in the hands of the controller eternally.

In addition, Article 12(1)(b) allows the data subject to demand the rectification or the deletion of their data when the processing of it is not in compliance with the Directive. If personal data is kept longer than what is allowed on the basis of the

[20] De Terwangne 2012, p. 110.

[21] Article 6(1)(b), (e) of the 95/46 Directive.

[22] De Terwangne 2012, p. 114.

purpose principle, the data subject may get such data erased. The current European Union framework provides sanctions in the case of infringement of these rules.[23]

These elements may be regarded as illustrative forms of a right to be forgotten in the Directive. They give the data controller[24] the role of verifying whether or not data is necessary for the purposes of the processing and whether the personal data should be deleted or anonymised. The right to be forgotten in this sense is assimilated to a right to deletion (of the data or at least of the identifying elements of it), inherent to the legal system of protection of personal data. The data subject does not have to do anything in order to have his/her data erased or anonymised. The data controller is the main actor in the right to be forgotten while the data subject is simply given a tool to see to it that the rule is respected and to obtain erasure of data in the case that the controller has not erased or anonymised it spontaneously.

There is another way of achieving the right to be forgotten in the Directive: through the right to object to the processing of personal data. This right is stated in Article 14 of Directive 95/46/EC. Data subjects have the right "to object at any time on compelling legitimate grounds relating to [their] particular situation to the processing of data relating to [them]. Where there is a justified objection, the processing instigated by the controller may no longer involve those data."[25] In this case, the active role is deferred to the data subject. The continued processing of personal data is considered legitimate until the data subject intervenes, unlike the case when data is kept after the necessary period to achieve the purposes of processing.

Both ways come to the conclusion that data processing is considered legitimate until a certain and specific moment: either when the purpose of processing is achieved (which includes the legal period of data retention for purposes of proof), or when the data subject objects on a compelling legitimate ground relating to his/her particular situation.

Notwithstanding the importance of the elements of a right to oblivion established by the Data Protection Directive, it shall be observed that the framework created in 1995 is old (adopted just before the societal diffusion of the Internet) and the provisions previously mentioned do not grant the data subject perfect and complete control over their data.[26] Should an individual object, for example, to the processing of his/her data, the individual must present compelling legitimate grounds. The "compelling" nature of the grounds is difficult to assess by someone outside of the processing. This difficulty has been taken into consideration in the Proposal of the General Data Protection Regulation, as will be seen below.

---

[23] Article 24 of the 95/46 Directive.

[24] A "controller" is "the natural or legal person, public authority, agency or any other body which alone or jointly with others determines the purposes and means of the processing of personal data; [...]" (Article 2, d) of the Directive.

[25] Article 14(1)(b) of the 95/46 Directive.

[26] Copeland 2012, p. 4.

Rapid technological developments have brought new challenges to the protection of personal data. Consequentially, it has been heavily debated whether or not it is appropriate to envisage an extension of the existing bits of the right to be forgotten in response to certain Internet specificities, particularly those linked to social networking services. As a result of the development of the Internet environment and of the limitation of current legislation, the European Commission, in its communication entitled "A comprehensive approach on personal data protection in the European Union",[27] concludes that the European Union needs a more comprehensive and coherent policy regarding the fundamental right to personal data protection.

9.4 The Right to Be Forgotten Under the Proposal for a General Data Protection Regulation

Due to the compelling developments in ICT since 1995 including the digitalisation of content and the proliferation of information, the need to revise the current legislative framework has become obvious. Concerns regarding the necessity to develop a genuine "right to be forgotten" have notably ensued from the multiplication of misadventures linked to SNS with the realisation that individuals may suffer grave consequences after the spontaneous disclosure of information at earlier stages. This is particularly evidenced upon understanding that it is impossible to entirely erase data once it is posted on Facebook.[28] The modification of the existing legislation revolves around the question of granting Internet users the possibility to take initiative regarding their personal data, and the possibility of deleting their data from websites, blogs and social networking sites.[29] The idea to attach a sort of expiration date to the data so that they are no longer usable after a certain time is also at issue.

9.4.1 An Article Specially Devoted to the Right to Be Forgotten and to Erasure

Article 17 of the Proposal for a General Data Protection Regulation[30] grants data subjects the right to have their personal data erased[31] when the data are no longer

[27] COM(2010)609 final.

[28] Van Alsenoy et al. 2009, pp. 65–79.

[29] Gomes de Andrade 2012, p. 124.

[30] Article 17.1. The data subject shall have the right to obtain from the controller the erasure of personal data relating to them and the abstention from further dissemination of such data, *especially in relation to personal data which are made available by the data subject while he or*

necessary for the purposes for which the data were collected or otherwise processed, where the data subject has withdrawn this/her consent for processing, when the data subject has objected to the processing of personal data concerning them or when the processing of their personal data otherwise does not comply with the rules set forth in the Regulation.

The situation does not differ considerably from that discussed above given that the purpose principle and the right to object are already present in Directive 95/46/EC. The right to object, however, will be more easily executed by the data subject as the grounds that he/she must present when objecting must no longer be "compelling and legitimate". Instead they must only relate to the particular situation of the data subject.[32] Recital 56 clearly states that "The burden of proof should be on the controller to demonstrate that their legitimate interests may override the interests or the fundamental rights and freedoms of the data subject".

On the other hand, what is openly welcomed is the clarification of the possibility to withdraw previously given consent. This is a key tool related to social networks as data processing in such a context partly relies on the consent of the data subject. The authors of the proposed Regulation underline that "This right is particularly relevant, *when the data subject has given their consent as a child*, when not being fully aware of the risks involved by the processing, and later wants to remove such personal data especially on the Internet."[33] That being said, one does not see the legal implication of saying that data subjects have the right to obtain the erasure of personal data on the part of the data controller, "especially in relation to personal data which are made available by the data subject while he or she was a child," as included in Article 17 of the Draft Regulation. Should it then be more difficult for the controller to demonstrate that its legitimate interest

(Footnote 30 continued)
she was a child, where one of the following grounds applies: (a) the data are no longer necessary in relation to the purposes for which they were collected or otherwise processed; (b) the data subject withdraws consent on which the processing is based according to point (a) of Article 6(1), or when the storage period consented to has expired, and where there is no other legal ground for the processing of the data; (c) the data subject objects to the processing of personal data pursuant to Article 19; (d) the processing of the data does not comply with this Regulation for other reasons. (emphasis added).

[31] Article 17 is entitled "Right to be forgotten and to erasure". One could wonder whether Article 17 establishes two separate rights. This is not the case as these two rights are merged in the view of the authors of the Regulation Proposal (see recital 54: "To strengthen the 'right to be forgotten' in the online environment, the right to erasure should also be extended […]." Also Opinion of the European Data Protection Supervisor on the data protection reform package (7 March 2012, point 146): "The right to erasure has been strengthened into a right to be forgotten to allow for a more effective enforcement of this right in the digital environment".

[32] Article 19.1 of the Regulation Proposal states: "The data subject shall have the right to object, on grounds relating to their particular situation, at any time to the processing of personal data which is based on points (d), (e) and (f) of Article 6(1), unless the controller demonstrates compelling legitimate grounds for the processing which override the interests or fundamental rights and freedoms of the data subject".

[33] Recital 53 (emphasis added).

overrides the data subject's interests when the data were made available when the latter was a child? The draft report of the Parliament on the Regulation Proposal has, in the same sense, stressed that there appears to be little specific value to demand 'particular' attention for children.[34] The Parliament is, in fact, concerned that this portion of text could implicitly lessen protection for adults.

To strengthen the 'right to be forgotten' on the Internet, Article 17.2 provides that, in case the data controller has made the personal data public or has authorised a third party to publish the personal data, he will be obliged to take all reasonable steps, including technical measures, to inform third parties who are processing such data, of the request from the data subject to erase any links to, or copies/replications of such personal data. Many commentators, among which is the European Data Protection Supervisor,[35] have noted that it may, in some cases, be an extensive effort to inform all third parties that may be processing such data, and that there will not always be clear understanding of where the data may have been disseminated. This is clearly the case with Internet pages open to the public. It should not, however, be applicable to the responsible operators of a social network having to warn application developers who process the data available in the network. Nevertheless, the "obligation of *endeavour* upon the controller is surely more realistic from a practical point of view than an obligation of *result*".[36]

A rapid analysis might lead us to believe that our children will now freely return to making mistakes and that as parents we can stop fearing that what they say may be used against them in the future.[37] But the right to be forgotten as outlined in the Proposal of Regulation indeed has limits.

9.4.2 Limits

1. The personal and household exemption

First of all, data protection principles, including the right to be forgotten, do not apply to individuals who process personal data exclusively for their own personal and domestic purposes. The application of this exemption to social networking sites has led to a fervent discussion.[38] What is the definition of personal or household activity? In the *Lindqvist* case, the European Union Court of Justice

[34] European Parliament, Draft Report on the Proposal for a General Data Protection Regulation, Committee on Civil Liberties, Justice and Home Affairs, Rapporteur: Jan Philipp Albrecht, 17 December 2012, Amendment 34.

[35] Opinion of the European Data Protection Supervisor of the data protection reform package, 7 March 2012, p. 148.

[36] Opinion of the European Data Protection Supervisor of the data protection reform package, 7 March 2012, p. 147.

[37] Koops 2011, available at www.ssrn.com.

[38] Moiny 2010, pp. 250–253; Van Alsenoy et al. 2009, pp. 65–79.

stated that the exception must be interpreted as relating only to activities which are carried out in the course of the private or family life of individuals, which is clearly not the case with the processing of personal data published online as those data are made accessible to an indefinite number of people.[39] Applied to the SNS context, this reasoning leads one to say that SNS users will not benefit from the exemption for personal use when their profile is 'public'. It is, however, debatable whether situations where access to data posted by a user is limited to self-selected contacts (e.g. friends) may benefit from this exception. In some cases users have an extensive number of contacts/friends, some of whom they may not actually know. "A high number of contacts could be an indication that the household exception does not apply."[40] Yet is there a minimum number of 'friends' one must have on a social network in order to be covered by data protection rules when the access is restricted by the use of privacy settings? Of course no such numerical threshold exists. The quality of the link with the recipients must also be taken into account. A sufficiently personal connection should thus be established in order to be exempted from data protection rules. In fact, it may also be argued that the publishing of information on sites such as Facebook, even if for purely personal reasons and even when restricted to a confined circle of persons, involves the disclosure of information and the storing of it by the *host*, in this case Facebook, an aspect that affects the application of the exemption. Finally, it should be clarified that what the social networking site does on its own initiative (copies of data, processing of data for marketing purposes, etc.) is not covered by the exemption.

To summarise, the right to withdraw one's consent or to object to the storage and publication of data cannot be invoked in situations where the personal exemption applies, i.e. in SNS cases where individuals disclose data and pictures inside a confined circle of *real* friends, family or relatives. Other legal tools from both civil and criminal law are then at the possible disposal of data subjects. An exemption for journalistic and artistic purposes as well as for literary expression also exists.

If the exemption for personal use does not apply, one must consider that the exception for journalistic purposes, artistic or literary expression may instead apply.

In the *Satamedia case*, the European Court of Justice provides a very broad understanding of what is to be covered by 'journalistic purposes'. For the Court this notion encompasses all activities whose objective is to disclose information, opinions or ideas to the public, irrespective of who carries out such activities (not necessarily a media undertaking), and of the medium used to transmit the processed data (it may be an electronic medium such as the Internet) and irrespective of the nature of those activities (profit-making or not).[41]

---

[39] ECJ, 6 November 2003 (*Lindqvist*), C-101-01, *Rec*. p. I-12971, § 47.

[40] Article 29 Data Protection Working Party, Opinion 5/2009 on online social networking, WP 163, p. 6.

[41] ECJ, 16 December 2008, *Tietosuojavaltuutettu v. Satakunnan Markkinapörssi Oy and Satamedia Oy*, C-73/07. See comment of this case by De Terwange 2008, *Satakunnan Markkinapörssi Oy et Satamedia Oy*, Affaire C-73/07, *R.D.T.I.*, 2010, n° 38, pp. 132–146.

The second part of the exception concerns the processing of personal data carried out solely 'for the purpose of artistic or literary expression'. The outline of this exception is still to be enlightened by the case law.

In the case that the first or second part of the exception is considered to apply to SNS activities, a balance between the freedom of expression and the rights of the data subject needs to be struck.[42]

2. Conflicts with other rights and interests

The right to be forgotten is not an absolute right. In fact, it is in major conflict and permanent tension with other rights and interests including the right to free speech, the right to information[43] and the duty to remember.[44] The question remains: "[s]*hould we have the right to remove … things from the Web or allow them to let be for the whole world to see until eternity…?*"[45]

Resolving such a conflict demands that the proportionality principle be respected. There should be no a priori and systematic pre-eminence given to one right over the others. A balancing test must be made in every case. It is true that where information regarding the life of a young person is at stake, most of the time priority will be given to the data subject's interest to erase it. There is indeed little chance that such information be linked to questions of public interest.

The proposed Regulation allows the further retention of personal data notably where it is necessary to exercise the right of freedom of expression, or for historical, statistical and scientific research purposes.

The text also provides that there may be cases where one could prefer restricting the processing of the data instead of erasing them. The text is not clear on what is meant by 'restricting the processing'. One should in any case understand that data remains stored but that access to it and use of it is restricted. This way of achieving the right to be forgotten is therefore a perfect illustration of the application of the proportionality principle.

3. Conflict with the economic model of SNS

The use of SNS appears to be free. The very efficient economic model of these services in fact relies on contextual advertising, i.e. the commercial exploitation of the information and digital traces left by users when using the service. SNS operators have an economic interest for not erasing personal data from their services since it represents a considerable economic asset.

---

[42] Article 29 Data Protection Working Party, Opinion 5/2009 on online social networking, WP 163, p. 6.

[43] In Google's legal advisor's view, there should be no expectation of privacy on the Internet and the right to oblivion represents the biggest threat to Internet free speech in our time, http://peterfleischer.blogspot.com/2011/03/foggy-thinking-about-right-to-oblivion.html; see also Mayes 2011.

[44] Gomes de Andrade 2012, p. 130.

[45] Daly 2011, available at http://emergingbusinessadvocate.wordpress.com/2011/03/15/le-doit-a-loubli-can-we-achieve-oblivion-on-the-internet/.

The General Data Protection Regulation proposal offers a strict answer to this economic activity when it regards children. Article 20 states that every natural person shall have the right not to be subject to measures based on profiling by means of automated processing. According to recital 58, such measures should be allowed in certain circumstances but never when a child is concerned.

4. Technical limits

In addition to these limitations one must be aware that there are serious technical limits to the implementation of the right to be forgotten: the deletion of data from the web is not as easy as it may appear. In fact, once data is removed by the controller, the information could be still available in cache memory. Moreover, during the time that data are available online, other individuals may download and re-publish the information without the data subject's consent, even without them being aware of such an action. At this point effective removal of the data could present intensive difficulties.[46] It is obvious that once data are made available on the Internet, it is a pure challenge to know where the data have been disseminated and to know who may be processing such data.[47] Entering in contact with these persons could therefore prove to be rather difficult or even impossible. In the same sense, the European Data Protection Supervisor and the Article 29 Working Party have welcomed the introduction of the right to oblivion but they have emphasised the necessity and challenge of its correct implementation.[48]

9.4.3 The Right to Be Forgotten by Default

Aside the right to have one's data erased upon request, the right to be forgotten could rely on the 'data protection by default' rule. Article 23.2. provides that "the controller shall implement mechanisms for ensuring that, by default, only those personal data are processed which are necessary for each specific purpose of the processing and are especially not [...] retained beyond the minimum necessary for those purposes, [...] in terms of [...] the time of their storage".[49] Article 17.7 more specifically asks the controller to implement mechanisms to ensure that the time limits established for the erasure of personal data and/or for a periodic review of the need for the storage of the data are observed.

[46] De Terwangne 2012, p. 117.

[47] See ENISA 2012, available at https://www.enisa.europa.eu/activities/identity-and-trust/library/deliverables/the-right-to-be-forgotten/.

[48] Opinion of the European Data Protection Supervisor on the data protection reform package, 7 March 2012, p. 24 and Article 29 Working Party Opinion 01/2012 on the data protection reform proposals, 23 March 2012, WP 191, p. 13.

[49] Also Article 17, § 7: "The controller shall implement mechanisms to ensure that the time limits established for the erasure of personal data and/or for a periodic review of the need for the storage of the data are observed."

Technical mechanisms should thus foresee that data storage automatically comes to an end as soon as the time necessary to achieve the purposes announced has been reached. It is important that social networking sites very carefully identify the different purposes linked to the processing of data as the time of retention will be determined accordingly. For example, certain sites keep all the data of individuals who choose to no longer utilize the given network, "sparing them the trouble of re-uploading everything if they want to come back". Even if one happens to consider this to be legitimate, it is clear that the retention time in such a case must be rather short. In cases where someone erases his/her messages exchanged via the SNS, there should be no justification to store these messages any longer given that the purpose of communication has expired and so has the time of storage.

In fact, the market already offers such possibilities to implement an automatic system of destruction of data with the data subject's consent.[50] As an illustration of such a system, the software X-Pire has been launched in Germany. It enables users to attach a digital expiry date to the images uploaded to social networking sites such as Facebook.

9.5 Conclusion

In a society where we are never truly forgotten, the right to oblivion represents a possible solution to problems raised by the "perfect" memory of the Internet combined with the power of search engines that lead to a de-contextualisation of data, notably data disclosed and processed within the framework of SNS.

Elements of a right to be forgotten are present in the current Data Protection Directive 95/46/EC. Rapid changes in the digital environment, and notably the impressive development of SNS, have highlighted the need to reconsider such an answer and to build a specific and augmented right to be forgotten. This new concept has appeared in the Proposal for a General Data Protection Regulation, but we have seen that the content of this concept is not so new. The right to be forgotten means that in different circumstances the data subject is given the possibility to obtain the deletion of his/her personal data. Due to the large number of children and young people active online, in particular on social networking sites, the need for a reinforced concept of right to oblivion gains even more importance.

There are, however, multiple difficulties of different nature for correct implementation of the right to be forgotten in the field of online social networks. First of all, the personal and household exception must be taken into consideration and it must be clarified whether and in which conditions a post on a social network is to be considered as a personal activity and consequently be exempted from data protection rules. Secondly, the implementation of the right to be forgotten faces serious technical limits for the practical deletion of data. Moreover, the erasure of

[50] www.x-pire.de/index.php?id=6&L=2.

personal data endues a potentially significant economic cost and loss, observing the fact that the economic model of the Internet relies heavily on behavioural and contextual advertising. While such difficulties are not insuperable, they strictly impose a realistic approach to the question at hand.

The last difficulty is that the right to be forgotten inevitably conflicts with other rights, such as the right to freedom of expression, to information and the duty to remember. Solving such conflicts implies the utilisation of a balancing test among all rights and interests at stake as well as respect of the principle of proportionality. The fact that the data subject disclosed data concerning him/her when he/she was a child should influence the balancing test in favour of the cancellation of such data as requested by the repentant adult.

Expressly instating such a right in a legal instrument will certainly not be enough to ensure that oblivion is part of digital relationships in the same way that it characterises natural relationships. Enforcement of the right to be forgotten requires different approaches and is not a one-way solution. The Recommendation of the Committee of Ministers of the Council of Europe to Member States on the protection of human rights with regard to social networking services[51] encourages, *inter alia*, self- and co-regulatory mechanisms. "Member States should co-operate with the private sector and civil society with a view to upholding users' right to freedom of expression. … The social networking service should enable users to control their information". Concerning the right to be forgotten, this Recommendation states that users should be informed of how to completely delete their profiles and all data stored about them in a social networking service.

Besides self- and co-regulation, privacy by design could certainly also help give life to the right to be forgotten, by giving an expiry date to any piece of information disclosed in SNS. Automatic deletion of the data could be an easy solution to the *eternity effect*, but it cannot be the general and systematic answer as there are cases where the deletion of data enters into conflict with overriding rights and interests.

When facing the question of the desire or necessity to delete data published at an earlier date in SNS, one should not forget the most fundamental piece of the puzzle: education that instils long-term and safe behaviour on social networks.

References

Casarosa F (2010) Child privacy protection online: how to improve it through code and self-regulatory tools. http://ssrn.com/abstract=1561570

Copeland N (2012) Online privacy: the right to be forgotten. Library of the European parliament

Daly S (2011) Le doit a l'oubli—can we achieve 'oblivion' on the internet? http://emergingbusinessadvocate.wordpress.com/2011/03/15/le-doit-a-loubli-can-we-achieve-oblivion-on-the-internet/

[51] Recommendation CM/Rec(2012)4 of the Committee of Ministers to member States on the protection of human rights with regard to social networking services.

De Terwangne C (2012) Internet privacy and the right to be forgotten/right to oblivion. Revista de internet, derecho y politica, pp 109–121. www.idp.uoc.edu

Dumortier F (2009) Facebook and risks of 'de-contextualization' of information. http://works.bepress.com/franck_dumortier/1

ENISA (2012) The right to be forgotten—between expectations and practice. https://www.enisa.europa.eu/activities/identity-and-trust/library/deliverables/the-right-to-be-forgotten/

European Commission (2010) A comprehensive approach on personal data protection in the European Union. COM (2010) 609 final

Gomes de Andrade NN (2012) Oblivion: the right to be different…from oneself reproposing the right to be forgotten. Revista de internet, derecho y politica

Koops B-J (2011) Forgetting footprints, shunning shadows. A critical analysis of the 'right to be forgotten' in big data practice. www.ssrn.com

Legrand F, Bellamy A (2012) Touche pas à ma e-réputation! Enquête. www.lesnumeriques.com/divers/touche-pas-a-e-reputation-enquete-a1548.html

Livingstone S, Haddon L, Görzig A, Ólafsson K (2011) Risks and safety on the internet: the perspective of European children. Full findings. LSE, EU kids online, London

Mayer-Schönberger V (2009) Delete—the virtue of forgetting in the digital age. Princeton University Press, Princeton

Mayes T (2011) We have no right to be forgotten online. The Guardian. www.theguardian.com/commentisfree/libertycentral/2011/mar/18/forgotten-online-european-union-law-internet

Moiny JP (2010) Facebook au regard des règles européennes concernant la protection des données. Eur J Consumer Law, 2: 235–271

Moiny JP (2012), Cloud based social network sites: under whose control? In: Dudley A, Braman J, Vincenti G (eds). Investigating cyber law and cyber ethics: issues, impacts and practices. Hershey, Information Science Reference, pp 147–219

Reding V (2010) Why the EU needs new personal data protection rules? In: the European Data Protection and Privacy Conference, Brussels, 30 November 2010, http://europa.edu/rapid/pressReleasesAction.do?reference=Speech/10/700, accessed 18 February 2014

Rouvroy A (2008) Réinventer l'art d'oublier et de se faire oublier dans la société de l'information?. http://works.bepress.com/antoinette_rouvroy/5/

Van Alsenoy B et al (2009) Social networks and web 2.0: are users also bound by data protection regulations? Springer, Heidelberg

Walz S (1997) Relationship between the freedom of the press and the right to informational privacy in the emerging information society. In: 19th International Data Protection Commissars Conference, Brussels

Chapter 10
Follow the Children! Advergames and the Enactment of Children's Consumer Identity

Isolde Sprenkels and Irma van der Ploeg

Contents

Isolde Sprenkels is a PhD researcher with the ERC funded DigIDeas project: Social and Ethical Aspects of Digital Identities. Towards a Value Sensitive Identity Management. This chapter is part of Isolde Sprenkel's dissertation. It features not only a study of multidisciplinary literature on children, advertising, new media and consumption, but it also has its base in the empirical research conducted for the aforementioned research project such as interviews with Dutch market practitioners and observations at marketing conferences.Irma van der Ploeg is an Associate Professor Infonomics and New Media at Zuyd University in The Netherlands, and principal investigator with the ERC funded DigIDeas project: Social and Ethical Aspects of Digital Identities. Towards a Value Sensitive Identity Management: www.digideas.com.

I. Sprenkels (✉)
Zuyd University, Limburg, The Netherlands
e-mail: isolde.sprenkels@zuyd.nl

I. van der Ploeg
Maastricht University, Maastricht, The Netherlands
e-mail: y.vanderploeg@maastrichtuniversity.nl

S. van der Hof et al. (eds.), *Minding Minors Wandering the Web: Regulating Online Child Safety*, Information Technology and Law Series 24, DOI: 10.1007/978-94-6265-005-3_10,

10.1 Introduction

In a society increasingly inundated with digital technology, children in the Netherlands learn from a very young age how to use new Information and Communication Technologies. These technologies offer them ways to play, learn, explore and develop their sense of identity, as well as interact and communicate with peers and adults. Using desktop, tablet, and laptop computers, smart phones, MP3 players and (handheld) video game consoles, children spend ever more time online. E-mail, messenger programmes, mobile app(lication)s, search engines, social networking websites, game portals, virtual (game) worlds and other types of websites are part of their everyday life.

Contemporary marketing strategies and advertising formats are increasingly designed with these developments in mind. Often part of a cross-media approach, market practitioners[1] employ diverse online means in order to connect with children. If they would have a credo for this, it could be 'We need to go where children are online'. Their online presence varies from banner advertisements, different forms of gamevertising, and branded social networking profiles, to viral video advertisements, brand presence within online virtual worlds, and websites aimed at children related for instance to food, beverage and toy brands or television programmes. It offers them ways to meet corporate goals, such as building brand awareness and stimulating product purchase amongst children and their parents. And it also enables them to collect valuable information about children; turning children's online playgrounds into sites for detailed surveillance.[2] This leads to a second possible credo 'What children do and care about online is worth monitoring'.

One type of game many children enjoy playing is online casual or mini-games. These short, 'free' and easy-to-learn games have friendly designs with bright colours and fun tasks to perform, and are developed to either entertain, to educate, or to deliver a particular commercial message. This chapter focuses on the latter, 'advertisement as game,' which is specially developed around a particular brand or product and is often referred to as 'advergame.'[3] We start with a preliminary analysis of a Dutch advergame, illustrating ways in which it aids in achieving a range of corporate objectives, which that go beyond advertising as such. In the sections that follow, we refer back to this, while, using insights from science and technology studies and surveillance studies, we show how the configuration of

---

[1] Daniel Cook defines the term market practitioners as "marketers, researchers, designers, manufacturers, and other market actors" as market practitioners; Cook 2011, p. 258.

[2] Chung and Grimes 2005; Steeves 2007.

[3] There are different understandings of what advergames are. Within this chapter we consider advergames to be online casual or mini-games specially developed around a particular brand or product. We consider them to be a particular form of gamevertising; with gamevertising in general being the promotional or advertising possibilities before, within or after an often already existing console, pc, or internet game; Hufen 2010.

advergames is part of enacting children's identities as consumers and 'media literates'. In addition, we discuss the issue of fairness of advertising and marketing to children. We show how market practitioners defend their practices by referring to images and conceptions of children as desiring and competent consumers which, we argue, are (partly) produced by the very practices they try to legitimise.

10.2 Inside an Icy Laboratory

In 2007, ice cream brand OLA and children's television channel Nickelodeon started the 'OLA Water Games'[4] campaign.[5] OLA was a sponsor of the Dutch Olympic Committee at the time, and felt inspired by the 2008 Beijing Olympic Games. Moreover, swimming was very popular as an Olympic sport among children, and many children associate the swimming pool with ice cream. Thus, OLA figured it had found a solid basis for a new campaign. Competition days were organised in swimming pools in the Netherlands, allowing children to play games based on Olympic sports and branded by OLA ice cream. Children were offered OLA (inflatable) water fun products as rewards, in order to stimulate children to exercise and play together, and of course, to enlarge the market share of OLA. With this campaign OLA tried to generate a positive brand image among children, connecting itself with sports and exercising, creating a healthy image for a product which normally isn't associated with a healthy lifestyle. Multiple channels were used to promote the OLA Water Games. For instance, the ice cream wrappings contained stamps called 'heartbeats', which could be saved for the inflatable water fun products used at the competition days. This campaign was also promoted in online parental communities. Nickelodeon reported on the Water Games during one of its best viewed shows named SuperNick, and a special OLA Water Games website was built with information about the competition days. In 2008, OLA added a gaming section to this website which immediately attracted many more visitors; in 2007, the site counted 156,000 unique visitors, in 2008, after adding the gaming section, 250,000 visitors were counted.[6]

The gaming section on the OLA Water Games website was considered a great success and OLA and Nickelodeon decided to build on this. As the Beijing Olympics were in the past, and OLA no longer a sponsor for the Dutch Olympic Committee, they decided to use associations children would have with OLA ice

[4] In Dutch: OLA 'Water Spelen'.

[5] OLA is the name under which the 'Heartbrand' operates in the Netherlands. The ice cream brand with the double lined red heart-shaped logo, is one of the food brands offered by multinational consumer goods company Unilever. Nickelodeon is a market-leading television channel for children, owned by Viacom International Media Networks Northern Europe.

[6] De Goeij and Kwantes 2009.

cream as a starting point for a new multimedia campaign in 2009 called OLA Ice Age,[7] with the specially designed gaming world www.olaijstijd.nl[8] at its centre. At Nickelodeon's Kids Insights day, a conference on 'kids marketing' trends in the same year, an OLA marketing manager gave a presentation on children's associations with ice, entitled 'the world of ice according to kids'. The presentation was illustrated with several pictures and drawings of ice caves, laughing children eating ice cream, a mammoth and a Neanderthal man.[9] Some of these associations may have been inspired by the Ice Age movies distributed by 20th Century Fox Film Corporation. OLA itself has a connection with Ice Age too, as they have promoted the Ice Age 3 movie on their product wrappings during 2009.[10] These associations were employed in the campaign, used as a starting point for the design of the gaming world OLA Ice Age, in order to appeal to children.

The leading role in the scenario for the OLA Ice Age campaign is taken by Professor Freeze,[11] playing the part of the ice cream professor and inventor of OLA ice cream. Professor Freeze is "taking children on an adventure and guides them through the games and activities on the website".[12] This fits Nickelodeon's self definition of being a 'crazy mentor'. In their brochure informing potential advertisers they explain that Nickelodeon is like a crazy mentor, taking children on an adventure within a secure and trusted environment, and bringing them back home safely afterwards.[13] Professor Freeze, the character representing the OLA brand,[14] is just like Nickelodeon presented as a mentor, a role model, someone to trust. Inviting children to engage in a trust relationship with a brand is a strategy used in marketing targeted at children. The concept of 'mentorship' is rooted in antiquity: it was Odysseus the father who placed his wise friend and trusted advisor Mentor in charge of his son Telemachus when he left for his years of wandering, his Odyssey. In OLA Ice Age, however, it is Professor Freeze, representing OLA, who pronounces himself mentor to children. Thus, children are encouraged to trust brands, consider them their mentors and friends, or, as Valerie Steeves argues: "as role models for the child to emulate, in effect embedding the product right into a child's identity".[15]

Professor Freeze's friends are living with him in his ice cave. Among these are a little woolly mammoth and a big Neanderthal man, at first sight playing no

---

[7] In Dutch 'OLA IJstijd'.

[8] The Dutch website is offline at time of finishing this chapter. Though the Belgian one is similar and online: www.olakids.be.

[9] Houben 2009.

[10] OLA 2009.

[11] Professor 'De Vries' in Dutch, which is actually a very common name in the Netherlands.

[12] OLAIJstijd 2010.

[13] MTV Networks 2009.

[14] Entertaining (cartoon) characters are often used in marketing campaigns to help sell a product, service or brand. Think of the Ronald McDonald character selling the McDonalds brand; Calvert 2008.

[15] Steeves 2006.

particular part at all, besides being considered part of children's associations with 'ice' and 'ice cream' perhaps.[16] At night, Professor Freeze drives around in his ice cream van to copy children's dreams. Back at his ice cave, he turns these dreams into ice cream by using his ice cream machine. When entering the website, an animation is showing Professor Freeze packing his bags, announcing that he is going on a vacation and in need of an assistant to operate the ice machine. Different badges can be earned on the website by playing games and quizzes, related to existing ice creams in OLA's assortment. Encouraging children to play with particular products enables them at a later point in time to identify the brand.[17] Other activities are earning badges and designing one's ultimate fantasy ice cream. When a child has earned all badges, he or she can become the assistant that professor Freeze is looking for. By ascribing a particular role to a child this way, a personal relationship with the brand is created.[18] This is a common strategy within advergames: children can, for example, become 'assistants', 'heroic riders' (www.raveleijn.nl) or 'arts and crafts champions' (www.knutselwereld.nl). They are asked to help out, are challenged, and offered a particular role to play.

Another feature of OLA Ice Age that illustrates this creation of a personal relationship is decorating "one's own room" by choosing particular colours for the elements in it. It is one of the first things a child is invited to do. A picture of this 'room' can be sent to friends, which allows OLA Ice Age to invite other children to the OLA Ice Age website. This is a form of viral marketing in which children are encouraged to share their experience and communicate with others about OLA. Friends receive a message such as "do you want to decorate your own room in the OLA Ice Age cave and play cool games? Go to…". Sharing one's gaming experience with others offers the possibility to collect personally identifiable information.[19] An arts and crafts competition can be entered here as well. In this competition children are asked to draw or glue together their own ice cream, take a picture of it and upload it to the website. Also, a competition was organised for which children were encouraged to buy a particular popsicle containing a code on its stick, required to enter into the competition. Such direct encouragement to product purchase is also a common strategy in advergames.[20] Within the ice cave, there are several games to play, wallpapers and ringtones to download, quizzes to enter and videos to watch. The videos contain the OLA Ice Age commercial and a realistic video about how ice cream is actually made, wrapped and transported to stores. Children can also upload their pictures or make a screenshot in order to 'shrek' themselves; colouring themselves green, adding 'ogor' ears and mouths, etc. And as OLA Ice Age contains multiple game levels, public displays of high

---

[16] OLA 2009.

[17] Grimes and Shade 2005.

[18] Steeves 2006.

[19] Gurău 2008.

[20] Moore 2004.

scores, and new games added on a regular basis, contact time with the brand is prolonged continuously.[21]

As the above illustrates, advergames are designed in such a way that they offer a brand the opportunity to reach a range of corporate goals, such as building brand awareness, creating a personal relationship with a brand, and stimulating product purchasing and consumption. There are other studies that illustrate the relationship between (adver)game design and reaching particular corporate goals, and although some of these studies have been conducted among adults, similarities are striking. Călin Gurău shows that there is a relationship between the capacity of the advergame to induce a state of flow, a mental state of subjective absorption within an activity, and a change in the buying behaviour of (adult) players.[22] This study shows similarities with research conducted by Natasha Dow Schull, demonstrating the connection between game design elements manipulating one's sense of space and time and the state of subjective absorption in play accelerating the extraction of money from players.[23] Advergame research also shows how some of these games include product-related polls or quizzes, offering valuable information for market research on children's habits and preferences.[24] As in OLA Ice Age, they may also encourage players to register and share their gaming experience with friends or family, thus enabling the collection of personally identifiable information.[25] Combined with an analysis of in-game-behaviour and activities, marketers are able to construct detailed consumer profiles, based on the aggregation of these behavioural data with demographic data.[26] Therefore, advergames can be described as Schull's "electronic surveillance devices",[27] as they enable tracking children's activities and whereabouts.

Notably, the OLA website contains no clear statement of these marketing purposes to either children or their parents. As the 'parents' section' on the website mentions, the goal is to "entertain children, stimulate their imagination and discover the world behind OLA ice cream". "Ice cream is not to be sold on the website, as it is only a fun world for children".[28] However, beyond a fun world for children, commercial ends are served as well. From plain advertising and getting children and their parents to buy a product or use a service, influencing their attitude towards a brand, to prolonging contact time with the brand, driving traffic to (brand)websites, automatically generating personally identifiable data, and building and expanding digital profiles of consumers using data mining and profiling techniques. While Professor Freeze grants children a warm welcome in his

[21] Moore 2004.

[22] Gurău 2008.

[23] Dow Schull 2005.

[24] Moore 2004; Grimes 2008.

[25] Gurău 2008.

[26] Grimes 2008; Chung and Grimes 2005.

[27] Dow Schull 2005.

[28] OLAIJstijd 2010.

ice cream laboratory, guiding them on a playful, and informative journey to become his assistant, in the background a business is running of which children have no clue.

Attempts to evaluate contemporary forms of marketing communication, especially those to children, from an ethical or moral point of view are rooted in a history of studying and questioning the fairness of advertising. Although discussed widely, a clear definition of the concept of fairness itself tends to be hard to find. Nonetheless, in what follows, we briefly summarise the main points made in this body of work, which, as Sonia Livingstone explains, merges "a philosophical question about ethics (is it fair to persuade those who are unaware of such efforts?) with an empirical question about influence (who is particularly susceptible to persuasive messages?)".[29] We then describe how market practitioners tend to respond to such ethical challenges with strategies and marketing research of their own, in an attempt to deflect moral criticism.

10.3 The Fun and Fairness of Advergames

10.3.1 Shaping Vulnerability

Assessing the fairness of advertising to children is usually based on certain presumed cognitive capacities of children, or lack thereof. Underlying this, and frequently referred to, is an age-stage evolution model of children's cognitive development from developmental cognitive psychology.[30] This model posits several developmental 'milestones',[31] the first of which is reached when a child is around 2 or 3 years old. This is the moment when a child is considered to be capable of distinguishing advertising from other media content. The moment a child can understand the selling and persuasive intent behind an advertisement, at around 8 years old, is considered to be the second milestone.[32] The third and final milestone is reached somewhere around age twelve, when a child is presumed to have acquired the ability to reflect on, weigh and refuse an advertisement.

The canonical argument about the fairness of advertising to children refers to this model, and states that those marketing campaigns can be considered 'fair' that respect the different levels of competency to understand techniques of persuasion. It can be dissected in three parts.[33] First, a literacy argument, which applies to

[29] Livingstone 2009a, p. 170.

[30] Nairn and Fine 2008.

[31] Lunt and Livingstone 2012, p. 147.

[32] Although, as David Buckingham explains, some studies suggest that this understanding is not necessarily used. He claims differences in these estimations are a consequence of research method; Buckingham 2009.

[33] Livingstone 2009a.

children until somewhere between 8 and 12 years of age and considers them unable to understand the persuasive and selling intent of advertising. Second, an influence argument, which claims that children in particular are susceptible to advertising since they lack adequate cognitive defences. And third, a fairness argument, which considers children to be both vulnerable and unable to defend themselves.

Several difficulties exist when using the above model as an ethical yardstick for assessing the fairness of advertising to children. For instance, by following this argument it is generally taken for granted that "those whose literacy is lower are assumed to be more susceptible to effects".[34] And, that "an increase in media or advertising literacy is assumed to reduce susceptibility to media effects".[35] Sonia Livingstone and Ellen Helsper found little empirical evidence for this claim. They argue that although teenagers are presumed to be more 'media literate', that does not mean that they are influenced less by advertising than younger children. They conclude that "different processes of persuasion are effective at different ages, precisely because literacy levels vary by age".[36] Which means that younger children, being less media literate, are merely persuaded differently than teenagers. Younger children tend to be persuaded by superficial or peripheral features of advertising, such as jingles and colourful and funny images, whereas teenagers tend to be persuaded by, for instance, strong arguments and references to peer-group approval.[37] Similarly, Elizabeth Moore found that 11–12 year olds were more susceptible to the entertainment provided by advertising and more likely to allow it to shape their interpretation for product use than younger children, even though their understanding, their 'literacy', was much richer and broader than the understanding of 7–8 year olds.[38]

Another difficulty has to do with contemporary advertising formats. Livingstone concludes that the age-stage evolution model of children's cognitive capabilities does not fit the diversity of the twenty-first century media environment anymore.[39] She claims that the idea of milestones related to age is not convincing, "both because there is no universal relation between understanding and age, and because persuasion occurs, in one way or another, across the range".[40] In saying this, she follows Agnes Nairn and Cordelia Fine, who doubt the possibility to establish any 'magical age' at which children are supposed to understand and resist persuasion,

[34] Advertising effects can be intended by advertisers, such as brand awareness and buying intent, and non-intended, such as materialism and family conflicts; Valkenburg 2002, p. 140. In this chapter we call intended effects by advertisers 'goals'.

[35] Livingstone and Helsper 2006.

[36] Livingstone and Helsper 2006.

[37] Here Livingstone and Helsper are inspired by Petty & Cacioppo's Elaboration Likelihood Model of Persuasion which distinguishes two routes of persuasion, a central one and the peripheral one; Livingstone and Helsper 2006.

[38] Moore 2004.

[39] Livingstone 2009a.

[40] Livingstone 2009a, p. 172.

as contemporary advertising formats often intentionally bypass children's explicit persuasion knowledge and instead persuade implicitly.[41] These formats tend to be more covert, by being integrated in non-commercial contexts, for example, which challenges not only younger and older children's cognitive defences, but those of teenagers and even adults as well.[42]

A theory on consumer behaviour that is well known among market practitioners is based on the 'persuasion knowledge model' developed by Friestad and Wright.[43] According to this model, consumers' knowledge of persuasion, marketing and advertising tactics influences the way they deal with attempts of persuasion. This means that when the persuasive intent behind a commercial message is recognised, people will deal with the message differently than when they do not recognise this intent. When they recognise the intent, they will change their attitude and will tend to resist the commercial message itself. We will leave aside whether this model is adequate or not. What is interesting is that it implies that by eliminating recognition of a commercial message market practitioners are more likely to succeed. This makes advergames an excellent tool for persuasion, marketing and advertising tactics, since the recognition of a commercial message is eliminated, and play and fun are probably the first and only thing children associate advergames with. Market practitioners tailor messages, design products, packages, websites, campaigns and advertisements in such a way that they appeal to children.[44] While advergames may be seen as an opportunity to play and have fun for free, children remain unaware of the commercial intent and goals behind the advergame. Market practitioners adapt online gaming technology, a technology generally understood and recognised by children as enabling play and fun, to serve quite different purposes. They appropriate and adapt this technology in such a way that it serves their needs for generating valuable consumer information, and for building a personal relationship between the brand they represent and a child playing the advergame.

When it comes to assessing fairness of marketing to children, Livingstone proposes a more explicit question: "Who can resist which type of persuasion under what circumstances?"[45] Framing the question this way addresses both difficulties mentioned. It leaves room for "multiple forms of vulnerability", as vulnerability depends on both an individual's cognitive/social resources and the (social or mediated) environment.[46] We want to expand on this emphasis on 'the environment' because it acknowledges that being able to recognise, understand and cope with advertising formats and tactics should not just be considered a function of the

---

41 Nairn and Fine 2008.

42 Fielder et al. 2007; Moore 2004; Nairn and Fine 2008.

43 Friestad and Wright 1994.

44 Cook 2011.

45 Livingstone 2009a, p. 172.

46 Livingstone 2009a.

individual child's cognitive/social resources.[47] An exclusive focus on skills and competences implies a rather instrumental view of technology, considering it to be inherently neutral, becoming 'good' or 'bad' dependent on, in this case, the literacy level of its user. Alternatively, we endorse Actor Network Theory's tenet that human and non-human actors ('the social' and 'the material') should be treated symmetrically.[48] We therefore propose to consider 'the fairness issue' as something that is also very much a function of the socio-material set of relations in which children's options, choices, and chances to resist are shaped, by the advertising tactics and formats.

In support of this line of reasoning, Livingstone has shown that the design of Internet environments can actually shape and limit media literacy.[49] 'Failing' to engage in such an environment, to 'read it correctly', is not just caused by a lack of competences or skills of an Internet user. One should also consider internet environments themselves and the ways in which they allow the user to 'read' these environments. Here she refers to the work of Steve Woolgar and the notion of 'technology-as-text'.[50] Woolgar's use of the metaphor of 'machine-as-text' is part of a semiotic approach to user-technology relations. It was introduced by Actor Network Theory scholars who have "extended semiotics – the study of how meanings are built – from signs to things".[51]

We consider a semiotic approach to user-technology relations to be very useful. In a similar type of reasoning, we follow a take proposed by Madeleine Akrich and Bruno Latour.[52] In their technology-as-text approach, technology is seen as a particular type of text; a film 'script',[53] within which both designers and users are inscribed as active agents in the shaping of a technology.[54] We propose to consider advergames as scripts, diverting correct recognition as commercial text. We stress that we can only see what this text does, the effects it produces in itself, we can't

---

[47] Nairn and Fine 2008; Rozendaal et al. 2011.

[48] The analytic symmetry between the social and material, between humans and non-humans, actors within and constituting networks, is part of a research approach or method called Actor Network Theory (ANT), originally developed by Bruno Latour (Latour 1987, 1991) and Michel Callon (Callon 1986). The title of this chapter refers to the ANT dictum to 'follow the actors' as well, describing and following any actor expressing itself when describing a network or relations.

[49] Livingstone 2009b, p. 195.

[50] Steve Woolgar "suggested that how users 'read' machines are constrained because the design and the production of machines entails a process of configuring the user" (Oudshoorn and Pinch 2005, p. 8), which means that both user and possible actions of the user are constructed in the design process.

[51] Oudshoorn and Pinch 2005, p. 7.

[52] Akrich and Latour 1992.

[53] Their notion of 'script' has its origins in ANT which is described in footnote 5. "Like a film script, technical objects define a framework of action together with the space of actors and the space in which they are supposed to act"; Akrich 1992, p. 208. "Technical objects participate in building heterogeneous networks that bring together actants of all types and sizes, whether humans of nonhumans"; Akrich 1992, p. 206.

[54] Oudshoorn and Pinch 2005.

say anything about the intentions behind it. Despite the careful avoidance of attributing intention here, there are some hints that suggest that some effects might not be entirely accidental. A comment from game advertising expert David Edery illustrates this for the general field of gamevertising. He states that "the whole point is to eliminate recognition".[55] As we have shown in the previous section on OLA Ice Age, this clever design consists of a putting 'reading clues' about fun and play in the foreground, while remaining silent on processes, activities and intentions in the background. This way, the 'script' of an advergame is written in such a way that it is likely to prevent children from identifying, understanding, and coping with the commercial message and its persuasive intent. In addition, it renders other marketing practices enabled by the digital networked character of advergames invisible. This leads us to consider advergames not just as 'advertisements as games', but as part of an implicit and broader marketing strategy. Children's vulnerabilities/literacies can be considered to be shaped by both children's cognitive/social resources and these cleverly designed 'texts'. We argue that the 'fairness issues' related to advergames cannot be adequately dealt with without considering the interplay of design, strategies, practices, knowledge, human and non-human actors within a network of relations configuring these contemporary marketing formats.

10.3.2 Legitimising Marketing While Shaping Play and Fun

Not only critics, but market practitioners themselves, too, address the question of fairness of advertising and marketing to children from time to time. However, they tend to deal with the issue by invoking images and conceptions of children as desiring consumers, as competent social actors.[56] There appears to be an assumption that it is perfectly legitimate to target children as long as this is based on and provides "what children want". Thus, the more they attempt to know what children think, want, and need, the better they will be able to provide this, and hence, the less reprehensible it is to use sophisticated marketing strategies on them. The 'knowledge' about children required for this, the 'listening' to their wants and needs, comes from their own marketing research[57] focused on children, i.e. (partly) from the very marketing practices in need of legitimisation. Daniel Cook describes this knowledge as 'commercial epistemologies of children's consumption'.[58] He discusses how knowledge derives in and from marketing

55 Edery 2009.

56 Cook 2011.

57 Isolde Sprenkels analyse the way in which market practitioners' research methods can be understood in a performative manner in her forthcoming dissertation, i.e. their research methods do not just represent a reality out there, but constitute or perform reality into being; Law 2009.

58 Cook 2011.

practice, how practices and discourses enact these epistemologies. We would like to take Cook's work a step further, and claim that contemporary marketers' constitution of children's preferences and identities as consumers, are actually socio-technical enactments enabled by the very marketing practices and research techniques under discussion. To then use children's identities as consumers as legitimisation of these same practices is circular, and one might argue, rather self-serving.

To a certain extent, market practitioners are also informed by academic research on children and their psychological and cognitive development, as mentioned in the previous section. However, they appear to do so rather selectively, as this academic discourse on children and advertising appears to have evolved, partly letting go the canonical argument mentioned earlier. Market practitioners, in contrast, seem to hang on to the age-stage evolution model in relation to advertising. Based on this model, they have put together codes of conduct. For instance the Dutch Advertising Code and its special section on children and advertising,[59] proposes to help children to differentiate content as it prescribes that the distinction between advertising and editorial content should always be made recognisable. For instance, television commercials are preferably clustered and banner and pop-up advertisements on the internet should be labelled with the word 'advertisement'. However, as mentioned above, when it comes to contemporary formats such as advergames, this Code is not honoured because the distinction is not made explicit in any way at all.[60] Not only do such 'seamless environments'[61] fail to honour the Code, this form of self-regulation advocates a strategy that runs exactly counter to what advergames are about, namely presenting advertisements as game. According to the code, market practitioners have agreed upon making advertisements recognisably distinct from other content. Advergames' design, as we have seen, obliterates this distinction, precisely because they are much more than plain advertisements, having corporate goals far beyond that.

The contemporary marketing practices described in this chapter are actually instrumental in creating children's 'interests', 'preferences' and 'choices', from which their identity as savvy consumers is construed, and subsequently are referred to in order to legitimise these very same practices. In other words, market practitioners are legitimising their actions by invoking 'contemporary realities' they have done their best to create themselves. Contemporary formats such as peer-to-peer marketing and viral marketing are, for instance, considered to be "all about empowerment – about children registering their needs, finding their voices, building their self-esteem, defining their own values and developing independence and autonomy".[62] Rather than being critically assessed in relation to the Code of

[59] Nederlandse Reclame Code.

[60] Fielder et al. 2007.

[61] Moore 2004.

[62] Buckingham 2007.

Conduct, these formats are reiterating the image of contemporary children turning into desiring, competent consumers by the age of 12. Together with uncritically accepting a discourse of digital natives, (which also has been strongly debunked by academics for some time now[63]), this can be considered quite problematic. Viewed this way, children do not need much protection, as they are assumed to be skilled consumers in the making, blossoming when sensitised with various forms of marketing and advertising practices.

10.4 Conclusion

During a presentation at the 2009 Brands and Games summit about the campaigns mentioned in this chapter, representatives from OLA and Nickelodeon claimed that "fun is very important, and if the brand is well integrated it doesn't matter to children that they are actually watching advertising".[64] As we have explained, children are not 'actually watching advertising', they are playing an advergame. Considering advergames to be 'advertisements as game', moves the far-reaching marketing practice and corporate objectives informing advergames further into the background. They are not only about plain advertising, about persuading people to buy a product, using a particular service, changing peoples' behaviour and with that, about the question whether or not children are recognising a form of marketing communication as advertisement, or whether or not they are capable of understanding and actively dealing with this persuasion. They are not even only about advertisements disguised as games, as play and fun, hiding this very same commercial message. They are cleverly designed in order to reach all sorts of corporate objectives, such as building brand awareness, creating a personal relationship with a brand, collecting personally identifiable data, and stimulating product purchasing and consumption.

In a blog about the 'number one kids and youth marketing conference' in the Netherlands, a marketing practitioner claims that her industry is 'more ethical' nowadays, as it is focusing less on 'encouraging sales' and more on cases related to forms of corporate social responsibility and consumer insights,[65] 'building relationships' with children. With OLA Ice Age, we have seen how a brand creates a 'personal relationship', a relationship of trust, fun and friendship, but that this relationship is embedded in a set of less innocent techniques, processes and practices in the background. In order to build the 'relationship', a particular kind of surveillance is needed, for which contemporary formats such as advergames lend themselves well. This monitoring actually produces a different set of ethical concerns in itself. While spending time within online environments such as

[63] Helsper and Enyon 2010; Bennet et al. 2008.

[64] Reintjes 2009.

[65] Jansen 2009.

advergames, children are leaving behind various types of personal information and are strongly encouraged to share their interests, preferences and (online) activities. The information generated by such marketing practices, together with other forms of market practitioners knowledge of children, can be considered the basis of how corporations and brands get to know and understand children as their (potential) customers. Thus, in line with the characteristics of 'the personal information economy',[66] economic value is generated from children's online play.

However, our argument goes even further: it is through these very monitoring practices, and the subsequent analysis of the data generated in terms of children's 'preferences', 'choices' and 'consumer behaviour' that children are enacted as full-fledged, competent consumers; a notion that is subsequently invoked to legitimise the very practices involved in its production. By rendering children in these consumerist terms, the difference between them and adults is played down, and hence, so is the moral significance of targeting them with tactics of persuasion and seduction acceptable when used on adults. Moreover, as this allows marketers to better 'know' and 'understand' what these 'preferences' are, and they use this to better serve children's 'consumer demands', the children get what they want. Don't they?

Acknowledgments The research leading to these results has received funding from the European Research Council under the European Union's Seventh Framework Programme (FP7/2007-2013)/ERC Grant no. 201853.

References

Akrich M (1992) The description of technical objects. In: Bijker WE, Law J (eds) Shaping technology/building society: studies in sociotechnical change. MIT Press, Cambridge, MA, pp 205–224

Akrich M, Latour B (1992) A summary of a convenient vocabulary for the semiotics of human and nonhuman assemblies. In: Bijker W E and Law J (eds) Shaping technology/building society: studies in sociotechnical change. MIT Press, Cambridge

Bennett S, Maton K, Kervin L (2008) The 'digital natives' debate: a critical review of the evidence. Br J Educ Technol 39(5):775–786

Buckingham D (2007) Selling childhood? Children and consumer culture. J Child Media 1(1):15–24

Buckingham D (2009) Beyond the competent consumer: the role of media literacy in the making of regulatory policy on children and food advertising in the UK. Int J Cult Policy 15(2):217–230

Callon M (1986) Some elements of a sociology of translation: domestication of the scallops and the fishermen of St Brieuc Bay. In: Law J (ed) Power, action and belief: a new sociology of knowledge?. Routledge, London, pp 196–223

Calvert SL (2008) Children as consumers: advertising and marketing. Future Child 18(1):205–234

[66] Elmer 2004; Perri6 2005; Pridmore 2012.

Chung G, Grimes SM (2005) Data mining the kids: surveillance and market research strategies in children's online games. Can J Commun 30(4):527–548

Cook DT (2011) Commercial epistemologies of childhood. 'Fun' and the leveraging of children's subjectivities and desires. In: Zwick D, Cayla J (eds) Inside marketing: practices, ideologies, devices. Oxford University Press, Oxford, pp 257–268

De Goeij M, Kwantes E (2009) Nickelodeon & OLA. Hoe betrek je kids écht bij je merk? Presentation at brands and games 2009. The game advertising network event. March 10, 2009. http://www.nlgd.nl/fog/pdf/bag09/BG8.pdf. Last accessed 10 June 2010

Dow Schull N (2005) Digital gambling: the coincidence of desire and design. Ann Am Acad Polit Soc Sci 597(1):65–81

Edery D (2009) Rethinking the impact and the potential of brands in games. Presentation at brands and games 2009. The game advertising network event. March 10, 2009

Elmer G (2004) Consumption in the network age: solicitation, automation, and networking. Profiling machines: mapping the personal information economy. MIT Press, Cambridge, MA, pp 52–71

Fielder A, Gardner W, Nairn A and Pitt J (2007) Fair game? Assessing commercial activity on children's favourite websites and online environments. Report National Consumer Council and Childnet International

Friestad M, Wright P (1994) The persuasion knowledge model: how people cope with persuasion attempts. J Consum Res 21(1):1–30

Grimes SM (2008) Kid's ad play: regulating children's advergames in the converging media context. Int J Commun Law Policy 12:161–178

Grimes SM, Shade LR (2005) Neopian economics of play: children's cyberpets and online communities as immersive advertising in neopets.com. Int J Media Cult Polit 1(2):181–198

Gurău C (2008) The Influence of advergames on players' behaviour: an experimental study. Electron Markets 18(2):106–116

Helsper EJ, Enyon R (2010) Digital natives: where is the evidence? Br Educ Res J 36(3):503–520

Houben J (2009) OLA IJstijd Kids campagne 2009. Presentation at kids insights day, October 21, 2009. http://media.mtvnetworks.nl/kidsday/kidsdayjoosthouben.pdf. Last accessed 1 June 2010

Hufen B (2010) Laat met je merk spelen. Games als marketingmiddel. Kluwer, Amsterdam

Jansen S (2009) Trends in kids- en jongerenmarketing. www.frankwatching.com/archive/2009/05/19/trends-in-kids-en-jongerenmarketing-2. Last accessed 20 April 2012

Latour B (1987) Science in action. How to follow scientists and engineers through society. Harvard University Press, Cambridge, MA

Latour B (1991) Technology is society made durable. In: Law J (ed) A sociology of monsters: essays on power, technology and domination. Routledge, New York, pp 103–131

Law J (2009) Seeing like a survey. Cultural sociology 3(2):239–256

Livingstone S (2009a) Debating children's susceptibility to persuasion—where does fairness come in? A commentary on the Nairn and Fine versus Ambler debate. Int J Advertising 28(1):170–174

Livingstone S (2009b) Children and the internet. Great expectations, challenging realities. Polity, Cambridge

Livingstone S, Helsper EJ (2006) Does advertising literacy mediate the effects of advertising on children? A critical examination of two linked research literatures in relation to obesity and food choice. J Commun 56(3):560–584

Lunt P, Livingstone S (2012) Media regulation. Governance and the interests of citizens and consumers. Sage, London

Moore ES (2004) Children and the changing world of advertising. J Bus Ethics 52(2):161–167

MTV Networks (2009) Adverteren bij MTV networks in 2010. www.mtvnetworks.nl/index.php?list/5. Last accessed 12 June 2010

Nairn A, Fine C (2008) Who's messing with my mind? The implications of dual-process models for the ethics of advertising to children. Int J Advertising 27(3):447–470

OLA (2009) 2009 Topjaar OLA ijs. www.unileverdirect.nl/OLA/images/misc/OLAverkoop Brochure2009.pdf. Last accessed 15 June 2010

OLAIJstijd (2010) Informatie voor ouders. www.olaijstijd.nl/ijstijd/info_ouders.html

Oudshoorn N, Pinch T (2005) Introduction: how users and non-users matter. In: Oudshoorn N, Pinch T (eds) How users matter. The co-construction of users and technology. MIT Press, Cambridge, MA, pp 1–28

Perri6 (2005) The personal information economy: trends and prospects for consumers. In: Lace S (ed) The glass consumer. Life in surveillance society. Policy Press, Bristol, pp 17–43

Pridmore J (2012) Consumer surveillance. In: Ball K, Haggerty KD, Lyon D (eds) Routledge handbook of surveillance studies. Routledge, New York, pp 321–329

Reintjes M (2009) Brands and games 2009: De cases. www.frankwatching.com/archive/2009/03/12/brands-and-games-2009-de-cases. Last accessed 12 September 2012

Rozendaal E, Buijzen M, Valkenburg P (2011) Children's understanding of advertisers' persuasive tactics. Int J Advertising 30(2):329–350

Steeves V (2006) It's not child's play: the online invasion of children's privacy. Univ Ottawa Law Technol J 3(1):169–188

Steeves V (2007) The watched child: surveillance in three online playgrounds. International conference on the rights of the child. Wilson Lafleur, Montreal, pp 119–140

Valkenburg P (2002) Beeldschermkinderen. Theorieën over kind en media. Boom, Amsterdam

Part IV
Cyberbullying

Chapter 11
Children and Peer-to-Peer Risks in Social Networks: Regulating, Empowering or a Little Bit of Both?

Eva Lievens

Contents

Dr. Eva Lievens is a Senior Research Fellow of the Research Fund Flanders at the Interdisciplinary Centre for Law and ICT—KU Leuven—iMinds.The research findings presented in this chapter are the result of her research project "Risk-reducing regulatory strategies for illegal and harmful conduct and content in online social network sites" (Postdoctoral research project funded by the Research Fund Flanders; www.fwo.be). The author wishes to thank Simone van der Hof and Bart Schermer for their valuable comments.

E. Lievens (✉)
Interdisciplinary Centre for Law and ICT, KU Leuven, Leuven, Belgium
e-mail: Eva.lievens@law.kuleuven.be

S. van der Hof et al. (eds.), *Minding Minors Wandering the Web: Regulating Online Child Safety*, Information Technology and Law Series 24, DOI: 10.1007/978-94-6265-005-3_11,

Social media mirror, magnify and complicate countless aspects of everyday life, bringing into question practices that are presumed stable and shedding light on contested social phenomena.

Nancy K. Baym and Danah Boyd (Baym and Boyd 2012, p. 320).

11.1 Introduction

Online social networking sites (SNS) provide individuals with the opportunity to share information on a previously unimaginable scale, by creating profiles, disclosing facts, emotions, or pictures and to interact in a highly sophisticated manner. During the past 5 years, the popularity of these SNS has expanded spectacularly, attracting an extraordinary number of users (e.g. almost 1,25 billion users for Facebook).[1] Among children and young people, social networking has become one of the preferred online activities.[2] The EU Kids Online study found that 77 % of 13–16 year olds and 38 % of 9–12 year olds have a social networking profile,[3] even though most SNS put the minimum age limit to create a profile at 13.

It has been argued that the blurring between 'public' and 'private' in SNS, the invisibility of audiences and the fact that information in such networks is persistent, replicable, searchable and visible on a large-scale[4] entail that risks in an SNS environment are significantly more complex than equivalent offline risks. Aside from providing greater access to certain (illegal or harmful) categories of content (e.g. hate speech), and the facilitation of certain behaviour such as sexting or grooming, an added complexity can be found in the fact that the increased interaction between minors may lead to more reciprocal harassment, blurring the lines between victims and offenders to a greater extent than in the offline world.[5,6]

This changing role of minors within social networks raises questions with regard to the applicability of the current legislative framework and liability for certain acts. This chapter will assess this applicability, to what extent minors may be held liable according to existing criminal or civil law for certain risk behaviour

---

1 Facebook statistics: www.facebook.com/press/info.php?statistics. Statistics for the end of December 2013.

2 Livingstone et al. 2011b, p. 1, www2.lse.ac.uk/media@lse/research/EUKidsOnline/ShortSNS.pdf.

3 Livingstone et al. 2011a, www2.lse.ac.uk/media@lse/research/EUKidsOnline/EU%20Kids%20II%20(2009-11)/EUKidsOnlineIIReports/Final%20report.pdf, p. 18.

4 boyd 2008, www.danah.org/papers/TakenOutOfContext.pdf.

5 Internet Safety Technical Task Force 2008, p. 33, http://cyber.law.harvard.edu/sites/cyber.law.harvard.edu/files/ISTTF_Final_Report.pdf.

6 Lampert and Donoso 2012, p. 147.

(e.g. bullying, posting of harmful/illegal comments or pictures) and whether third parties, such as parents, may be held liable for the behaviour of minors on SNS. This will be illustrated by means of provisions from Belgian (civil and criminal) law. Given the specific nature of SNS, the use, and especially the implementation and enforcement of, traditional types of legislation are neither obvious nor desirable.[7] It is the aim of this chapter to explore a number of regulatory and other strategies that may be adopted instead to deal with risk behaviour of young SNS users without depriving them of the undeniable benefits and opportunities that SNS provide them with. This includes a discussion of the potential of self- and co-regulation and non-regulatory mechanisms, such as improving media literacy skills or providing efficient reporting tools, for the development of (regulatory) strategies, which reduce peer-to-peer risks in user-centric environments.

11.2 Children and SNS Risks: Victims, Participants, Offenders, …?

As in most environments in which children and young people are present (e.g. the street, school, playground, in front of the television, etc.), risks may occur in social networks. Recent research has found that children who use SNS encounter more risks online than those who do not,[8] but this substantially depends on how they use these services. Moreover, the exposure to risks does not automatically lead to harm. As Staksrud et al. put it: “Risk may, therefore, be safely encountered by many, and only in a proportion of cases (depending on the action of both protective and risk factors) does it result in harm.”[9]

Examples of risks that may occur in SNS are bullying, sexting, posting hurtful comments, sharing of or being tagged in pictures without permission and targeted advertising.[10] Whereas children used to be predominantly regarded as victims of certain risks, in need of protection, increasingly, and this has become very visible in the SNS environment, they may adopt different roles depending on the activities they perform. According to the ‘three C’s classification’ of online risks developed by the EU Kids Online study children may be recipients (Content), participants (Contact) or actors (Conduct) with regard to various risks.[11]

---

[7] Lievens 2010, Article 4.

[8] Staksrud et al. 2013, pp. 40, 48.

[9] Staksrud et al. 2013, p. 41.

[10] See also European Commission 2012, p. 5, http://eur-lex.europa.eu/LexUriServ/LexUriServ.do?uri=COM:2012:0196:FIN:EN:PDF.

[11] Hasebrink et al. 2009, http://eprints.lse.ac.uk/24368/1/D3.2_Report-Cross_national_comparisons-2nd-edition.pdf, p. 24.

Although (inappropriate or harmful) content and contact (with adult strangers, so-called 'stranger danger'[12]) have traditionally been the major causes of concern for policy makers and parents, empirical research has shown that the risks that upsets minors the most often occur between peers.[13] Sexting, i.e. the communication of "sexually explicit content [...] via text messages, smart phones or visual and Web 2.0. activities such as social networking sites"[14] and cyberbullying are prime examples of this type of risks. Scholars have found, for instance, that, similarly to bullying that occurs offline, around 60 % of children that bully online have been the target of bullies themselves.[15,16] Children thus engage in both functions (victim—bully),[17] and these multiple roles are considered to be "fluid over time and across different contexts".[18] Other situations where peers may be considered 'actors' are when pictures or video clips are posted, shared or tagged without the consent of the child that is portrayed. This may, for instance, be the case with regard to types of secondary sexting,[19] where sexually suggestive pictures that are sent voluntarily by someone are forwarded by the receiver of the picture, or incidents of 'happy slapping', where bullying scenes or assaults in the offline world are filmed with a digital or often a phone camera and then shared online. Especially in SNS, which are increasingly accessed through smart phones,[20] such actions may have significant consequences that are often not anticipated by the 'actor'. Once content is uploaded on an SNS it can be shared

---

[12] Barbovschi et al. 2012, pp. 177 and 186: "The EU Kids Online findings show that 'stranger danger', although high on the Internet safety agenda, affects only a few children in Europe."

[13] Internet Safety Technical Task Force 2008, p. 4; Livingstone et al. 2011a, www2.lse.ac.uk/media@lse/research/EUKidsOnline/EU%20Kids%20II%20(2009-11)/EUKidsOnlineIIReports/D4FullFindings.pdf, p. 6.

[14] Ringrose et al. 2012, p. 9.

[15] Görzig 2011, http://eprints.lse.ac.uk/39601/1/Who%20bullies%20and%20who%20is%20bullied%20online%20%28LSERO%29.pdf, p. 1.

[16] They have been called 'bully-victims'. Other additional roles children may adopt in a bullying situation have also been identified: e.g. assistants, reinforcers, defenders, onlookers. Levy et al. 2012, http://cyber.law.harvard.edu/sites/cyber.law.harvard.edu/files/FINAL_BTWF_LitReview_091212-1.pdf, p. 15.

[17] Lampert and Donoso 2012, p. 147; OECD 2012, pp. 29 and 31.

[18] Levy et al. 2012, p. 15.

[19] When looking at sexting from a legal perspective it is helpful to distinguish between primary and secondary types of sexting; the first meaning that minors take pictures of themselves and share these pictures with their peers themselves, the second meaning that someone forwards or further shares a picture that was sent to him by a person that took a picture of him or herself. Whereas primary sexting can be consensual (unless of course it is the result of coercion), secondary sexting is likely not to be consensual, but rather part of a revenge action (for instance by a previous love interest) or bullying behaviour, and may have a grave impact on the person in the image.

[20] Ringrose et al. 2012, p. 26.

very quickly with a very large audience,[21] and it is often very difficult to completely remove it. Moreover, content may already have been copied or forwarded before it is erased by a SNS provider, something of which children and young people are often not aware.[22]

11.3 Legal Implications

Translated to the legal context the various roles a child may adopt in the SNS environment, e.g. active creator, perpetrator or 'data controller', may—in theory—entail different legal consequences and the applicability of specific legislation. Of course, it is necessary to take into account that, because of their age, or potential lack of legal capacities,[23] they may not be considered liable for their actions. Consequently, this raises questions with regard to the liability of parents or other caretakers.

11.3.1 Applying Existing Legislative Provisions to Unwanted Behaviour

The fact that SNS constitute a global, vast communication platform with millions of users in countries across the world does not entail that this environment finds itself in a legal vacuum. If an offense is committed on a SNS, the existing legal framework may be applied if certain conditions laid down in the law in question are fulfilled. Depending on the national circumstances, legislation may be formulated in a technology-neutral manner, may be interpreted in an evolutionary manner or may even be drafted especially with new media environment in mind (e.g. provisions with regard to electronic stalking or harassment).[24]

In Belgium, for instance, a number of articles of the Criminal Code may be relevant with regard to sexting. Article 383 criminalises the display, sale or

[21] A recent example of how fast information that is shared by teenagers on an SNS can spread and how this may lead to unintended and unforeseen consequences is the *Project X Haren Party* case in the Netherlands. A party invitation of a teenage girl on Facebook that was not set to private on the event page went viral, attracted several thousands of youngsters and ended in riots. For more information, cf. www.bbc.co.uk/news/world-europe-19684708.

[22] Sacco et al. 2010, http://cyber.law.harvard.edu/sites/cyber.law.harvard.edu/files/Sacco_Argudin_Maguire_Tallon_Sexting_Jun2010.pdf, pp. 3–4.

[23] In Belgium, for instance, according to Article 1124 of the Civil Code, minors are in principle legally incapable of entering into contracts. In practice, however, courts will take the level of discernment of the minor in question into account when deciding upon the nullity of contracts.

[24] In Belgium, the Act of 13 June 2005 on electronic communications contains an article, which criminalises 'harassment by electronic communication means' (Article 145 §3bis).

distribution of writings or images that are indecent. If this is done in the presence of minors below the age of 16, more severe sentences are imposed according to Article 386. In addition, Article 384 stipulates that the production of indecent writings or images is also a criminal offence. Child pornography is addressed in Article 383bis of the Criminal Code. This article criminalises the display, sale, rental, distribution, transmission, delivery, possession or (knowing) obtainment of access of or to images that depict poses or sexual acts with a pornographic character which involve or depict minors. These articles are formulated in a technology-neutral and broad manner, so in theory they could be applied to cases of sexting in SNS. In addition to criminal provisions, legislation with regard to the processing of personal data or portrait rights may be violated in cases where images are shared or distributed without the consent of the person that is portrayed. Whether or not these existing legislative provisions are applicable in certain situations will be judged on a case-by-case basis.

However, the application of existing legislation may have unintended consequences. In case of primary sexting, for instance, it seems to be disproportionate to apply legislative provisions that aim to address child pornography and to punish adults who intend to sexually abuse children, to situations where minors send or post sexually suggestive pictures to each other.[25] Not only may such behaviour possibly "be part of the developmentally necessary exploration and experimentation that enables the emergence of sexual identity",[26] but even when considered imprudent or unwise taking into account the spiralling loss of control of a picture once uploaded on a SNS, criminally prosecuting and punishing minors may also be counterproductive and over-reaching.[27]

In addition, practical obstacles may arise when an attempt is made to enforce national legislative provisions. Often SNS providers are located in another jurisdiction than the victim and declare in their Terms and Conditions that disputes need to be brought before the courts of their country of establishment.[28] Moreover, in the SNS environment perpetrators may act anonymously (for instance by means of a fake profile), making it very difficult to find and punish them. Other complicating factors may be that victims have not succeeded in obtaining evidence of certain acts (because the offending content has been deleted by the perpetrator or

[25] Schmitz and Siry 2011, Article 3, p. 9. Note that whereas cases of secondary sexting (cf. n. 19) could be more problematic and may cause actual harm, the question remains whether this type of 'offenses' should be dealt with on the basis of the criminal provisions that are aimed at fighting child pornography. A new, carefully tailored legal provision, in addition to the use of empowerment strategies (discussed below) may be more appropriate to address cases where malignant intent is undeniable and the (moral) damage significant.

[26] Livingstone and Görzig 2012, p. 152.

[27] Van der Hof and Koops 2011, pp. 16–17, 19, 23.

[28] However, in a case in France, a judge declared himself competent in a dispute concerning Facebook (Court of Appeal of Pau, First Chamber, Judgement of 23 March 2012, www.legalis.net/spip.php?page=breves-article&id_article=3382 [in French]). It remains to be seen whether this will be upheld in the future.

by the victim itself), that law enforcement and magistrates are not sufficiently aware of the characteristics of the SNS environment or that children do simply not report or file a complaint when they have been the victim of harmful acts.

11.3.2 Responsibility and Liability of Minors, Parents and Teachers

1. Criminal liability

Even if certain acts may fall within the scope of application of existing criminal provisions, this will not automatically mean that children can be held responsible or liable. This will depend on the age of criminal responsibility, i.e. "the age at which children are deemed to have the capacity to be legally responsible for breaches of the criminal law",[29] that is adopted in each national jurisdiction, as there is no commonly accepted age of criminal responsibility in international or European legislative or policy documents.[30] In order to determine this age it should be assessed "whether a child, by virtue of her or his individual discernment and understanding, can be held responsible for essentially anti-social behaviour".[31]

In Belgium, for instance, the Youth Protection Act of 1965 states that minors cannot be put on a par with adults with regard to the degree of liability and the consequences of their actions (Preamble, para 4). However, if a minor commits an 'act that is described as a crime' they should be made aware of the consequences of that offence. As a result, the Youth Protection Act imposes other measures, including supervision, education, disciplinary measures, guidance, advice or support instead of the punishments of the Criminal Code.[32] Measures can be imposed on parents or on the minors themselves. The age of the minor in question is taken into account; different measures will be imposed before and after the age

---

[29] Van Bueren 2007, p. 58. Cf., Article 40 §3 United Nations Convention on the Rights of the Child: "States Parties shall seek to promote the establishment of laws, procedures, authorities and institutions specifically applicable to children alleged as, accused of, or recognized as having infringed the penal law, and, in particular: (a) The establishment of a minimum age below which children shall be presumed not to have the capacity to infringe the penal law."

[30] Van Bueren 2007, p. 106.

[31] United Nations Standard Minimum Rules for the Administration of Juvenile Justice ("The Beijing Rules"), 1985, www.un.org/documents/ga/res/40/a40r033.htm.

[32] Cf. Article 40 §3 United Nations Convention on the Rights of the Child: "(b) Whenever appropriate and desirable, measures for dealing with such children without resorting to judicial proceedings, providing that human rights and legal safeguards are fully respected. 4. A variety of dispositions, such as care, guidance and supervision orders; counselling; probation; foster care; education and vocational training programmes and other alternatives to institutional care shall be available to ensure that children are dealt with in a manner appropriate to their well-being and proportionate both to their circumstances and the offence."

of 12 years (Article 37). If possible, the judge may give preference to victim-offender mediation (Article 37bis).

2. Civil liability

In addition to potential criminal liability, depending on the system of law of a particular country, minors may be held civilly liable for 'wrongful acts' or acts that have caused damage. In order to assess whether this will be the case in a specific situation, a child's age and maturity will be taken into account to determine whether he or she had the ability to discern the scope of his or her actions. In Belgium, for instance, judges have held that this may be as early as the age of seven.[33] On the basis of Article 1382 and 1383 of the Belgian Civil Code, to be held liable the victim must prove the offence and the causal link with the damage that this offence has caused. This entails that the offender has not acted as a normal, reasonable and careful person that he or she acted freely and consciously and that he or she must have been able to foresee that his or her behaviour would cause damage to the victim.[34] Judges will need to evaluate this element of foresee ability, taking into account the specific and concrete circumstances of each case. One may wonder, for instance in the case of sexting, whether minors can reasonably foresee the consequences of their actions. It is conceivable that it is hard for minors (or even adults) to grasp what it means to forward or post an intimate picture of someone else, as the loss of control over content that is made public in the digital sphere is so vast and irreversible.

3. Liability of parents and teachers

Moreover, in certain circumstances parents and teachers may be held liable for the acts of their children or pupils. In Belgium, for parents as well as teachers an assumption of liability has been included in Article 1384 of the Civil Code. This means that, in order not to be held liable, the parents and teachers in question must prove that they did not commit a mistake in raising or supervising the child.[35] Walrave et al. have argued that supervision with regard to a child's activities online is very difficult and advocate evolving towards a liability system without fault that would require an obligatory insurance.[36]

11.3.3 Reflections

First of all, it is important to emphasise that many cases that may be perceived as involving a peer-to-peer risk will not fall inside the scope of the legislative

[33] Walrave et al. 2009, www.internet-observatory.be/internet_observatory/pdf/brochures/Boek_cyberpesten_nl.pdf, pp. 101–102.

[34] Walrave et al. 2009, p. 102.

[35] Walrave et al. 2009, pp. 103–111.

[36] Walrave et al. 2009, p. 107.

framework because they lack gravity (even if the victim in question may experience harm). Second, whereas in theory it is possible to apply existing legislation to peer-to-peer risks in SNS, in practice the enforcement may run into various obstacles, rendering the law ineffective, or the side-effects may be undesirable. In addition it may be argued that with regard to such risks the application of criminal law provisions and the use of court procedures should be considered an *ultimum remedium*,[37] and be limited to very serious cases, where malignant intent is undeniable and the (moral) damage significant. Other types of intervention, both ex ante and ex post, will in most cases be more appropriate and effective.

11.4 The Use of Self- and Co-regulation

Policies aimed at a safer Internet for children have over the past 15 years put significant emphasis of alternative regulatory instruments such as self- and co-regulation.[38,39] This was again confirmed in the Commission Communication on a European strategy for a better Internet for children of May 2012, which stated that "[l]egislation will not be discarded, but preference will be given to self-regulation, which remains the most flexible framework for achieving tangible results in this area".[40] Furthermore, the Commission underlined that "[o]ngoing effective industry self-regulation for the protection and empowerment of young people, with the appropriate benchmarks and independent monitoring systems in place, is needed to build trust in a sustainable and accountable governance model that could bring more flexible, timely and market-appropriate solutions than any regulatory initiatives".[41]

Examples of 'ongoing' industry self-regulation are the Safer Social Networking Principles for Europe,[42] the CEO Coalition[43] and the ICT Coalition,[44] three 'coalitions' that consist of different constellations of companies (some companies, such as Facebook, are a member of all three coalitions). They put forward largely similar principles, albeit with different emphasis, to make the Internet in general, or SNS in particular, safer for children, such as the promotion of privacy-friendly

[37] Van der Hof and Koops 2011, p. 13.

[38] Lievens 2010, p. 208. Cf. also recital 44 of the Audiovisual Media Services Directive.

[39] For a comprehensive overview of policy history in this field, Lievens 2010.

[40] European Commission 2012, p. 6.

[41] European Commission 2012, p. 16.

[42] European Social Networking Task Force 2009, http://ec.europa.eu/information_society/activities/social_networking/docs/sn_principles.pdf.

[43] Coalition to make the Internet a better place for kids 2011, Statement of purpose and work plan. http://ec.europa.eu/information_society/activities/sip/docs/ceo_coalition_statement.pdf.

[44] ICT Coalition 2012.

default settings, age-appropriate content, reporting mechanisms, content classification and parental controls.

The reference to the need for independent monitoring systems with regard to self-regulatory initiatives in the Commission Communication is crucial. Up until now in reality the results of the coalitions' work leave significant room for improvement. Independent assessments of the implementation of the Safer Social Networking Principles for instance have shown that with regard to reporting mechanisms, in 2010, only 9 out of 22 sites responded to complaints submitted by minors asking for help,[45] and in 2011, only 17 out of 23 services responded to complaints or reports, sometimes taking up to 10 days to do so.[46] The results of the CEO Coalition were assessed in July 2012 and in 2013. The conclusion of these assessments was that progress can be observed, but that tangible results remain limited.[47]

The results of these evaluations raise the question of the effectiveness of this type of regulatory initiative: although the commitment of the SNS providers to take steps to make their services safer is to be applauded, the concrete implementation of such safety measures is of course crucial in order to achieve actual protection. It is our view that the European Commission should play a role in observing and guiding the various existing initiatives in order to avoid fragmentation, discrepancies or contradictions, and should consider moving towards a stronger co-regulatory[48] framework if independent evaluations keep demonstrating that self-regulation does not reach the policy objectives in this area.

In addition to monitoring and evaluating self- (and/or co-)regulatory systems in this domain, it is, very important, from a human rights perspective, to be aware that if such systems have an impact on fundamental rights, such as freedom of expression and the right to privacy,[49] certain safeguards or procedural guarantees, laid down for instance in the European Convention on Human Rights (ECHR), need to be respected.[50] It has been emphasised by the Council of Europe Committee of Ministers in its Recommendation on the protection of human rights with regard to social networking services that it is important that "procedural safeguards are respected by these mechanisms, in line with the right to be heard and to

[45] Staksrud and Lobe 2010, http://ec.europa.eu/information_society/activities/social_networking/docs/final_report/first_part.pdf, p. 8.

[46] Donoso 2011a, http://ec.europa.eu/information_society/activities/social_networking/docs/final_report_11/part_one.pdf, p. 10 and Donoso 2011b, http://ec.europa.eu/information_society/activities/social_networking/docs/final_reports_sept_11/report_phase_b_1.pdf, p. 10.

[47] X 2012a, http://ec.europa.eu/information_society/activities/sip/docs/ceo_coalition/report_11_july.pdf.

[48] Lievens 2010.

[49] An example of such a situation may be where content is blocked, filtered or removed by a SNS provider.

[50] Lievens 2010.

review or appeal against decisions, including in appropriate cases the right to a fair trial, within a reasonable time, and starting with the presumption of innocence".[51]

11.5 Empowerment Strategies

Influenced by increasingly available high-quality empirical social science research, such as the EU Kids Online project, the debate on the 'regulation' of the digital and social media environment to protect minors has shifted its focus away from legislation and regulation towards empowerment and the improvement of digital skills and media literacy over the past 5 years. As Livingstone et al. have emphasised: "[w]hile recognising that measures to reduce specific risks have their place, it is also important to develop strategies to build children's resilience and to provide resources which help children to cope with or recover from the effects of harm".[52] Moreover, "the more that children are equipped to work out solutions for themselves – through skills, greater resilience or access to online resources to support them – the less others will need to step into guide or restrict their online activities".[53]

Policy documents in this area at different levels highlight the importance of empowering children and young people. The Council of Europe already issued a Recommendation on empowering children in the new information and communications environment in 2006.[54] More recently, the OECD Council Recommendation on the protection of children online, for instance, stated that "policies to protect children online should empower children and parents to evaluate and minimise risks and engage online in a secure, safe and responsible manner".[55] Furthermore, in its Strategy for a better Internet for children the European Commission very clearly emphasises that "[r]egulation remains an option, but, where appropriate, it should preferably be avoided, in favour of more adaptable self-regulatory tools, and of education and empowerment".[56]

A number of empowerment strategies could help reduce peer-to-peer risks in SNS.

---

[51] Council of Europe, Recommendation CM/Rec(2012)4 of the Committee of Ministers to member States on the protection of human rights with regard to social networking services, https://wcd.coe.int/ViewDoc.jsp?id=1929453&Site=CM.

[52] Livingstone et al. 2012, www2.lse.ac.uk/media@lse/research/EUKidsOnline/EU%20Kids%20III/Reports/EUKidsOnlinereportfortheCEOCoalition.pdf, p. 5.

[53] Livingstone and Haddon 2012, p. 8.

[54] Council of Europe, Recommendation Rec(2006)12 of the Committee of Ministers to member states on empowering children in the new information and communications environment, https://wcd.coe.int/ViewDoc.jsp?Ref=Rec(2006)12&Sector=secCM&Language=lanEnglish&Ver=original&BackColorInternet=9999CC&BackColorIntranet=FFBB55&BackColorLogged=FFAC75.

[55] OECD Council 2012.

[56] European Commission 2012, p. 2.

1. Improving media literacy skills

Media literacy[57] and skills are of the utmost importance to children's use of the Internet.[58] In the context of SNS, media literacy has been argued to be especially important "in order to make the users aware of their rights when using these tools, and also help them acquire or reinforce human rights values and develop the behaviour necessary to respect other people's rights and freedoms".[59] With regard to peer-to-peer risks such as bullying or sexting, this last element is of particular importance. This relates to a basic principle that children are taught in the offline world as well: 'do not do to others what you would not want others do to you'. This should also be a golden rule with regard to SNS, but for children and young people it is much more difficult to estimate the consequences and potential grave impact of their actions in this environment. Hence, raising awareness of children from a very early age about the particular characteristics of SNS and the potential long-term impact of a seemingly trivial act is crucial. Furthermore, children are often completely unaware of a number of basic legal principles, such as portrait rights or the right to privacy. However, it is crucial that they have a clear understanding of the fact that certain acts in SNS may have legal implications, and this should be conveyed to them in an age-appropriate, clear and understandable manner.

2. Providing information

The idiom 'knowledge is power' is often used in relation to the information society. It is undeniable that if we want to empower children and young people to act appropriately in SNS, providing them with information is essential. Not only parents and teachers can play a role in this. SNS providers should provide understandable and accessible information about the types of behaviour that are not tolerated in their networks or that may infringe on legal provisions.[60] This is now often included in the Terms and Conditions section of their network. However, these Terms and Conditions remain notoriously unread and un-understood.

---

[57] Media literacy has been defined as the "ability to access the media, to understand and to critically evaluate different aspects of the media and media contents and to create communications in a variety of contexts" in the Commission Communication on A European approach to media literacy in the digital environment: European Commission, Communication from the Commission to the European Parliament, the Council, the European Economic and Social Committee and the Committee of the Regions, A European approach to media literacy in the digital environment, COM(2007) 833 final, http://ec.europa.eu/culture/media/literacy/docs/com/en.pdf.

[58] European Commission 2012, p. 8.

[59] Council of Europe 2012 at point 4.

[60] See also: Council of Europe 2012 at point 10: "member States should take appropriate measures to ensure children and young people's safety and protect their dignity while also guaranteeing procedural safeguards and the right to freedom of expression and access to information, in particular by engaging with social networking providers to carry out the following actions: provide clear information about the kinds of content or content-sharing or conduct that may be contrary to applicable legal provisions; [...]".

"Rais[ing] awareness of safety education messages and acceptable use policies to users, parents, teachers and carers in a prominent, clear and age-appropriate manner" is the first principle of the Safer Social Networking Principles (supra). An independent assessment of the implementation of this principle found that whereas safety information is often available (although only in half of the cases easy to find) on SNS, the Terms of Use, Community guidelines, Statement of Rights and Responsibilities and/or House rules are "either difficult to access and/or difficult to understand, especially for younger audiences".[61] There are, however, SNS that provide child-friendly versions of the Terms of Use, sometimes even presented in audio–visual format. Given the importance of this information, not only with regard to peer-to-peer risks but for instance also with regard to the protection of personal data and privacy, SNS providers should be encouraged to adopt innovative strategies to make children read and above all understand their Terms of Use. Empirical research on such strategies is urgently needed.

3. Providing efficient reporting mechanisms

Whereas the provision of information usually takes place before certain acts are carried out (*ex ante*), reporting mechanisms allow users to complain about certain content or report about conduct or content *ex post*. With regard to social media, the use of reporting mechanisms is increasingly promoted. The Council of Europe, for example, has emphasised that in order to protect children and young people against harmful content and behaviour "while not being required to control, supervise and/or rate all content uploaded by its users,[62] social networking service providers may be required to adopt certain precautionary measures (for example, comparable to 'adult content' rules applicable in certain member States) or take diligent action in response to complaints (*ex-post* moderation)".[63] To do this, the setting up of easily accessible reporting mechanisms is actively encouraged.[64] The CEO Coalition (*supra*) also put forward the development of simple and robust reporting tools for users as one of its action points, and the provision of such tools is one of the core Safer Social Networking Principles as well. In addition, the European Commission has advocated the establishment and deployment of reporting tools for users, and added that for children in particular, these mechanisms should be "visible, easy to find, recognisable, accessible to all and available at any stage of the online experience where a child may need it".[65]

---

[61] Donoso 2011a, at p. 8.

[62] Please note that on the basis of Article 15 of the E-Commerce Directive hosting providers do not have a general obligation to monitor content or search for illegal activities. In this context the European Court of Justice confirmed that Netlog, a SNS based in Belgium, could not be obliged to install a filtering/blocking system in order to prevent the unlawful use of musical and audiovisual works (European Court of Justice, *SABAM v. Netlog*, C-360-10. 16 February 2012).

[63] Council of Europe 2012 at point 8.

[64] Council of Europe 2012 at point 10.

[65] European Commission 2012, p. 10.

With regard to peer-to-peer risks, such as sexting or cyberbullying the importance of mechanisms to report behaviour or acts that are experienced as being harmful or hurtful cannot be overestimated. At the moment, research shows that the use of these tools by children is still rather low. The EU Kids Online study found for instance that only 9 % of those upset by bullying messages have used the available reporting tools, leaving significant scope for awareness-raising concerning availability and use.[66] SNS providers, however, seem to be increasingly committed to providing users with reporting possibilities.[67,68] Of course, in addition to making such tools available it is also essential that if SNS providers receive complaints about problematic peer-to-peer behaviour they promptly act upon them,[69] provide support for the victims, warn the offenders that this type of behaviour is not tolerated and apply sanctions if necessary. Such sanctions (such as removing content, suspending or deleting accounts) are often included in the Terms and Conditions, another reason why it is very important that steps be taken to ensure that users are aware of these terms and that they understand them.

Moreover, the action that is taken by a SNS provider should be carefully considered. First, with regard to the removal of content there should there be transparent procedures that include the possibility to appeal certain decisions in order to keep private censorship at bay. Second, with regard to serious cases, where actual harm seems to occur,[70] SNS providers should cooperate with other actors such as law enforcement agencies (LEA). Whereas many SNS providers are already working together with LEA, it is important that the criteria that are used to assess content and to decide whether to escalate reports to LEA are made very clear.[71] Assessing to what extent certain behaviour has actual legal implications should not and cannot be left to private actors.

4. Peer-to-peer strategies

In order to address peer-to-peer risks, advantage could also be taken from peer-to-peer opportunities, such as peer mentoring schemes,[72] peer-based

[66] Livingstone et al. 2012, p. 5.

[67] Cf. for instance www.facebook.com/report or http://www.youtube.com/t/community_guidelines. Cf. also X 2012b, http://ec.europa.eu/information_society/activities/sip/docs/ceo_coalition/reporting_tools_progress_report.pdf.

[68] Please note that there are also initiatives by NGOs and law enforcement, which enable young people to report illegal or harmful behaviour, for instance, https://www.ecops.be/ in Belgium and http://www.meldknop.nl/ in The Netherlands.

[69] Livingstone et al. 2012, p. 8; Ringrose et al. 2012, p. 59.

[70] For instance, in cases of secondary sexting. A recent example occurred in Belgium, when suggestive (webcam) pictures of teenage girls were posted on a Facebook page titled 'Antwerp whores'; for more information www.expatica.com/be/news/belgian-news/Antwerp-whores-Facebook-fan-page-under-investigation-_254445.html.

[71] X 2012b, p. 2.

[72] Görzig 2011, p. 1.

learning[73] or peer education.[74] In such schemes (usually older) children provide support and advice to other (younger) children, based on the idea that they may be better able to get a certain message across than parents or teachers.

Currently, these types of systems are being promoted with regard to the online environment, for instance by the European Commission in its European strategy for a better Internet for children.[75] In some member states initiatives have already been taken, such as the Cybermentors[76] project in the United Kingdom, which is an online forum where 'cybermentors' chat with their peers about negative online experiences such as cyberbullying and provide support for each other.[77]

Peer-monitoring or peer support mechanisms have been used for some time to address traditional bullying, and have generally been proven to be effective in reducing bullying, empowering children and creating more positive peer relations, for instance in a school environment.[78] However, some scholars have warned that such schemes may also have unintended consequences, such as reinforcement of aggressive behaviour and thus an increase in bullying, when implemented in certain circumstances and that their implementation should thus be carefully considered.[79] Empirical research into the uptake and success of these types of systems to reduce peer-to-peer risks in the SNS environment should be encouraged.

11.6 Conclusion

In the context of the protection of children and young people in the digital environment, multi-stakeholder involvement has long been put forward as a key principle. It should also be considered as such with regard to peer-to-peer risks. In many cases that involve such risks legal, and certainly criminal, action is not desirable. Moreover, although certain acts may fall within the scope of the legislative framework, the enforcement thereof, where warranted, may run into

---

[73] De Zwart et al. 2011, http://newmediaresearch.educ.monash.edu.au/moodle/pluginfile.php/2117/mod_label/intro/SNSandRisks_REPORT.pdf, p. 10.

[74] European Commission 2012, p. 9.

[75] European Commission 2012, p. 9.

[76] See: www.cybermentors.org.uk/.

[77] Hathcote and Hogan 2011, p. 103.

[78] Van der Zwaan et al. 2010, http://bnaic2010.uni.lu/Papers/Category%20A/Zwaan_et_al.pdf, p. 1; Hinduja 2010, http://cyberbullying.us/blog/peer-mentoring-as-a-strategy-to-address-cyberbullying.html; Banerjee et al. 2010, www.sussex.ac.uk/Users/robinb/bbreportsummary.pdf, p. 4; Cowie 2012, http://surrey.academia.edu/HelenCowie/Papers/1306578/Peer_support_systems_to_counteract_bullying, p. 6.

[79] Bradshaw and Waasdorp 2012, www.stopbullying.gov/at-risk/groups/lgbt/white_house_conference_materials.pdf, p. 47; Boyd and Palfrey 2012, http://cyber.law.harvard.edu/sites/cyber.law.harvard.edu/files/Necessary_Info.pdf, point 9.

practical obstacles that undermine its effectiveness. Notwithstanding these findings, policy makers at national level need to make clear decisions regarding the application of criminal law to situations where peer-to-peer risks lead to serious harm (such as secondary sexting), taking into account the interests of both minor victims and offenders. Ambiguous situations, which leave doubt as to the possible application of certain criminal law provisions (e.g. with regard to child pornography) to minor offenders should be avoided.

Many steps can be taken, however, to attempt to prevent peer-to-peer risks from occurring: starting from instilling in children from a very early age basic principles such as empathy and respect for one another,[80] to gradually increasing their media literacy skills, which should include an understanding of the characteristics of the digital environment in general, and SNS environments in particular, as well as a basic insight into and awareness of a number of potential legal implications of certain behaviour. Whereas parents and teachers would seem the most suitable actors to do this, research has found that their capacities are limited,[81] both in relation to skills as to time. Their efforts should thus be complemented by industry commitment to keep improving their services and providing users with clear information and tools that empower them. In addition, governmental actors must encourage educational institutions and civil society organisations to implement empowerment strategies and provide them with the resources to do so.

Given the importance of providing children with a positive online environment, in our view, policy makers should consider establishing strong co-regulatory mechanisms in this context. Such mechanisms can take various forms and can be organised at different levels, but should at least entail that all initiatives that are taken are evaluated independently, and that there are safety-net procedures if these evaluations show that the actors that are involved do not take up their responsibility. Although the European Commission hints at such an approach in its 2012 European strategy on a better Internet for children, by referring to considering regulatory or legislative measures if industry initiatives fail to deliver,[82] this remains too vague and open-ended. A transparent co-regulatory framework, with an unambiguous division of responsibilities, strong incentives to comply and clearly defined evaluation criteria, would lead to more accountability and certainty for all actors involved and would thus, in our view, be in everyone's best interest.

Finally, it remains crucial that both quantitative and qualitative empirical research is undertaken in this domain. A comprehensive and efficient strategy to reduce risks and empower young users can only be developed on the basis of sound evidence on the occurrence of certain practices, the actual harm they cause, and the concrete impact of initiatives of different actors.

---

[80] Boyd 2012, www.aplatformforgood.org/blog/entry/three-conversations-for-parents-navigating-networked-publics.

[81] Livingstone and Haddon 2012, p. 9.

[82] European Commission 2012, pp. 10–13.

References

Banerjee R, Robinson C, Smalley D (2010) Evaluation of the beatbully peer mentoring programme. www.sussex.ac.uk/Users/robinb/bbreportsummary.pdf

Barbovschi M, Marinescu V, Velicu A, Laszlo E (2012) Meeting new contacts online. In: Livingstone S, Haddon L, Görzig A (eds) Children, risk and safety on the internet. The Policy Press, Bristol, pp 177–189

Baym NK, Boyd D (2012) Socially mediated publicness: an introduction. J Broadcast Electron Media 56:320–329

boyd d (2008) Taken out of context: American teen sociality in networked publics. Ph.D. thesis. University of California, Berkeley. www.danah.org/papers/TakenOutOfContext.pdf

boyd d (2012) Three conversations for parents: navigating networked publics. www.aplatformforgood.org/blog/entry/three-conversations-for-parents-navigating-networked-publics

boyd d , Palfrey J (2012) What you must know to help combat youth bullying, meanness, and cruelty. http://cyber.law.harvard.edu/sites/cyber.law.harvard.edu/files/Necessary_Info.pdf

Bradshaw C, Waasdorp T (2012) Effective strategies in combating bullying. White paper prepared for the White House Conference on bullying prevention, pp 43–49. www.stopbullying.gov/at-risk/groups/lgbt/white_house_conference_materials.pdf

Coalition to make the Internet a better place for kids (2011) Statement of purpose and work plan. http://ec.europa.eu/information_society/activities/sip/docs/ceo_coalition_statement.pdf

Council of Europe (2006) Recommendation Rec(2006)12 of the Committee of Ministers to member states on empowering children in the new information and communications environment. https://wcd.coe.int/ViewDoc.jsp?Ref=Rec(2006)12&Sector=secCM&Language=lanEnglish&Ver=original&BackColorInternet=9999CC&BackColorIntranet=FFBB55&BackColorLogged=FFAC75

Council of Europe (2012) Recommendation CM/Rec(2012)4 of the Committee of Ministers to member states on the protection of human rights with regard to social networking services. https://wcd.coe.int/ViewDoc.jsp?id=1929453&Site=CM

Cowie H (2012) Peer support systems to counteract bullying. http://surrey.academia.edu/HelenCowie/Papers/1306578/Peer_support_systems_to_counteract_bullying

De Zwart M, Lindsay D, Henderson M and Philips M (2011) Teenagers, legal risks & social networking sites. http://newmediaresearch.educ.monash.edu.au/moodle/pluginfile.php/2117/mod_label/intro/SNSandRisks_REPORT.pdf

Donoso V (2011a) Assessment of the implementation of the safer social networking principles for the EU on 14 websites: Summary report. http://ec.europa.eu/information_society/activities/social_networking/docs/final_report_11/part_one.pdf

Donoso V (2011b) Assessment of the implementation of the safer social networking principles for the EU on 9 services: Summary report. http://ec.europa.eu/information_society/activities/social_networking/docs/final_reports_sept_11/report_phase_b_1.pdf

European Commission (2007) Communication from the Commission to the European Parliament, the council, the European Economic and Social Committee and the Committee of the Regions. A European approach to media literacy in the digital environment, COM(2007) 833 final. http://ec.europa.eu/culture/media/literacy/docs/com/en.pdf

European Commission (2012) Communication from the Commission to the European Parliament, the Council, the European Economic and Social Committee and the Committee of the Regions. European strategy for a better internet for children, COM(2012) 196 final. http://eur-lex.europa.eu/LexUriServ/LexUriServ.do?uri=COM:2012:0196:FIN:EN:PDF

European Social Networking Task Force (2009) Safer social networking principles for the EU. http://ec.europa.eu/information_society/activities/social_networking/docs/sn_principles.pdf

Görzig A (2011) Who bullies and who is bullied online?: a study of 9–16 year old internet users in 25 European countries. EU kids online, London. http://eprints.lse.ac.uk/39601/1/Who%20bullies%20and%20who%20is%20bullied%20online%20%28LSERO%29.pdf

Hasebrink U, Livingstone S, Haddon L, Ólafsson K (2009) Comparing children's online opportunities and risks across Europe: cross-national comparisons for EU kids online, 2nd edn. Deliverable D3.2. LSE, EU kids online, London. http://eprints.lse.ac.uk/24368/1/D3.2_Report-Cross_national_comparisons-2nd-edition.pdf

Hathcote A, Hogan K (2011) Resource guide on cyberbullying. Preventing Sch Fail Altern Educ Child youth 55:102–104

Hinduja S (2010) Peer mentoring as a strategy to address cyberbullying. http://cyberbullying.us/blog/peer-mentoring-as-a-strategy-to-address-cyberbullying.html

ICT Coalition (2012) http://www.ictcoalition.eu

Internet Safety Technical Task Force (2008) Enhancing child safety and online technologies: final report of the ISTTF to the multi-state working group on social networking of state attorney generals of the United States. Berkman Center for Internet and Society. http://cyber.law.harvard.edu/sites/cyber.law.harvard.edu/files/ISTTF_Final_Report.pdf

Lampert C, Donoso V (2012) Bullying. In: Livingstone S, Haddon L, Görzig A (eds) Children, risk and safety on the internet. The Policy Press, Bristol, pp 141–150

Levy N, Cortesi S, Gasser U, Crowley E, Beaton M, Casey J, Nolan C (2012) Bullying in a networked era: a literature review. http://cyber.law.harvard.edu/publications/2012/kbw_bulling_in_a_networked_era

Lievens E (2010) Protecting children in the digital era: the use of alternative regulatory instruments. Martinus Nijhoff Online, Leiden

Livingstone S, Görzig A (2012) 'Sexting': the exchange of sexual messages online among European youth. In: Livingstone S, Haddon L, Görzig A (eds) Children, risk and safety on the internet. The Policy Press, Bristol, pp 151–164

Livingstone S, Haddon L (2012) Theoretical framework for children's internet use. In: Livingstone S, Haddon L, Görzig A (eds) Children, risk and safety on the internet. The Policy Press, Bristol, pp 1–14

Livingstone S, Haddon L, Görzig A, Ólafsson K (2011a) Risks and safety on the internet: the perspective of European children: full findings. EU kids online, London. www2.lse.ac.uk/media@lse/research/EUKidsOnline/EU%20Kids%20II%20(2009-11)/EUKidsOnlineIIReports/D4FullFindings.pdf

Livingstone S, Ólafsson K, Staksrud E (2011b) Social networking, age and privacy. EU kids online, London. www2.lse.ac.uk/media@lse/research/EUKidsOnline/ShortSNS.pdf

Livingstone S, Ólafsson K, O'Neill B, Donoso V (2012) Towards a better internet for children. EU kids online, London. www2.lse.ac.uk/media@lse/research/EUKidsOnline/EU%20Kids%20III/Reports/EUKidsOnlinereportfortheCEOCoalition.pdf

OECD Council (2012) The Protection of Children Online: Recommendation of the OECD Council. http://www.oecd.org/sti/ieconomy/childrenonline_with_cover.pdf

Ringrose J, Gill R, Livingstone S, Harvey L (2012) A qualitative study of children, young people and 'sexting'—a report prepared for the NSPCC. www.nspcc.org.uk/Inform/resourcesforprofessionals/sexualabuse/sexting-research-report_wdf89269.pdf

Sacco DT, Argudin R, Maguire J, Tallon (2010) Sexting: youth practices and legal implications. Cyberlaw clinic, Harvard Law School. http://cyber.law.harvard.edu/sites/cyber.law.harvard.edu/files/Sacco_Argudin_Maguire_Tallon_Sexting_Jun2010.pdf

Schmitz S, Siry L (2011) Teenage folly or child abuse? state responses to 'sexting' by minors in the U.S. and Germany. Policy Internet 3:Article 3

Staksrud E and Lobe B (2010) Evaluation of the implementation of the safer social networking principles for the EU, Part 1: general report. http://ec.europa.eu/information_society/activities/social_networking/docs/final_report/first_part.pdf

Staksrud E, Ólafsson K, Livingstone S (2013) Does the use of social networking sites increase children's risk of harm? Comput Hum Behav 29:40–50

United Nations Standard Minimum Rules for the Administration of Juvenile Justice (1985).The Beijing Rules. www.un.org/documents/ga/res/40/a40r033.htm

Van Bueren G (2007) Child rights in Europe: convergence and divergence in judicial protection. Council of Europe Publishing, Strasbourg

Van der Hof S, Koops B-J (2011) Adolescents and cybercrime: navigating between freedom and control. Policy Internet 3:Article 4

Van der Zwaan J, Dignum V, Jonker C (2010) Simulating peer support for victims of cyberbullying. Paper at the 22nd Benelux conference on artificial intelligence. http://bnaic2010.uni.lu/Papers/Category%20A/Zwaan_et_al.pdf

Walrave M, Demoulin M, Heirman W, Van der Perre A (2009) Onderzoeksrapport cyberpesten [Research report cyberbullying]. www.internet-observatory.be/internet_observatory/pdf/brochures/Boek_cyberpesten_nl.pdf

X (2012a) Report of mid-term review meeting of the CEO coalition to make the Internet a better place for kids. http://ec.europa.eu/information_society/activities/sip/docs/ceo_coalition/report_11_july.pdf

X (2012b) Action 1 simple and robust reporting tools for users progress report. http://ec.europa.eu/information_society/activities/sip/docs/ceo_coalition/reporting_tools_progress_report.pdf

Chapter 12
On Technology Against Cyberbullying

Janneke M. van der Zwaan, Virginia Dignum, Catholijn M. Jonker and Simone van der Hof

Contents

Janneke van der Zwaan is a Ph.D. Candidate in Human–Computer Interaction at Delft University of Technology.Virginia Dignum is Associate Professor at the Faculty of Technology, Policy and Management, Delft University of Technology. Catholijn Jonker is Full Professor of Man–Machine Interaction at the Faculty of Electrical Engineering, Mathematics and Computer Science of the Delft University of Technology. Simone van der Hof is Full Professor of Law and Information Society and chair of eLaw, the Center for Law in the Information Society, Leiden University.An extended version of this chapter will appear in Van den Hoven et al. (forthcoming) *Responsible Innovation* Volume 1: Innovative Solutions for Global Issues.

J. M. van der Zwaan (✉) · V. Dignum · C. M. Jonker
Delft University of Technology, Delft, The Netherlands
e-mail: J.M.vanderZwaan@tudelft.nl

S. van der Hof
Center for Law in the Information Society, Leiden University, Leiden, The Netherlands

S. van der Hof et al. (eds.), *Minding Minors Wandering the Web: Regulating Online Child Safety*, Information Technology and Law Series 24, DOI: 10.1007/978-94-6265-005-3_12,

12.1 Introduction

Nowadays, many children and adolescents spend a lot of time online.[1] The Internet is used not only as an educational tool, but also for fun, games and to develop and maintain social contacts. One of the risks children and adolescents run online is to become a victim of cyberbullying. Cyberbullying can be defined as 'any behavior performed through electronic or digital media by individuals or groups that repeatedly communicates hostile or aggressive messages intended to inflict harm or discomfort on others'.[2]

Recently, cyberbullying gained a lot of attention. There have been a number of cases involving online bullying with extreme consequences for those involved that have received extensive media coverage in the US and Western Europe. Additionally, in the academic world, studies are conducted to map the problem of cyberbullying and its consequences for victims, bullies, and bystanders. With victimization rates ranging from 20 to 40 %,[3] cyberbullying is a common risk for children and adolescents. In addition, recent findings from the EU Kids Online II survey indicate that cyberbullying has a high impact on victims.[4]

Antisocial behavior such as cyberbullying can be regulated socially, legally, and/or technologically.[5] Social norms play an important role in regulating behavior in general. Law also regulates behavior; "[different] laws all continue to threaten ex post sanction for the violation of legal rights".[6] Technology can control or steer social behavior through functionalities in the software design (coined 'code as law' by Lessig[7]) or through exerting social influence (persuasive technology[8]). The different modalities are connected and their interaction is complex.[9] Generally, complex problems such as cyberbullying cannot be solved by measures from a single modality alone; better solutions may be found in a combination of measures from different modalities.

This chapter focuses on using technology to protect and empower children and adolescents against cyberbullying. So far, this topic has received little attention).[10]

---

1 The Gallup Organisation 2008; Eurobarometer 2007.

2 Tokunaga 2010.

3 Tokunaga 2010.

4 Livingstone et al. 2010.

5 Instead of three, Lessig distinguishes four modalities for regulation: social norms, the law, architecture and the market; Lessig 2000. In the case of cyberbullying, the market is not or less relevant as a modality for regulation and will therefore not be addressed in this chapter.

6 Lessig 2006, p. 124.

7 Lessig 2000.

8 Fogg 2002.

9 Lessig 2006.

10 Exceptions are Internet Safety Technical Task Force 2008; Szwajcer et al. 2009; Mesch 2009.

However, recently different initiatives have started to investigate the regulation of cyberbullying through technology, such as AMiCA[11] and Friendly ATTAC.[12] Existing work seems to rely on the assumption that general Internet safety technologies can be used as protection against cyberbullying as well. In this chapter, we show that this assumption is mostly unfounded and propose an alternative approach to addressing cyberbullying with technology.

This chapter is organized as follows. In Sect. 12.2, we provide a background on Internet safety technology and cyberbullying. In Sect. 12.3, this information is used to construct a framework of characteristics that technology against cyberbullying should have to be able to protect against cyberbullying. In Sect. 12.4, we use the framework to discuss the expected effectiveness of existing Internet safety technologies against cyberbullying. Finally, in Sect. 12.5, we present our conclusions.

12.2 Background

12.2.1 Internet Safety Technology

Online safety of children and adolescents concerns risks such as harassment, bullying, sexual solicitation, exposure to problematic and illegal content (including pornography, and violence), malicious software (for instance, viruses), hackers, and online delinquency (for example, identity theft). In their review of existing Internet safety technology, the Technology Advisory Board of the Internet Safety Technical Task Force distinguished the following functional goals[13]:

- Limit harmful contact between adults and minors,
- Limit harmful contact between minors,
- Limit/prevent minors from accessing inappropriate content on the Internet,
- Limit/prevent minors from creating inappropriate content on the Internet,
- Limit the availability of illegal content on the Internet,
- Prevent minors from accessing particular sites without parental consent,
- Prevent harassment, unwanted solicitation, and bullying of minors on the Internet.

These goals show that Internet safety technology is restrictive; they clearly intend to restrict online behavior. This view on technology corresponds to the aforementioned 'code as law' perspective from Lessig. Web filtering software is an example of restrictive technology; a Web filter blocks access to websites based on certain criteria.

[11] See www.clips.ua.ac.be/amica/.

[12] See www.friendlyattac.be/en/.

[13] Internet Safety Technical Task Force 2008.

Different types of Internet safety technologies can be distinguished, including[14]:

- Content and behavior analysis,
- Filtering,
- Monitoring,
- Blocking undesirable contacts,
- Reporting,
- Age/identity verification, and
- Educational technology.

Some technologies, such as age/identity verification, require storing personal data, which raises privacy concerns. Monitoring online behavior or automatically analyzing online communication might also invade privacy. In addition, restrictive technology could violate the rights to freedom of information and expression. Children's privacy and their rights to freedom of information and expression must be balanced against the potential benefits of Internet safety technologies. In some cases it might be appropriate to restrict behavior, for example, to protect younger children, whereas for older children and adolescents protecting their privacy and/or freedom of information and expression might be more important.

12.2.2 Cyberbullying

Research on cyberbullying is still in the early stage. Little is known beyond prevalence, frequency among specific groups, and negative outcomes.[15]

1. Compared to traditional bullying

Cyberbullying—by definition—is a type of bullying. According to Olweus,[16] bullying is aggressive behavior or intentional 'harm doing' which is carried out 'repeatedly and over time' and in an interpersonal relationship characterized by an imbalance of power. Additionally, cyberbullying has some specific characteristics. First, cyberbullies can remain anonymous relatively easy.[17] Another important difference is the lack of physical and social cues in online communication.[18] This prevents the bully from being confronted with the consequences of the harassments[19] and could also lead to misinterpreting messages as cyberbullying when in

[14] Internet Safety Technical Task Force 2008; Szwajcer et al. 2009.

[15] Tokunaga 2010.

[16] Olweus 1999.

[17] Ybarra and Mitchell 2004; Patchin and Hinduja 2006; Kowalski and Limber 2007; Shariff 2008.

[18] Ybarra and Mitchell 2004; Patchin and Hinduja 2006; Kowalski and Limber 2007; Kowalski et al. 2008.

[19] Kowalski et al. 2008.

fact they were not intended to be.[20] A third difference is the 24/7-attainability provided by online communication.[21] Traditional bullying is usually characterized by a confined period of time during which bullies have access to their victims. In most cases, victims of traditional bullying are safe at home. This is no longer the case with cyberbullying. Other differences between traditional bullying and cyberbullying are the quick distribution of electronic messages to (potentially) infinite audiences[22] and the permanent nature of information on the Internet.[23]

2. Types, Media, and Methods

Cyberbullying refers to bullying through electronic communication devices. It happens through different media, such as e-mail, instant messenger applications, social networking websites, blogs, chat rooms, online games, virtual worlds, and mobile phones (sms). Cyberbullying can be communication-based or content-based. Methods used for online bullying include name-calling, gossiping, ignoring, threatening, spreading personal conversations, manipulating and spreading pictures, creating defamatory websites, and sending sexual comments.[24]

3. Victims

Prevalence rates of cyberbullying victimization vary among studies. In a recent review of existing research, Tokunaga reports victimization rates of 20–40 %.[25] Cyberbullying victims tend to be heavier Internet users than youth that is not victimized.[26] Victims of traditional bullying and those that bully others online are also more likely to be cyberbullied.[27]

4. Bullies

Online bullies are typically the same age as their victims.[28] And even though anonymity is often viewed as integral to cyberbullying, it seems that cyberbullying often takes place in the context of social groups and relationships.[29] Online bullying has a strong connection with the offline world; between 44 and 82 % of cyberbullying victims know their bullies offline.[30]

---

[20] Ybarra et al. 2007.

[21] Patchin and Hinduja 2006; Kowalski and Limber 2007.

[22] Kowalski and Limber 2007; Kowalski et al. 2008; Shariff 2008.

[23] Shariff 2008.

[24] Dehue et al. 2008; Vandebosch and Cleemput 2008.

[25] Tokunaga 2010.

[26] Smith et al. 2008.

[27] Ybarra et al. 2006; Li 2007.

[28] Patchin and Hinduja 2006; Wolak et al. 2006; Kowalski and Limber 2007; Hinduja and Patchin 2009.

[29] Mishna et al. 2009.

[30] Wolak et al. 2006; Hinduja and Patchin 2009.

5. Tackling Cyberbulling

Because cyberbullying is a phenomenon that only recently emerged, validated approaches to stop or prevent it do not yet exist. However, some researchers made suggestions on how to tackle the problem.

Many studies stress the importance of education and awareness to reduce and prevent cyberbullying. Ybarra et al. support the idea to include cyberbullying prevention in conventional anti-bullying programs.[31] It is important to educate both children and adults (e.g., teachers and parents).[32] Educating parents and other adults might make it easier for children and adolescents to talk to them about their negative online experiences.[33] Teaching technological skills—again, both to children and adults—deserves special attention, so children and adults know what can be done in certain situations.[34]

12.3 The Framework

In order to discuss the expected effectiveness of existing technology against cyberbullying, we constructed a framework consisting of desired characteristics of technology against cyberbullying. These characteristics are derived from important topics that emerge from the literature on Internet safety technology and cyberbullying when taking the perspective of a (potential) cyberbullying victim and looking at the direct consequences for his/her online experience. To identify the desired characteristics, we started with the following basic questions: what are the online behaviors that can be characterized as cyberbullying?, who are the bullies?, and when do users need protection? While using the literature to answer these questions, we took as a starting point the principle that all Internet users (including bullies and victims) should be restricted in their behavior as little as possible and that it is better to learn potential victims to deal with antisocial behavior such as cyberbullying than to attempt preventing them from coming into contact with these types of behavior at all. Subsequently, we identified some risks associated with online technology in general.

Online behaviors that can be characterized as cyberbullying are diverse; different types, media and methods can be used to cyberbully others. Like traditional bullying, cyberbullying usually is communication-based (for example, name-calling in chat conversations or sending threatening e-mails), but content-based cyberbullying also occurs (for example, creating a fake profile on a social network or posting manipulated pictures). Technology against cyberbullying should take

[31] Ybarra et al. 2006.

[32] Ybarra et al. 2006; Dehue et al. 2008.

[33] Ybarra et al. 2006.

[34] Finkelhor et al. 2000; Smith et al. 2008.

into account different types, media, and methods of cyberbullying and at least target online communication.

Recent studies reveal that many of the online threats experienced by children and adolescents are perpetrated by peers, including sexual solicitation[35] and online harassment.[36] Additionally, victims usually know their bullies in real life.[37] Therefore, technology against cyberbullying should at least take into account relationships with known and unknown peers.

Cyberbullying can occur at any moment. This 24/7 attainability of cyberbullying is enabled by technology. Technology against cyberbullying should also be available at any moment and/or be able to intervene at any moment. In other words, technology against cyberbullying should provide real-time support.

Technology in general has some risks that might limit its suitability to protect against cyberbullying. For example, in Sect. 12.2 we observed that existing Internet safety technology always restricts users in some way. A disadvantage of restrictive technology is that it can be circumvented relatively easily by computer-savvy users. It is very hard to force people to use some technology. Therefore, it is suggested that technology against cyberbullying should rely on voluntary use. Victims (and potentially bystanders) are motivated to use some technology if they have something to gain (they want to stop the bullying), while cyberbullies are less likely to participate voluntarily, because bullying is an intentional act.

Additionally, technology might invade privacy and/or limit freedom of expression. Although these issues are beyond the scope of this chapter, they are very important. Children's privacy and their right to freedom of expression should be balanced carefully against the potential benefits of technology against cyberbullying. Therefore, protection of privacy and freedom of expression are included in the framework.

The desired characteristics are summarized in Table 12.1. We would like to emphasize that this list should not be regarded as the only one possible or as a definitive set of characteristics for technology against cyberbullying. Instead, it is intended as a starting point for discussing technology in the context of cyberbullying. In the next paragraph, these characteristics are used to assess the expected effectiveness of existing technology against cyberbullying.

12.4 Existing Internet Safety Technologies

This paragraph reviews existing Internet Safety technologies and discusses their expected suitability against cyberbullying based on the framework proposed in Sect. 12.3. The following technologies are discussed: content and behavior

---

[35] Wolak et al. 2006.

[36] Smith et al. 2008; Hinduja and Patchin 2009.

[37] Mishna et al. 2009.

Table 12.1 Desired characteristics for technology against cyberbullying

Characteristics
a. Suitable for different types, media and methods
b. Take peer contact into account
c. Real-time
d. Voluntary use
e. Protecting the user's privacy
f. Protecting the user's freedom of speech

analysis, filtering, monitoring, blocking undesirable contacts, reporting, age/identity verification, and educational technology. Most existing parental control applications, such as Net Nanny[38] or Cyber Patrol,[39] combine multiple technologies, including content and behavior analysis, filtering, and monitoring in one product. Below, we focus on the separate technologies, not complete applications.

12.4.1 Content and Behavior Analysis

Content and behavior analysis are about automatically extracting meaningful information from data, such as text, images, video material, and network traffic. Potentially, these techniques can also be used to detect cyberbullying in text-based conversations.

Preliminary results on related tasks show that it is rather difficult to automatically recognize different types of harassment. Pendar used a statistical approach to automatically distinguish between communication of sexual predators and victims.[40] Classifier performance ranged from 40 to 95 %. Kontostathis et al. also attempted to recognize sexual predation and the resulting classifier correctly predicted predator speech 60 % of the time.[41] These results seem promising, however, these studies have some limitations. First, the datasets used for the experiments were small (701 and 25 conversations respectively[42]). Standard corpora for text classification contain hundreds of thousands texts (e.g., the Reuters corpus[43]). Second, the data used consisted of conversations that were known to be malicious; most online conversations are not. Data imbalance (data sets containing

[38] See www.netnanny.com/.

[39] See www.cyberpatrol.com/.

[40] Pendar 2007.

[41] Kontostathis et al. 2009.

[42] Pendar 2007 and Kontostathis et al. 2009 both used data made available by Perverted Justice (www.perverted-justice.com/).

[43] Lewis et al. 2004.

only a few objects that need to be detected) is a well-known problem in machine learning that leads to suboptimal classifier performance.[44]

In 2009, the Content Analysis for the Web 2.0 Workshop (CAW2.0) offered a shared task on misbehavior detection.[45] Yin et al. trained classifiers to identify harassing messages in chat and online discussion forums.[46] Performance was between 25 and 40 %, so, there is much room for improvement.

Automatically recognizing cyberbullying or other harmful content could be a first step in protecting children and adolescents against these threats. As mentioned before, most applications for parental control employ some form of content analysis. Content and behavior analysis can be used to detect different forms of cyberbullying, both communication-based and content-based. However, related work shows that detecting different types of harassment is not trivial and needs to be improved before it can be used as (partial) protection against cyberbullying. The technology can be applied to all communication, including peer communication. In addition, content and behavior analysis can be both used voluntary and non-voluntary. It can be applied in real-time. Because technology for content and behavior analysis stores and interprets online behavior, which can be considered personal data, the privacy of users might be invaded. Detecting inappropriate data does not limit the freedom of expression per se, but actions taken after something has been detected might.

12.4.2 Filtering

Web-filtering software blocks access to websites with inappropriate content, such as pornography. Filtering techniques include white lists (lists of websites the user is allowed to visit), black lists (lists of websites the user is not allowed to visit), and content analysis (the content analysis algorithm decides whether the user is allowed to visit a website, e.g., based on the occurrence of certain key words). Common problems with Web filtering are underblocking (fail to block access to websites with inappropriate material) and overblocking (block websites that do not contain inappropriate material). Hunter evaluated four commercial Web-filtering applications. He found the applications blocked 75 % of a collection of inappropriate material and 21 % of a collection of appropriate material.[47]

Filtering is a preventive measure. It does not specifically target communication, but filtering incoming and/or outgoing communication could limit or prevent harmful contact between minors and between minors and adults. However, automatically recognizing either communication-based or content-based cyberbullying is not a trivial task (see Sect. 12.4.1). Filtering technology does not exclude

---

[44] Chawla et al. 2004.

[45] See http://caw2.barcelonamedia.org/.

[46] Yin et al. 2009.

[47] Hunter 2000.

communication between peers. Because users do not get the choice to apply filtering or not before they go online, filtering does not rely on voluntary use. Filtering software may be circumvented. For example, it is very easy to substitute terms that are filtered for unfiltered terms that are equally offending, for example 'loser' becomes 'l o s e r', 'L0S3R', 'looser', etc. Filtering software is real-time technology; websites are blocked and/or communication is filtered instantaneous. Since filtering software does not store personal data to block access to certain online resources, privacy is not at stake. However, blocking communication or preventing access to websites may affect freedom of information and expression.

12.4.3 Monitoring

Monitoring software informs parents about their children's online activities by recording websites addresses and online communication (for example instant messaging). Most parental control software allows monitoring online activities. A recent study found the use filtering and/or monitoring software does not correlate with less cyberbullying victimization.[48]

Monitoring software is preventive and works based on the assumption that users will adapt their behavior if they know their online activities are being watched. Because all online activity is stored, monitoring software theoretically targets all types, media, and methods of cyberbullying. In practice, however, cyberbullying incidents will have to be extracted by hand or automatically (see Sect. 12.4.1). Since cyberbullying might be hard to recognize and cyberbullying may only be a small part of all online activity, this is a tedious job. Because all online activities are recorded, peer communication is taken into account. Monitoring software does not rely on voluntary participation, users usually do not know or notice being monitored. Activities are recorded in real-time, however, action can be taken only after the records have been reviewed by an external party (for example a parent). For monitoring, privacy is an issue, because all online activities, which can be considered personal data, are recorded and stored for reviewing. Freedom of expression is not at stake.

12.4.4 Blocking Undesirable Contacts

Most instant messaging applications (e.g., Windows Live Messenger[49]), chat rooms, and social networking sites (e.g., Facebook[50] and MySpace[51]) give users

---

[48] Mesch 2009.

[49] See http://explore.live.com/windows-live-messenger.

[50] See www.facebook.com/.

[51] See www.myspace.com/.

the possibility to block other users, in order to prevent them from being contacted by these people. Many social networking sites also provide the possibility to restrict unknown users from contacting them and accessing their profile.

Blocking happens in response to incidents and limit harmful contact between minors and both minors and adults. Blocking contacts is suitable only for communication-based cyberbullying in applications where blocking options are available. It does take into account contact between peers. In fact, blocking bullies is a common advice for stopping cyberbullying.[52] Blocking is a voluntary act that allows users to control who can contact them. Users can block contacts whenever they want; in that sense blocking is real-time. Blocking users does not invade privacy or restrict freedom of expression.

12.4.5 Reporting Content

Many social Web applications (e.g., Facebook and MySpace) provide the possibility to report inappropriate and illegal content, for instance, by clicking a button labeled 'report abuse'. Reports are sent to community moderators that manually review reported content and decide whether or not to remove it. Some social networking sites, chat rooms, online games, and forums also allow users to report others when they break the rules, for example, by cyberbullying. Moderators decide whether and how to punish offenders.

Reporting tools can be useful for limiting access to inappropriate material, including some forms of content-based cyberbullying (for instance happy slapping videos or fake profiles on social networking sites). Reporting communication-based cyberbullying is only possible if moderators are available in the application and communication records exist. Everybody can report content they feel is inappropriate, so this technology relies on voluntary use. Because moderators have to check reports manually, it may take some time before reported content is removed. Therefore, reporting is not real-time. Privacy is not at risk, since no personal data needs to be stored for reporting (reporters may be anonymous). Removing content might interfere with freedom of expression. Therefore, in the case of cyberbullying, content will only be removed in obvious and/or extreme cases of content-based cyberbullying.

12.4.6 Age/Identity Verification

Age and/or identity verification technologies aim at restricting inappropriate contact between minors and adults as well as preventing minors to access

[52] See for example http://cybermentors.org.uk, www.stopcyberbullying.org and www.cybersmart.gov.au/.

inappropriate content. For example, in Second Life,[53] users must be 18 years old to view mature content. These technologies are preventive. Age and/or identity verification often use public or private databases containing information on either minors (for example school records) or adults (such as known sex offenders). People in the database (for instance minors or sex offenders) or people of certain ages (for example adults) are either allowed or not allowed to contact certain other people (such as minors) or access certain material (for example pornography).

Age and/or identity verification technologies do not target various forms of cyberbullying, such as content-based cyberbullying and harmful contact between peers. Age and/or identity verification may rely on voluntary participation (for example by becoming a member of a social network that applies age restrictions). In other cases participation may not be voluntary, for example if a school only allows its pupils to use the school's social networking website. This technology works online. However, since verifying age or identity requires gathering and storing personal data, the privacy of users might be at risk. Freedom of speech is not threatened.

12.4.7 Educational Technology

Education is another approach to improving the online safety of minors. Since the topic of this chapter is technology, the discussion below is limited to educational technology, such as interactive computer games.

FearNot! is an Intelligent Virtual Environment (IVE) in 3D, where synthetic characters act out bullying scenarios.[54] The application was designed for children 8–12 to witness the events from a third-person perspective. After a bullying episode, the victimized character turns to the user to ask for advice. The IVE offers children a safe environment that supports social and emotional learning. A controlled trial conducted in Germany and the UK established a short-term effect of escaping victimization for a priory identified victims of bullying and a short-term overall prevention effect for UK children,[55] demonstrating the potential of IVEs to support anti-bullying activities.

Other applications aimed at educating minors about online safety include Mr Ctrl[56] (not available anymore) and Internet Safety with Professor Garfield.[57] Mr Ctrl was a chatbot that answers questions about online safety. Internet Safety with Professor Garfield is a series of online interactive lessons about different topics concerning Internet safety. This type of applications can be used individually, but

[53] See http://secondlife.com/.

[54] Paiva et al. 2005.

[55] Sapouna et al. 2010.

[56] See http://mrctrl.spaces.live.com/ (in Dutch).

[57] See www.infinitelearninglab.org/.

also provide teaching material for classroom use. To the best of our knowledge, these applications have not been evaluated.

Because education is aimed at stimulating the right behavior in general, it basically targets all types, media and methods of cyberbullying. From the examples given here, it is not clear to what extend peer communication is explicitly taken into account. However, it would be easy to do so. Educational programs are usually mandatory, so there is no voluntary participation. Educational technology is designed to support traditional classroom teaching and not to protect or empower pupils at the same time they use the Internet. Finally, privacy and freedom of expression are not at risk in normal educational settings.

Another concern regarding education and/or educational technology is its effectiveness. Mishna et al. performed a systematic review of interventions against cyber abuse of youth.[58] Three educational programs were selected for review. Mishna et al. concluded that participation in cyber abuse prevention and intervention strategies is associated with an increase in Internet safety knowledge, but changes to Internet risk attitudes and behavior are not significant.[59] So, increased knowledge about safe Internet use does not necessarily correlate with less risk taking (or other behavior changes) online.

12.4.8 Summary

In this section, we discussed the expected effectiveness of different existing Internet safety technologies against cyberbullying. The results of this discussion are summarized in Table 12.2. While all technologies satisfy at least some of the desired characteristics from the framework we proposed, we expect their effectiveness against cyberbullying to be limited. Technologies such as age/identity verification, filtering and monitoring, reporting, and blocking undesirable contacts have not been designed to protect against cyberbullying, but with other online risks in mind. Some of these technologies primarily target access to undesirable content. Their success in protecting against cyberbullying, which is mostly communication-based, is therefore limited. According to our criteria, blocking undesirable contacts is the most promising approach.

One of the most salient features of existing Internet safety technology is its attempt to steer the behavior of users by restricting them. While in certain cases restricting bullies and/or victims might be useful, teaching them to deal with cyberbullying incidents seems a better approach. This viewpoint is supported by the literature. For example, Shariff argues that incidents of cyberbullying potentially are valuable learning experiences.[60] This potential, however, is ignored by

---

[58] Mishna et al. 2010.

[59] Mishna et al. 2010.

[60] Shariff 2008.

Table 12.2 Match between characteristics of existing technologies and the desired characteristics of technology against cyberbullying

	Different forms	Peer communication	Voluntary use	Real-time	Protect privacy	Protect freedom of expression
Content and behavior analysis	±	+	–	+	±	+
Filtering	±	+	–	+	+	–
Monitoring	±	+	–	–	–	+
Blocking contacts	–	+	+	+	+	+
Reporting	–	+	+	–	+	–
Age/identity verification	–	–	±	+	–	+
Educational technology	+	?	–	–	+	+

+: good match; ±: partial match; –: no match; ?: unknown

existing technologies. Additionally, Thierer claims education (media literacy) is the primary solution against online risks.[61] In his view, the role of technology is to supplement (but never to supplant) education. Educational technology (Sect. 12.4.7) is a primary example of using technology to supplement education.

Our discussion was focused on the separate existing Internet safety technologies. One might argue that combining multiple technologies, as is done in existing parental control software, might increase performance compared to individual technologies. However, the main issues, i.e., using technology that has been designed for other risks and restricting users instead of empowering them, will not be tackled by combining restrictive technologies.

Finally, we would like to emphasize that our discussion is limited to the expected effectiveness of technologies against cyberbullying. We do not claim the technologies discussed in this paragraph should not be used; they might be very effective against other online risks, such as exposure to problematic and illegal content or identity theft. However, based on the characteristics proposed in the framework, we expect that the effectiveness of existing Internet safety technology against cyberbullying is limited.

12.5 Conclusion

This chapter makes two contributions. First, we presented a framework of desired characteristics of technology against cyberbullying based on a review of literature on Internet safety technology and cyberbullying. Second, we discussed the

[61] Thierer 2009.

expected effectiveness of existing Internet safety technologies based on this framework. The results indicate that these technologies are not effective against cyberbullying, mainly because they restrict online behavior that is not related to cyberbullying.

The framework was constructed based on literature on Internet safety technology and cyberbullying. The framework consists of desired characteristics that were formulated by taking the perspective of a potential cyberbullying victim and making sure his/her online experience is not restricted too much. The following desired characteristics for technology against cyberbullying emerged: technology should be suitable for different types, media and methods of cyberbullying (at least communication-based cyberbullying), it should take into account peer contact, it should rely on voluntary use, it should be real-time, and user's privacy and freedom of expression should be balanced against restriction. These characteristics are not a definitive list; rather they should be seen as a first contribution in an ongoing discussion of technology against cyberbullying.

Our review of existing Internet safety technologies shows that all of them satisfy at least some of the characteristics from our framework. However, we conclude that the effectiveness of these technologies against cyberbullying is still limited. Technologies such as age/identity verification, filtering and monitoring, reporting, and blocking undesirable contacts have not been designed to protect against cyberbullying, but with other online risks in mind. Some of these technologies primarily target access to undesirable content. Their success in protecting against cyberbullying, which is mostly communication-based, is therefore limited. Blocking undesirable contacts is the most promising approach. Additionally, apart from education, none of the technologies discussed are designed to empower children and adolescents. Rather, the technologies restrict the behavior of bullies and/or victims (filtering and monitoring, age/identity verification, blocking undesirable contacts). While in some cases restricting the behavior of bullies and/or victims might be useful, incidents of cyberbullying potentially can be valuable learning experiences,[62] which are currently ignored by technology.

The results of our review of existing technologies indicate that prevention and detection of cyberbullying do not suffice. Five online safety task forces agree and conclude that empowerment, i.e., education and awareness, is a primary solution strategy to protect children and adolescents against online risks.[63] Technology can be used to supplement education and awareness. However, it is important to emphasize that technology alone can never solve a complex problem such as cyberbullying. A combination of social, legal, and technological measures is required for best results.

Technology does not have to be restrictive to influence behavior. Persuasive technology steers behavior by exerting social influence. In previous work, we presented a design for a virtual empathic buddy that provides emotional support

---

[62] Shariff 2008.

[63] Thierer 2009.

and practical advice to children that are victims of cyberbullying.[64] The buddy is a virtual character that 'lives' on the screen of potential cyberbullying victims. At the user's request, it provides emotional support and practical advice on how to deal with the incident.[65] A preliminary study suggests adolescents recognize the emotional cues emitted by the buddy.[66] Further research is required to assess the effectiveness of this kind of technology.

Acknowledgments This work is funded by NWO under the Responsible Innovation (RI) program via the project 'Empowering and Protecting Children and Adolescents Against Cyberbullying'.

References

Chawla NV, Japkowicz N, Kotcz A (2004) Editorial: special issue on learning from imbalanced data sets. SIGKDD Explor Newsl 6(1):1–6

Dehue F, Bolman C, Völlink T (2008) Cyberbullying: youngsters' experiences and parental perception. Cyberpsychol Behav 11(2):217–223

Eurobarometer (2007) Safer internet for children, qualitative study in 29 European countries, national analysis, The Netherlands. http://ec.europa.eu/information_society/activities/sip/surveys/qualitative/index_en.htm

Finkelhor D, Mitchell KJ, Wolak J (2000) Online victimization: a report on the nation's youth. www.unh.edu/ccrc/pdf/Victimization_Online_Survey.pdf

Fogg B J (2002) Persuasive technology: using computers to change what we think and do, chapter computers as persuasive social actors. ACM, New York

Hinduja S, Patchin JW (2009) Bullying beyond the schoolyard: preventing and responding to cyberbullying. Corwin Press, Thousand Oaks

Hunter CD (2000) Internet filter effectiveness (student paper panel): testing over and underinclusive blocking decisions of four popular filters. In: CFP'00: Proceedings of the tenth conference on computers, freedom and privacy, pp 287–294, ACM

Internet Safety Technical Task Force (2008) Enhancing child safety and online technologies: final report of the internet safety technical task force to the multi-state working group on social networking of state attorneys general of the United States. Technical report. http://cyber.law.harvard.edu/pubrelease/isttf/

Kontostathis A, Edwards L, Leatherman A (2009) Chatcoder: toward the tracking and categorization of Internet predators. In: Proceedings of the 7th text mining workshop

Kowalski RM, Limber SP (2007) Electronic bullying among middle school students. J Adolesc Health 41(6, Supplement 1):22–30

Kowalski RM, Limber SP, Agatston PW (2008) Cyber bullying: bullying in the digital age. Wiley Blackwell, Malden

Lessig L (2000) Code and other laws of cyberspace. Basic Books, New York

Lessig L (2006) Code: and other laws of cyberspace, version 2.0. Basic Books, New York

---

[64] Van der Zwaan et al. 2010.

[65] We would like to emphasize that the buddy is not intended as a replacement for professional help or human support. Instead, the buddy should be seen as an additional, easily accessible support channel for cyberbullying victims.

[66] Van der Zwaan et al. 2012.

Lewis DD, Yang Y, Rose TG, Li F (2004) RCV1: a new benchmark collection for text categorization research. J Mach Learn Res 5:361–397

Li Q (2007) New bottle but old wine: a research of cyberbullying in schools. Comput Hum Behav 23(4):1777–1791

Livingstone S, Haddon L, Görzig A, Ólafsson K (2010) Risks and safety on the internet: the perspective of European children. Initial findings. http://eprints.lse.ac.uk/33731/

Mesch GS (2009) Parental mediation, online activities, and cyberbullying. Cyberpsychol Behav 12(4):387–393

Mishna F, Saini M, Solomon S (2009) Ongoing and online: children and youth's perceptions of cyber bullying. Child Youth Serv Rev 31(12):1222–1228

Mishna F, Cook C, Saini M, Wu MJ, MacFadden R (2010) Interventions to prevent and reduce cyber abuse of youth: a systematic review. Res Soc Work Pract 21(1):5–14

Olweus D (1999) The nature of school bullying: a cross-national perspective, chapter Sweden. Routledge, London, pp 7–27

Paiva A, Dias J, Sobral D, Aylett R, Woods S, Hall L, Zoll C (2005) Learning by feeling: evoking empathy with synthetic characters. Appl Artif Intell Int J 19(3):235–266

Patchin JW, Hinduja S (2006) Bullies move beyond the schoolyard: a preliminary look at cyberbullying. Youth Violence Juv Justice 4(2):148–169

Pendar N (2007) Toward spotting the pedophile telling victim from predator in text chats. In: ICSC'07: Proceedings of the international conference on semantic computing. IEEE Computer Society, pp 235–241

Sapouna M, Wolke D, Vannini N, Watson S, Woods S, Schneider W, Enz S, Hall L, Paiva A, Andre E, Dautenhahn K, Aylett R (2010) Virtual learning intervention to reduce bullying victimization in primary school: a controlled trial. J Child Psychol Psychiatry 51(1):104–112

Shariff S (2008) Cyber-bullying: issues and solutions for the school, the classroom and the home. Routledge, London

Smith PK, Mahdavi J, Carvalho M, Fisher S, Russell S, Tippett N (2008) Cyberbullying: its nature and impact in secondary school pupils. J Child Psychol Psychiatry 49(4):376–385

Szwajcer E, Ebbers W, Oostdijk M, Wartena C, Hulsebosch B (2009) Kinderen en nieuwe media—technische and socio-technische oplossingsmogelijkheden voor gevaren in de online wereld. www.novay.nl/medialibrary/documenten/originelen/Eindrapportage_kinderen_en_nieuwe_media.pdf

The Gallup Organisation (2008) Towards a safer use of the Internet for children in the EU—a parents' perspective. http://ec.europa.eu/public_opinion/flash/fl_248_en.pdf

Thierer AD (2009) Five online safety task forces agree: education, empowerment & self-regulation are the answer. Progress & freedom foundation progress on point paper, vol 16, issue no. 13

Tokunaga RS (2010) Following you home from school: a critical review and synthesis of research on cyberbullying victimization. Comput Hum Behav 26(3):277–287

Van den Hoven J, Koops B-J, Romijn H, Swierstra T, Doorn N (2013, forthcoming) Responsible innovation volume 1: innovative solutions for global issues. Springer, Dordrecht

Van der Zwaan JM, Dignum V, Jonker CM (2010) Simulating peer support for victims of cyberbullying. In: Proceedings of the 22st Benelux conference on artificial intelligence (BNAIC 2010)

Van der Zwaan JM, Geraerts E, Dignum V, Jonker CM (2012) User validation of an empathic virtual buddy against cyberbullying. Stud Health Technol Inform 181:243–247

Vandebosch H, Cleemput KV (2008) Defining cyberbullying: a qualitative research into the perceptions of youngsters. Cyberpsychol Behav 11(4):499–503

Wolak J, Mitchell KJ, Finkelhor D (2006) Online victimization of youth: five years later. www.unh.edu/ccrc/pdf/CV138.pdf

Ybarra ML, Mitchell KJ (2004) Youth engaging in online harassment: associations with caregiver-child relationships, Internet use, and personal characteristics. J Adolesc 27(3):319–336

Ybarra ML, Mitchell KJ, Wolak J, Finkelhor D (2006) Examining characteristics and associated distress related to internet harassment: findings from the second youth internet safety survey. Pediatrics 118(4):1169–1177

Ybarra ML, Diener-West M, Leaf PJ (2007) Examining the overlap in internet harassment and school bullying: implications for school intervention. J Adolesc Health 41(6, Supplement 1):42–50

Yin D, Xue Z, Hong L, Davison BD, Kontostathis A, Edwards L (2009) Detection of harassment on web 2.0. In: CAW 2.0'09: Proceedings of the 1st content analysis in web 2.0 workshop

Chapter 13
Violent Video Games and Cyberbullying: Why Education Is Better than Regulation

Sarah Genner

Contents

13.1 Introduction

Online safety for youth is a growing concern for parents, educators, and policymakers. Legal regulation of online risks and youth protection are often well intentioned, but not effective as this chapter shows using the example of violent shooter games and cyberbullying in Switzerland. Politicians demand bans and regulations in spite of the limited success of previous youth protection laws. A closer look at Swiss public debates on the ban on "killer games" unveils that regulation concerning youth and media is very complex and influenced by political interests of certain policymakers. Research on media effects shows that risks are highly interconnected with psychological resilience. Resilient youth are less susceptible to negative effects of media violence and cyberbullying.

Sarah Genner is a senior researcher in media psychology at Zurich University of Applied Sciences and a Ph.D. Candidate at Zurich University. The title of her Ph.D. is 'ON/OFF—online connectivity behavior and regulations'.

S. Genner (✉)
Zurich University for Applied Sciences, Zurich, Switzerland
e-mail: sarah@genner.cc

S. van der Hof et al. (eds.), *Minding Minors Wandering the Web: Regulating Online Child Safety*, Information Technology and Law Series 24, DOI: 10.1007/978-94-6265-005-3_13,

The chapter summarizes research to date on violent games (which are increasingly played online) and cyberbullying, analyzes the political public debate and, finally, emphasizes why educational measures and focusing on fostering psychological resilience are more effective than legal regulation in the long run to reduce online risks.

Following shocking events, such as school shootings like 'Columbine' in 1999 in the United States or murder cases similar to Zurich-Hoengg in Switzerland in 2007,[1] journalists and experts look for explanations and politicians for solutions. Intuitive explanations are usually more quickly available than scientific evidence—especially when the general public is still perplexed and the motives of the murderers are hard to explain. After both tragic events mentioned above, violent computer games[2] were found at the killers' homes. This leads to the widespread conclusion that these games are the cause for the atrocities, or at least made significant contributions. In fact, the murder in Zurich-Hoengg and a similar case in Central Switzerland were the main reasons for Swiss politicians to put a ban of violent computer games on the political agenda.[3]

Cyberbullying is another widely discussed subject in the Swiss political debate on youth and harmful effects of digital media. This form of bullying occurs through information and communication technologies, which include the Internet and the use of mobile phones for phone calls and texting. National MPs[4] called for effective measures at the political level to preemptively proceed against cyberbullying.

The next two sections of this chapter present research results on violent video games and the corresponding legislation process. Section 13.4 summarizes research results on cyberbullying and political attempts to pass regulations. Sections 13.5 and 13.6 argues how education and fostering resilience are more advantageous than laws and regulations.

---

[1] The Columbine High School massacre was a school shooting on April 20, 1999, at Columbine High School in Colorado, USA. Parents of some of the victims filed several unsuccessful lawsuits against video game manufacturers. A Swiss army soldier killed a 16-year-old girl with an assault rifle while waiting for the bus on November 23, 2007 in Zurich-Hoengg in Switzerland.

[2] In this chapter, the terms "first-person shooter," "killer games," and "violent computer games" are used synonymously to describe computer games including virtual killing through a first-person perspective. Players experience the action through the eyes of the protagonist. Many of these games are played online in multiplayer versions. Examples of such games are e.g., *Call of Duty, Counterstrike, Battlefield, or Doom*. "Killer games" is the concept of opponents and "first-person shooter" rather the term of the proponents.

[3] Ban of "killer games" in Switzerland: www.parlament.ch/D/Suche/Seiten/geschaefte.aspx?gesch_id=20073870/Media violence and youth violence—The murderer in Ried-Muotathal: www.medialegewalt.ch/artikel_presse/analyse_toetungsdelikt_muotathal.pdf.

[4] MPs in this context refer to members of the Swiss national parliament (Federal Assembly consisting of National Council and Council of States).

13.2 Violent Computer Games

In 2012, 68 % of Swiss teens played video games on a regular basis, 70 % of which indicate having played games for which they were too young.[5] A large variety of games get played by Swiss teens. The favorite genre is first-person shooter games (e.g., Battlefield, Call of Duty), followed by the genres casual games (e.g., Angry Birds, Guitar Hero), sport games (e.g., FIFA, NHL), and action games (e.g., Grand Theft Auto, Uncharted). The shooter game Call of Duty is by far the favorite game of Swiss 12- to 19-year olds, although the age rating of Call of Duty is 18 years and above.[6] There is a gender gap in using video games. While 59 % of male teens play daily or several times a week, only 19 % of female teens do.[7] Playing first-person shooters is a particularly male activity: 50 % of male teens in Germany play violent video games versus 10 % of female teens.[8] While 79 % of Swiss teens play video games, only 52 % of 18 to 19 year olds do.[9]

In summary, a majority of teens play video games, especially males and young teens, and they prefer violent first-person shooter games to any other genre (Fig. 13.1).

In spite of heated debates, the scientific community agrees that the use of violent computer games alone will not lead to violence. In other words, the stimulus–response model clearly does not apply. The model's assumption that using violent media content automatically leads to imitation and delinquent behavior has been refuted in research on media effects, but scientists agree that the use of media violence can have negative effects under specific circumstances.[10] Explaining the effects of violent media exposure on real-life aggressive behavior is only the beginning of the scientific debate. While some researchers emphasize the only marginal influence of violent computer games on aggressive behavior, others advise against trivializing potential negative effects.

The high-risk group approach gets increasingly recognized in computer game violence research. According to this approach, for any assessment of media effects, a combination of certain social, personal, and medial factors have to be taken into account. The following factors constitute the high-risk group related to harmful media use[11]:

---

5 These numbers are taken from the representative youth and media survey in Switzerland (JAMES—Youth, Activities, Media—Survey Switzerland) conducted by the research team at Zurich University of Applied Sciences of which the author is part. Every second year, a representative and randomized sample of 1,200 Swiss teens from 12 to 19 years fill out a 45-min questionnaire on their media use. Willemse et al. 2012, p. 42.

6 Willemse et al. 2012, p. 45.

7 Willemse et al. 2012, p. 16.

8 Feierabend et al. 2012, p. 50.

9 Willemse et al. 2012, p. 42.

10 Kunczik and Zipfel 2006, p. 13.

11 Steiner 2009, p. XV; Merz Abt 2009, p. 7

Fig. 13.1 Examples of present day first-person shooter games: Call of Duty and Counter-Strike. They can be played offline and online. Download is not necessary to play shooter games online

1. Social factors:
   - Climate of violence in the personal environment (family, peer group, everyday; experience), and view on violence in society perceived through media;
   - Tensions, conflicts, and violence within the family, parental neglect, and rejection, stressed parent–child communication;
   - Lack of interest of parents for media consumption or lack of control of media consumption;
   - Low media literacy of parents, particularly in relation to new media;
   - High or excessive media consumption of parents as well as the parents of their peers.
2. Personal factors:
   - Early use of violent media content (especially younger than age 12, before moral values are established);
   - Personality factors: trait aggressiveness (aggressive attitude), increased irritability;
   - The tendency to "sensation seeking" (strong desire for new, intense, and complex experiences);
   - Male gender;
   - High or excessive consumption: more than 2 h daily is considered to be problematic;
   - Introversion, anxiety, decreased frustration tolerance;

- Limited social skills and intellectual capacity, inability to distinguish between reality and fiction;
- Restricted repertoire of behavior, poor social problem-solving skills;
- Excessive computer game consumption, strong preference for violent games;
- Missing or weak emotional competence, low empathy, emotion regulation problems, emotional labiality;
- Values that legitimize violent behavior.

3. Media factors:

- Depiction of violence taken out of context;
- Lack of victim perspective;
- Highly realistic representation of violence;
- Availability of audio-visual media (especially in children's bedroom).

In contrast to computer game violence research, television violence research has a longstanding tradition. Researchers claim that results from it can be transferred for various reasons and that the effects of media violence in computer games are even stronger for the following reasons[12]:

- Computer games require higher activity and attention compared to pure watching;
- More intense emotional reactions due to higher identification with characters;
- Direct reward for aggressive behavior (as opposed to TV) or lack of punishment (violence often has no negative consequences for the aggressor, but is sometimes even the main goal of the game);
- Identification with the aggressor is usually preset by the game (as opposed to film and television, where identification with other characters is possible);
- Simultaneity of different parts of the learning process (observe model, encouragement, exhibit behavior), which is significant according to the concept of model learning;
- Training effects and continuity: computer games allow proper training, all sequences of a killing act can get repeated (e.g., procure and load weapons, make sacrifices, aim, pull the trigger, etc.), players can play the same game for a long time;
- Violent content: violence is pervasive in many games, the frequency of violent scenes are usually higher compared to television.

Short-term and long-term effects can be distinguished for violent video game use. According to Hartmann, the following short-term effects were measured in previous research[13]:

---

[12] Kunczik and Zipfel 2006, p. 295.

[13] Hartmann 2006, p. 89.

- Short-term increase of aggressive thoughts and aggressive emotional state of mind;
- Activity in the brain area of aggression while playing computer games;
- Overestimation of hostile intentions of others;
- Increased expectation that other people will react violently to problems and conflict and not defensively;
- Intensified self-perception of the user as aggressive person;
- Increased likelihood that aggressive behavior is exhibited;
- Short-term decrease of pro-social behavior.

In longitudinal studies, long-term effects of violent video game use have been explored. Gentile, Saleem, and Anderson and Hopf, Luber and Weiß clearly indicate a relationship between long-term use of violent games and personality changes (e.g., decrease in empathy).[14] Hopf et al. concluded in their longitudinal study that increased exposure to media violence has effects on violent behavior: "Of particular importance are the findings that playing violent electronic games is the strongest risk factor of violent criminality and both media-stimulated and real experiences of aggressive emotions associated with the motive of revenge are core risk factors of violence in school and violent criminality."[15] Although, especially for high-risk groups, statistical correlations between playing violent video games and violence have been found, these research results underestimate the personality and the social circumstances of players, and therefore the actual impact of violent computer games on aggressive behavior often gets misinterpreted. Correlation is not causality. If murderers play first-person shooter games, the reverse is not true—not every consumer of violent games will automatically become a murderer. Long-term studies[16] estimate that 5–10 % of the increase in aggression can be explained by the influence of media violence and the remaining 90–95 % by other factors, i.e., personality, social environment.[17]

In recent years, research on violent games also showed positive effects. Playing first-person shooter video games is associated with superior mental flexibility. Compared to non-players, players of such games were found to require significantly shorter reaction time while switching between complex tasks.[18]

Conclusively, negative media effects are rather weak compared to variables such as parental neglect and rejection, lack of parental involvement and control, family conflict, and family violence. High-risk adolescents under psychological pressure with an aggressive personality preferably turn to media violence. Playing

[14] Gentile et al. 2007 and Hopf et al. 2008.

[15] Hopf et al. 2008, p. 79.

[16] E.g., Johnson et al. 2002.

[17] Bonfadelli 2004, p. 268.

[18] Colzato et al. 2010, p. 1.

violent games may be described as a symptom of many modern real-life aggressors. However, the games' contribution to explaining real-life aggression is comparatively insignificant.

13.3 Why MPs Called for a Ban

In the name of youth protection, Swiss MPs demanded banning so-called "killer games" (opponents deliberately chose the dissuasive term). Politicians took action backed by the "association against media violence." By calling for a ban, they hoped to encourage preventive effects related to youth violence.

However, bans often have counterproductive effects as the following example shows. Since 1972, there is an index in Germany by the Federal Department for Youth and Harmful Media Content ('Bundesprüfstelle für jugendgefährdende Medien'). In the 1980s, an album of the popular German music band, Die Ärzte, which included adult texts, was placed on the index. The album turned out to be very successful because of the index.[19] Although the list of banned violent games in Germany is confidential, news of games on the index spreads fast in the online gamer community and this serves as an unintended recommendation making it even more attractive.

Bans may indeed send a social signal, but they can—especially in the Internet age—by no means prevent the spreading of the games that are played online ("massively multiplayer online first-person shooters") or can be bought online. National laws often fail in a transnational network infrastructure.

Moreover, article 135 of the Swiss Penal Code is in force since 1990 after a national political debate about splatter movies. Article 135 bans "video recordings, pictures, and other objects or performances that, without having legitimate cultural or scientific value, represent cruel violence against humans or animals." Anyone who provides, shows or advertises such content "shall be punished with imprisonment up to 3 years or a fine".[20] More than 20 years of experience with this law proves its rather symbolic nature. Almost no verdicts have been passed, and the ban of the extremely violent movie "Blutgeil" in the early 1990s created a lot of national attention instead of it disappearing from the limelight. The Internet certainly did not make article 135 less challenging to enforce.

The Swiss parliament voted in favor of a nationwide ban on violent computer games for youth in 2010. Experts were against the ban, and even the government had strongly recommended to the parliament not to pass the law, claiming article 135 was sufficient and could apply to violent games, too. Still, the law was passed.

How to explain this? One explanation suggests that parliament and government have different objectives. MPs are elected by Swiss citizens. As a result, it is quite

[19] Beckedahl and Lüke 2012, p. 44.

[20] Swiss Penal Code, Article 135, depiction of violence: www.admin.ch/ch/d/sr/311 0/a135.html.

Fig. 13.2 "Association against media violence" and its founder, politician Roland Näf, during an election campaign posing with a rose instead of a gun as a pacifist James Bond (*screenshots*)

rational for them to tackle popular issues, such as youth violence, and to put forward solutions. In a public debate about youth violence, Swiss MPs raised the issue of media violence. In fact, the ban of "killer games" was born as a way of combating youth violence. The popular view, that shooter games are the cause of violent behavior in real life, helped politicians in election campaigns. The president of the "association against media violence" used "the ban of killer games" as his national election campaign issue (Fig. 13.2).

Most MPs who voted for the ban may indeed have realized that it is not an effective solution against youth violence. Nevertheless, they must have known that voting against the ban—especially in the current political climate and often one-sided media reports—could get interpreted as a vote for, or at least not a clear enough stand against, violence. This made it difficult for opponents of the ban among MPs to vote against it. The seven members of the Swiss government get elected by the parliament and not by the Swiss population. Therefore, the government could more easily accommodate the complex reasoning and recommend rejecting the ban.

13.4 Cyberbullying

Cyberbullying is a rising online safety concern as media reports on teen suicide as a consequence of online bullying increase. It can be defined as

> any behavior performed through electronic or digital media by individuals or groups that repeatedly communicates hostile or aggressive messages intended to inflict harm or discomfort on others. In cyberbullying experiences, the identity of the bully may or may not be known. Cyberbullying can occur through electronically mediated communication at school; however, cyberbullying behaviors commonly occur outside of school as well.[21]

[21] Tokunaga 2010, p. 278.

Youth bullying involvement can be characterized by four basic roles: (1) Bully; (2) Victim; (3) Bully-victim (actors who both bully and are victimized by others); (4) Bystander. Over time and across different contexts, youth can be involved in multiple roles.[22]

Although cyberbullying is a relatively new phenomenon, research has already produced important results. A key finding, based on data from the U.S. and Europe, is that face-to-face bullying remains the dominant mode of bullying despite the rapid uptake of technologies.[23] Although many studies present numbers to show the prevalence of cyberbullying, they can hardly be compared. As definitions of cyberbullying vary (some including the upload of pictures without asking permission as a form of cyberbullying), measured prevalence varies largely.

Numbers published in Switzerland in 2012 show that 17 % of Swiss teens have experienced bullying online (including chat and social networks, such as Facebook), 3 % reported that hurtful content about them has been spread online.[24] The Swiss EU Kids Online survey 2012 found a prevalence of 5 % of Swiss 9–16 year olds that have been bullied online.[25] Youth self-reporting is a method typically used (by reporting one's own versus other's involvement in cyberbullying). Data from EU Kids Online suggests that youth self-reporting and reporting by parents differ. Most parents in the Swiss survey were not aware that their child had been subject to cyberbullying.[26]

An Australian study found that 83 % of students, who bully other students online, also bully them offline. And 84 % of students who were bullied online were also bullied offline.[27] In most cases, online bullying co-exists with offline bullying. These results are confirmed by new findings from a large study that identifies longitudinal risk factors for cyberbullying: "Those who attack others in the real world today are more than four times as likely to do so in cyberspace a few months later."[28] The same study also confirms findings from previous studies suggesting that "adolescents who display some form of antisocial behavior in the real world are at increased risk of involvement in cyberbullying."[29]

The main differences between traditional and online bullying are:

- Bullies online usually remain anonymous (although most bullies know their victims in real life);
- Harmful content can get distributed online 24/7;
- Content may remain online for a long time;
- Physical absence and anonymity encourage non-sympathetic behavior.

---

22 Levy et al. 2012, p. 17.

23 Ybarra et al. 2012, p. 57.

24 Willemse et al. 2012, p. 34.

25 Hermida 2013, p. 14.

26 Hermida 2013, p. 14.

27 Cross et al. 2009.

28 Sticca et al. 2012, p. 11.

29 Sticca et al. 2012, p. 11.

Sticca and Perren[30] found that the perceived severity of cyberbullying varies largely: “Cyberbullying is not a priori perceived as worse than traditional bullying. Instead, bullying is perceived as worst if it is public (as opposed to private) and if anonymous (as opposed to non-anonymous).” Evidence suggests that cyberbullying can have profoundly damaging consequences for youth. In a recent study with 1,320 students from Switzerland and Australia, victims of cyberbullying reported significantly higher levels of depressive symptoms, even when controlling for the involvement in traditional bullying. This result was the same for Swiss and Australian teens, which suggests that this statistical connection is not culturally dependent.[31]

In the wake of a handful of high-profile cyberbullying incidents, some lawmakers in the United States began floating legislation to address the issue suggesting the creation of a new federal felony to punish cyberbullying including fines and jail time for violators.[32] In Switzerland, a Swiss national MP demanded the Federal Council in 2008 to prepare a report on cyberbullying that:

- Shows the prevalence of cyberbullying in Switzerland;
- Provides an overview of measures already taken at federal, cantonal, and municipal or local level;
- Compares various old and new measures; and
- Shows concrete and effective ways how cyberbullying can be prevented.[33]

The corresponding report by the Swiss Federal Council,[34] published in 2010, claimed no further legal regulation is necessary as cyberbullying can get included in existing laws in the Swiss Penal Code such as defamation (‘Üble Nachrede’, Article 173; ‘Verleumdung,’ Article 174), calling names (‘Beschimpfung’, Article 177), threat (‘Drohung’, Article 180), constraint (‘Nötigung’, Article 181). The report concludes that the most effective measures to prevent cyberbullying are transmission of knowledge and media literacy for children and teens, but also for parents and teachers.

MPs in Switzerland have called for a “cyberbullying officer” in 2010, but the Federal Council rejected the initiative.[35] In fall 2012, “Pro Juventute,” a Swiss non-governmental youth organization, launched the first national prevention campaign on cyberbullying in Switzerland. It raises awareness for teen suicide as a cause of cyberbullying (Fig. 13.3).

---

[30] Sticca and Perren 2012, p. 10.

[31] Perren et al. 2010, p. 8.

[32] Szoka and Thierer 2009, p. 1.

[33] Schmid-Federer 2008, www.parlament.ch/d/suche/seiten/geschaefte.aspx?gesch_id=20083050.

[34] Report of the Federal Council 2010, www.ejpd.admin.ch/content/ejpd/de/home/dokumentation/info/2010/ref_2010-06-02.html.

[35] Schmid-Federer 2010, www.parlament.ch/d/suche/seiten/geschaefte.aspx?gesch_id=20103856.

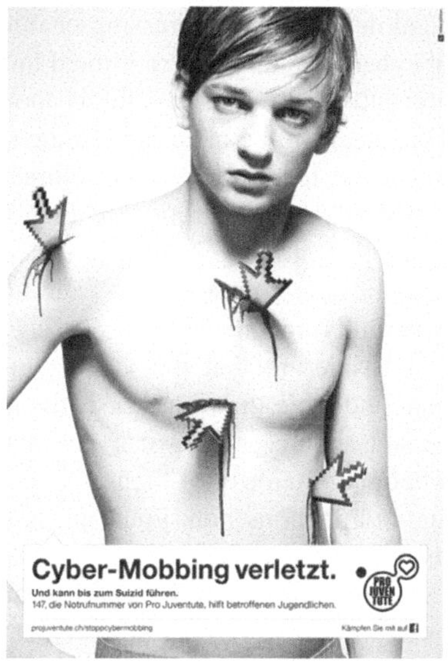

Fig. 13.3 "Cyberbullying hurts. And can lead to suicide." Information campaign (online and offline) for cyberbullying prevention in Switzerland (press photo Pro Juventute)

13.5 Why Education and Parenting Is Better than Legal Regulation

Although policymakers tend to create new laws for online risks, existing laws from the pre-Internet age generally apply to both online and offline. National law enforcement has become even more difficult, as companies like Facebook (which is often involved in cyberbullying cases) and video games played online escape national boundaries and legislation. Thus, effective political regulation of digital media is hardly possible and bans remain largely symbolic political acts.

Struggling to enforce the ban on "killer games," the Swiss Federal Council has initiated the program "Youth and Media" focusing on prevention and educational measures. As a national framework, the program is intended to connect existing services primarily in the field of media literacy promotion and provide information services for teachers, parents, and mental health professionals. The educational approach of "Youth and Media" is in line with reports and research publications suggesting education-based Internet safety programs as effective ways to reduce cyberbullying.[36] No report suggests criminalizing cyberbullying in additional laws, or at least any legal regulation is qualified as premature. Researchers Szoka and Thierer even take a clear stand against legal regulation of cyberbullying: "Criminalizing what is mostly child-on-child behavior will not likely solve the age-old problem of kids mistreating each other, a problem that has traditionally been dealt with through counseling and rehabilitation at the local level. Moreover, criminalization could raise thorny free speech and due process issues related to

[36] Szoka and Thierer 2009; Cross et al. 2009; Levy et al. 2012.

legal definitions of harassing or intimidating speech."[37] The considerable overlap of cyberbullying with traditional bullying shows that an effective way is to develop preventive activities in schools about bullying in general, including cyberbullying. This means to be clear among the school community about the school's stance on this issue, fostering a school climate in which students feel comfortable reporting cyberbullying, teaching safe Internet use, including privacy and protection, and promoting bullying bystander education. Authorities can help support antibullying activities in schools, but additional laws will certainly not help prevent cyberbullying.

Considering that the video game industry in Switzerland generates approximately double the turnover of the movie industry, it is hardly surprising that first-person shooter games can be found in many teens' homes. Luckily, an overwhelming majority of them plays without any violent behavior in real life. It is an age-old phenomenon: youth pushing limits, trying to shock parents and others of their generation in order to find their own identities and proof of masculinity. Especially, the use of first-person shooter games is a means for many youngsters to make an implicit but clear statement of an activity that their parents most probably would not engage in and do not approve of. Research shows that the use of video games decreases while teens get older. An overwhelming number of teens though play violent games that are not appropriate for their age. The self-regulation of the gaming industry with PEGI[38] ratings fails if parents do not make sure their children only play games suitable for their age. Research results show the relative insignificance of playing violent games compared to other risk factors, such as real-life violence within the family and parental neglect. A more promising approach than a legal ban is supporting and educating parents. A good example for this is the British online safety initiative "Munch Poke Ping." It provides resources on underage use of games for parents, parent education in schools, and all those working with children.[39]

13.6 Protecting Kids by Fostering Their Resilience

Parents and educators can help foster children's psychological resilience in general but also as a way to reduce negative media effects. The concept of psychological resilience does not assess risk but focuses on how individuals cope

[37] Szoka and Thierer 2009, p. 1.

[38] The Pan-European Game Information (PEGI) age rating system was established to help European parents make informed decisions on buying computer games. It was launched in spring 2003 and replaced a number of national age rating systems with a single system now used throughout in thirty European countries.

[39] "Munch Poke Ping"—Underage use of Games: Resources, www.carrick-davies.com/downloads/Underage_gamingHow_to_support_young_people_teachers_and_parents.pdf.

with stress and protect themselves. According to Brooks and Goldstein resilient children[40]:

- Are optimistic, have high self-esteem, are aware that they are important;
- Build on their success and maintain a constructive attitude toward mistakes, consider them challenges;
- Have a good problem-solving ability and experience;
- Focus on what they can change in their own lives and not on with what is immutable;
- Know their strengths and their weaknesses;
- Have confidence in their own abilities;
- Can set realistic and achievable goals;
- Are able to empathize with other people;
- Know effective ways to resolve conflicts;
- Have communication skills;
- Feel responsible for their actions;
- Can assess the impact of their behavior on others.

Taub and Pearrow mention internal and external protective factors associated with resilience. Internal factors are within the individual (e.g., impulse control, social problem solving, ability to form positive relationships with others). External factors include e.g., families, schools, and their ways of setting and enforcing clear boundaries, norms, and rules, and fostering encouraging supportive and caring relationships with others and possessing values of altruism and cooperation.[41] The authors "strongly believe that such programs [school-based programs targeted at violence and bullying prevention] contribute, directly or indirectly, to the reduction of factors related to violence in schools, as well as the promotion of factors related to resilience in our nation's student population."[42]

Research clearly shows that resilient teens deal much better with adversities in general and with negative media effects in particular. Resilient adolescents are embedded in a stable social environment and have active stress-coping strategies. Instead of legal regulations, it takes the attitude of parents, schools, and other educators to support and listen to children and teens and to talk to them about their joys and sorrows. Parents have to set clear boundaries in media exposure regarding time and content, respecting the age classifications of games and to actively engage with teens' experiences with and without digital media. Schools, parents, and other educators need to be empowered to teach children and adolescents traditional values and standards like respect in terms of behavior and communication. Those values are a means to prevent violence and (cyber)bullying even if parents, teachers and other educators (who did not grow up with digital media themselves) do not understand the details about online gaming and

---

[40] Brooks and Goldstein 2002.

[41] Taub and Pearrow 2013, p. 372.

[42] Taub and Pearrow 2013, p. 371.

communication. The *New York Times* wrote about the role of the Internet in the "Boston Bombings" in 2013:

> And that is why the faster, more accessible and ultramodern the Internet becomes, the more all the old-fashioned stuff matters: good judgment, respect for others who are different and basic values of right and wrong. Those you cannot download. They have to be uploaded, the old-fashioned way, by parents around the dinner table, by caring but demanding teachers at school and by responsible spiritual leaders in a church, synagogue, temple, or mosque.[43]

The challenge of the educational approach promoted by the Swiss federal program "Youth and Media"—as of any prevention and information campaign—remains to reach high-risk teens and parents. It seems vital to provide schools with enough human and financial resources in order to support youth by including anti-bullying prevention, mandatory media literacy classes, and by supporting adolescents to become responsible, respectful, and resilient adults.

References

Beckedahl M, Lüke F (2012) Die digitale Gesellschaft. Recht & Freiheit im Internet. dtv premium

Bonfadelli H (2004) Medienwirkungen II: Anwendungen in Politik, Wirtschaft und Kultur. UVK UTB 2615

Brooks R, Goldstein S (2002) Raising resilient children. McGraw-Hill, New York

Colzato LS, van Leeuwen PJA, van den Wildenberg W, Hommel B (2010) DOOM'd to switch: superior cognitive flexibility in players of first person shooter games. Frontiers in cognition 1:Article 8. www.frontiersin.org/Journal/DownloadFile.ashx?pdf=1&FileId=12504&articleId=1515&Version=1&ContentTypeId=15&FileName=fpsyg_2010_00008.pdf

Cross D, Shaw T, Hearn L, Epstein M, Monks H, Lester L, Thomas L (2009) Australian covert bullying prevalence study (ACBPS). Child Health Promotion Research Centre, Edith Cowan University, Perth. www.deewr.gov.au/Schooling/NationalSafeSchools/Pages/research.aspx

Federal Council (2010) Report Schutz vor Cyberbullying. www.ejpd.admin.ch/content/ejpd/de/home/dokumentation/info/2010/ref_2010-06-02.html

Feierabend S, Karg U, Rathgeb T (2012) JIM 2012. Jugend, Information, (Multi-)Media Basisstudie zum Medienumgang 12- bis 19-jähriger in Deutschland. Medienpädagogischer Forschungsverbund Südwest. www.mpfs.de/fileadmin/JIM-pdf12/JIM2012_Endversion.pdf

Friedman TL (2013) Judgment not included. New York Times. www.nytimes.com/2013/04/28/opinion/sunday/friedman-judgment-not-included.html

Gentile DA, Saleem M, Anderson CA (2007) Public policy and the effects of media violence on children. Soc Issues Policy Rev 1:15–61

Hartmann T (2006) Gewaltspiele und Aggression. Aktuelle Forschung und Implikationen. In: Kaminski W, Lorber M (eds) Clash of realities: Computerspiele und soziale Wirklichkeit. Kopäd, pp 81–99

Hermida M (2013) EU kids online: Schweiz. Schweizer Kinder und Jugendliche im Internet: Risikoerfahrungen und Umgang mit Risiken. www.eukidsonline.ch

[43] Friedman 2013, www.nytimes.com/2013/04/28/opinion/sunday/friedman-judgment-not-included.html.

Hopf W, Huber G, Weiß R (2008) Media violence and youth violence. A 2-year longitudinal study. J Media Psychol 20(3):79–96

Johnson JG, Cohen P, Smailes EM, Kasen S, Brook JS (2002) Television viewing and aggressive behavior during adolescence and adulthood. Science 295:2468–2471. www.sciencemag.org/content/295/5564/2468

Kunczik M, Zipfel A (2006) Gewalt und Medien. Ein Studienhandbuch. UTB

Levy N, Cortesi S, Gasser U, Crowley E, Beaton M, Casey JA, Nolan C (2012) Bullying in a networked era: a literature review. Harvard Berkman Center Research Publication no. 2012-17. http://ssrn.com/abstract=2146877

Merz-Abt T (2009) Killerspiele und ihre Herausforderungen für Schule und Eltern. Theoretische Reflexion und medienpädagogische Handlungsempfehlungen. www.medienheft.ch/dossier/bibliothek/d09_Games_Merz-AbtThomas.pdf

Perren S, Dooley J, Shaw T, Cross D (2010) Bullying in school and cyberspace: associations with depressive symptoms in Swiss and Australian adolescents. Child Adolesc Psychiatry Mental Health 4:28. www.ncbi.nlm.nih.gov/pmc/articles/PMC3003626/pdf/1753-2000-4-28.pdf

Schmid-Federer B (2008) Postulat 'Schutz vor Cyberbullying'. www.parlament.ch/d/suche/seiten/geschaefte.aspx?gesch_id=20083050

Schmid-Federer B (2010) Einsetzung eines eidgenössischen Mobbing- und Cyberbullying-Beauftragten. www.parlament.ch/d/suche/seiten/geschaefte.aspx?gesch_id=20103856

Steiner O (2009) Neue Medien und Gewalt. Beiträge zur sozialen Sicherheit. Expertenbericht 04/09 des Eidgenössischen Departements des Innern., Bern. www.bsv.admin.ch/praxis/forschung/publikationen/index.html?lang=de&bereich=4&jahr=2009

Sticca F, Perren S (2012) Is cyberbullying worse than traditionional bullying? Examining the differential roles of medium, publicity, and anonymity for the perceived severity of bullying. J Youth Adolescence. doi:10.1007/s10964-012-9867-3

Sticca F, Ruggieri S, Alsaker F, Perren S (2012) Longitudinal risk factors for cyberbullying in adolecence. J Commun Appl Soc Psychol. doi:10.1002/casp.2136

Szoka BM, Thierer AD (2009) Cyberbullying Legislation: why education is preferable to regulation. Progress & freedom foundation progress on point paper 16(12). http://papers.ssrn.com/sol3/papers.cfm?abstract_id=1422577

Taub J, Pearrow M (2013) Resilience through violence and bullying prevention in schools. In: Goldstein S, Brooks R (eds) Handbook of resilience in children. Springer Science and Business Media, New York, pp 371–386

Tokunaga RS (2010) Following you home from school: a critical review and synthesis of literature on cyberbullying victimization. Comput Hum Behav 26(3):277–287

Willemse I, Waller G, Süss D, Genner S, Huber A (2012) JAMES 2012. Youth, activities media—survey Switzerland. Zurich University of Applied Sciences. www.psychologie.zhaw.ch/JAMES

Ybarra ML, boyd d, Korchmaros JD, Oppenheim J (2012) Defining and measuring cyberbullying within the larger context of bullying victimization. J Adolesc Health 51:53–58

Chapter 14
Addressing Cyberbullying Using a Multi-Stakeholder Approach: The Flemish Case

Heidi Vandebosch

Contents

14.1 Introduction

Cyberbullying is a common phenomenon amongst youngsters,[1] which is often connected to traditional (school) bullying.[2] Therefore, many scholars plea for an "integrative" anti-bulllying approach.[3] In this chapter, we argue that to address cyberbullying effectively, it is necessary to take into account the specific characteristics of this type of bullying.

First of all, these specific characteristics have consequences for the different actors that should be involved. Because cyberbullying is mostly initiated at home,

---

Heidi Vandebosch is Associate Professor at the Department of Communication Studies at the University of Antwerp (Belgium). She is a member of the Research Group MIOS (Media and ICT in Organisations and Society).

---

[1] Kowalski and Limber 2007; Tokunaga 2010.
[2] Juvonen and Gross 2008; Li 2007; Vandebosch and Van Cleemput 2009.
[3] Agatson et al. 2007; Mason 2008.

H. Vandebosch (✉)
University of Antwerp, Antwerp, Belgium
e-mail: heidi.vandebosch@uantwerpen.be

S. van der Hof et al. (eds.), *Minding Minors Wandering the Web: Regulating Online Child Safety*, Information Technology and Law Series 24, DOI: 10.1007/978-94-6265-005-3_14,

is only directly observable online, and often done by a perpetrator who takes advantage of the relative anonymity provided by ICT, school staff is probably less aware of this type of bullying and less able to react immediately. Therefore, other types of actors—i.e. parents, Internet Service Providers and the police—should also be engaged in actions aimed at the prevention, detection and solution of cyberbullying. Mass media too, may play an important role, by putting cyberbullying on the general public's and policy makers' agenda.

Second, addressing cyberbullying requires adjustments in the contents of anti-bullying programs. To prevent, to detect and to solve cyberbullying, all parties involved should be aware of what cyberbullying actually is, which students are at risk of becoming a perpetrator or a victim, what causes cyberbullying and what can be done to prevent or solve it. Hence the importance of (academic) research in this field, that provides the necessary input for evidence-based interventions.

In this chapter, we will illustrate the role of students, school staff, parents, the police, Internet Service Providers (ISP's), e-safety organisations, the mass media, policymakers and academics with regard to cyberbullying by referring to research findings and concrete intervention initiatives (especially in Flanders—Belgium).

14.2 Cyberbullying and Traditional Bullying: A Story of Differences and Similarities

Research on cyberbullying is from a relatively recent date. Based on the observation that information and communication technologies (such as the internet and the mobile phone) had become very popular amongst youngsters, researchers started to investigate some of the negative side-effects or risks of these new media. In line with a well-known form of offline peer-to-peer-aggression, scholars identified cyberbullying as an important issue. The 24/7 character, the anonymity, the lack of cues, the mediated form, the replicability and the potentially worldwide audience of (some of) the technologies, were hypothesised to distinguish cyberbullying from traditional or offline bullying.[4]

These technological attributes led, for instance, to discussions about the definition of cyberbullying (how can the typical characteristics of traditional bullying—i.e. repetition, power imbalance, intention to hurt—be translated to the cyber context?),[5] and to the identification of new forms of bullying (such as 'masquerade' and 'outing').[6] With regard to the prevalence of cyberbullying, it was hypothesised that the high penetration of ICT amongst youngsters, together with its (perceived) anonymity and mediated character (often regarded as potential

---

[4] Patchin and Hinduja 2006; Heirman and Walrave 2008; Dooley et al. 2009.

[5] Vandebosch and Van Cleemput 2008; Menesini and Nocentini 2009; Menesini et al. 2011; Langos 2012.

[6] Vandebosch and Van Cleemput 2009.

triggers for bullying),[7] might lead to high(er) perpetration and victimisation rates. The profile of the cyberbullies and the cybervictims, too, was predicted to be different from that of offline bullies and victims. Given the fact that ICTs were especially popular amongst older children and adolescents (who had the skills to go online), the average age of those involved in cyberbullying was expected to be higher than that of those involved in traditional bullying.[8] Moreover, the anonymity of the internet and the mobile phone was hypothesised to empower some categories of students (e.g. girls and victims of traditional bullying), who were less involved as perpetrators in (some types of) traditional bullying, to become cyberbullies (i.e. the 'revenge of the nerds' hypothesis).[9] Furthermore, the fact that the internet allows youngsters to communicate with people they have only met online seemed to broaden the scope of bullying. Instead of being bullied by or bullying peers known from offline contexts (e.g. school), the internet also made it possible for youngsters to become involved in cyberbullying incidents with people they had never met in person. Finally, the impact of cyberbullying was thought of as being different from that of traditional bullying.[10] The 24/7 character of the internet and mobile phones could make cyberbullying almost inescapable (while the home was considered a safe place for those who were, for instance, being bullied at school). The (potential) worldwide audience was considered to be another worsening aspect.

The studies on cyberbullying that tested these hypotheses were mainly quantitative in nature, with a focus on cross-sectional, online or school surveys. The results of these studies seem to indicate that cyberbullying is a common problem (although the prevalence rates differ significantly amongst studies, because of different conceptualisations and operationalisations of cyberbullying,[11] but is still less prevalent than traditional bullying. The fact that most youngsters spend relatively more time with peers in offline contexts, such as school, where they—unlike in online environments—can less easily avoid individuals they actually do not like, might explain these findings. With regard to the most common forms of cyberbullying, it is clear that verbal, direct forms of cyberbullying (such as insulting or threatening somebody) are popular.[12] Studies on the platforms or applications that are most frequently used to cyberbully, reflect the shifts in popularity of technologies. For instance, while Instant Messaging was a very popular place to cyberbully in some of the earlier studies,[13] more recent research indicates that much of the cyberbullying takes place on Social Network Sites (such as Facebook).[14] With regard to the profile of cyberbullies, the following trends

[7] Heirman and Walrave 2008.

[8] Salmivalli and Pöyhönen 2010.

[9] Vandebosch and Van Cleemput 2009.

[10] Campbell 2005.

[11] See for instance, Kowalski et al. 2008; Tokunaga 2010.

[12] Wegge et al. 2013.

[13] Kowalski and Limber 2007.

have been observed: perpetrators of cyberbullying are also often more involved as perpetrators in traditional bullying,[15] and as victims or bystanders in cyberbullying; they often make more use of the internet or certain types of applications; they report less parental supervision (on their online activities)[16]; and they are more often involved in other problematic behaviours, such as substance use and delinquent behaviour.[17] Perpetrators often cyberbully anonymously,[18] and most of their actions are targeted towards victims they know in person. With regard to the age and the gender of the cyberbullies, the findings are less clear-cut. Nevertheless many of them seem to indicate a peak in cyberbullying behaviour between the age of 12 and 15,[19] and—compared to traditional bullying—a relatively high involvement of girls as perpetrator (who often seem to draw level with or even outrun boys in cyberbullying). Perpetrators report they cyberbully because it makes them feel powerful, popular, better than other students[20]; for fun, because they feel bad about themselves[21]; to redirect feelings, out of boredom, to protect themselves from being picked on by others[22]; to vent anger and frustration[23]; to get back at someone they are mad at[24] and out of jealousy.[25] Victims of cyberbullying have often been observed to be: more often involved as victims in traditional bullying[26] and as perpetrators and bystanders of cyberbullying; and more frequent users of the internet (or certain types of applications).[27] Again, the findings with regard to the age and the gender of the victims are less clear-cut, but (also) seem to point to a relatively high victimisation degree amongst early adolescents of both genders (although there are some indications that girls—like in traditional bullying—report more victimisation).[28]

The evidence on the precise impact of cyberbullying is still scarce. Cross-sectional studies reveal that cyberbullying is related to similar types of health- and school-related problems as traditional bullying.[29] The severity of the impact (compared to traditional bullying) might, however, be highly dependent on the

---

[14] Livingstone et al. 2011.

[15] Dehue et al. 2008; Li 2007; Raskauskas and Stoltz 2007; Smith et al. 2008.

[16] Vandebosch and Van Cleemput 2009.

[17] Ybarra and Mitchell 2004.

[18] Patchin and Hinduja 2006; Wegge et al. 2013.

[19] Slonje and Smith 2008; Williams and Guerra 2007.

[20] Mishna et al. 2010.

[21] Raskauskas and Stoltz 2007.

[22] Varjas et al. 2010.

[23] Hinduja and Patchin 2009.

[24] Raskauskas and Stoltz 2007.

[25] Varjas et al. 2010.

[26] Dehue et al. 2008; Juvonen and Gross 2008; Li 2007; Vandebosch and Van Cleemput 2009.

[27] Ybarra 2004; Juvonen and Gross 2008.

[28] For an overview see Tokunaga 2010.

form of cyberbullying that was used. In the study of Smith et al.,[30] for instance, picture or video clip bullying was perceived by students as having more impact than traditional bullying, while chatroom bullying was perceived as having less impact (all other kinds of cyberbullying, e.g. text message bullying or e-mail bullying, were thought to have a similar impact as traditional bullying). Research on the coping strategies of victims distinguishes four subcategories: confronting a bully, doing nothing or ignoring, technical strategies, and seeking instrumental and emotional support. Preliminary results (again based on what victims perceive as helpful) seem to indicate that technical solutions such as "blocking" the perpetrator[31] and (especially) "telling someone" are most effective.[32]

The above-mentioned findings seem to indicate, on the one hand, that there is a considerable overlap between traditional bullying and cyberbullying (e.g. regarding the profile of bullies and victims, the type of consequences, et cetera), but, on the other hand, that cyberbullying also has some distinctive features (e.g. its 24/7 character, potentially worldwide audience, mediated form and anonymity). This observation also has consequences for interventions aimed at tackling cyberbullying.

14.3 Tackling the 'Bullying' and the 'Cyber' Part of 'Cyberbullying'

Since many cases of cyberbullying are an extension of traditional school bullying (with the same pupils bullying the same other pupils offline and online)[33] and also have an influence on students' functioning at school,[34] many researchers[35] as well as legal experts[36] argue that schools have an important responsibility in addressing this problem. Schools are also considered central actors, because they have experience with traditional anti-bullying programmes. Scholars, therefore, often suggest that schools should adapt an integrated anti-bullying programme, which aims at tackling both traditional and new forms of bullying. Starting from what has proven to be most effective in tackling traditional bullying, that is a "whole school approach",[37] such a programme should rely on the cooperation of different types

[29] For an overview see Tokunaga 2010.

[30] Smith et al. 2008.

[31] Price and Dalgleish 2010.

[32] Price and Dalgleish 2010; Machmutow et al. 2012.

[33] Juvonen and Gross 2008; Smith et al. 2008; Mishna et al. 2010; Erentaite et al. 2012; Wegge et al. 2013.

[34] Beran and Li 2007; Marsh et al. 2010.

[35] Agatston et al. 2007; Diamanduros et al. 2008.

[36] Lane 2011.

of actors (students, school staff, parents and the wider community) and include different types of actions (preventive, detective, reactive).

However, to address cyberbullying effectively, it is necessary to take into account the specific characteristics of this type of bullying when developing such an integrated anti-bullying approach. First of all, these specific characteristics have consequences for the different actors that should be involved. Because cyberbullying is mostly initiated at home, is only directly observable online, is often done by a perpetrator who takes advantage of the relative anonymity provided by ICT and aimed at a victim who does not know how to adequately protect him or herself online, school staff (and parents) alone are not always able to prevent, discover and react to this type of bullying. Therefore, other types of actors—e.g. Internet Service Providers, the police, e-safety organisations—should also be engaged. Second, the (preventive, detective and curative) actions should take into account the specific characteristics of cyberbullying. For instance, to prevent cyberbullying, it is not only important to inform pupils, parents and teachers about the general social mechanisms that underlie bullying behaviour, but also on the ways in which features of the online environment (e.g. the perceived anonymity, and the mediated character) might facilitate these. Likewise, students can be taught how to decrease the chance of being victimised online (e.g. by using privacy settings on SNS) or how to react appropriately to online bullying (e.g. by reporting incidents offline and online). In other words, to address cyberbullying adequately, insights from traditional bullying programmes should be complemented with insights from e-literacy programmes (as, for instance, created by e-safety organisations, and/or implemented in schools).

Figure 14.1 gives an overview of all the actors that should be involved to adequately tackle cyberbullying (amongst youngsters). These actors are situated at different levels. The first level consists of students, staff and parents (together constituting the school environment). At the second level, we can find actors such as mental-health organisations, and (especially relevant for cyberbullying) the police, ISP's and e-safety organisations. On an even higher level, mass media may play an important role in creating awareness about (cyber)bullying and setting the public (and policy) agenda. Policymakers, in turn, may undertake several types of actions (based on the scientific knowledge about the problem), such as: creating laws against cyberbullying, stimulating education about e-safety, demanding actions from ISPs to decrease the prevalence and the impact of cyberbullying amongst youngsters. Together with these traditional and 'new' actors, two types of expertise—on bullying and on the 'cyberworld'—are combined. We will describe the role of the different actors at each level in the following sections, and illustrate these with examples stemming from Flanders (the Dutch-speaking part of Belgium).

[37] Samara and Smith 2008.

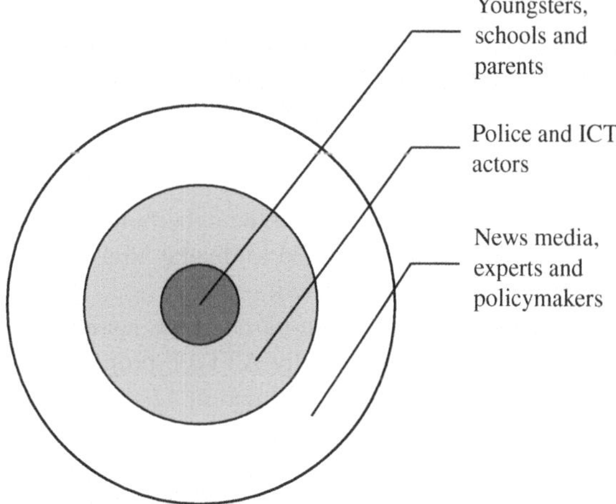

Fig. 14.1 Overview of stakeholders needed to address cyberbullying

14.4 The School Environment and Cyberbullying: Involving Students, Staff and Parents

The ultimate goal of anti-cyberbullying programmes is to reduce the prevalence and the impact of cyberbullying amongst youngsters. This goal can be reached by targeting youngsters themselves, but also by targeting important actors in youngsters' direct environment (such as their parents and teachers), who—through their own behaviours—affect the likelihood of youngsters being involved in and suffering from cyberbullying.

1. Youngsters

Youngsters can be addressed in their role(s) of (potential) victims, bystanders and perpetrators of cyberbullying.[38] (Potential) perpetrators should be made more aware of the negative impact of cyberbullying on the victim and of the possible negative consequences of the cyberbullying behaviour for themselves (e.g. rejection by peers, punishments by parents and teachers, exclusion from online services by ISPs when Users Terms are violated, or legal consequences when their cyberbullying constitutes criminal behaviour). They should also be taught what is socially acceptable behaviour on the internet and what is not (e.g. 'netiquette'), how to ventilate possible negative emotions (which may underly the cyberbullying behaviour) in a different way and how to restore their past bullying behaviours. (Potential) victims should be informed about the possible negative consequences of internet-related risk behaviour (such as sharing passwords, and putting very personal information online). They should also be taught how to use adequate

[38] Vandebosch and Poels 2012.

coping strategies. Victims, for instance, should get a more realistic picture of the size and the attitude of the audience witnessing the bullying behaviour online (cognitive component). They should also learn how to act appropriately to cyberbullying behaviour (e.g. by seeking support from friends, parents, teachers or professionals, rather than taking (online) revenge). Bystanders should be persuaded that they can (and should) play an important role in cyberbullying situations. If they overtly condemn the cyberbullying behaviour and defend the victim, the bully will be less inclined to display this negative behaviour in the future and the victim will feel supported.

In Flanders, an evidence-based game against cyberbullying is currently being developed within the Friendly ATTAC project (www.friendlyattac.be). The main goal of this game (which is aimed at 12–15 year olds) is precisely to modify the above-mentioned determinants (e.g. attitudes and knowledge) of behaviours related to cyberbullying, by means of highly personalised virtual experience scenarios, providing players with immediate feedback in a safe computer-mediated environment. This game can be incorporated in (school-based) programmes against cyberbullying.

2. Schools

As indicated in the section above, schools are thought to be important actors in anti-cyberbullying programmes. They can undertake several actions to promote a positive school climate and reduce (the prevalence and impact of) negative social behaviours, such as traditional bullying.[39] Indirectly—since bullying through the internet or through mobile phones is often an extension of traditional bullying—this may also affect the prevalence of cyberbullying amongst pupils. However, as argued above, the specific characteristics of cyberbullying, also require specific attention. Schools should raise awareness about cyberbullying (what is it?, what are its causes and effects? and what can be done about it?) amongst their pupils (and the parents of their pupils), promote reporting cases of cyberbullying to the school staff, and try to adequately deal with cyberbullying incidents that occur. However, according to some authors, "schools have been slow to respond to the increased incidences of cyberbullying"[40] and are now only "beginning to extend their bullying policies to include the Internet".[41] The study of Vandebosch, Poels and Deboutte amongst principals of primary and secondary schools in Flanders, partially confirms this.[42] Compared to the initiatives on traditional bullying (aimed at students, teachers or parents), the number of activities specifically dealing with cyberbullying is still rather limited. This study also shows that this is not due to an underestimation of the cyberbullying problem by schools, nor to the fact that they do not feel responsible for bullying that takes place outside school (hours). The

39 Samara and Smith 2008.

40 Aoyama and Talbert 2010.

41 Sharples et al. 2009.

42 Vandebosch et al. 2011.

main reason for this relatively limited attention for cyberbullying is—according to the principals—the lack of professional support and concrete materials in this area. Schools are looking forward to evidence-based intervention programmes that are appealing for their students.

These results seem to indicate that the existing initiatives of anti-bullying and e-safety organisations on cyberbullying (see infra), are not well-known or considered insufficiently by school principals. They also suggest that the current policy of the Flemish Ministry of Education—which has undertaken some anti-cyberbullying initiatives, but leaves the main responsibility to tackle (cyber)bullying in the hands of schools—has serious shortcomings. A more directive policy approach, which gives clear instructions to schools on how to handle (cyber)bullying without suppressing (additional) local initiatives, might be more effective in dealing with this important issue.

3. Parents

Apart from schools, parents should be involved in anti-cyberbullying programmes. Given the fact that cyberbullying often takes place outside school (hours), their role is even more important than in traditional bullying programmes. Parental-mediation styles with regard to their children's ICT use may lower the chance of involvement in and the impact of cyberbullying and other online risk behaviours. In the literature, several forms of parental mediation have been distinguished, such as active co-use, interactional restriction, technical restriction and monitoring.[43] The mediation styles that parents apply seem to be dependent on, amongst others, gender, Socio-Economic Status (SES) and their perception of the risks associated with the use of ICT. With regard to cyberbullying, it appears that parents do consider cyberbullying a serious problem.[44] Their (consequential?) parental involvement with their children's ICT use is also associated with a lower risk of cyberbullying perpetration[45] and victimisation.[46] Research furthermore shows that when youngsters—perhaps despite precautionary measures of their parents—become the victim of cyberbullying, they not always tell their parents,[47] for instance, because they have the feeling that their parents will not be able to help them. This "not reporting" may also explain why parents underestimate their own children's involvement in cyberbullying as a victim (and as a perpetrator).[48] Creating awareness amongst parents about how to prevent their children from being the perpetrator or victim of cyberbullying, about how to decode signals of their children being involved in cyberbullying incidents and about how to solve these problems adequately is thus a crucial aspect in anti-cyberbullying strategies.

---

[43] Livingstone and Helsper 2008.

[44] Livingstone et al. 2011.

[45] Vandebosch and Van Cleemput 2009.

[46] Mesch 2009.

[47] Li 2006.

[48] Dehue et al. 2008.

In Flanders, examples of such (research-based) advices aimed at parents can, for instance, be found on the website of the Internet Observatory.[49]

14.5 The Role of the Police, ISPs and e-Safety Organisations

On the second level (see Fig. 14.1), three other categories of actors are important to tackle cyberbullying amongst youngsters: the police, Internet Service Providers (ISPs) and e-safety organisations. As will be demonstrated below, these actors often already cooperate on this issue.

1. The police

Although there are a number of arguments that would plea against the involvement of the police in cyberbullying amongst youngsters (e.g. the fact that (cyber)bullying is to some degree "normal" in the social development of youngsters and that offenders should thus not be criminalised, and the fact that not all forms of cyberbullying (e.g. massively defriending someone) constitute a criminal offence), there are also some arguments that plea in favour. As mentioned before, since most cyberbullying takes place outside school and outside school hours, it may not always be so evident for schools to mediate between, for instance, the victim and the perpetrator (and their respective parents). Hence, the (local) police might fulfil this role. The involvement of the police is also necessary in those cases where cyberbullying does represent a serious threat to the mental and/or physical health of the victim, and fast cooperation with the ISPs is needed to identify the perpetrator and to stop the crime. To summarise: the police should be contacted when cyberbullying is (expected to constitute) a criminal offence,[50] and could be contacted for more ambiguous cases (and for tips on how to prevent all types of cyberbullying).

In Belgium, both the federal police (more in particular, the Federal Computer Crime Unit (FCCU)) and the local police are involved in cyberbullying prevention, detection and solution.[51] The FCCU and (some) local police departments (especially those in large towns with a considerable amount of young people, such as Antwerp and Leuven) have first-hand knowledge on cybercrime (in general), which they can draw upon in their prevention activities. During their information sessions (often in collaboration with schools), and in their brochures and radio

[49] www.internet-observatory.be/internet_observatory/pdf/faq_cards/parents/Cyberharcelement_parents_web_nl.pdf.

[50] For more information on the legal qualification of different types of cyberbullying in different countries, see Walrave et al. 2009; Kowalski et al. 2008; Stefkovich et al. 2010; Shariff 2008; Campbell et al. 2008.

[51] For an extensive overview, see Vandebosch et al. 2012.

programmes, the police refer to concrete examples, make suggestions on how to behave safely, and give tips on what to do and whom to contact in case of victimisation. Besides preventive actions, the police are also involved in detecting instances of cyberbullying. Crucial for the detection of this (and other online criminal) behaviour are user notifications. The FCCU is often informed about cyberbullying by bystanders or victims using the online reporting system, eCops (www.ecops.be). On this online platform, users can report crimes (but not officially file complaints) committed on or through the internet. Additional notifications (on serious abuses) reach eCops via Child Focus (an e-safety organisation, cf. infra) and Netlog (a social networking site), who also have their own "reporting systems". To officially file a complaint (which requires a signed declaration and is necessary for some types of crimes), cyberbullying victims have to contact their local police department. Law enforcement officers then first have to evaluate whether (and how) the reported behaviour can be qualified as an offence. If the reported cyberbullying behaviour is indeed an offence, the police can continue their work. Often, they will have to try to identify the perpetrator by relying on evidence from the side of the victim (e.g. records of the abuse: dates, times and virtual places, the content of the message(s), user names, e-mail addresses and phone numbers). Starting from these traces, the police then usually have to cooperate with (different types of) Internet Service Providers (i.e. access providers, who provide a link from the customer to the internet, and content providers, such as social network sites, photo sharing sites, messaging services, who both offer and receive (user-generated) content). Cooperation with content providers is also necessary to mitigate the problem (i.e. to remove certain (illegal) contents).

2. Internet Service Providers

Content providers, however, do not only rely on notifications from the police to remove illegal and harmful content (cf. the Notice and Takedown regimes[52]). Many of them (like Facebook, for instance) also provide possibilities to their users to (directly) report abuses to them. Furthermore, they often actively screen the (public) contents themselves (by using human or automatic monitoring). On the basis of these reports and detections, they can remove certain content (which represents illegal content or breaches of the terms of use), and/or take other measures, such as excluding the offender from further use of their services (based on the same terms of use).[53] Content (and access) providers also undertake many preventive actions. By creating specific technical features (such as privacy settings), they allow their users to better protect themselves. Furthermore, these ISPs (and their associations, e.g. ISPA Belgium) are also very active in awareness-raising campaigns about cyberbullying (and other online risks).

[52] See Ahlert et al. 2004; Lievens et al. 2006.

[53] Walrave et al. 2009; Durrant 2010.

3. e-Safety organisations

Apart from the industry, other (non-profit or governmental) organisations are involved in promoting e-safety. In Belgium, Child Focus (Foundation for Missing and Sexually Exploited Children) is the Belgian Safer Internet Center since 2000. It has a website (www.clicksafe.be/splash/nl_BE) with information on e-safety for children, adolescents, parents and professionals; developed a course package on cyberbullying (that teachers can use in their classes); and (since June 2011) operates a specific helpline for questions regarding internet safety. Only recently, Child Focus and the six most important content and access providers in Belgium (Belgacom, KPN Group Belgium/Base, Microsoft, Mobistar, Netlog and Telenet) signed the "E-safety charter". This e-safety charter is a self-regulatory instrument (cf. the "Safer Social Networking Principles", developed by the social networking sites in consultation with the European Commission) to enhance the safety of children and young people using their services.[54] In this charter, these content and access providers commit themselves, amongst others, to raising awareness about Internet-related risks, and empowering users through tools and technology (e.g. privacy settings).

14.6 The Role of News Media, Policymakers and Researchers

1. News media

News media, too, may play an important awareness-raising role. The amount of attention that they pay to cyberbullying, and the ways in which they frame the issue may influence the general public's and policymakers' perceptions (and concurrent actions).

Content analyses reveal that news media pay considerable attention to stories on internet-related risks and children, especially those involving sex (e.g. grooming) and aggression (e.g. cyberbullying).[55] A recent study on Flemish newspapers' reporting on cyberbullying[56] shows that the first stories on bullying through ICT appeared in 1998. The media attention for cyberbullying increased significantly in 2005, when a large-scale study on cyberbullying amongst Flemish youngsters, which was commissioned by the Flemish government, was conducted. Since that time, the attention for the issue has remained high. Newspapers mostly pay attention to Flemish or Belgian news with regard to cyberbullying. Stories on "cases", "research" and "policy" are equally present.

[54] Child Focus 2011.

[55] Haddon and Stald 2009; Mascheroni et al. 2010.

[56] Vermeulen and Vandebosch 2012.

With regard to the way news media portray ICT-related risks, it is clear that there are some indications of a "moral panic framing".[57] News media often focus on youngsters, not only in the role of victims but also as perpetrators (e.g. in the case of "sexting" or "cyberbullying"). Furthermore, the news stories on cases often refer to those with very severe consequences (e.g. cyberbullying cases associated with suicide, or suicidal attempts of the victim).[58]

With regard to the potential effects of the amount of news media coverage on cyberbullying, the agenda-setting theory suggests that the media determine what people think about. Issues that are high on the media agenda will also be high on the public's agenda (and—consequently—on policymakers' agenda, cf. infra). The way the media frame the issue (by selecting information, mentioning certain causes, "effects" and solutions) may also have an impact on how people think about the issue, on their knowledge, attitudes and actions with regard to the "problem". As mentioned by Haddon and Stald parents, for instance, might be influenced by the news media: "For something as new and challenging as the Internet, it is likely that news stories and media values will be particularly important in contextualising how parents reflect on the issues that arise for their children and influence any decisions to monitor and mediate their children's use of the Internet, which in turn could have a bearing on children's behaviour online."[59]

2. Policymakers

The media's attention for cyberbullying might not only influence the public's agenda, but also policymakers' agenda. Policymakers may use the so-called "stick", "sermon" and "carrot" instruments to tackle a societal problem, such as cyberbullying. Their actions determine the general framework within which the other actors (e.g. schools, the police and ISPs) have to operate. They can, for instance, create new criminal laws (e.g. "anti-cyberbullying" laws), fund awareness-raising initiatives and stimulate the implementation of cyberbullying programmes in schools.

In Flanders, the Commission for Culture, Youth, Sport and the Media of the Flemish Government commissioned the first large-scale study on cyberbullying amongst youngsters in Flanders (funded by viWTA, and conducted by the University of Antwerp) in 2005. Since that date, actions against cyberbullying (and other online risks or health problems amongst youngsters) have become a priority on the policy agenda of several Ministries. For instance, the Ministry of Education has formulated ICT-related learning objectives for both primary and secondary education in Flanders. One of these objectives is that: "Pupils are able to use ICT to communicate in a safe, sensible and appropriate way."[60] Currently, the policy initiatives in the field of education focus on three aspects: (1) Strengthening the ICT-policy and infrastructure of schools, (2) Improving teachers' expertise and

---

[57] Lynn 2010.

[58] Thom et al. 2011.

[59] Haddon and Stald 2009, pp. 379–380.

[60] De Craemer 2010, p. 7.

providing teaching resources and (3) Monitoring ICT infrastructure and education. The Department of Education also provides some supporting activities, such as KlasCement (an educational portal site that functions as an electronic knowledge centre, with teaching aids and software and exchanges of good practices), and the E-safety guide and website.[61] With regard to cyberbullying, specifically, the Department of Education has financed the publication and the distribution of the course pack on cyberbullying (developed by ChildFocus), and organised a colloquium (aimed at teachers). The Flemish Minister for Innovation, Government Investments, Media and Poverty, on the other hand, has announced the creation of a knowledge centre for media literacy ('Kenniscentrum Mediawijsheid'). Dealing with mental health issues amongst youngsters (such as depression, possibly caused by (cyber)bullying) is, furthermore, a key issue for the Flemish Minister of Well-being, Health and Family.[62] One notable similarity in the policy plans and initiatives of the three above-mentioned Ministries is their intention to stimulate the use of digital games for learning and health amongst youngsters (an idea that is also present in the above-mentioned Friendly Attack project against cyberbullying).

3. Researchers

Finally, the role of researchers should be acknowledged. To address cyberbullying adequately, thorough knowledge of the problem is necessary (cf. the idea of "evidence-based interventions"). The first scientific publications on cyberbullying appeared around 2004 (see for instance the article of Ybarra on "internet harassment").[63] Since that date, there has been an explosive growth of research in this field. International cooperation between scholars working in this domain has also been promoted by initiatives, such as the European COST action IS0801 "Cyberbullying: coping with negative and enhancing positive uses of new technologies, in relationships in educational settings". The knowledge on the phenomenon of cyberbullying should, of course, also be disseminated beyond the academic borders. Researchers have the duty to inform policymakers (and inspire the measures they undertake), and to help create awareness on cyberbullying amongst the general public (for instance, by operating as a media source or giving presentations about their research topic to the general public).

14.7 Conclusion

In this chapter, we focused on cyberbullying, which is a common phenomenon amongst youngsters (especially early adolescents) and may have a serious impact on the victim's school functioning and (mental and physical) health. Since

[61] Vlaams Parlement 2009a.

[62] Vlaams Parlement 2009b.

[63] Ybarra 2004.

cyberbullying is often an extension of traditional bullying in schools, the typical "whole-school approach" on bullying (involving different types of activities (prevention, detection and solution) and actors (students, school staff, parents and the wider community) is often considered to be a good starting point for addressing cyberbullying. However, the specific features of cyberbullying also ask for an adjustment of this traditional approach, both with regard to the content of the activities, as well as with regard to the actors involved. Knowledge on "bullying" has to be combined with knowledge on "e-safety", and apart from traditional partners, a cooperation with "new", ICT-related, actors (such as the (cyber)police, Internet Service Providers and e-safety organisations) is necessary.

Starting from an ecological view, we described in this chapter that when we ultimately want to reduce the prevalence and the impact of cyberbullying amongst youngsters, we should not only focus on modifying the knowledge, (internet) skills, attitudes, norms and (eventually) the behaviours of youngsters themselves, but also of actors constituting their (social) environment (which—through their own behaviours—modify the chances of youngsters being involved in and affected by cyberbullying).

We described what should be done on each level (by different actors) as to address cyberbullying adequately, and also mentioned what is already being done or being prepared (in Flanders). As is clear from this overview, there is still a contrast between the ideal situation and the current situation. For instance, in many schools the number of activities specifically being organised on cyberbullying prevention, detection or solution is (still) quite limited compared to the activities with regard to traditional bullying. A main reason for this is the (perceived) lack of professional support for schools in this area. A second observation holds to effectiveness and efficiency of the initiatives that are already being undertaken (in Flanders and elsewhere). Many of the awareness-raising activities (from, for instance, schools, e-safety organisations and ISPs) are not always based on (scientific) knowledge on the problem, nor evaluated in terms of their effectiveness (do they reach the goals they are designed for, i.e. increase awareness, and (in this way) influence the behaviours of the target groups?). The current shift in academic cyberbullying research from problem-focused research to research on the development and evaluation of "evidence-based" programs against cyberbullying may help to solve this problem. With regard to efficiency, it is clear that the multitude of actors involved in addressing cyberbullying has also led to a proliferation of activities. These activities often overlap with each other (e.g. several schools developed their own—but in fact a quite similar—anti-cyberbullying strategy), in other cases they are not tuned into each other (e.g. when students are being advised in a campaign to tell their parents they are being victimised, this requires that parents know what to do about cyberbullying) and sometimes even contradict each other (e.g. the police may recommend victims to "save the evidence", while school psychologists might, for instance, advice the victim to delete the hurtful contents they received). Although there is already (some) cooperation between (some) large actors (e.g. ISPs, e-safety organisations, such as Child Focus, and the police) in the field, this cooperation should be extended (to other actors and other levels) and coordinated (e.g. by policymakers).

References

Agatston PW, Kowalski R, Limber S (2007) Students' perspectives on cyber bullying. J Adolesc Health 41:S59–S60

Ahlert C, Marsden C, Yung C (2004) How 'liberty' disappeared from cyberspace: the mystery shopper tests Internet content self-regulation. http://pcmlp.socleg.ox.ac.uk/sites/pcmlp.socleg.ox.ac.uk/files/liberty.pdf. Accessed 22 August 2011

Aoyama I, Talbert TL (2010) Cyberbullying internationally increasing: New challenges in the technology generation. In: Zheng R, Burrow-Sanchez J, Clifford D (eds) Adolescent online social communication and behavior: relationship formation on the internet. Information Science Reference, Hershey, pp 184–200

Beran T, Li Q (2007) The relationship between cyberbullying and school bullying. J Stud Wellbeing 1:15–33

Campbell MA (2005) Cyber bullying: an old problem in a new guise? Australian J Guidance Couns 15:68–76

Campbell MA, Butler DA, Kift SM (2008) A school's duty to provide a safe learning environment: does this include cyberbullying? Australia N Z J Law Educ 13:21–32

Child Focus (2011) Signature e-safety charter press release—23/06/2011. www.clicksafe.be/splash/uploads/Persbericht%20ondertekening%20echarter%20EN.pdf. Accessed 22 August 2011

De Craemer J (2010) Belgium (Flemish community). Country report on ICT in education. European schoolnet. www.ond.vlaanderen.be/ict/english/Insight_Country_%20Report_Flanders_June2010.pdf. Accessed 2 November 2010

Dehue F, Bolman C, Völlink T (2008) Cyberbullying: Youngsters' experiences and parental perception. Cyberpsychol Behav 11:217–223

Diamanduros T, Downs D, Jenkins SJ (2008) The role of school psychologists in the assessment, prevention, and intervention of cyberbullying. Psychol in the Schools 45:693–704

Dooley JJ, Pyżalski J, Cross D (2009) Cyberbullying versus face-to-face bullying: a theoretical and conceptual review. Zeitschrift für Psychologie/J Psychol 217:182–188

Durrant P (2010) Cyberbullying: the legal and technical constraints for ISPs. Keynote presentation at the COST-workshop on legal issues regarding cyberbullying. Antwerp

Erentaite R, Bergman LR, Zukauskiene R (2012) Cross-contextual stability of bullying victimization: a person-oriented analysis of cyber and traditional bullying experiences among adolescents. Scand J Psychol 53:181–190

Haddon L, Stald G (2009) A comparative analysis of European press coverage of children and the internet. J Child Media 3:379–393

Heirman W, Walrave M (2008) Assessing concerns and issues about the mediation of technology in cyberbullying. Cyberpsychol J Psychosoc Res Cyberspace 2:1–12

Hinduja S, Patchin JW (2009) Bullying beyond the schoolyard. Preventing and responding to cyberbullying. Corwin Press, Thousand Oaks

Juvonen J, Gross EF (2008) Extending the school grounds? Bullying experiences in cyberspace. J Sch Health 78:496–505

Kowalski RW, Limber SP (2007) Electronic bullying among middle school students. J Adolesc Health 41:S22–S30

Kowalski RM, Limber SP, Agatston PW (2008) Cyber bullying. Bullying in the digital age. Blackwell, Malden

Lane DK (2011) Taking the lead on cyberbullying: why schools can and should protect students online. Iowa Law Rev 96:1791–1811

Langos C (2012) Cyberbullying: the CHALLENGE to define. Cyberpsychol Behav Soc Netw 15:285–289

Li Q (2006) Cyberbullying in schools. A research of gender differences. Sch Psychol Int 27:157–170

Li Q (2007) New bottle but old wine: a research of cyberbullying in schools. Comput Hum Behav 23:1777–1791

Lievens E, Dumortier J, Ryan PS (2006) The co-protection of minors in new media: a European approach to co-regulation. UC Davis J Juv Law Policy 10:97–151

Livingstone S, Helsper EJ (2008) Parental mediation of children's internet use. J Broadcast Electron Media 52:581–599

Livingstone S, Haddon L, Görzig A, Olafsson K (2011) Risks and safety on the internet. The perspective of European children. Full findings. EU kids online, London

Lynn R (2010) Constructing parenthood in moral panics of youth, digital media, and 'Sexting'. Paper presented at the 105th annual meeting of the American Sociological Association, Atlanta, Georgia

Machmutow K, Perren S, Sticca F, Alsaker FD (2012) Peer victimisation and depressive symptoms: can specific coping strategies buffer the negative impact of cybervictimisation? Emotional Behav Diffic 17(3–4):403–420

Marsh L, McGee R, Nada-Raja S, Williams S (2010) Brief report: text bullying and traditional bullying among New Zealand secondary school students. J Adolesc 33:237–240

Mascheroni G, Ponte C, Garmendia M, Garitaonandia C, Murru MF (2010) Comparing media coverage of online risks for children in southern European countries: Italy, Portugal and Spain. Int J Media Cult Polit 6:25–44

Mason KL (2008) Cyberbullying: a preliminary assessment for school personnel. Psychol Sch 45:323–348

Menesini E, Nocentini A (2009) Cyberbullying definition and measurement: some critical considerations. Zeitschrift für Psychologie/J Psychol 217:230–232

Menesini E, Nocentini A, Calussi P (2011) The measurement of cyberbullying: dimensional structure and relative item severity and discrimination. Cyberpsychol Behav Soc Netw 14:267–274

Mesch GS (2009) Parental mediation, online activities, and cyberbullying. Cyberpsychol Behav 12:387–393

Mishna F, Cook C, Gadalla T, Daciuk J, Solomon S (2010) Cyber bullying behaviors among middle and high school students. Am J Orthopsychiatr 80:362–374

Patchin JW, Hinduja S (2006) Bulies move beyond the schoolyard. A preliminary look at cyberbullying. Youth Violence Juv Justice 4:148–169

Price M, Dalgleish J (2010) Cyberbullying. Experiences, impacts and coping strategies as described by Australian young people. Youth Stud Aust 29:51–59

Raskauskas J, Stoltz AD (2007) Involvement in traditional and electronic bullying among adolescents. Dev Psychol 43:564–575

Salmivalli C, Pöyhönen V (2010) Cyberbullying in Finland. In: Li Q, Cross D, Smith PK (eds) Bully goes to the cyber playground: research of cyberbullying from an international perspective. Guilford, New York

Samara M, Smith PK (2008) How schools tackle bullying, and the use of whole school policies: changes over the last decade. Educ Psychol 28:663–676

Sharples M, Graber R, Harrison C, Logan K (2009) E-safety and web 2.0 for children aged 11. J comput assisted Learning 16(25):70–84

Shariff S (2008) Cyber-bullying. Issues and solutions for the school, the classroom and the home. Routledge, New York

Slonje R, Smith PK (2008) Cyberbullying: another main type of bullying? Scand J Psychol 49:147–154

Smith PK, Mahdavi J, Carvalho M, Fisher S, Russell S, Tippet N (2008) Cyberbullying: its nature and impact in secondary school pupils. J Child Psychol Psychiatry 49:376–385

Stefkovich JA, Crawford ER, Murphy MP (2010) Legal issues related to cyberbullying. In: Shariff S, Churchill AH (eds) Truths and myths of cyberbullying. Peter Lang, New York, pp 139–158

Thom K, Edwards B, Nakarada-Kordic I, McKenna B, O'Brien A, Nairn R (2011) Suicide online: portrayal of website-related suicide by the New Zealand media. New Media Soc 13(8):1355–1372. doi:10.1177/1461444811406521

Tokunaga RS (2010) Following you home from school: a critical review and synthesis of research on cyberbullying victimization. Comput Hum Behav 26:277–287

Vandebosch H, Van Cleemput K (2008) Defining cyberbullying: a qualitative research into the perceptions of youngsters. Cyberpsychology & Behavior 11:499–503

Vandebosch H, Van Cleemput K (2009) Cyberbullying among youngsters: profiles of bullies and victims. New Media Soc 11:1349–1371

Vandebosch H, Poels K (2012) Friendly ATTAC: virtuele scenario's tegen cyberpesten. In: Goossens F, Vermande M, van der Meulen M (eds) Pesten op school. Achtergronden en interventies. Boom/Lemma, Den Haag, pp 181–186

Vandebosch H, Poels K, Deboutte G (2011) Cyberpesten bij jongeren: een zaak voor de school? Welwijs 22:15–18

Vandebosch H, Beirens L, D'haese W, Wegge D, Pabian S (2012) Police actions with regard to cyberbullying: the Belgian case/Acciones policiales relacionadas con cyberbullying: el caso belga. Psicothema 24:646–652

Varjas K, Talley J, Meyers J, Parris L, Cutts H (2010) High school students' perceptions of motivations for cyberbullying: an exploratory study. West J Emerg Med 11:269–273

Vermeulen A, Vandebosch H (2012) Flemish press coverage on cyberbullying. Paper presented at the International conference on cyberbullying—COST IS0801. Paris

Parlement Vlaams (2009a) Beleidsnota Onderwijs. Flemish Government, Brussel

Parlement Vlaams (2009b) Beleidsnota Volksgezondheid & Gezin. Flemish Government, Brussel

Walrave M, Demoulin M, Heirman W, Van der Perre A (2009) Cyberpesten: pesten in bits & bytes. Observatorium van de Rechten op het Internet, Brussel

Wegge D, Vandebosch H, Eggermont S (2013) Offline netwerken, online pesten: Een social netwerkanalyse van cyberpesten in de schoolcontext. Tijdschrift voor communicatiewetenschap 1

Williams KR, Guerra NG (2007) Prevalence and predictors of internet bullying. J Adolesc Health 41:S14–S21

Ybarra ML (2004) Linkages between depressive symptomatology and internet harassment among young regular internet users. Cyberpsychology & Behav 7:247–257

Ybarra ML, Mitchell KJ (2004) Online aggressor/targets, aggressors, and targets: a comparison of associated youth characteristics. J Child Psychol Psychiatry 45:1308–1316

Part V
Online Grooming

Chapter 15
Regulating Online Sexual Solicitation: Towards Evidence-Based Policy and Regulation

Leontien M. van der Knaap and Colette M.K.C. Cuijpers

Contents

Leontien M. van der Knaap is Associate Professor at the International Victimology Institute Tilburg (INTERVICT) at Tilburg University. Colette Cuijpers is Assistant Professor at TILT—the Tilburg Institute for Law, Technology, and Society at Tilburg University.

L. M. van der Knaap (✉)
INTERVICT, Tilburg University, Tilburg, The Netherlands
e-mail: l.m.vdrknaap@tilburguniversity.edu

C.M.K.C. Cuijpers
TILT Tilburg Institute for Law, Technology, and Society, Tilburg University, Tilburg, The Netherlands

S. van der Hof et al. (eds.), *Minding Minors Wandering the Web: Regulating Online Child Safety*, Information Technology and Law Series 24, DOI: 10.1007/978-94-6265-005-3_15,

The challenge is to protect children from rare but harmful occurrences without limiting the opportunities of the majority.

(Livingstone et al. 2011a, p. 42)

15.1 Introduction

Recent research from the EU Kids Online Project shows that Internet use by children is increasingly individualised, privatised and mobile.[1] Some striking figures demonstrate the extensive Internet use by children. Aged 9–16, children spend 88 minutes per day online, on average. Half of the children who go online (49 %) do so in their bedroom, suggesting unsupervised Internet access.[2] In accordance with the rise in children's Internet use, concerns about the risks the Internet poses to children have increased. One major concern regards online sexual solicitation.[3] Often defined as 'requests to engage in sexual activities or sexual talk or to give personal sexual information that were unwanted or, whether wanted or not, were made by an adult'[4] many parents and policy makers also worry about adolescents' online sexual communication in general. Already a prominent concern on the agenda of policy makers, the attention for the phenomenon is further triggered by the increased number of children who own a mobile device for this trend is considered to bear extra risks in respect of online sexual solicitation.[5]

In response to public and policy concern, a number of legislative initiatives have been taken to curtail online sexual solicitation of children and youth. For Europe, the Lanzarote Convention is the first piece of regulation regarding online sexual solicitation.[6] In addition, numerous campaigns have been initiated to educate children about the risks of the Internet.

Even though concerns regarding the risks related to online sexual solicitation appear valid at face value, little is actually known about the consequences of online sexual solicitation or about how many children and youth actually come to harm as a result of online sexual solicitation.[7] This means that important

[1] Livingstone et al. 2011a.

[2] Livingstone et al. 2011a, p. 12.

[3] Eurobarometer 2008; Kierkegaard 2008.

[4] Mitchell et al. 2001, p. 3012.

[5] Livingstone et al. 2011a, p. 12; CHILDWISE Monitor Trends Report 2012, key trends; Europol Child Sexual Abuse Fact Sheet 2012, p. 5.

[6] Council of Europe Convention on the Protection of Children against Sexual Exploitation and Sexual Abuse (CETS 201). Available from: http://conventions.coe.int/Treaty/Commun/QueVoulezVous.asp?NT=201&CM=1&DF=&CL=ENG.

[7] Livingstone 2010; Livingstone and Haddon 2009.

regulatory initiatives are developed without substantiating empirical evidence of the risk and protective factors that bear relevance to the actual conduct of victims and offenders. From a regulatory perspective, this raises several questions regarding the European regulatory strategies adopted to curtail online sexual solicitation.

In this chapter, we first describe the criminalisation of online sexual solicitation in the Lanzarote Convention and Directive 2011/93/EC.[8] Subsequently, a review is presented of recent empirical research on the prevalence and nature of online sexual solicitation and we will analyse what is known about the interrelationship between online sexual solicitation and psychosocial development. In Sect. 15.4 the relation between the EU legislation and the existing empirical research is discussed. This discussion reveals the underlying assumptions, scope and proposed regulatory mechanisms within the EU legislation and how they can benefit from empirical substantiation. We conclude that the sharing of knowledge between the fields of social science and law is essential to develop promising regulation strategies for protecting youth from harmful consequences of online sexual solicitation, without overly curtailing normal sexual exploration by adolescents.

Before addressing existing regulation strategies to combat online sexual solicitation, it is important to make a note in respect of terminology. In the extant literature, in addition to online sexual solicitation, the term grooming is also used. Even though some scholars differentiate between grooming and online sexual solicitation, in a sense that grooming is a narrower concept reflecting the criminalisation of certain behaviour as described in Article 23 of the Lanzarote Convention,[9] we do not make this distinction. We will not refer to grooming, but use the term 'online sexual solicitation' in the broadest sense. We are perfectly aware that just part of what constitutes online sexual solicitation is criminalised in the Lanzarote Convention. However, as will be discussed in the next paragraphs, the scope of criminalisation of online sexual solicitation is one of the regulatory issues in need of empirical substantiation. Moreover, public concern is not limited to grooming but also extends to receiving (and sending) sexual images and messages.

---

[8] Directive 2011/92/EU of the European Parliament and of the Council of 13 December 2011 on combating the sexual abuse and sexual exploitation of children and child pornography, and replacing Council Framework Decision 2004/68/JHA, OJ 2011 L 335 of 2011-12-17, pp. 1–17. Corrigendum to Directive 2011/92/EU of the European Parliament and of the Council of 13 December 2011 on combating the sexual abuse and sexual exploitation of children and child pornography, and replacing Council Framework Decision 2004/68/JHA, OJ 2012 L 18 of 2012-01-21, p. 7. This corrigendum states that the Directive is numbered Directive 2011/93/EU instead of 2011/92/EU. Directive available from: http://eur-lex.europa.eu/LexUriServ/LexUriServ.do?uri=OJ:L:2011:335:0001:01:EN:HTML.

[9] Kool 2011, pp. 48–49.

15.2 Present Regulation Strategies Targeting Online Sexual Solicitation

Since the adoption of the Joint action to combat trafficking in human beings and sexual exploitation of children in 1997, both the Council of Europe and the European Union have launched several initiatives to strengthen judicial cooperation,[10] as well as to harmonise substantive law, in the field of child protection against sexual abuse and sexual exploitation. In 2001 the Cybercrime Convention was adopted,[11] and in 2003 the EU Council Framework Decision on 'combating the sexual exploitation of children and child pornography'.[12] Even though both fall outside the scope of this chapter, as online sexual solicitation is not specifically addressed, these documents are important from the perspective of procedural law. The first EU legal document to explicitly criminalise online sexual solicitation of children is the 2007 Lanzarote Convention.[13] Article 23 of the Lanzarote Convention states: 'The intentional proposal, through information and communication technologies, of an adult to meet a child for the purpose of engaging in sexual activities or producing child pornography, where this proposal has been followed by material acts leading to such a meeting.' As the Council of Europe Convention is only binding upon those Members that ratify it, and the rate of ratification remained low, the EU in 2011 decided to adopt Directive 2011/93/EU.[14] In general, the Directive is in line with the Lanzarote Convention. However, some minor differences are interesting in view of the issues we want to raise in this chapter. We will focus our discussion of these documents to the way in which regulatory strategies are addressed and, of course, the provisions relevant to online sexual solicitation.

Directive 2011/93/EU will replace the earlier mentioned Framework Decision of 2003. Article 6 of the Directive criminalises online sexual solicitation:

> 1. Member States shall take the necessary measures to ensure that the following intentional conduct is punishable: the proposal, by means of information and communication technology, by an adult to meet a child who has not reached the age of sexual

---

[10] E.g. Joint Action 2008/976/JHA and the Council Decision of 29 May 2000 to combat child pornography on the Internet. Available from: http://europa.eu/legislation_summaries/justice_freedom_security/fight_against_trafficking_in_human_beings/l33138_en.htm.

[11] Convention on Cybercrime, CETS No. 185. Available from: http://conventions.coe.int/Treaty/en/Treaties/Html/185.htm.

[12] Council framework Decision 2004/68/JHA of 22 December 2003 on combating the sexual exploitation of children and child pornography, OJ L013, 20/01/2004, pp. 0044–0048.

[13] Council of Europe Convention on the Protection of Children against Sexual Exploitation and Sexual Abuse (CETS 201). Available from: http://conventions.coe.int/Treaty/Commun/QueVoulezVous.asp?NT=201&CM=1&DF=&CL=ENG.

[14] The Directive must be implemented ultimately December 2013.

consent, for the purpose of committing any of the offences referred to in Article 3(4) and Article 5(6), where that proposal was followed by material acts leading to such a meeting, shall be punishable by a maximum term of imprisonment of at least 1 year.

2. Member States shall take the necessary measures to ensure that an attempt, by means of information and communication technology, to commit the offences provided for in Article 5(2) and (3) by an adult soliciting a child who has not reached the age of sexual consent to provide child pornography depicting that child is punishable.

Both the Lanzarote Convention and the Directive define a child as anyone younger than 18 years of age. However, by referring to the 'age of sexual consent', the Directive leaves the actual scope of application to the discretion of the Member States, as the age of sexual consent is defined as: "(...) the age below which, in accordance with national law, it is prohibited to engage in sexual activities with a child". This relates to the fact that depending on culture, but also over time, perceptions of decency, but also perceptions in respect of when and how minors are deemed to be able to consent to sexual activity, change.[15]

From the preamble of the Lanzarote Convention, it becomes clear that the Convention is based on the assumption that children and youth are harmed by online sexual solicitation. This assumption also lies at the basis of EU Directive 2011/93/EU. Even though eminent in relation to actual child sexual abuse and exploitation, with regard to the field of online sexual solicitation several questions can be raised regarding this assumption, as well as to the scope of criminalisation of online sexual solicitation, in both the Lanzarote Convention and the Directive. The scope is limited to the act of online sexual solicitation by adults, but how many children actually receive sexual messages from adults? Furthermore, the premise underlying criminalisation is that receiving sexual messages online is detrimental to children in general, but what do children actually say about the harm that online sexual solicitation causes them? And what do we really know about the consequences for children's psychosocial development? Finally, the general nature of the criminalisation carries the presumption that all children are at risk, but which children are really at risk of receiving (aggressive) online sexual solicitation?

Before assessing underlying presumptions, scope and regulatory strategies within the Lanzarote Convention and Directive 2011/93/EU in view of online sexual solicitation further, we will first discuss the empirical evidence relating to three aspects of existing regulation strategies: (1) the focus on adults and strangers, (2) the assumption that all children are at risk and (3) the assumption that children are harmed by online sexual solicitation. With regard to the latter assumption, a distinction will be made between short-term and long-term consequences of receiving sexual messages online.

[15] Koops 2009, p. 67.

15.3 Youth and Online Sexual Solicitation

15.3.1 Prevalence and Nature of Online Sexual Solicitation

A number of studies have reported on the prevalence of online sexual solicitation. For instance, in a nationally representative telephone survey among 1,500 10 to 17-year-old U.S. Internet users conducted in 2005, 13 % of youth reported unwanted sexual solicitation in the previous year.[16] A study among British 9 to 17-year-old youth reports that 23 % of them ever received unwanted sexual comments over the Internet[17] and in a recent study among Dutch adolescents aged 12–17 years, Baumgartner, Valkenburg and Peter reported six-month prevalence rates of unwanted online sexual solicitation of 5.6 % for male adolescents and 19.1 % for female adolescents.[18] Similar results were reported by Helweg-Larsen, Schütt and Larsen in their study among Danish adolescents (aged 14–17 years): 5.4 % of boys and 16.2 % of girls reported having received online sexual propositions from an unknown person, albeit in the previous year.[19] A recent Swedish survey, conducted in 2010, found that 26 % of 12 to 16-year-old adolescents had ever talked about sex with someone on the Internet.[20] A third of these conversations were with total strangers (8 % of the total sample). The most recent figures on the prevalence of online sexual solicitation that we are aware of have been reported by Kerstens and De Graaf.[21] Collected between January and April 2011, these figures come from a sample of 6,299 Dutch youth (aged 8–18 years) who completed an online questionnaire on a range of aspects of their online behaviour. One in five children (19.2 %) had ever received online requests to engage in sexual activities or sexual talk or to give personal sexual information. The majority of these online requests to engage in sexual talk or sexual activities were done by peers (70.8 %) and a small subset of 7.3 % was sent by someone who was at least five years older than the respondent. A quarter of the adolescents who ever received such a request, reported that this request was sent by someone they did not know in person but only communicated with on the Internet (25.4 %). This percentage is higher among younger adolescents and drops with age: Older adolescents (aged 15 years and older) more often receive an online request about sex or sexuality from someone they also know offline. These are mainly friends, dating partners or peers they know from school.

As a result of differences in definitions, sampling strategies and the exact wording of questions, it is difficult to compare the results from individual studies.

---

[16] Wolak et al. 2006.

[17] Livingstone 2006.

[18] Baumgartner et al. 2010.

[19] Helweg-Larsen et al. 2012.

[20] Medierådet 2010.

[21] Kerstens and De Graaf 2012.

Large-scale research in 25 European countries,[22] however, reported prevalence rates that were fairly similar to those reported in the separate studies discussed in the previous paragraph. Livingstone and her colleagues found that 15 % of European children aged 11–16 years old have seen or received sexual messages on the Internet in the 12 months preceding their study.[23] Prevalence rates ranged from 4 % for Italian youth to 22 % for Romanian youth, but between-country differences were relatively minor with about two-thirds of the countries' prevalence rates ranging between 14 and 20 %. Most common among these experiences is being sent a sexual message, while only 2 % of all European adolescents aged 11–16 report that they have been asked to talk about sexual acts with someone on the Internet. An equal percentage reported to have received a request to show a photo or video of their genitals in the previous 12 months.

Despite societal concern about the risk that online sexual solicitation might lead to sexual abuse in real life, research describes a rather different reality. With regard to receiving an invitation to meet in person with someone a youngster met online, Kerstens and De Graaf report that 15.4 % of their respondents had received such a request in the previous year.[24] One in ten of these invitations was sexually motivated (for ethical reasons, this response option was not provided to primary school aged children). Instead, many invitations were intended to engage in shared leisure activities, such as gaming, shopping or seeing a movie (44.1 %). Other, perhaps more ambiguously phrased, response options that were frequently ticked included 'because the other person likes me' (39.8 %) and 'because the other person wants to date me' (14.3 %). Although not all respondents who received an invitation to meet in person knew the age or gender of the person inviting them, the majority of invitations was sent by a peer (75 %). Of the respondents who received an invitation to meet in person with someone a youngster met online, Kerstens and De Graaf reported that two in five agreed to meet the other person (40.6 %). Most respondents who agreed to a meeting did so on the basis of mutual consent. A small group, however, felt forced to comply or was threatened by the other person (2.3 % of all youth who agreed to a meeting). Approximately 1 in 20 youngsters who agreed to a meeting reported that this meeting was a negative experience (5.6 %). This negative experience was caused by the other person wanting to have sex for 5 of the 22 respondents who reported such a negative experience. Each of these five respondents were boys and two of them reported to have been forced to have sex. Although these two represent two victimised adolescents who should not have been victimised, they also constitute an extremely small proportion of the entire group of respondents (0.03 %).

Taking a different approach to this issue, Wolak, Finkelhor and Mitchell studied the characteristics of Internet-initiated sex crimes against minors.[25] They

---

[22] Livingstone et al. 2011b.

[23] Livingstone et al. 2011b.

[24] Kerstens and De Graaf 2012.

[25] Wolak et al. 2004, 2008.

concluded that the majority of these crimes involved offenders who were considerably older than their victims but who could not be characterised as true paedophiles, as their victims were mainly adolescents. Furthermore, most offenders did not deceive their victims about their age or sexual intentions. This is in accordance with results reported by Noll, Shenk, Barnes and Putnam who found that adolescents who were more likely to agree to offline meetings had also experienced relatively high rates of online sexual advances.[26] According to these authors, this would suggest that "such adolescents may have some inkling as to the potential sexual agenda of offline encounters".[27] As a matter of fact, in synthesising their results, Wolak et al. concluded that offenders who use the Internet to meet and groom a victim could not be labelled as strangers, because these offenders typically spend a lot of time building a relationship with their victim.[28]

15.3.2 Risk Factors for Receiving Online Sexual Solicitation

As is clear from the previous paragraph, a substantial group of children and adolescents never receive requests to engage in sexual activities or sexual talk or to give personal sexual information on the Internet. From a regulatory point of view, the question should then be which children are at risk of receiving online sexual solicitation. There is a growing body of literature on the relation between online solicitation and adolescent risk-taking behaviour.[29] This research indicates that posting personal information, by itself, does not make youth particularly vulnerable, nor do social networking sites appear to have increased the risk of victimisation. Rather, patterns of risky behaviour make youth vulnerable, including talking online with unknown people about sex, sending personal information (e.g. name, telephone number, pictures) to unknown people and visiting chat rooms.[30] Wolak and her colleagues warn, however, that youth who engage in these types of online interactions are not typical adolescent Internet users. Most young people do not interact online in such ways,[31] while young people who are most at risk of receiving online sexual solicitations appear to engage in a wide range of risky behaviour, both online and offline.[32]

Along similar lines, research has also shown that children who have been victimised offline are significantly more likely to experience online sexual solicitation. For instance, Noll, Shenk, Barnes and Putnam found that adolescent girls

[26] Noll et al. 2009.

[27] Noll et al. 2009, p. 1082.

[28] Wolak et al. 2004.

[29] Baumgartner et al. 2010; Mitchell et al. 2008; Wolak et al. 2008.

[30] Wolak et al. 2008.

[31] Ybarra et al. 2007.

[32] Wolak et al. 2008.

who have experienced childhood abuse were significantly more likely than non-abused girls to have experienced online sexual advances.[33] Moreover, they were also more likely to have met someone offline whom they previously only knew online. Research by Livingstone and her colleagues showed that children who experience more psychological problems are more vulnerable to receive sexual messages on the Internet.[34]

15.3.3 Youngsters' Assessment of and Coping with Online Sexual Solicitation

Several studies that asked whether receiving online sexual requests affected youth have reported that, in fact, a (significant) minority of children say that they were upset or bothered. Livingstone and her colleagues report that 25 % of children who saw or received sexual messages were bothered by this.[35] They found that girls were more likely to be bothered than boys, and that younger children were more often bothered than older adolescents. In addition, children from lower socio-economic families were more likely to be bothered than children from medium or higher socio-economic families. However, being bothered is not synonymous to being upset: Nearly half of all children who were bothered by seeing or receiving sexual messages reported that they were very or fairly upset. The other half was either a bit upset (47 %) or not upset at all (7 %).

Research by Mitchell et al. showed that 25 % of solicited youth reported high levels of distress after solicitation incidents with distress being more common among younger (10–13 years) youth and those experiencing an aggressive solicitation.[36] Similarly, De Graaf and Vanwesenbeeck report that youth are not easily upset by unwanted sexual solicitation on the Internet: Even youth who indicate they experienced an incident of sexual solicitation that they did not like, are not necessarily upset by these experiences.[37] According to De Graaf and Vanwesenbeeck, whether or not youth are upset by unwanted online sexual solicitation depends on their reactions to the incident: When youth feel they adequately dealt with the solicitation, for instance by ignoring a sexual request, they less often report being upset. Furthermore, even upsetting incidents are rarely discussed with others because youth do not regard their experiences as anything worth talking about to other people.[38]

---

[33] Noll et al. 2009.

[34] Livingstone et al. 2011a.

[35] Livingstone et al. 2011b.

[36] Mitchell et al. 2001.

[37] De Graaf and Vanweesenbeeck 2006.

[38] Livingstone 2010.

In the study by Kerstens and De Graaf, the majority of adolescents who ever received an online sexual request, rated these requests as 'normal' or 'fun'.[39] Slightly less than one third of the respondents who ever received such a request, reported that they experienced this as something negative or unpleasant (31.8 %). However, almost half of the girls negatively evaluated the experiences (47.9 %) and only a small minority of girls rate their experiences as 'fun' (9.2 %). Boys were more likely to positively evaluate receiving online sexual requests (26.2 %) and the majority of boys considered receiving those requests as normal (57.0 %). Younger respondents more often than older respondents said that receiving such a request was a negative experience and a similar relation existed with educational level: Respondents in higher level education less often reported receiving the requests as negative. In addition, Kerstens and De Graaf found that youth's behaviour online was significantly associated with negative assessments of online experiences: More frequent use of instant messaging, compulsive Internet behaviour and feeling less inhibited while being online were all related to more negative experiences. Finally, adolescents with lower self-control and decreased psychosocial well-being more often reported being upset by receiving online requests of a sexual nature. These findings are in line with the results reported by Livingstone and her colleagues who also found that children with little self-efficacy or psychological problems felt more intensively upset.[40]

When asked by Kerstens and De Graaf how they responded to online sexual solicitation, almost half of the children who ever received such a request replied that they only commented on the things they wanted to talk about (45.9 %).[41] There is a strong effect for age in this regard: With increasing age, the percentage of respondents who only discuss what they want to increases. Younger children more often 'de-friend' someone who sends them online sexual requests, while older respondents rarely do so. Almost a quarter of the adolescents who had received an online sexual request, answered all questions they were asked, with a clear effect for gender: Boys more often than girls were willing to reply to every question or request. According to Kerstens and De Graaf, this gender difference is probably related to the gender difference in the evaluation of the requests (with boys more often positively labelling their experience).

Kerstens and De Graaf also asked respondents who replied to online sexual requests they received about their reasons to reply. One third of these youth responded to the requests because they liked the person who sent the request (33.6 %) and an equal share of respondents indicated that they thought it was fun or exciting to reply to the request they received (33.7 %). Respondents were allowed to give more than one reason so there is no way to distinguish unique groups. About a quarter replied because they were bored and one in ten did not want to appear a bore. Only a small minority of youth replied because they felt

[39] Kerstens and De Graaf 2012.

[40] Livingstone et al. 2011a.

[41] Kerstens and De Graaf 2012.

forced or threatened by the one who sent the request (2.1 %). What is worrying, though, is that negative reasons for replying, specifically not wanting to appear a bore and feeling forced or threatened, were quite prevalent among young children (8–10 years old): 36.4 and 18.2 %, respectively, of young children who ever responded to sexual requests did so because of these reasons. These figures, however, are based on a very small number of respondents and should therefore be interpreted with great caution. Moreover, we should keep in mind that young children often refused to reply to a sexual message and that many of them went on to block or de-friend the sender.

Specifically focusing on children's coping responses when they feel upset after exposure to online risks, Livingstone and her colleagues distinguish between fatalistic, communicative and proactive coping strategies.[42] They conclude that younger children were more likely to use fatalistic coping strategies such as hoping the problem would go away or not using the Internet for a while. Older adolescents were more likely to talk to someone if they were upset about sexual images (communicative strategy) or to block the sender (proactive strategy). Boys were more likely than girls to hope upsetting sexual messages will go away, while girls more often talked to somebody about online harms and were more likely to adopt proactive strategies to deal with unwanted online experiences. Not surprisingly, children higher in self-efficacy more often adopted a proactive approach and tried to fix the problem themselves, while children lower in self-efficacy preferred fatalistic responses. This was also true for children with more psychological difficulties.

15.3.4 Consequences for Children's Psychosocial Development

Despite the existing research on prevalence and adolescent online risk-taking behaviours, to date there is little empirical research available on the effects of online sexual solicitation on youth.[43] There is some correlational evidence that online sexual solicitation is associated with depressive symptomatology,[44] substance abuse[45] and post-traumatic stress[46] but there are no studies that prospectively link online victimisation of sexual solicitation to psychosocial well-being.[47] As a result, it remains unclear whether victimisation is causally related to

42 Livingstone et al. 2011a.

43 Livingstone 2010.

44 Mitchell et al. 2007.

45 Mitchell et al. 2007.

46 Wells and Mitchell 2007.

47 Sumter et al. 2012.

psychosocial problems in youth or whether, for example, pre-existing mental health problems add to the risk of online victimisation.

15.4 Filling the Gaps in Empirical Knowledge

While it is difficult to compare separate studies because of differences in the exact formulation of questions as well as differences in samples, the available research on the prevalence and nature of online sexual solicitation clearly shows that online sexual solicitation of youth may be less wide-spread than public anxiety may lead people to believe. Moreover, although receiving sexual messages and requests certainly is a part of everyday life for a substantial minority of youth, most requests are sent by peers and in the majority of cases the sender is also known to youth in the offline context. A large proportion of youth who receive such messages feel free to choose whether or not to respond to online sexual solicitation and if they do, most of them do so because they liked the other person or thought it was fun or exciting to do so. In addition, youth who most often receive requests of a sexual nature are most likely to rate these experiences as positive. A minority of children are upset by receiving online sexual requests and an even smaller group of children feels forced to respond to online sexual solicitation. This, of course, is a group policy makers should be especially worried about, but more knowledge about who constitutes this group is necessary. There is a clear relation with gender, age and educational level, but as yet we do not know enough to ensure that regulatory policies sufficiently target the most vulnerable groups.

Even though the EU Kids Online project, as well as the Online Grooming project, have clarified several aspects of the phenomenon of online sexual solicitation and communication, important gaps in the existing knowledge still remain.[48] To fill in these gaps is especially important as youth development is increasingly influenced by interactions and experiences in online environments. In this respect, research that contributes to the understanding of how to create a safer online environment for youth is beneficial to society as a whole. Brown and Bobkowski rightfully state that: '[…] to fully understand the process of media effects on adolescents, longer-term longitudinal studies that include accurate measures of media use as well as other contextual and individual difference variables are necessary'.[49] Longitudinal studies can fill an important gap in social-scientific knowledge on the effects of online sexual solicitation of minors by offering insight into negative consequences and risk and protective factors for experiencing negative effects of online sexual solicitation.

---

[48] See www2.lse.ac.uk/media@lse/research/EUKidsOnline/Home.aspx and www.european-online-grooming-project.com/.

[49] Brown and Bobkowski 2011, p. 107.

15.4.1 Linking Regulation and Empirical Knowledge

Longitudinal research into the developmental consequences of online sexual solicitation will not only enrich psychological research, but will also be beneficial in view of the assessment and development of regulation strategies. There is a strong correlation between behaviour and regulation. Regulation tries to curb certain behaviour, while at the same time the way in which people behave, and how they respond to regulation, is important information in the development of regulation strategies. In order for such strategies to be effective in practice, they should be based upon factual evidence of risks and protective factors within the realm of the behaviour to be regulated, in our case being online sexual solicitation. In order to prevent harm related to online sexual solicitation, it is necessary to gain insight into the forms of online sexual solicitation that actually constitute a risk of harm, what type(s) of harm may be caused and the characteristics of youth who are at risk of suffering harm.

Even without an in-depth analysis, three aspects of the current EU legislation can already be mentioned for which a stronger connection to existing and future empirical evidence will be valuable: (1) overregulation, (2) underregulation (3) and the type of regulation to be deployed.

In principle, Article 23 of the Lanzarote Convention applies to all solicitations by adults of minors. This implies that a 20-year-old who contacts a 17-year-old could be committing an offence (depending on the national implementation—the Convention leaves room for exceptions), whereas this behaviour could simply be part of normative sexual development. Similarly, authors like Ost[50] and Gooren[51] warn against the danger of overprotection and overregulation, as adolescents can engage in autonomous sexual expression, and too far-reaching criminalisation of such behaviour can be counterproductive for child protection. Koops remarks that there is a very delicate line between what constitutes healthy sexual exploration and what constitutes a crime because a boundary of age, consent or abuse of power has been crossed. As mentioned before, perceptions of decency can differ over time and depending on culture. The same holds true for perceptions regarding when and how minors are deemed to be able to consent to sexual activity.[52] In these respects, the regulatory strategy adopted in the Lanzarote Convention carries the impression of overregulation—constraining normative sexual development—based on an unsubstantiated and one-sided view of the detrimental effects that online sexual solicitation is presumed to have upon all minors alike. Even though the Directive leaves some room to the Member States to decide where to draw the boundaries of age of sexual consent—an important aspect to take into account when discussing possible overregulation—empirical knowledge on the conditions

[50] Ost 2009.

[51] Gooren 2011.

[52] Koops 2009, p. 67.

for actual harm to occur and on the group of youth who are vulnerable to harm would substantially increase the relevance of existing regulatory initiatives.

While these regulatory initiatives require empirical research with respect to possible overregulation, at the same time, research should consider the question whether the regulatory strategy might be too restrictive given the requirements to be fulfilled in order for behaviour to qualify as criminalised online sexual solicitation. First, criminalisation is restricted to those situations where a physical meeting is intended and prepared. This may be deficient, if the act of solicitation itself has negative consequences for victims: Empirical research will have to shed light on the forms of online sexual solicitation that constitute actual harm. Second, criminalisation will only be effective if it is enforced in practice, and this is particularly difficult in that it requires intervention after a meeting has been planned but before the meeting actually takes place.[53] In these respects, the regulatory strategy carries the impression of underregulation.

In relation to the third aspect, the type of regulation strategy, it is important to note that regulatory theory suggests that rule setting is only one of the available modalities to curb (harmful) behaviour. Besides legal rules, Lessig distinguishes between social norms, markets and architecture as modalities of regulation.[54] A suitable framework for discussing regulatory strategies, which can involve any of these regulatory modalities, to address online sexual solicitation is the ‘situational crime prevention framework’ developed by Clarke.[55] The object of situational crime prevention is to reduce crime by removing the opportunity to carry it out.[56] Within Clarke’s framework, four major strategies are defined to minimise the occurrence of crime: increasing the effort; increasing the risk; removing excuses; and reducing the rewards. Within these four broad strategies, several options can be specified; for example, reducing rewards can be done through target removal, identifying property, removing inducements and rule setting.[57] This framework of four broad strategies to minimise crime provides a useful heuristic to discuss regulation strategies for online sexual solicitation, to put into perspective the potential overregulation and underregulation of the Lanzarote Convention. For instance, empirical knowledge regarding the characteristics of youth who are at risk of experiencing harm may inform secondary prevention strategies such as Internet safety education programmes and as such facilitate a form of target removal. Along similar lines, such knowledge may also be used to sensitise practitioners who work with vulnerable youth to recognise potential risks in their clients’ online behaviour. As a way of increasing the risk, one could consider

[53] Koops 2009.

[54] Lessig 1999.

[55] Clarke 1995, 1997.

[56] Felson and Boba 2010, p. 177.

[57] Clarke 1997; see also Felson and Boba 2010.

removing from the legislation the legal requirement that actual contact needs to have taken place between the 'solicitor' and the victim—provided that social scientific findings substantiate our concern of underregulation and reveals that a meeting is no necessary condition for harm to arise.

In line with the Lanzarote Convention, Directive 2011/93/EU suggests a whole array of measures to be taken by the Member States such as preventive measures, specialised authorities and co-ordinating bodies, protective measures and assistance to victims. However, there is no direction on prioritising the measures, the mutual relation between the measures or positive and negative factors of the measures in relation to actual prevention of child sexual abuse. Also, no guidance is given in view of what measures best to explore in relation to specific crimes. Empirical research can provide such guidance by providing answers to the question which youth are at risk of experiencing what forms of harm from which types of online sexual solicitation.

15.5 Conclusion: The Need for Future Research

Given the reasons to question the general assumption underlying current legislation that online sexual solicitation should be generically governed because it harms children and adolescents, research on the effects of online sexual solicitation on adolescents is called for. Furthermore, considering the possible overregulation as well as underregulation offered by the Lanzarote Convention and Directive 2011/93/EU, a discussion is needed regarding possible regulation strategies that might lead to a more effective way of protecting youth from negative consequences of online sexual solicitation. In order to achieve insights into risk and protective factors, research should be carried out regarding the interrelationship between online sexual solicitation and psychosocial development. Such studies should identify what youth experience as distressing incidents of online sexual solicitation. Where do they deem the boundary to be between normal sexual exploration and criminal behaviour? Is there a general understanding or do differences exist in view of the type of youth (culture, age, sex etc.)? In other words, more insight is needed regarding which youth experience harm as a result of online sexual solicitation and what the negative consequences are for them as a result of online sexual solicitation. In this respect it is necessary to identify the risk and protective factors that are associated with the chance of youth experiencing harm from online sexual solicitation.

Subsequently, the results of the research proposed above should form the basis for analysing possible regulation strategies that might lead to a more effective way of protecting youth from negative consequences of online sexual solicitation, while at the same time avoiding curtailing the normal development of youth's sexuality.

References

Baumgartner SE, Valkenburg PM, Peter J (2010) Unwanted online sexual solicitation and risky sexual online behavior across the lifespan. J Appl Dev Psychol 31:439–447

Brown JD, Bobkowski PS (2011) Older and newer media: Patterns of use and effects on adolescents' health and well-being. J Res Adolesc 21:95–113

CHILDWISE Monitor Trends Report 2012 (2012) http://www.childwise.co.uk/childwise-published-research-detail.asp?PUBLISH=53. Accessed 22 Sept 2012

Clarke RV (1995) Situational crime prevention. In: Tonry M, Farrington DP (eds) Crime and justice. Building a safer society: strategic approaches towards crime prevention. Chicago University Press, Chicago, pp 91–150

Clarke RV (ed) (1997) Situational crime prevention: successful case studies, 2nd edn. Criminal Justice Press, Monsey

De Graaf H, Vanweesenbeeck I (2006) Seks is een game: gewenste en ongewenste seksuele ervaringen van jongeren op internet. Rutgers Nisso Groep, Utrecht

Eurobarometer 2008 (2010) How do young Europeans use online and mobile technologies? http://ec.europa.eu/information_society/activities/sip/surveys/index_en.htm. Accessed 10 Sept 2010

Europol Child Sexual Abuse Fact Sheet 2012 (2012) https://www.europol.europa.eu/content/publication/child-sexual-exploitation-fact-sheet-2012-1727. Accessed 22 Sept 2012

Felson M, Boba R (2010) Crime and everyday life, 4th edn. Sage, Thousand Oaks

Gooren JCW (2011) Deciphering the ambiguous menace of sexuality for the innocence of childhood. Crit Criminol 19(1):29–42. doi: 10.1007/S10b12-010-g102-2

Helweg-Larsen K, Schütt N, Larsen HB (2012) Predictors and protective factors for adolescent internet victimization: results from a 2008 nationwide Danish youth survey. Acta Paediatr 101:533–539

Kerstens J, de Graaf H (2012) Jongeren en online seksuele activiteiten. In: Kerstens J, Stol W (eds) Jeugd en cybersafety. Online slachtoffer- en daderschap onder Nederlandse jongeren. Boom Lemma uitgevers, Den Haag, pp 135–179

Kierkegaard S (2008) Cybering, online grooming and ageplay. Comput Law Secur Rep 24(1):41–55. doi: 10.106/j.clsr.2007.11.004

Kool R (2011) Prevention by all means? A legal comparison of the criminalization of online grooming and its enforcement. Utrecht L Rev 7(3):46–69. http://ssrn.com/abstract=1949762. Accessed 22 Sept 2012

Koops B-J (2009) Sex, kids, and crime in cyberspace: some reflections on crossing boundaries. In: Lodder AR, Oskamp A (eds) Caught in the cybercrime act. Kluwer Juridisch, Deventer, pp 63–76

Lessig L (1999) Code and other laws of cyberspace. Basic Books, New York

Livingstone S (2006) Drawing conclusions from new media research: reflections and puzzles regarding children's experience of the internet. Inf Soc 22:219–230

Livingstone S (2010) eYouth: (Future) policy implications: reflections on online risk, harm and vulnerability. http://eprints.lse.ac.uk/27849/. Accessed 12 Aug 2010

Livingstone S, Haddon L (2009) EU Kids online: final report 2009. www2.lse.ac.uk/media@lse/research/EUKidsOnline/EU%20Kids%20Online%20reports.aspx. Accessed 22 Sept 2012

Livingstone S, Haddon L, Görzig A, Ólafsson K (2011a) EU kids online final. www2.lse.ac.uk/media@lse/research/EUKidsOnline/EU%20Kids%20Online%20reports.aspx

Livingstone S, Haddon L, Görzig A, Ólafsson K (2011b) Risks and safety on the internet: the perspective of European children. Full findings. www2.lse.ac.uk/media@lse/research/EUKidsOnline/EU%20Kids%20Online%20reports.aspx

Medierådet (The Swedish Media Council) Ungar och medier (2010) Fakta om barns och ungas användning och upplevelser av medier [Young persons and media 2008. Facts about childrens' and young person's use and experience of media]. The Swedish Media Council, Stockholm

Mitchell KJ, Finkelhor D, Wolak J (2001) Risk factors for and impact of online sexual solicitation of youth. J Am Med Assoc 285:3011–3014

Mitchell KJ, Ybarra M, Finkelhor D (2007) The relative importance of online victimization in understanding depression, delinquency, and substance use. Child Malt 12:314–324

Mitchell KJ, Wolak J, Finkelhor D (2008) Are blogs putting youth at risk for online sexual solicitation or harassment? Child Abuse Negl 32:277–294

Noll JG, Shenk CE, Barnes JE, Putnam KT (2009) Childhood abuse, avatar choices, and other risk factors associated with Internet-initiated victimization of adolescent girls. Pediatrics 123:e1078–e1083

Ost S (2009) Child pornography and sexual grooming: legal and societal responses. Cambridge University Press, Cambridge

Sumter SR, Baumgartner SE, Valkenburg PM, Peter J (2012) Developmental trajectories of peer victimization: off-line and online experiences during adolescence. J Adolesc Health 50:607–613

Wells M, Mitchell KJ (2007) Youth sexual exploitation on the Internet: DSM-IV diagnoses and gender differences in co-occurring mental health issues. Child Adolesc Soc Work J 24:235–260

Wolak J, Finkelhor D, Mitchell KJ (2004) Internet-initiated sex crimes against minors: implications for prevention based on findings from a national study. J Adolesc Health 35:424.e11–424.e11

Wolak J, Mitchell KJ, Finkelhor D (2006) Online victimization of youth: five years later. National Center for Missing and Exploited Children, Alexandria. www.missingkids.com/en_US/publications/NC167.pdf. Accessed 22 Sept 2009

Wolak J, Finkelhor D, Mitchell KJ, Ybarra ML (2008) Online 'predators' and their victims: myths, realities, and implications for prevention and treatment. Am Psychol 63:111–128

Ybarra ML, Mitchell KJ, Finkelhor D, Wolak J (2007) Internet prevention messages: Targeting the right online behaviors. Arch Pediatr Adolsec Med 16(12):138–145

Chapter 16
Protecting Children from the Risk of Harm? A Critical Review of the Law's Response(s) to Online Child Sexual Grooming in England and Wales

Jamie-Lee Mooney

Contents

16.1 Introduction

The increased utilisation and integration of communication via online communication technology[1] in society has facilitated opportunities for individuals to gain access to children for sexual abuse.[2] This chapter analyses the growing recognition

---

Jamie-Lee Mooney is a Lecturer in Law at the University of Liverpool.

---

[1] Online communication will be referred to in this analysis as opposed to communication via the 'Internet', as online communication encompasses all modern communication processes that use Internet mediums in order to work. It is acknowledged that this excludes text messages from the scope of this analysis but includes email, chat rooms, social networking sites, games consoles (live), 3G technology, websites and message boards.
[2] Wolak et al. 2008, p. 111.

J.-L. Mooney (✉)
Liverpool University Law School, Liverpool, UK
e-mail: Jamielee.Mooney@liverpool.ac.uk

S. van der Hof et al. (eds.), *Minding Minors Wandering the Web: Regulating Online Child Safety*, Information Technology and Law Series 24, DOI: 10.1007/978-94-6265-005-3_16,

of the prevalence of online child sexual grooming[3] in a context that explores how online communication can accelerate progression through the grooming stages, with a view to establishing to what extent these forms of communication have increased the potential risk of harm to children. Ultimately, this chapter demonstrates that online technology makes it easier for individuals to groom children and thus increases the chances of successfully grooming a child, i.e. gaining access for sexual abuse.[4]

In the early 2000s, the phenomenon of 'grooming' attracted much attention in the UK[5] following calls from child protection agencies[6] for legal acknowledgment of the significant risk of harm posed to children by grooming online in particular. The increased societal awareness of grooming was further reflected in judicial[7] recognition of the associated 'harms' of grooming behaviour, leading to the announcement and enactment of an offence related to grooming under Section 15 of the Sexual Offences Act 2003 (SOA). The principal aim of this chapter is to explore the current limitations of Section 15 offence in relation to grooming. The analysis will emphasise that the exemption of the early stages of the grooming process from the offence's scope has exacerbated the lack of clarity and understanding about this phenomenon.

The chapter will also consider two particular examples of grooming, which fall outside Section 15's scope. First, the discussion will focus on 'third party grooming'. This term is employed to refer to a 'form' of grooming arising where the grooming is directed at a child (B) with intent to subsequently facilitate a meeting with another child (C), for example, B's younger sibling or a friend, in order to commit a sexual offence against C. Section 15 fails to address this situation, recently highlighted by the UK's Child Exploitation and Online Protection Centre (CEOP),[8] in which children are targeted and groomed in order to gain access to other children for sexual abuse.

The second example relates to an arrangement to meet a child in the 'virtual world'. For instance, a groomer may gain the child's trust by befriending him/her, which could then result in an arranged virtual meeting via webcam. This chapter will consider the potential risk of harm these virtual meetings pose to children, whilst also drawing attention to the possibility of this grooming behaviour being caught by other statutory provisions under the SOA. It will be argued that judicial support for the utilisation of other offences under the SOA for targeting grooming behaviour underplays the government's rationale for and relevance of Section 15 offence in providing a greater level of protection to children from grooming behaviour.

[3] 'Grooming' will be referred to throughout the analysis, unless otherwise stated, it should be taken to mean online child sexual grooming.

[4] As will be shown, this abuse could take place 'online' or 'offline'.

[5] Ost 2003, p. 150.

[6] E.g. The Taskforce on Child Protection on the Internet and Childnet International.

[7] Re Attorney General's Reference (No. 41 of 2000) [2001] 1 Cr. App. R. (S) 372.

[8] See Sect. 16.4.1.

16.2 The Phenomenon of Online Child Sexual Grooming

Understanding of the grooming process and the ability to identify sexual grooming behaviours is crucial, not only if children are to be protected from child sexual abuse, but also to gain an increased understanding of what has so far been shown to be a rather complex and misunderstood phenomenon. Whilst grooming is an increasingly discussed issue within society, there is still little legal and societal understanding about this phenomenon as a 'distinct behaviour type'.[9] Importantly, child sexual grooming is not a 'modern' concept, nor is it limited to the use of online communication. What is clear is that grooming is a necessary prerequisite in many cases for child sexual abuse[10]; an opportunity to sexually abuse a child is more likely to emerge following a period of sexual grooming.[11]

Grooming is the preparatory act that will allow an individual to gain access to a child with the intent of committing sexual abuse. Ost argues that 'like child pornography, "sexual grooming" is a label that has very broad application' therefore, '[a]ny behaviour that is designed to build up a relationship of trust with a child with the longer-term goal of [sexually abusing her/him] could constitute grooming'.[12] Thus, it is important that grooming is conceived as a 'process' rather than a singular event, although defining this process is problematic since it is not possible to identify exactly where grooming begins or ends,[13] nor is it possible to illustrate the fluidity of grooming behaviours within one precise 'model'[14] of offending behaviour. Craven et al. explain that there are three types of sexual grooming present in the literature: self-grooming; grooming the child; grooming the environment and significant others. The term 'self-grooming' is problematic when discussed in relation to grooming that occurs online, since the analysis provided by Craven et al. seems to be specifically directed at grooming that occurs face to face. Self-grooming can be said to relate to the justification or denial of offending behaviour[15] and although this may be the case for some individuals, justification and denial is by no means a straightforward linear process. Indeed, not all groomers may progress through this stage during the grooming and/or abuse.[16]

Turning to grooming the child, as will be shown, the groomers' victim selection has been reported to often include targeting children who have particular vul-

---

9 Gillespie 2006, p. 412.

10 See Sect. 16.4.1.

11 Durkin 1997, pp. 14–18.

12 Ost 2009, p. 3.

13 Gillespie 2004, p. 239.

14 Craven et al. 2006, p. 289 and Ost 2009, p. 32.

15 Craven et al. 2006, pp. 291–292.

16 See Finkelhor 1984. Also see Suler 2004, p. 321.

nerabilities, such as low confidence, emotional deprivation or a broken family background.[17] The grooming process can be directed by the offender to create an impression that it is a mutually enjoyable 'relationship' or 'courtship' between the victim and the perpetrator. The emphasis on the 'exclusivity' of the relationship helps create 'distance' between the child and their parents/carers, making it less likely that the latter will discover the individual's communications with the child and report their suspicions to the police. Further to this, the use of threats[18] or bribery could maintain a child's compliance and secrecy in order to continue and develop the abusive cycle, for example, encouraging victims to send explicit images or exposing themselves online.[19] Arguably, the use of threat and bribery to exploit children in these ways exceeds online grooming and could even lead to the production and distribution of indecent images of children.[20]

By grooming 'significant others', groomers who target children offline or who use both online communication and face-to-face contact to groom a child, can integrate themselves within the family or those who have care over the child. Research has shown that child sexual offenders will often select single parent families,[21] allowing groomers to gain the parent's/carer's trust and, therefore, encouraging unsupervised contact with the child to give groomers an opportunity to introduce sexual activity.

Besides the groomer directly grooming the child's family, particularly in cases of face-to-face grooming, the community in which the individual belongs may also be groomed. Research suggests that some groomers assess what the community needs and what they can offer in this regard,[22] thereby placing themselves in close proximity to children whilst also creating the perception within the community that they are trustworthy, allowing for increased contact with children without raising concerns. What should thus be apparent is that the way in which a groomer can manipulate the child, himself/herself, the parent, the community and the environment adds to the complex nature of grooming.

Developing a greater understanding of the opportunities presented by online communication and the subsequent use of this form of communication within the grooming of children should at least result in a better awareness of how to protect children from this particular risk of harm.[23] The aim of the following section is to illustrate the specific opportunities that online communication provides within the grooming process.

---

[17] Elliot et al. 1995, p. 584.

[18] Ost 2009, p. 35. Also see Pryor 1999, as cited in Robertiello and Terry 2007, p. 512.

[19] Gillespie 2008, p. 59.

[20] Quale and Taylor 2003, p. 93.

[21] McAlinden 2006, p. 347.

[22] Hare and Hart 1993, pp. 104–115. As referenced by Craven et al. 2006, p. 298.

[23] Craven et al. 2006, p. 297.

16.3 Grooming via Online Communication Technology

The 'dangers of the Internet' and the associated risk of harms posed by grooming are reiterated frequently in the media.[24] Online communication has revolutionised the way in which individuals can target and groom children for sexual abuse. There are a number of ways in which the relative anonymity afforded to groomers makes it easier for them to befriend a child from a relatively safe distance by concealing their 'true identity', thus minimising the chances of detection and assisting them to successfully achieve their ultimate goal. Groomers can withhold their identity until the later stages in the grooming process, when their 'relationship' with the child is strong enough to withhold such a discovery,[25] increasing their chance of success. Moreover, it is not uncommon for online groomers to target several children at once,[26] allowing them to perfect their grooming technique in order to progress quickly through the grooming stages. Contact with multiple children online also ensures that if one child disengages, others are readily available.[27]

Being able to conceal their identity by, for example, posing as someone who is of similar age to the victim could enable the groomer to convince the child to meet them in person. Groomers can utilise the child's greater willingness to meet another 'child' rather than an adult to their advantage. In *R v. Gray*,[28] the 52-year-old defendant posed on the Internet as 'Robbie', a 17-year-old boy. The effective use of online communication to arrange a subsequent 'offline' meeting, particularly when the groomer poses convincingly as a child, ultimately puts children at serious risk of sexual abuse. Recent studies have shown how online groomers can use online gaming platforms to make contact with young boys,[29] concealing their identity by using online 'Avatars'[30] and gaming profile names.[31]

Indeed, this method of grooming is an ongoing concern for CEOP[32] and, as part of the effort to tackle grooming and the risk posed to children by grooming,

---

[24] BBC News 2010. Available at http://news.bbc.co.uk/1/hi/england/cornwall/8652124.stm; Dorsetpolice.uk 2006, 'Teenage victim warns others after Internet grooming'. Available at www.dorset.police.uk/default.aspx?page=3644.

[25] Ost 2009, pp. 49–51.

[26] McAlinden 2006, p. 346.

[27] BBC News 2011b. Available at www.bbc.co.uk/news/uk-england-tees 15642789.

[28] [2007] EWCA Crim 1411.

[29] Webster et al. 2012, p. 17. Available at www.europeanonlinegroomingproject.com/wp-content/file-uploads/European-Online-Grooming-Project-Final-Report.pdf.

[30] Online game console users can create graphical representations of themselves that are visible to other users. Users are able to customise age, gender, hairstyle, body shape, clothing and even behaviour (See new technology for Xbox Kinect Avatar).

[31] See O'Connell 2003. Available at http://image.guardian.co.uk/sys-files/Society/documents/2003/07/24/Netpaedoreport.pdf.

[32] 'CEOP target 'anonymous' online child sex offenders' CEOP Media Centre. Available at http://ceop.police.uk/Media-Centre/Press-releases/2012/CEOP-target-anonymous-online-child-sex-offenders/.

researchers have recently developed a tool, which enables law enforcement to detect adults posing as children in chat rooms.[33] The increased societal awareness of this danger has led to classes promoting safe use of online communication in high schools across the UK.[34] However, whilst steps are thus being taken to respond to this particular form of grooming behaviour, concealing identity is not the only way in which a groomer can develop effective online grooming techniques.

As stated above, research suggests that groomers appear to target children with obvious vulnerabilities.[35] The unique way of sharing information via online communication allows groomers to easily locate vulnerable children by simply browsing children's personal profiles and status updates on social networking sites.[36] Groomers can become adept at quickly identifying vulnerabilities that make certain children more susceptible to grooming and they could then manipulate their grooming technique in a way that is tailored to meet a particular child's needs.[37] This could result in a child having a sense of a more exclusive, reliant bond with the groomer, making it easier for the groomer to 'control the child',[38] and therefore increasing the likelihood of subsequent sexual abuse.

Even if a child appears to have no obvious vulnerability, the open nature of sharing information via 'personal profiles' means that groomers are presented with a catalogue of information that allows them to target a child's particular interest(s) in order to strike up initial conversations. Groomers who use social networking sites to identify and befriend victims can thus readily appear as if they know or share common interests with the child, even before any form of communication is exchanged,[39] rapidly moving from being 'strangers' to online friends.[40] Furthermore, some children post photographs on social networking sites/personal profiles, sometimes of a provocative nature,[41] thereby enabling groomers to identify a child who is perhaps more naive. And concerns have been raised about the use of social networking sites to post images with 'geo-tagging'[42], which provides the geographical location at which a photograph was taken which, when combined with

---

[33] 'Protecting Children Online', ISIS Forensics. Available at http://isis-forensics.com/childprotection/.

[34] 'Teach Online Safety', Staysafeonline.org. Available at http://staysafeonline.org/teach-online-safety/landing/.

[35] Ost 2009, p. 76.

[36] Most common examples: Facebook, Bebo, Twitter and MySpace.

[37] Craven et al. 2006, p. 296.

[38] Palmer 2004, p. 27.

[39] BBC News 2011a. Available at www.bbc.co.uk/news/uk-england-derbyshire-15735519.

[40] Davidson and Martellozzo 2005. Available at http://westminsterresearch.wmin.ac.uk/1737/1/Davidson_Martellozzo_2005_final.pdf, p. 6.

[41] See ABC News 2012, http://abcnews.go.com/blogs/headlines/2012/03/facebook-shuts-down-most-beautiful-teen-page/.

[42] Herald Sun 2012. Available at www.heraldsun.com.au/technology/photograph-uploads-put-kids-at-risk/story-fn7celvh-1226331243923.

information such as 'taken at his favourite park', could be used to identify children even from their parents' profiles. Similarly, the use of 'Foursquare'[43] and other location based services[44] can create networks for rapid identification of potential victims, including other children that the groomer could gain access to, for example, a sibling or a friend of the child that the groomer is communicating with.[45]

Webwise have revealed that adolescents adopt more risky behaviour when using online communication and have demonstrated a culture of acceptance, along with a degree of expectation, of receiving sexual communications whilst using the Internet.[46] Moreover, some adolescents seek (virtual) adult-like relationships.[47] Indeed, Salter refers to the grooming process as 'emotional seduction',[48] illustrating that forming the illusion of an intimate relationship is one of the most effective ways to manipulate adolescents. In some cases, this might lead to a child acquiescing in explicit conversations,[49] taking and/or sending explicit images.[50] These images could then be used to reinforce the 'adult-like' relationship whilst desensitising the child to sexual activity,[51] or could be used as a threat in order to ensure further compliance.[52] Sexting can be used as a 'tool of coercion, threat and power'[53] within the grooming of children means that more young people are being encouraged to send and receive explicit images and messages because they believe their groomer is in fact their boyfriend. Adolescents who perceive their grooming as 'analogous to adult courtship'[54] might believe they are a 'consenting' party[55] to the relationship, which could prevent them from recognising and disclosing the nature of their abuse.

Another way in which grooming is facilitated is by the use of 3G technology, which can enable a more rapid progression through the grooming stages than if a groomer had more limited contact with a child.[56] Whilst parents may have become

---

[43] Foursquare is downloadable Smartphone app with over 25 million users worldwide that allows users to share their location with others.

[44] See: https://www.facebook.com/about/location.

[45] See Sect. 16.4.1.

[46] Webwise 2006, www.webwise.ie/article.aspx?id=4526.

[47] BBC News 2011c. Available at www.bbc.co.uk/news/uk-england-somerset-16215914.

[48] Salter 1995, p. 74.

[49] Otherwise known as 'Sexting' which involves the sharing of sexually suggestive/explicit messages or images electronically.

[50] 'The Guardian 2011. Available at www.guardian.co.uk/uk/2011/jun/07/nursery-worker-admits-raping-toddler.

[51] Ost 2009, p. 80.

[52] BBC News 2011d. Available at www.bbc.co.uk/news/uk-scotland-glasgow-west-14929227.

[53] 'Sexting and Sexual Grooming', House of Commons, Hansard, 25 April 2012, Col. 279–281WH.

[54] Howitt 1995, p. 176.

[55] BBC News 2006b. Available at http://news.bbc.co.uk/1/hi/wales/south_west/5159190.stm.

[56] Gillespie 2008, p. 19.

more vigilant about the dangers posed to adolescents accessing the Internet on home computers through public education programmes,[57] the added risks of 3G technology may be overlooked. Recent newspaper reports have commented on the way smart phone features such as 'BBM'[58] have been used by groomers to 'summon friends to join in'[59] with the abuse. It is thus important to recognise the risk of harm to children that can be facilitated by online communication, not only in terms of the grooming process but also their continued abuse and exploitation.

Whilst the above discussion has made reference to instances where groomers seek to identify and communicate with children whom they have never met, this is not the only way that the opportunities presented by online communication can be exploited. Academic literature has emphasised the importance of recognising that children are more likely to be groomed and abused by someone they know rather than a stranger.[60] Groomers who already have access to a child, e.g. through employment or family/friends, can complement the grooming that they have already implemented by using online communication. They can become proficient at communicating with the children[61] using various forms of communication, which could rapidly ensure and bestow a great level of trust[62] by maintaining constant communication. This could increase the likelihood of sexual abuse at a much earlier stage in the grooming process, far more quickly than could be achieved offline.[63]

Given these risks of harm that grooming poses, the legislative response in England and Wales has been to create an offence directed towards online grooming in particular. However, as will now be discussed, the ambiguity created by the offence related to grooming could be argued to place children at further risk of harm.

16.4 Limitations of the Offence Relating to Grooming

Prior to the SOA 2003, no specific offence existed under English law[64] directed towards the grooming of a child. The inclusion of such a specific offence in the 2003 legislation was a significant development in child protection, designed to allow intervention at an earlier stage in the preparatory process of gaining access

57 ThinkUknow XXXX. Available at https://www.thinkuknow.co.uk/parents/parentsguide/.

58 Black Berry Messenger.

59 The Telegraph 2012. Available at www.telegraph.co.uk/news/uknews/crime/9327534/Child-abuse-taking-place-in-every-town-village-and-hamlet-in-England.html.

60 Grubin 1998, p. 15.

61 Ost 2009, p. 49.

62 Davidson and Martellozzo 2005.

63 In *R v. Gray*, the child had 'Robbie's' mobile number stored in her phone as 'hubby'.

64 Gillespie 2001, p. 435.

to children for sexual abuse.[65] However, as the analysis will show, the limitations of the 'so-called' grooming offence[66] have further exacerbated the lack of clarity and understanding of grooming.

Section 15 offence (as amended)[67] provides that

> an individual aged 18 and over (A) commits an offence of 'meeting a child following sexual grooming' if:
>
> (a) A has met or communicated with another person B on at least two occasions and subsequently
>
> (i) A intentionally meets B,
> (ii) A travels with the intention of meeting B in any part of the world or arranges to meet B in any part of the world, or
> (iii) B travels with the intention of meeting A in any part of the world,
>
> (b) A intends to do anything to or in respect of, during or after the meeting mentioned in paragraph (a) (i) to (iii) and in any part of the world, which if done will involve the commission by A of a relevant offence,
> (c) B is under 16, and
> (d) A does not reasonably believe that B is 16 or over.

Despite claims that Section 15 offence would make it a crime to groom children under 16 for sex,[68] it is notable that the offence only targets the arranging of and/or meeting a child, with the coupled intent, following a period of grooming. Although Section 15 is rather misleadingly headed '*meeting* a child following sexual grooming etc.',[69] there is no requirement that the grooming behaviours employed by a groomer are sexual in nature.[70] Rather the word 'etc.' in the title indicates that communication should not be excluded from the offence if seemingly innocent in nature.[71] It could be argued that the section's misleading title could result in some instances of grooming being overlooked if they contain no sexual content. Moreover, ambiguity could also arise as the title of the section makes it unclear that the act of arranging a meeting falls within Section 15's scope.[72]

---

[65] Hansard 2003. Available at www.publications.parliament.uk/pa/ld200203/ldhansrd/vo030401/text/30401-28.htm.

[66] McAlinden 2006, p. 347.

[67] The Criminal Justice and Immigration act 2008, c.4, sch 15, para 1, extended the scope of Section 15 to include a groomer arranging to meet a child following grooming and also a child travelling to an arranged meeting with a groomer.

[68] Home Office 2002, Protecting the Public', para 54.

[69] My emphasis.

[70] Ormerod 2011, p. 342.

[71] *R v. G* [2010] EWCA Crim 1693.

[72] There are multiple reasons for a perpetrator not being able to abuse the child. E.g. the child does not go to the meeting; the meeting gets interrupted or the child alerts others of meeting. This is not an exhaustive list.

Evidence of ulterior intent to commit a relevant offence could be derived from the surrounding circumstances,[73] including any transcripts of online conversations, prior convictions or items found in the groomer's possession.[74] Ost correctly states that such evidence is unlikely to be available in all cases, since groomers could be aware of what would be deemed 'incriminating evidence'.[75] Potentially, 'savvy' groomers who use online communication could ensure that most, if not all, of their communications are specifically non-sexual, or have at the very least a deniability element to them.[76] This might provide groomers with a sense of security, a security gained through an awareness of the difficulty of establishing a harmful interior intent for the purposes of the offence. It will be argued in the remainder of this section that two specific forms of grooming that fall outside the ambit of Section 15 add to the current ambiguity surrounding the offence.[77]

16.4.1 Third Party Grooming

The notion of a third party being involved within the grooming process has received little attention by the academic or awareness-raising literature and thus, rather unsurprisingly, is not a situation currently covered by Section 15. In a study of children and the Internet, CEOP found that over 25 % of children met up with someone they met online, with 8 % taking someone along with them.[78] This illustrates the possibility that groomers could target third parties: they communicate with children online, and subsequently arrange to meet them as well as another child whom they actually intend to sexually abuse.

As part of the EU Safer Internet Day campaign in 2009, CEOP released a thought-provoking advert, 'Where's Klaus?',[79] to raise parental awareness of the dangers of children communicating online. The advert highlights the situation where an adult communicates with a child online (B), but has the intention to target another child (C) for sexual abuse. Online communication could thus provide groomers with a way of targeting children who are, for example, too young to communicate online or have no access, by encouraging older children to introduce them or bring them along to pre-arranged meetings. A groomer could then employ

---

[73] See Guidance to Part 1 of the Sexual Offences Act 2003, Home Office, p. 17.

[74] Sexual Offences Act: Explanatory Notes 2004: para 29.

[75] Ost 2009, p. 76.

[76] E.g. content is not unambiguously of a sexual nature.

[77] Other difficulties regarding the offence as it relates to all forms of CSG are discussed by Gillespie 2008, p. 61.

[78] CEOP, Thinkuknow Parents Quiz answers. Available at https://www.thinkuknow.co.uk/Parentsold/quiz_answers/.

[79] CEOP, Thinkuknow, Internet Safety Film 'Where's Klaus? Available at https://www.thinkuknow.co.uk/Parentsold/film/.

grooming techniques towards this child, establishing a relationship of trust, which could lead to the child acquiescing in sexual activity.

Research suggests that offenders will get victims to recruit other children by offering incentives, or by threats and by giving bribes and gifts to the children recruited.[80] Recent examples of groomers targeting children on the street and then grooming them online[81] highlight how vulnerable[82] children can be groomed in order to recruit other victims. Groomers who reward children with gifts[83] and flattery[84] for bringing younger friends along to pre-arranged meetings for sexual abuse may be able to gain access to children who might have previously been unavailable.[85] This grooming technique is evidenced in *R v. LB*,[86] where the groomer abused his granddaughters and subsequently abused their younger school friend. The defendant supplied the girls with cigarettes and alcohol in order to maintain their secrecy and reward them for sexual activity. Section 15 could only apply in such a situation,[87] if the communication, the arrangement/meeting and the ulterior intent were directed at B. Therefore, in a situation of third party grooming, where communication with B is coupled with an arrangement to meeting with B and C for the purpose of committing a relevant offence against C, Section 15 offence does not apply.

It is possible that this form of grooming could be criminalised under Section 14 SOA,[88] which makes it an offence for an individual to intentionally arrange or facilitate any action which he intends to do or intends another person to do or believes that another person will do, in any part of the world, if this action will involve the commission of a sexual offence. Despite the Court of Appeal previously referring to Section 14 as the 'offence of grooming',[89] the guidance, which accompanies the SOA makes no suggestion that Section 14 was intended to capture grooming behaviour within its scope. Importantly, under Section 14,

---

[80] Elliot et al. 1995, p. 584.

[81] 'BBC News 2012a. Available at www.bbc.co.uk/news/uk-england-17993003.

[82] *R v. Mohammed* [2006] EWCA Crim 1107—The victim had severe learning difficulties and behavioural problems.

[83] Berliner and Conte 1990, p. 35.

[84] Ost 2009, p. 76.

[85] E.g. do not have access to the Internet or is under parental control.

[86] [2010] EWCA Crim 1233. Although no online communication was used in the commission of the offence, the point that groomers can target younger children via third parties remains valid. Also see: *R v. Connolly* [2007] EWCA Crim 1880 where the defendant used text messaging to contact a friend of a third party and subsequently was charged with two counts of engaging in sexual activity with a child and one count of causing or inciting a child to engage in sexual activity against both the third party and her friend.

[87] In *R v. LB* the appellant was charged with the S.14 offence because sexual abuse had occurred. See *R v. Harrison* [2005] EWCA Crim. 3458. However, the case still illustrates how third party grooming can be used to gain access to subsequent victims.

[88] Arranging or facilitating the commission of a child sex offence.

[89] *R v. Harrison* [2005] EWCA Crim. 3458.

similarly to Section 15, no offence needs to have been committed towards a child in order to satisfy the offence. Arguably, Section 14 is better able to capture instances of grooming since no arrangement to meet needs to take place before the offence comes into play. However, if Section 14 is used to prosecute third party grooming, it is arguable that this could seriously undermine the relevance of Section 15 and fail to recognise the harm that the sophisticated levels of grooming employed could have caused to B[90] in the commission of the relevant offence against C.

Despite the failure to recognise the potential existence of third party grooming within the victim selection/recruitment process, it is debatable whether third party grooming could ever be accounted for under Section 15 due the difficulty in gaining evidence of and differentiating ulterior intent between both B and C. But given that it was specifically targeted at online grooming,[91] it is worrying that Section 15 is limited to the communication and grooming of one child (B), despite the evidence that a groomer could groom one child online in order to gain access to another. If a groomer successfully recruits other victims through a third party, it is possible that this could reinforce offending behaviour,[92] allowing a groomer to further develop their technique and subsequently placing further children at risk of harm.

16.4.2 'Virtual' Meetings

Despite the government's acknowledgment of the dangers the Internet poses to children,[93] Section 15 seems to be limited and only provides protection from meetings, following a period of grooming that occurs face-to-face. Limiting the pre-emptive strike of Section 15 to face-to-face meetings arguably undermines the government's aim to provide greater protection to children,[94] potentially failing to protect children from the risks of harm that meetings in the virtual world pose, risks which will now be discussed.

During a virtual 'meeting', the child may be exposed to sexually explicit communication or even pornographic images, which could desensitise her/him to sexual abuse and/or encourage her/him to become sexually explicit, and thereby form part of the grooming process.[95] Albeit not specifically in relation to grooming, research into child Internet-related experiences has found that 15 % of

---

[90] See BBC News 2012b. Available at www.bbc.co.uk/news/uk-england-manchester-17914138.

[91] Hansard 2003 at para 27. See also McAlinden 2006, p. 342.

[92] Ost 2009, p. 3.

[93] Home Office 2002, 'Protecting the Public', para 54. Available at www.archive2.official-documents.co.uk/document/cm56/5668/5668.pdf.

[94] See Hansard 2003.

[95] See O'Connell 2003.

11–16 year olds have received sexual messages and images of people engaging in sexual activity and 3 % have sent naked images to others online.[96] The concern is that such risk-taking activity could increase a child's vulnerability to grooming behaviour.[97] Davidson et al. have proposed that groomers who use online communication are defined by their intention to initiate contact with a child online, establish a sexual relationship in order to engage in cybersex and/or offline sexual abuse.[98]

However, it is important to recognise that online 'meetings' might not necessarily be sexual in nature. Yet even non-sexual meetings online could pose a threat by desensitising a child to the groomer, making it more likely that s/he will agree to meet the groomer in person.[99] Meetings could be arranged and occur through webcams and, more recently, through the use of 'Skype' on a mobile phone,[100] recordings of which could be posted on the Internet and shared with other abusers.[101] Furthermore, the problematic nature of obtaining forensic evidence[102] of the content of Skype meetings may make this an even more attractive opportunity for groomers and could increase the likelihood of them avoiding detection.

If the grooming is successful and the child acquiesces to sexual activity via a webcam, it is likely that this will reinforce the groomer's perceptions of their behaviour, allowing them to develop their technique and potentially placing further children at risk of abuse. Furthermore, any recordings or pictures taken by webcam may be used as bribes or threats towards a child to ensure compliance and secrecy. This would increase the possibility that the grooming behaviour would not be detected until a sexual offence has been committed.[103] One victim of a virtual meeting described her ordeal as 'Internet rape',[104] a violation of her bodily integrity without any physical contact, demonstrating the level of control a groomer can gain over a victim without any physical meeting taking place.

The act of arranging a child to watch or perform a sexual act through the use of a webcam could be subject to other provisions within the SOA. Virtual meetings could be arranged and activity could take place, which would constitute an offence under Section 11 (engaging in sexual activity in a child's presence), Section 12 (causing a child to watch a sexual act) or Section 10 (causing or inciting a child to engage in sexual activity), if that activity was for the purpose of sexual

---

[96] Haddon and Livingstone 2012. Available at www2.lse.ac.uk/media@lse/research/EUKids Online/EU%20Kids%20III/Reports/PerspectivesReport.pdf.

[97] Haddon and Livingstone 2012, p. 3.

[98] Davidson et al. 2012. Available at www.europeanonlinegroomingproject.com/wp-content/file-uploads/EOGP-Literature-Review.pdf, p. 8.

[99] Gillespie 2008, p. 60.

[100] See 'About Skype' at http://about.skype.com/.

[101] NY Daily News, 2012. Available at http://articles.nydailynews.com/2012-05-10/news/31659087_1_sexual-exploitation-child-skype.

[102] BBC News 2012c. Available at www.bbc.co.uk/news/magazine-16505791.

[103] Ost 2009, p. 77.

[104] BBC News 2006a. Available at http://news.bbc.co.uk/1/hi/england/derbyshire/6133360.stm.

gratification. However, it is concerning that neither of these sections protect children before any harm occurs. As already mentioned, it is Section 14 that allows the police to act before an arrangement to meet takes place, arguably providing a better level of protection to children. However, Section 14 could only be used to criminalise the arrangement of a virtual meeting that occurs following a period of grooming, if evidence was available to prove that the meeting would involve a Section 10 or a Section 12 offence. Moreover, the nature of 'virtual meetings' is that the abuse is likely to have occurred before law enforcement officials are notified, and thus before Section 14 can be utilised. Furthermore, Section 14 would not cover non-sexual meetings that occur in order to desensitise the child, even if these were for the purpose of encouraging the child to meet the groomer in person.

Section 15 was created to enable a pre-emptive strike, rendering behaviour that could lead to harm unlawful.[105] Its later amendments[106] potentially allow the police to intervene at an early stage, thus minimising the risk of a physical meeting and, subsequently, any abuse taking place. However, it seems that Section 15 offence was only designed to target specific sexual behaviour over the Internet and arguably offers limited protection to children who are groomed to meet with an adult over the Internet.

16.5 Conclusion

This chapter has analysed the risk of harm posed by grooming via online communication and the particular limitations of Section 15 offence in targeting online grooming. Article 1 of the Council of Europe Convention on the Protection of Children against Sexual Exploitation and Abuse[107] (the Convention) states that the Convention's purpose is to ensure the prevention of and to combat child sexual abuse and exploitation. It is clear that the use of online technology for third party grooming could further advance the victim recruitment process for child sexual groomers, subsequently placing more children at risk of harm. Section 15 does not prevent the risk of harm to C following third party grooming, neither does Section 15 or any other provision under the SOA account for harm suffered by B either by third party grooming, or as a consequence of virtual meetings that form part of the grooming process. Thus, some child exploitation by way of grooming appears to fall outside the criminal law's grasp in England and Wales.

[105] Ost 2009, p. 90.

[106] The Criminal Justice and Immigration act 2008, c.4, sch 15, para 1.

[107] UK signed the convention 05/05/2008. Convention entered into force 1 December 2009. Also see Directive 2011/92/EU of European Parliament and of the Council of 13 December 2011 on combating the sexual abuse and sexual exploitation of children and child pornography and replacing the Council Framework Decision 2004/68/JHA.

Arguably, a greater level of protection would be afforded to children, if the actual grooming were criminalised rather than a subsequent (arranged) meeting. It could be argued that besides arranging to meet, meeting a child or travelling to meet a child, the 'grooming itself should constitute an offence'.[108] However, it is acknowledged that this would be no easy task given the ambiguity and fluidity of grooming behaviour presented alongside practical issues surrounding evidence of ulterior intent. One option is to broaden Section 15's scope in order to provide a greater level of protection to children from third party grooming and virtual meetings.[109] Further extending the scope of the offence would act to reinforce not only the preventative measures laid down by the Convention, but also the UK government's rationale for implementing an offence related to grooming.

Admittedly, incorporating these forms of grooming into Section 15 could further complicate the offence, leading to greater ambiguity and failing to offer children any better protection from harm. Perhaps, therefore, Section 15 provides the best level of protection that is legislatively possible, despite the arguments made in this chapter. However, where grooming does come to the attention of prosecutors and Section 15 does not apply, they should ensure they make use of the other potential offences, such as Section 14, where applicable. Whilst the limitations of Section 15 are largely a result of the complexities posed by the phenomenon of grooming, it remains the case that Section 15 only targets certain abusive behaviours and largely excludes the use of online technology in the commission of sexual offences against children. This, it is suggested, is an oversight that will lead to further children being at risk of harm from sexual abuse.

References

ABC News (2012) Facebook shuts down 'most beautiful teen' page. http://abcnews.go.com/blogs/headlines/2012/03/facebook-shuts-down-most-beautiful-teen-page/

BBC News (2006a) Internet groomer handed jail term. http://news.bbc.co.uk/1/hi/england/derbyshire/6133360.stm

BBC News (2006b) Jail for internet teen 'groomer'. http://news.bbc.co.uk/1/hi/wales/south_west/5159190.stm

BBC News (2010) Cornwall postman used fake names to groom victims. http://news.bbc.co.uk/1/hi/england/cornwall/8652124.stm

BBC News (2011a) Bieber fan web grooming man jailed. www.bbc.co.uk/news/uk-england-derbyshire-15735519

[108] Ost 2009, p. 72.

[109] Although space limits discussion, the following amendment could be proposed: Following Section 15 (a)(iii) insert: (iv) A arranges to meet B in order to gain access to another child (C), or (v) A arranges or facilitates the use of a webcam to communicate with B, for the purpose of obtaining sexual gratification. However, it is noted that the latter provision might perhaps be too broad, as it could catch 'innocent', non-harmful conversations with B via a webcam if A obtains sexual gratification from these.

BBC News (2011b) Stockton man Dennis Forster jailed for web grooming' BBC news, 8 Nov 2011. http://www.bbc.co.uk/news/uk-england-tees-15642789
BBC News (2011c) Saltford church youth leader jailed for sex offences. www.bbc.co.uk/news/uk-england-somerset-16215914
BBC News (2011d) Brandon Watson guilty of grooming girls online for sex. www.bbc.co.uk/news/uk-scotland-glasgow-west-14929227
BBC News (2012a) Rochdale grooming trial: nine men jailed. www.bbc.co.uk/news/uk-england-17993003
BBC News (2012b) Rochdale grooming case: victim's story. www.bbc.co.uk/news/uk-england-manchester-17914138
BBC News (2012c) Why crimes on skype leave witnesses but no evidence. www.bbc.co.uk/news/magazine-16505791
Berliner L, Conte JR (1990) The process of victimization: the victim's perspective. Child Abuse Negl 14:35
CEOP Media Centre (2012) CEOP target 'anonymous' online child sex offenders. http://ceop.police.uk/Media-Centre/Press-releases/2012/CEOP-target-anonymous-online-child-sex-offenders/
CEOP. Thinkuknow parents quiz answers. https://www.thinkuknow.co.uk/Parentsold/quiz_answers/
CEOP. Thinkuknow, internet safety film 'where's Klaus?. https://www.thinkuknow.co.uk/Parentsold/film/
CEOP. Growing up online. The parent's and carer's guide. https://www.thinkuknow.co.uk/parents/parentsguide/
Craven S, Brown SJ, Gilchrist E (2006) Sexual grooming of children: review of literature and theoretical considerations. J Sex Aggression 12(3):287–299
Davidson J, Martellozzo E (2005) Policing the internet and protecting children from sex offenders online: when strangers become 'virtual friends. Cybersafety conference. http://westminsterresearch.wmin.ac.uk/1737/1/Davidson_Martellozzo_2005_final.pdf, p 6
Davidson J, Grove-Hills J, Bifulco A, Gottschalk P, Carretti V, Pham T, Webster S (2012) EU overview of policy, legislation and safety practice. www.europeanonlinegroomingproject.com/wp-content/file-uploads/EOGP-Literature-Review.pdf, p 8
Dorsetpolice.uk (2006) Teenage victim warns others after internet grooming. www.dorset.police.uk/default.aspx?page=3644
Durkin KF (1997) Misuse of the internet by paedophiles: implications for law and empowerment. Fed probation 61(3):14–18
Elliot M, Browne K, Kilcoyne J (1995) Child sexual abuse prevention: what offenders tell us. Child Abuse Negl 19(5):584
Finkelhor D (1984) Child sexual abuse: new theory and research. Free Press, New York
Gillespie A (2001) Children, chatrooms and the law. Crim Law Rev 435
Gillespie A (2004) Tackling grooming. Police J 77(3):239
Gillespie A (2006) Indecent images, grooming and the law. Crim Law Rev 412
Gillespie AA (2008) Child exploitation and communication technologies. Russell House Publishing, Dorset, pp 59–61
Grubin D (1998) Sex offending against children: understanding the risk. Police research series paper 99, Home Office, London, p 15
Haddon L, Livingstone S (2012) EU kids online: national perspectives. http://www2.lse.ac.uk/media@lse/research/EUKidsOnline/EU%20Kids%20III/Reports/PerspectivesReport.pdf
Hansard HL (2003) Sexual offences bill, Lord Falconer of Thoroton, Column 1257. www.publications.parliament.uk/pa/ld200203/ldhansrd/vo030401/text/30401-28.htm
Hare RD, Hart SD (1993) Psychopathy, mental disorder and crime. In: Hodgins S (ed) Mental disorder and crime. Sage, Thousand Oaks, pp 104–115
Herald Sun (2012) Police warn photos of kids with geo-tagging being used by paedophiles. www.heraldsun.com.au/technology/photograph-uploads-put-kids-at-risk/story-fn7celvh-1226331243923

Home Office (2002) Protecting the public, para. 54. www.archive2.official-documents.co.uk/document/cm56/5668/5668.pdf
Howitt D (1995) Paedophiles and sexual offences against children. Wiley, New York, p 176
McAlinden A-M (2006) Setting 'em up': personal, familial and institutional grooming in the sexual abuse of children. Soc Leg Stud 15(342):346–347
NY Daily News (2012) Babysitter streamed rape of 5 year old girl over Skype. http://articles.nydailynews.com/2012-05-10/news/31659087_1_sexual-exploitation-child-skype
O'Connell R (2003) A typology of child cybersexploitation and online grooming practices. Cyberspace Research Unit, University of Central Lancashire. http://image.guardian.co.uk/sys-files/Society/documents/2003/07/24/Netpaedoreport.pdf
Ormerod D (2011) Sexual offences: meeting a child following sexual grooming. CLR, Case comment, p 342
Ost S (2003) Getting to grips with sexual grooming? the new offence under the Sexual Offences Act 2003. J Soc Welf Family Law 26(2):150
Ost S (2009) Child pornography and sexual grooming, legal and societal responses. Cambridge University Press, Cambridge
Palmer T (2004) Just one click: sexual abuse of children and young children through the internet and mobile technology. Barnardos, London, p 27
Pryor D (1999) Unspeakable acts. NYC Press, New York
Quale E, Taylor M (2003) Model of problematic internet use in people with a sexual interest in children. Cyberpsychol Behav 6(1):93
Robertiello G, Terry KJ (2007) Can we profile sex offenders? A review of sex offender typologies. Aggress Violent Behav 12:512
Salter A (1995) Transforming trauma: a guide to understanding and treating adult survivors of child sexual abuse. Sage, Newbury Park, p 74
Suler J (2004) The online disinhibition effect. Cyberpsychol Behav 7(3):321
The Guardian (2011) Nursery worker admits raping child. www.guardian.co.uk/uk/2011/jun/07/nursery-worker-admits-raping-toddler
The Telegraph (2012) Child abuse is taking place in every town, village and hamlet in England. www.telegraph.co.uk/news/uknews/crime/9327534/Child-abuse-taking-place-in-every-town-village-and-hamlet-in-England.html
Webster S, Davidson J, Bifulco A, Gottschalk P, Caretti V, Pham T. Grove-Hills J, Turley C, Tompkins C, Ciulla S, Milazzo V, Schimmenti A, Craparo O (2012) European grooming project online: final report. www.europeanonlinegroomingproject.com/wp-content/file-uploads/European-Online-Grooming-Project-Final-Report.pdf
Webwise (2006) Survey of children's use of the internet: investigating online risk behaviour. www.webwise.ie/Webwise2006Survey.pdf
Wolak J, Finkelhor D, Mitchell KJ, Ybarra ML (2008) Online 'predators' and their victims. Myths, realities, and implications for prevention and treatment. Am Psychol 63(2):111

The manufacturer's authorised representative in the EU is Springer Nature Customer Service Centre GmbH, Europaplatz 3, 69115 Heidelberg, Germany. If you have any concerns regarding our products, please contact ProductSafety@springernature.com

Printed and bound by CPI Group (UK) Ltd, Croydon, CR0 4YY
29/04/2026
02099460-0009